Industrial Ecology

Series Editor

Syed Abdul Rehman Khan, Tsinghua University, Beijing, China

Industrial ecology and circular economy is a peer-reviewed book series that focuses on different disciplinary approaches to waste management, sustainable practices & strategies on different scientific, societal, pyschological, technological, economic, governance, and cultural and political aspects of the ongoing and emerging debate. This primary goal of this series is to offer scientists from different school of thoughts and institutions a platform for scientific analysis and debate.

Undeniably, Industrial ecology is a rapidly growing field that systematically examines local, regional and global materials and energy uses and flows in products, processes, industrial sectors and economies. It focuses on the potential role of industry in reducing environmental burdens throughout the product life cycle from the extraction of raw materials, to the production of goods, to the use of those goods and to the management of the resulting wastes. Industrial ecology is ecological in that it (1) places human activity -- industry in the very broadest sense -- in the larger context of the biophysical environment from which we obtain resources and into which we place our wastes, and (2) looks to the natural world for models of highly efficient use of resources, energy and byproducts. By selectively applying these models, the environmental performance of industry can be improved. Industrial ecology sees corporate entities as key players in the protection of the environment, particularly where technological innovation is an avenue for environmental improvement. As repositories of technological expertise in our society, corporations provide crucial leverage in attacking environmental problems through product and process design.

Syed Abdul Rehman Khan ·
Adnan Ahmed Sheikh · Oluwaseun Kolade ·
Sachin Kamble
Editors

Circular Economy and Technological Innovation

The Regional Implications

Springer

Editors
Syed Abdul Rehman Khan
School of Engineering and Management
Xuzhou University of Technology
Xuzhou, China

Adnan Ahmed Sheikh
College of Business
University of Buraimi
Al Buraimi, Oman

Oluwaseun Kolade
Sheffield Business School
Sheffield Hallam University
Sheffield, UK

Sachin Kamble
Operations and Supply Chain Management
EDHEC Business School
Roubaix, France

ISSN 2730-5775 ISSN 2730-5783 (electronic)
Industrial Ecology
ISBN 978-981-96-5649-3 ISBN 978-981-96-5650-9 (eBook)
https://doi.org/10.1007/978-981-96-5650-9

This Springer imprint is published by the registered company Springer Nature Singapore Pte Ltd.
The registered company address is: 152 Beach Road, #21-01/04 Gateway East, Singapore 189721, Singapore

Acknowledgements

We appreciate the authors for their submission of state-of-the-art research work, which contributed to the success of this book project. We also express our gratitude to the reviewers for their voluntary participation in the evaluation process. Furthermore, we express our gratitude to the publishing team for their ongoing collaboration and assistance in facilitating the successful production of this book.

This book is partially supported by the National Natural Science Foundation of China (No. 72250410375).

Contents

About the Editors

Dr. Syed Abdul Rehman Khan is a Full Professor of Supply Chain Management at Xuzhou University of Technology. His research primarily focuses on the circular economy, sustainable manufacturing, waste treatment, and green supply chains. He has published over 150 academic works, including book chapters and articles. Additionally, Professor Khan serves on the editorial boards of several international publications.

Dr. Adnan Ahmed Sheikh is a seasoned academic and professional with extensive expertise in digitalization, marketing, supply chain management, and sustainable business practices. Dr. Sheikh earned his Ph.D. from Universiti Utara Malaysia and is currently affiliated with the University of Buraimi, Sultanate of Oman, as an Associate Professor of E-Marketing. With thirteen years of combined academic and industry experience, he has authored more than 60 research publications, including journal articles and book chapters.

Dr. Oluwaseun Kolade is affiliated with Sheffield Hallam University as a Full Professor of Entrepreneurship and Digital Transformation. He has published more than 110 academic outputs, including journal articles, book chapters, and technical reports. He is the co-editor of *Digital Innovations for a Circular Plastic Economy in Africa* (2023). He holds editorial roles in several international journals.

Dr. Sachin Kamble is a Professor of Strategy (Operations and Supply Chain Management) at EDHEC Business School, Roubaix, France. He holds a Ph.D. in Management, an MBA in Operations, and a bachelor's degree in mechanical engineering. Before joining EDHEC, he worked with the National Institute of Industrial Engineering (NITIE), Mumbai, India. Dr. Sachin's teaching and research interests include Operations Management, Supply Chain Management, Big Data Analytics, Industry 4.0, and Digital Transformation. He has more than 50 authored or co-authored publications in international journals, including high-impact journals such as Int. J of Production Economics, Int. J of Production Research, Computers in Industry, Int. J of Information Mgmt. and Process

Safety & Env. Mgmt. Dr. Sachin has completed more than 25 consultancy assignments for leading manufacturing and service organizations across various sectors, including cement, oil refineries, fertilizers, seaports, textiles, tires, and pharmaceuticals.

Foundations of Circular Economy and Technological Innovation

Introduction: Circular Economy and Technological Innovations: Synergies and Regional Implications

Syed Abdul Rehman Khan, Oluwaseun Kolade, and Adnan Ahmed Sheikh

Abstract The sustainability agenda has taken the central stage on the global agenda amid heightened concerns that the planet's resources are being stretched to the limit. In the past few centuries, and especially since the beginning of the twentieth century, the global economy has seen astronomical industrial growth powered by advances in technological innovations across a whole spectrum of industries.

1 Circular Economy and the Promise and Challenge of Technological Innovations

The sustainability agenda has taken the central stage on the global agenda amid heightened concerns that the planet's resources are being stretched to the limit. In the past few centuries, and especially since the beginning of the twentieth century, the global economy has seen astronomical industrial growth powered by advances in technological innovations across a whole spectrum of industries. These technologies have revolutionized mass production, created new markets, and instigated new habits of consumption across the countries of the world. As corporate industrial giants sought to consolidate their gains and expand market opportunities, they instigated new production processes and market dynamics underpinned by strategies such as planned obsolescence, vertical and horizontal integration, monopolization and cartel formation, and tied selling and bundling. Geopolitical forces and interests also reinforced this evolution of the global economy as leading countries seek to outrun one another in a frantic race to the bottom.

S. A. R. Khan
School of Engineering Management, Xuzhou University of Technology, Xuzhou, China

O. Kolade (✉)
Sheffield Business School, Sheffield Hallam University, Leicester, UK
e-mail: s.kolade@shu.ac.uk

A. A. Sheikh
College of Business, University of Buraimi, Al Buraimi, Sultanate of Oman
e-mail: adnan.a@uob.edu.om

S. A. R. Khan et al. (eds.), *Circular Economy and Technological Innovation*, Industrial Ecology, https://doi.org/10.1007/978-981-96-5650-9_1

The result of this is a linear economy characterized by centralized mass production and large inventory stocking powered by the economy of scale. This make-take-dispose paradigm has invariably instigated increased waste production and associated waste management problems that have increasingly worsened as more countries industrialize and harness the benefits of existing technologies. The lock-in to the linear economy technologies continued apace as creators and adopters of the technologies aggressively promoted them and influenced later adopters. The aggregate of the ensuing network externalities and the increasing returns associated with these old technologies have induced the global economy to outcomes that are at once inferior and difficult to alter. With considerable capital sunk into these linear technologies and the significant political capital that comes with the investments, along with entrenched consumption habits associated with them in the absence of attractive market options, the linear economy has become a difficult nut to crack.

The promise of the circular economy is set against this backdrop of the entrenched linear economy. In place of the make-take-dispose paradigm associated with the linear economy, the circular economy is underpinned by three core R's: Reduce, Reuse, Recycle; or, in its more expanded form, include other R's such as recover, re-manufacture, repair, repurpose, and refurbish (Zhang et al. 2024). By prioritizing resource efficiency and waste minimization, the circular economy is seen by many stakeholders as the economy of the future. At the heart of this paradigm is the prioritization of planetary health and human needs in a positive sum game in which one outcome does not have to suffer to realize the other: that humans produce what they need while taking care of the planet and considering the needs of future generations.

The circular economy, thus, sets a new agenda for technological progress. It does not advocate for a drawdown on technological ambitions. Instead, it sets a new direction and target for it—underpinned by the mutually reinforcing pillars of humancentric and eco-priority. Technology has, therefore, emerged as a principal ally, rather than an adversary, in the drive to break the lock-in to the linear economy. It is this theme that this book draws its attention. Across the globe, technological innovations are playing a critical role in the campaign to drive the transition to the circular economy (Hassan et al. 2023). The outcomes and challenges are not homogenous. Still, the emerging directions of impact offer a window into key areas that should attract the attention of scholars, policymakers, and practitioners.

1.1 Breaking Free from the Linear Model: Digital Innovations in Action

The advent of digital transformation, accelerated since the beginning of the millennium, provides an auspicious opportunity to upend the linear economy in this age of disruptions. Old technologies are falling apart at a rapid pace, and new ones are taking command at the forefront of the global economy. These disruptive technologies are not necessarily eco-friendly and, in some cases, have exacerbated the challenges and problems of the linear economy as they push the frontiers of efficiency of mass production, promote shortened product lifespan, and make worse an endemic global waste problem. Still, others are eco-oriented technologies, prioritizing resource efficiency over production maximization. In effect, digital transformation is a battleground of disruption, where ambitious eco-friendly innovations challenge the onslaught of a digitally powered linear economy for market leadership. The following is a highlight of key areas where circular innovations are gaining traction:

Firstly, as linear economy technologies prioritize resource extraction and disposal, they invariably create inefficiencies and environmental burdens. In response, digital technologies such as IoT and blockchain prioritize the optimization of material flows, thereby minimizing waste and maximizing reuse. The second example contrasts centralized high-volume production with decentralized, customized manufacturing. The former, underpinned by traditional manufacturing, creates waste from inefficient resource use but is also more intensive in energy and ancillary resource consumption associated with long supply chains and economies of scale. On the other hand, frontier digitally enabled technologies like 3D printing to minimize resource use and disrupt traditional supply chains through decentralized manufacturing and the economy of one (Oyinlola et al. 2022). Thirdly, digital innovations are challenging ownership-based consumption by enabling servitization models where consumers can access services without ownership, thereby reducing waste while extending the product lifecycle. The past decade has seen a remarkable growth of multi-sided digital platforms powering collaborative consumption in what has been described as the sharing economy (Oyinlola et al. 2022). Fourthly, while linear economies typically operate reactively, the boom in AI and machine learning technologies has driven new predictive applications in predictive maintenance, thereby reducing time and material use and addressing problems in advance before they escalate.

1.2 Challenges to Technology-Enabled Circularity

While the potential of digital innovations to drive the CE transition is evident, numerous challenges hinder their widespread adoption and effectiveness. First, the digital divide remains a significant barrier, particularly in developing regions. The ability of many countries and communities to realize benefits from the technologies is limited by inadequate digital infrastructures, lack of meaningful internet connectivity, and inadequate digital literacy. This is exacerbated by the uneven distribution of technological expertise and financial resources, further marginalizing disadvantaged regions and populations. Regulatory and institutional barriers also pose significant challenges. Globally, many countries lag in the policy frameworks required to incentivize circular economy practices. For instance, the lack of extended producer responsibility regulations in several African countries undermines efforts to hold manufacturers accountable for the lifecycle impacts of their products.

The given regulatory frameworks need to understand the utility of technology-led solutions in the given geographical proximity. Meanwhile, firms that have spent money on traditional operational formations are usually reluctant to adopt emerging technologies, considering the cost and risk associated with them. Likewise, the global corporate landscape also reflects stats in line with linear technologies, with a slight tilt in favour of emerging circular sustainable technologies (Khan et al. 2024). Conversely, to counter the prevailing linear technology-led mindset, there is a dire need for public–private collaboration (Kolade et al. 2024).

1.3 Regional Nuances and Progress in the Circular Economy Transition

The advancements and developments surrounding the circular economy process vary from one region to another. These variations are developed due to several factors, including the level of economic development, the nature of industrial frameworks, and the unique sociocultural environments. In Europe, the concept of circular economy has its place within regional policy frameworks because of initiatives like the European Green Deal. This policy framework focuses on the need to adopt circular practices across industries to emphasize a collective commitment to sustainability. Digital innovations receive substantial backing from funding initiatives such as Horizon Europe, which offers vital resources for the research and development of circular technologies.

Initiatives such as Woelabs in Togo, which focuses on constructing 3D printers from electronic waste, have achieved impressive results. They highlight the potential of resource-limited settings to foster innovative solutions and promote circular economy principles.

Southeast Asia faces the significant challenge of addressing both the substantial amounts of plastic waste generated and the need to shift towards more sustainable circular systems.

In the same way, geographical areas like Africa and Southeast Asia are faced with challenges of varying nature and intensity, which set the direction for its development. According to the article, grassroots support and informal industrial formations for circular economic nourishment. Similarly, the stated grassroots initiatives hold notable strength in causing a change in Favor of a circular economy. However, challenges prevail, including the availability of supporting policies, infrastructure, and financial subsidies. There are also signs of slow yet steady technological growth within the developing region for the adoption of sustainable business practices.

Likewise, Indonesia and Vietnam have also adopted digital technologies for managing their waste, which marks a significant step in the direction of sustainable development. Though corresponding challenges, including non-existent policies and social support, do undermine the positive, sustainable step, the given limitations also underscore the developments in Favor of technological advancements and ask for prompt community engagements and mass education in Favor of the subject matter.

1.4 A Multi-Sectoral, Multi-Stakeholder Approach to Circular Economy Transitions

The intermix of technological advancements and circular economic development has a promising prospect for sustainable orientation. Yet, to make the maximum of the given potential, there is a dire need for coordinated efforts across the layers of the social fabric. Public offices are required to legislate in favor of circular economic practices and related technological adoption. It also asks for formalizing the public and private partnerships for digital infrastructure development, which in turn encourages sustainable consumption practices. Businesses, still sticking with conventional value chains, are supposed to rethink their corporate formations for improved performance outcomes. Firms are required to absorb technologies that facilitate the optimum utilization of resources, which ignites efficiency. This leads to rethinking products, with increased reliability and reusability, through effective integration with chain-wide stakeholders.

Academic institutions do have a role to play in pursuit of shaping the future, which would be sustainable. Developing a curriculum that will focus on developing digital competencies will surely play its part in nurturing generations that will be more innovative and would have more inclination toward sustainable innovation (Okoya et al. 2024). Similarly, the influx of 3D printing within the given education landscape has the potential to cause sustainable transformation (Bañón and Raspall 2022).

The integration of technological advancement and the emergence of circular economic principles hold the definite potential to address sustainable issues faced by the present-day world. With the effective use of emerging technologies, firms can likely ensure the transition towards circular economic systems, which ensures optimum utilization of resources, reduced waste, and the development of self-sustaining systems (Oyinlola et al. 2022). The materialization of the given sustainable aspirations demands countering the regulatory, technological, and industrial challenges at hand. Varying geographical formations ask for tailored policies that propagate the practical usage of prevailing advantages in order to counter existing challenges. The given intellectual compilation digs deep into the process, which aspires to craft a sustainable future with a reasonable focus on innovation and circular corporate formation.

The upcoming sections present an overview of the chapters, emphasizing the connections and complementary insights that exist among them. Additionally, they will address the gaps and opportunities that arise in the context of circular economy transitions across various regional and geopolitical landscapes.

2 Introduction to the Chapters

The given edited compilation presents a mindfully crafted list of chapters that explore the interrelationship between the concepts of circular economy and technological enhancement. The dispersed contributions highlight the utility of nexus in encouraging sustainable development across the region. Chapters also unbox the challenges posed and prevailing opportunities, which are both the by-products of the transition from linear to comparative circular and resource-smart systems.

Similarly, the initial chapters, titled Circular Economic and Technological Innovation in Industry 4.0 and 5.0 Revolution, which proves to be the stepping stone that sets the tone for discovering the connection between technological enhancement and the idea of circular economic development, the given book also explores the actions, through which AI, blockchain, and Internet of things (IoT), contributes towards transparent supply chains. Therefore, the given industrial developments are critical for transforming industries by reducing their carbon footprints. This sets the robust foundation for the book's exploration of innovative circular practices.

Expanding on this foundation, the third chapter, *Insights into Eco-Product Designs and Eco-Business Model Strategies*," examines the design strategies and business models that underpin the circular economy. With the traditional "take-make-dispose" model proving unsustainable, the chapter demonstrates how industries can adopt circular product design and eco-business strategies to mitigate resource depletion and environmental degradation. This resonates with the practical deployment of Industry 4.0 tools discussed in this chapter, which highlights the interaction between technological and design innovations.

The initial chapters investigate behavioral and logistical aspects of circular economy practices. The chapter title, Online to Offline Recycling—An Analysis of Recycling Waste in an Internet-Integrated World, explores how digital platforms influence consumer recycling behavior, demonstrating the role of Internet-enabled services in promoting sustainability. This is especially true among younger demographics, who are strongly represented in the frontline of sustainability and circularity campaigns. The chapter titled *Environmental Sustainability: Nexus between Green Conscientiousness, Green Motivation, Green Altruism, Green Attitudinal Purchase Intention, and Green Brand Evangelism*, analyses consumer attitudes and motivations. The authors underline the effective role of "green evangelists" and promoters of circular consumption habits among the population. Together, these chapters connect technological infrastructure with consumer-centric insights, illustrating the behavioral and digital dimensions of circular transitions.

Higher education emerges as a pivotal actor in the other two chapters. Chapter title, *Circular Economy and Commitment of Asian, South American, and Middle Eastern Higher Education Institutions to Sustainability Agenda*, investigates how regional higher education institutions (HEIs) embed sustainability principles into their strategies. Using content analysis, the chapter identifies regional variations in how HEIs align with Sustainable Development Goals (SDGs). Chapter title, *Assessing Publication Trends in MIS, Economics, and Management: Exploring the Impact of Sustainable Practices, Circular Economy, and Digitalisation*, underscores the intellectual contributions of academia to advancing circular economy research, tracing publication trends and emerging themes in sustainability and digitalization. These chapters highlight the role of knowledge systems and education in driving systemic change.

Two chapters focus on organizational and consumer dynamics within circular transitions. Chapter title: *The Impact of Integration, Hyper Agility, and Resilience Capability on Agile Strategy: Leading Towards Firms' Sustainable Performance*, examines how firms navigate global supply chain disruptions using agility and resilience capabilities. The findings underscore the necessity of dynamic capabilities to achieve sustainable performance. Chapter title, *Determinants of Consumer Green Product Consumption: Analysing the Role of Green Marketing and Consumer Attitudes*, explores the factors driving consumer preferences for green products. These chapters emphasize the interplay between organizational strategies and consumer engagement in fostering circular economies.

The following three chapters offer insightful regional perspectives that focus on the sustainability challenges and opportunities. The chapter titled "The Complex Nexus of Military Spending, Economic Growth, Energy Consumption, and Environmental Sustainability: Insights from India and China" focuses on the intricate association between economic development and environmental impact, specifically on India and China. A chapter titled "A Multivariate Analysis of Economic Growth, Energy Consumption, and Carbon Emissions in Highly Mountainous Economies: An Empirical Evidence" focuses on the environmental Kuznets curve within mountainous regions. The chapter examines the intricate association between economic activities and their influence on carbon emissions by providing valuable insights. Chapter titled "Environmental Kuznets Curve in Pacific Nations: ICT and Renewable Dynamics" delves into the intricate association between information and communication technology (ICT) and renewable energy by exploring their roles in shaping environmental sustainability across East Asia and the Pacific region. These chapters together highlight the specific details of regional paths, demonstrating how socioeconomic and environmental contexts bring circular economy practices in the implementation process.

The concluding chapters focus on transformative opportunities. Revolutionising Agriculture: Harnessing High-Performance Computing and Artificial Intelligence for Innovative Farming Practices" explores how AI and high-performance computing can transform agriculture, enhancing resource use efficiency and reducing environmental impacts. The next chapter, *Revolutionising Sustainability: The Impact of Circular Economy Innovations on CO2 Emissions*, examines circular economy innovations' macroeconomic and environmental benefits, particularly in reducing carbon emissions. Further, in a chapter titled: *3D Printing and the Circular Plastic Economy: Challenges and Opportunities in Nigerian Universities*, the authors explore how universities can drive sustainability through 3D printing technologies. Analyzing data from 151 students in Nigeria, the chapter highlights the critical role of knowledge in plastic waste management while uncovering systemic gaps in infrastructure and policy. It advocates multi-sectoral partnerships to enhance innovation and entrepreneurship in resource-constrained settings.

In the last chapter, *Greening the Workforce for Product Recycling and Energy Conservation,* addresses the human capital dimension, highlighting the importance of workforce greening and green human resource management practices in achieving organizational sustainability goals.

While these chapters span diverse topics, they are united by a common thread: the recognition that technological innovations are indispensable for advancing circular economy principles. The role of digital platforms in recycling and AI-driven agricultural solutions highlights the importance of integrated approaches in achieving circular transitions. These contributions illustrate that such transitions necessitate a harmonious blend of technological, organizational, and behavioral dimensions. The chapters simultaneously highlight the difficulties posed by established linear economic models, the variations across regions, and the pressing requirement for both policy and educational interventions.

3 Introduction to Book Sections

The following sections represent three emerging domains that capture the interconnectedness and critical aspects of circular economy and technological innovation discussed in the above-mentioned chapters. The transformative potential of digital technologies in circular practices is significant. Themes such as these serve as a guide for comprehending and tackling the intricate challenges associated with implementing a circular economy in various settings.

3.1 Foundations of Circular Economy and Technological Innovation

The foundational chapters of this book revealed that technological innovations have considerable potential in the enhancement of circular economy (CE) practices. These innovative technologies have the potential to deal with inefficiencies found in traditional business models and to leverage sustainable resource utilization. Innovations concerning circular practices play a significant role in the design, implementation, and scaling of circular business models by transforming global economies and shifting to sustainability initiatives. Other researchers have indicated that the incorporation of digital solutions within circular economy frameworks improves resource efficiency, aids in waste reduction, and encourages innovative opportunities for reuse, reform, and recycling (Khan et al. 2024; Khan et al. 2024; Khan et al. 2024; Zhang et al. 2024).

Furthermore, the first section of the book discusses the growth and development of the circular economy and innovations in technology, particularly their use in industries 4.0 and 5.0. This section also emphasizes insights into eco-product designs and eco-business model strategies. Additionally, it emphasizes the trends in MIS, economics, and management by Redefining the role of sustainable practices, circular economy, and digitalization. Innovative technologies such as Industry 4.0 and 5.0 possess the capacity to disrupt and transform conventional industrial methods. Innovative tools like AI-enabled blockchain technologies enhance supply chain visibility and transparency.

Meanwhile, additive manufacturing plays a significant role in remanufacturing, showcasing its practical relevance in promoting circularity. Similarly, recent studies have highlighted that the transparency offered by blockchain technology plays a crucial role in enabling closed-loop supply chain systems, thereby ensuring traceability throughout the recycling and remanufacturing processes (Khan et al. 2024; Rehman Khan et al. 2022). Despite these challenges, significant opportunities for innovation can arise. Digital technologies have the potential to connect infrastructural gaps and inspire local innovations by encouraging collaborations among various stakeholders and incorporating circular economy practices into broader socio-economic strategies. Current research shows that these methods enable informal and small-scale participants to engage in circular value chains, fostering inclusive economic ecosystems. The literature highlights the crucial requirement to leverage digital technologies for logical systemic change. However, this approach fosters not only strong circular economy practices but also tackles global sustainability concerns affecting us all.

3.2 Sustainability Practices Across Industries and Regions

As global challenges like the climate crisis and the ongoing pandemic intensify, scholars are calling for modernizing regional development strategies. Issues such as rising inequalities and the depletion of critical resources have often been overlooked in mainstream economic discussions despite their profound socio-spatial impacts (Oyinlola et al. 2022). To address these challenges, we propose a framework for transformative regional development. This approach emphasizes innovation and socio-technical system changes that align with ecological boundaries and address major crises like climate change. It adopts a clear normative stance, integrating ecological and social dynamics into regional development concepts.

A connection is made between the principles of regional industrial growth and the objectives of transitions toward sustainability through transformative regional development. Even though recent research has shed light on the overlap between these domains, there is still a lack of comprehensive and integrated approaches. There is an urgent requirement for a comprehensive plan that investigates the dynamic relationship between regional industrial pathways and the broader sociological and spatial environments in which they are situated. The trajectories of regions are interrelated and influence one another across various spatial scales. Regions do not exist in isolation from one another. Even while there is a growing awareness of these interdependencies, the crucial role that natural resources play in supporting economies and lifestyles is sometimes underestimated. The true meaning of transformative regional development is acknowledging the profound interconnectedness of ecological boundaries with human systems while respecting those boundaries.

3.3 Innovations Driving Green Transformation

A core idea of circular economy models is optimizing product use, not just production, with consumer behaviour playing a crucial role in the adoption of green and innovative products. This shift emphasizes an "attitude to care," treating end-of-life goods as items for reuse rather than waste. Reintegrating these goods into new cycles reduces waste and promotes sustainability. Studies explore what influences consumers' attitudes toward product care, and green marketing has fostered a segment of environmentally conscious consumers. These individuals consider the ecological impact of their choices, challenging traditional views by recognizing humanity's connection with nature and prioritizing sustainability in their decisions.

Green consumers embody a sense of responsibility at three levels: to themselves, others, and the environment. This convergence between green and ethical consumerism underscores the link between self-care, health, and a shift toward sustainable consumption. However, challenges remain, such as the "rebound effect," where access to eco-friendly products may encourage overconsumption, offsetting environmental benefits. Sustainable marketing highlights that consumer responsibility extends beyond personal actions, emphasizing choices' broader societal and environmental impact. Principles like fairness, respect, and justice define the consumer-citizen, whose decisions aim to create a positive social and ecological balance within a win–win framework.

4 Conclusion

This introductory section explains the essential relationship between the concepts of a circular economy, technological innovation, consumer responsibility, and regional development concerning sustainability and circular economy practices. The book chapters majorly focus on addressing pressing global issues like technology and green transformation, climate change, resource depletion, responsible consumption, environmental impacts, industry transformation, circular product designing, green workforce, and many other insights. This book majorly focuses on the importance of circular economy practices in changing the production paradigms from traditional production to the optimum utilization of resources to reduce wastage and make materials reusable to conserve natural resources and achieve sustainable development goals. Further, the circular economy encourages us to view products that have completed their lifecycle not as waste but as a valuable opportunity to reuse such products and to conserve resources by optimizing the use of raw materials through the concept of recycling and reform. The emergence of technological innovations and depletion of resources has raised a lot of environmental concerns and led consumers to be more environmentally conscious, specifically enabling them to make responsible decision-making. Therefore, in this book, chapters address a comprehensive framework for tackling the sustainability issues offered based on regional development. Collectively, these concepts chart a pathway toward a future that is more sustainable, balanced, and resilient.

References

Bañón C, Raspall F (2022) 3D printing floating modular farms from plastic waste. Mater Today: Proc 70:560–566. https://doi.org/10.1016/j.matpr.2022.09.591

Hassan NM, Khan SAR, Ashraf MU, Sheikh AA (2023) Interconnection between the role of blockchain technologies, supply chain integration, and circular economy: A case of small and medium-sized enterprises in Pakistan. Sci Prog 106(3):1–22. https://doi.org/10.1177/00368504231186527

Khan FA, Sheikh DAA, Zainab F (2024) The impact of smes capability for service innovation and its tactical green marketing on sustainable business performance. J Small Bus Strat 34(2):2024. https://doi.org/10.53703/001c.117659

Khan SAR, Sheikh AA, Tahir MS (2024b) Corporate social responsibility-an antidote for sustainable business performance: interconnecting role of digital technologies, employee eco-behavior, and tax avoidance. Environ Sci Pollut Res Int 31(3):4365–4383. https://doi.org/10.1007/S11356-023-31377-9

Khan SAR, Tahir MS, Sheikh AA (2024) Sustainable performance in SMEs using big data analytics for closed-loop supply chains and reverse omnichannel. Heliyon 10(16). https://doi.org/10.1016/j.heliyon.2024.e36237

Kolade O, Oyinlola M, Ogunde O, Ilo C, Ajala O (2024) Digitally enabled business models for a circular plastic economy in Africa. Environ Technol Innov 35:103657. https://doi.org/10.1016/j.eti.2024.103657

Okoya SA, Oyinlola M, Ajala O, Kolade O, Adefila A, Akinlabi E (2024) Assessing the determinants of participation in the circular plastic economy by Nigerian students. Int J Sustain High Educ. https://doi.org/10.1108/IJSHE-04-2023-0132

Oyinlola M, Schröder P, Whitehead T, Kolade O, Wakunuma K, Sharifi S, Rawn B, Odumuyiwa V, Lendelvo S, Brighty G, Tijani B, Jaiyeola T, Lindunda L, Mtonga R, Abolfathi S, Hofstetter JS (2022) Digital innovations for transitioning to circular plastic value chains in Africa. Afr J Manag 8(1):83–108. https://doi.org/10.1080/23322373.2021.1999750

Rehman Khan SA, Ahmad Z, Sheikh AA, Yu Z (2022) Digital transformation, smart technologies, and eco-innovation are paving the way toward sustainable supply chain performance. Sci Prog 105(4):1–26. https://doi.org/10.1177/00368504221145648

Zhang Y, Hassan NM, Sheikh AA (2024) Unboxing the dilemma associated with online shopping and purchase behavior for remanufactured products: A smart strategy for waste management. J Environ Manag 351. https://doi.org/10.1016/j.jenvman.2023.119790

Technological Innovation in Industry 4.0 and 5.0 Revolution

Hina Zafar, Bader Unnisa Mehdi, Adnan Ahmed Sheikh, and Noor E Sahar

Abstract This chapter discusses the relationship between technological innovation and the principles of the circular economy, highlighting its role in addressing global challenges and advancing sustainable development. It elaborates on how Industry 4.0, with its focus on automation, digitalization, and data-driven processes, and Industry 5.0, with its innovation-centric and human-centered transformation drive the world toward a shift from linear to circular economic models. These models prioritize waste reduction and resource optimization, facilitated by transparent supply chains enabled through smart technologies such as artificial intelligence (AI), blockchain, and the Internet of Things (IoT). It also refers to how it can be applied with circular economy sustainable production in conjunction with steps that could provide extra length of life to the product life cycles and lives of the products to neutralize the adverse impacts on the environment. This chapter explores the possibility of combining technological advancement with the principles of circular economy to overcome issues related to global environmental concerns. It is more generally predicated on the transformation of traditional linear forms of the economy into increasingly circular forms by transformative impacts from Industry 4.0 technologies through to those from Industry 5.0. This discussion critically examines technologies like blockchain, IoT, and AI to determine whether they reduce waste, improve resource efficiency, and enhance supply chain visibility. Various research studies have been conducted implementing such resources in harmony with principles based on the circular economy regarding

H. Zafar
University of Newcastle, Callaghan, Australia
e-mail: hina.zafar@newcastle.edu.au

B. U. Mehdi
Western Sydney University, Sydney, Australia
e-mail: b.unnisa@westernsydney.edu.au

A. A. Sheikh
College of Business, University of Buraimi, Al Buraimi, Sultanate of Oman
e-mail: Adnan.a@uob.edu.om

N. E. Sahar (✉)
Benazir Bhutto Shaheed University Lyari, Karachi, Pakistan
e-mail: noor.sahar@bbsul.edu.pk

S. A. R. Khan et al. (eds.), *Circular Economy and Technological Innovation*, Industrial Ecology, https://doi.org/10.1007/978-981-96-5650-9_2

sustainable production, prolonged lifetime of the products, and least damaging environmental effects.

Keywords Circular Economy · Sustainable Manufacturing · Industry 4.0 · Industry 5.0 · Digital Transformation · Technological Innovation · Artificial Intelligence

1 Introduction

This chapter explores the synergy between technological innovation and circular economy strategies, focusing on how these developments critically influence the march toward a sustainable future. It is because of the accelerated rate that the world depletes and degrades its natural resources that accelerates globalization towards sustainability. It allows for more sustainable action regarding the challenges posed by this shift because of the interplay of the principles defining circular economy with technological innovation (Rehman Khan et al. 2022). Therefore, circular economy strategies increase this concept of resource usage in a much better way, reduce waste, and save the environment in response to the fact that the industry is now shifting from the back end to receive, produce, and dispose of models of the past. Transformability is found in such new technologies, which greatly enhance resource management effectiveness and the ability of sustainable systems to adapt to production conditions (Khan et al. 2023; Khan et al. 2024).

Technological development not only facilitates the circular economy but also forms its fundamental foundation. Consequently, innovations pertaining to sustainable development include, on one side, Industry 4.0—the unformulated characteristics of smart manufacturing technologies, digitalization, and automation—and the emerging paradigm of Industry 5.0, which emphasizes human-centric innovation. Such technologies fit these industries with tools that optimize, extend the lifecycle, and reduce the carbon footprint of products. These circular economy principles begin to resonate with modern technology, becoming a fuel for the transition of organizations toward more sustainable resource-efficient, and competitive business models.

The organization of this chapter is designed to be expressive so as briefly to show an understanding of the relationship between technological innovation and circular economy principles. **Section** 2 demonstrates comprehensive conceptions of the circular economy and its alignment with new technology in the transition from traditional linear economic models to resource-efficient circular ones. **Section** 3 discusses Industry 4.0 as an enabler of sustainable production, the sense that is about aspects that relate to the transformative power of some of these technologies—improve resource use, reduce wastes in generation, and increase efficiency in production through IoT, AI, and big data analytics. **Section** 4 deals with the progression towards Industry 5.0, emphasizing human-centric innovation and sustainability by emphasizing the collaboration between human intellect and machine capabilities to promote environmentally friendly behaviors. **Section** 5 discusses the technological novelties towards achieving the goals of the purposes for the circular economy, including blockchain, AI, and smart systems for better decisions in real-time and hence promoting greater transparency and sustainability designs for products. Finally, **Sect.** 6 concludes with a discussion of the challenges that these adopted technologies of Industry 4.0 and 5.0 pose in reaching the circular goals, such as the lack of skills and cost, and also with remedies to facilitate this transition into a more sustainable future.

1.1 The Intersection of Circular Economy and Technological Revolutions

Market instability and rising geopolitical tensions are being fueled by fast-depleting essentials like freshwater, rare earth elements, and fossil fuels (Shahzad et al. 2023; Xiong et al. 2023). A novel idea has emerged, known as the "circular economy," which addresses these challenges and offers a far more sustainable alternative to the traditional system that depletes the limited resources of the environment. It is not an insignificant shift, one of real transformation that will be in response to the requirement facing the globe to solve pending issues that will make the future more sustainable and just, also ecologically balanced (Mukherjee et al. 2023). The circular economy tries to minimize waste and pollution, healthier communities, and strengthen resilience in social and economic systems. As De Pascale et al. (2023) suggest that the circular economy is a description of how improvement in sustainability thrives on reusing, recycling, and regenerating activities that separate economic growth from the depletion of natural resources. That transformation is much needed for environmental sustainability.

According to Charlier and Fizaine (2023), the activities of business enterprises may stabilize markets and materials because the business organizations will lessen their demand for these very valuable but very limited resources. In the long run, this will finally make their activities less destructive to the environment. As per predictions, the world will achieve its goals regarding the availability, usage, and management of water resources along with combating climatic change conditions by 2030 (Khajuria et al. 2022). Adopting circular economy principles presents a golden opportunity for businesses to align with sustainable practices while achieving economic growth (Hassan et al. 2023; Zhang et al. 2024).

Technical innovations would be the key to formulating and implementing strategies in a circular economy. In this context, innovations investigate circular systems to improve sustainability and efficiency. Additionally, it is considered essential for promoting innovation in sustainable production and resource management. Innovations in this domain are necessary to facilitate material reuse, enhance manufacturing processes, and explore new avenues for resource management, sustainable design, and recycling within the organization. According to Sánchez-García et al. (2024) and

Sehnem et al. (2022), the technological innovations have been incorporated into the circular economy, which encourages sustainable production and job opportunities for developing countries. This shift is vital to bringing more sustainable business practices into usage (Khan et al. 2024). Such emerging technology is enabling the growth of circular practices in the social spheres of society because such potential technological change influences social systems, industries, and economies in general (Sánchez-García et al. 2024).

As per Oluleye et al. (2023), blockchain and AI are more promising for promoting sustainable industrial methods. Artificial intelligence can change industrial processes, manage product life cycles better, predict behavioral trends, and manage resource distribution appropriately. According to Singh and Sarkar (2023), the goals of the circular economy may be directly advanced by enhancing the efficacy and efficiency of recycling and material reuse. Blockchain technology is important to make it possible to monitor and responsibly administer materials throughout their lifecycles. Resources will be more efficiently and responsibly used with supply chain transparency and accountability.

Technological advancement significantly impacts everyday life in our digital environment, enhancing a sense of belonging. It is now quite simple to communicate with people in ways that were just a dream a short time ago, and it does not need as much effort as it did in the past. Another unanticipated consequence of such access is the accumulation of electronic garbage, which is a growing problem (Rajesh et al. 2022). Rapid integration of emerging technology is fast becoming a contributory factor to the proliferation of electronic waste, which is a formidable challenge for sustainability. In that regard, there has been some progress in the integration of technological advancements with principles of a circular economy, which is helping pave the way to a sustainable path. Organizations of many sectors can apply innovations to resource efficiency, waste reduction, and a way of supporting sustainability through circular economy frameworks (Bhardwaj et al. 2025). Their interconnection would most likely drive innovation, form the underpinning of growth in the economy, and help to solve some of the severely important environmental issues we are going to have to deal with now. The key assumption underlying the circular economy is that technology will be a tool through which the current "receive, produce, dispose" paradigm can be transitioned to a more sustainable and circular one.

According to Khong (2023) and Özçatalbaş (2023), digital technologies track the availability of resources used by companies, unlock recycling and reusing possibilities, and evaluate products throughout their whole lifecycle. This implies that, on the whole, these technologies are much needed to form a better economy and an efficient one by making it easy for companies to make smarter and more informed decisions. Renewable energy technology is the core nucleus of the circular economy structure. Jakubelskas and Skvarciany (2023) and Santos et al. (2023) hold the view that the transition to renewable energy reduces dependence on fossil fuels and brings it into tenets of circular economy as it allows for sustainable usage of resources and waste reduction. This would then go further to bolster the foundation for more sustainable production which is necessarily efficient. It reduces the environmental impacts that will be associated with production and thus, contributes to more sustainable overall supply chains. Rejeb and Appolloni (2022) assert that this circular economy transition has accelerated, led mostly by the advancement of Industry 4.0 technologies that were supposed to have potential positive impacts on business and societal goals through an opportunity for sustainable system development with a focus on fairness.

Through predictive analytics, which encompass AI and machine learning, firms or businesses optimize their resource allocation without waste or excess expenditure. Taking the same with blockchain technology, new levels of transparency and accountability will emerge herein for inventory management that is traceable from the point of manufacture to final disposal (Khan et al. 2024). As stated by Wang and Yu (2023), integrating AI with blockchain also increases data security and efficiency in operation, more vital components for a sustainable circular economy. On the other hand, new features in product life cycle management allow it to be easier to disassemble and reuse parts, and therefore, materials acquired from re-manufacturing become even more appealing. Knoth et al. (2022) and Sánchez-García et al. (2024) argue that firms are now capable of making strategic decisions in stimulating the circular economy by handling data collected at each step of a product's lifecycle through the application of big data analytics. Some of the short-term impacts of such a change are new business models, industrial process improvement, cooperation on value chains, and reduced environmental impact.

Kamalaldin et al. (2020) and Dana et al. (2022) argued that the organization needs to have a plan of action properly, not to be at the back of competition within sustainable markets. However, challenges are found with a circular economy. A circular model requires much change in workflow, and companies have to face heavy initial investment to adopt such advanced technology in their systems. The another limitation is the change in the mindset of people who get aligned and back traditional models of production and consumption (Hu et al. 2018). This calls for significant collaboration and workplace innovation.

There has been a tremendous push for implementing circular economy concepts, including the active participation of relevant stakeholder groups, cutting-edge technological solutions, and the mobilization of educational resources to create a new workforce. Business development needs a greater number of experts skilled in the methodologies and tools of the circular economy. According to Muriithi and Ngare (2023), students could learn to integrate a module on sustainability, circular design, and innovation technology. Integrating modules on sustainability, circular design, and innovative technology into education can prepare professionals to implement circular economy practices effectively.

The promising path toward long-term success comes when there is a reconciliation between the principles of the circular economy and technological innovation. This brings the best improvements in resource efficiency and waste minimization and is very much needed to stimulate economic growth. There will be a need for governments, businesses, and consumers to work together in harmony, ensuring alignment through education and practices regarding sustainability goals. In building long-term values for society, businesses that embrace this circular economy model thus benefit the planet's well-being—with the approach of the circular economy coupled with technology, issues such as electronic waste can be addressed through alternative methods, considered urgent worldwide. If appropriately used, then maybe a better change will be introduced in the environment as an application of technology would open doors to growth opportunities. With effective use of technology, issues like e-waste can be mitigated, fostering innovation and growth opportunities that require unified efforts from all stakeholders.

1.2 Industry 4.0: Foundations for Sustainable Manufacturing

Industry 4.0 is changing sustainable manufacturing with advanced technology in addition to more efficiency in operations, waste minimization, and activities of the environment. The fourth industrial revolution enables the use of cutting-edge digital technologies in production processes, compelling industries to change the way they work. This change allows companies to increase their operational efficacy and practice more sustainable production. As per Raja Santhi and Muthuswamy (2023), these technologies are transforming the industrial landscape by transforming traditional manufacturing methods into intelligent, adaptable, and highly responsive systems, thereby enabling industries to better align with sustainability goals and enhance productivity.

One of the major advantages of Industry 4.0 in terms of maximizing resource use and reducing waste is the automation and real-time data analysis it offers. Devices made possible by the IoT allow for continuous monitoring of industrial processes and equipment performance, which helps reduce unexpected downtime and enables predictive maintenance (Rehman and Alfaify 2023). Such preventive interventions are encouraged under welfare guidelines as a means to facilitate sustainability objectives by extending equipment life, minimizing energy demand, and enhancing operational performance (Larsen et al. 2023). For instance, some tools are used to measure and manage inefficient efficiency by comparing the consumption of energy with the required levels so that operations are located and reduce carbon emissions (Shadravan and Parsaei 2023).

Artificial intelligence and machine learning change processes by acquiring smarter decision-making, optimizing the use of resources, and enhancing operational efficiency. Such high technology further improves manufacturing through developing adaptive systems able to adjust dynamically to changing conditions and demands. These technologies can produce bespoke products with relatively low resource use, in line with the principles of a circular economy (Patalas-Maliszewska and Kłos 2019). In order to promote recyclability and repair flexibility, the process of developing and producing goods with longer lifespans is much less difficult. This results in reduced complexity. Additionally, the environmental effect of these items is greatly reduced with time (Acerbi et al. 2021). This strategy not only meets regulatory requirements but also aligns with the rising customer desire for green goods (Sherif et al. 2023).

Despite the hype, industry investment in Industry 4.0 holds serious challenges for its implementation. The high capital-intensive nature of initial investments is paired with a scarcity of competent manpower, not to mention an unstable disposition to retain traditional processes, most of which have turned out ineffective. It just pushes more companies away (Shadravan and Parsaei 2023). To develop competent manpower, organizations have to train their workforce by investing in massive human resource training and development expenditures. However, innovation and collaboration may also be encouraged within the business entity to facilitate ease of new practices adoption and implementation into the organization (Chonsawat and Sopadang 2020).

The integration of Industry 4.0 technologies also acts as an enabler for implementing circular economy practices in manufacturing. Industry 4.0 improves resource use and also facilitates traceability of the product lifecycle. In this process, it facilitates recycling, re-manufacturing, and resource recovery (Ghaithan et al. 2023). For instance, through advanced analytics, customer engagement in design can be facilitated to address end-of-life needs early on in the design phase. Moving towards these circular economy approaches saves natural resources while simultaneously promoting creativity and building new competitive market advantages (Rusmayadi et al. 2023). However, the integration of Industry 4.0 into green manufacturing is not without any challenges. Some of them are very high initial capital expenditure, lack of proficient employees, and reluctance to discontinue the use of traditional manufacturing systems, among others (Torbacki 2021). This will only be the case if businesses begin investments in training and development procedures, equipping employees to function in the use of cutting-edge manufacturing technology. An emerging culture that encourages collaboration fosters the assimilation of new and emerging technologies, such as sustainability.

Collaboration along the supply chain is equally important for the smooth implementation of Industry 4.0. Manufacturers must collaborate with suppliers, customers, and technology providers to develop an ecosystem that fosters sustainable practices (Akundi et al. 2022). Such a partnership builds innovative business models that involve resource efficiency and sustainability, yielding competitive advantages in the marketplace (Katrakazas et al. 2021). Industry 4.0 provides the blueprint for sustainable manufacturing because it places advanced digital technologies and innovative practices within its framework. However, challenges are still apparent while at the same time presenting numerous opportunities for improved performance operations with minimal impacts on the environment and supporting sustainability. Industry 4.0 allows for more productive production and contributes positively to achieving global environmental performance by embracing its principles and tools.

1.3 The Transition to Industry 5.0: Human-Centric Innovation

Industry 5.0 is a great change in industrial development, oriented towards human-centered innovation and sustainability. It is a way of implementing new technologies into daily life beyond technological advancement, improves human ability, increases cooperation between human beings and machines, and brings about the realization of sustainability across many different sectors. Human-centric innovation emphasizes creating new products and services that revolve around the needs, wants, and behaviors of end users (Carayannis et al. 2022). By placing humans at the center of the design process, Industry 5.0 ensures that solutions are customized to address specific needs, enhancing the meaning, utility, and value of businesses for their customers.

At its core, Industry 5.0 views human workers are considered core contributors to the production process, not just machine operators but innovators and decision-makers. This shift depicts an ever-increasing need for building resilient and adaptable production systems that are responsive to dynamic market demands and environmental challenges (Aguilar Esteva et al. 2021). This would include using AI, robotics, and IoT within an organization to enhance human capacity so that the employee is freed to work on higher value creation involving creativity, critical thinking, and problem-solving (Jones and Wynn 2021).

Industry 5.0 aligns seamlessly with the principles of circular economy and rests on efficiency, reduction in waste, and sustainability of products. The induction of circular economy concepts in Industry 5.0 frameworks helps in designing products and processes for which organizations are coming up with environment-friendly output with the minimum wasteful usage of resources (Ghaithan et al. 2023). For instance, the automotive sector has been embracing circular economy principles through material efficiency, recycling activities, and designing products for durability and reparability (Aguilar Esteva et al. 2021). Such efforts enhance sustainability and offer a competitive advantage for businesses in an increasingly changing environment.

However, transitioning to Industry 5.0 and a circular economy poses several challenges. For instance, it demands massive investments in developing new technologies, a qualified enough workforce, and a readiness to give up the much-practiced manufacturing system (Awan et al. 2021). In this process, education and training programs should be on the top agenda of companies that help employees function well in a human-centered, technology-driven environment (Alfarizi et al. 2023). Companies need to focus education and training programs on employees to allow them to thrive in a human-centered technological environment. To promote the widespread adoption of innovative methodologies and practices, it is essential to cultivate an atmosphere that fosters creative problem-solving and collaboration (Saeed et al. 2023).

Industry 5.0 and circular economy will become effective if collaborations up and down the supply chain increase. The involvement of customers, suppliers, and technology vendors for their support creates an ecosystem to endorse sustainability and innovation (Aguilar Esteva et al. 2021; Akkad et al. 2022). Such collaborative engagements are likely to bring new sustainable business models and resource utilization-based business models to tap the sustainability performance of an enterprise. Therefore, it takes it from the step of human-centric innovations and sustainability going forward toward human-centricity in building toward Industry 5.0, meaning it will change to promote improvement in sustainability competitiveness for human power empowerment at the advanced technology level while integrating as well as focusing on principles of the circular economy. Indeed, challenges abound, but the scope for innovation and better environmental outcomes underscores the need to adopt Industry 5.0 as a critical framework for the future of manufacturing and beyond.

1.4 Technological Innovations Driving the Circular Economy

Technological advancements are among the most significant catalysts for converting the world to a circular economy, maximizing the use of resources and waste minimization, thereby making it feasible for many sectors. Classical linear economic models have evolved into an efficient system much more effortlessly than by implementing new technology like artificial intelligence, blockchain, and the Internet of Things. The digital tools in use are probably the most impactful technologies that would enable the circular economy. Digitalization brings a connection of growth and sustainability for organizations, making operations smoother and lowering the impact of an organization on its surroundings. For instance, IoT enables organizations to get insights into how resources flow through them and pinpoint inefficiency in real time, correcting those mistakes promptly (Cahayani et al. 2023). This is one of the most important capabilities toward maximizing a principle of waste reduction and resource efficiency that is very much in line with the ideals of a circular economy.

This technological innovation brings about transformation concerning a circular economy because the same can make businesses able to reduce their waste, save their resources, and minimize impacts on the environment (Greene et al. 2024). The IoT, AI, and advanced manufacturing technologies transform linear production systems into sustainable, circular models. For instance, IoT-connected products enable companies to monitor in real-time how their products are being used and how they are performing. This encourages predictive maintenance and optimal resource consumption, extending the life of their products and reducing excess production and material consumption. Technologies like 3D printing improve resource efficiency through on-demand manufacturing without material waste and customized sustainability goals. Overall, all these factors benefit companies to produce products to be used for long periods, restored, and recycled, ultimately making the transition to a more circular economy easier.

Blockchain technology is instrumental in ensuring supply chain transparency and traceability. Decentralized and tamper-proof transaction records made available by blockchain enable tracing from source to product life cycles to ensure proper reusing and recycling of materials and products. Such a breakthrough can help consumers create confidence in the origin and the sustainability practices associated with the product through verifiable information that is in line with circular economy principles (Batool et al. 2023; Priyana et al. 2023). The creation of innovation goes beyond assurance against the principles of the circular economy while making consumer confidence based on verifiable origins as well as sustainable practices of the business enterprise (Batool et al. 2023). In that perspective, AI and ML technologies support a more effective utilization in decision-making through both consumption and product design. Through this, AI can process vast data to optimize the processes of production and reduce energy usage as well as waste formation (Onyeaka et al. 2023). AI-based predictive analytics allows firms to predict demand with more accuracy and thus manage operations for further achievement of circular economy goals (Ghaithan et al. 2023).

Changes to consumer and industry behavior come along with the integration of the practice of the circular economy with technology tools (Henao-Hincapié et al. 2024). For example, intelligent technologies such as blockchain—provide beyond-compare levels of transparency across a supply chain while tracing the lifecycle of the material for compliance in their respective sustainability standards. For a similar reason, digital platforms help improve the product-sharing model and the reverse logistics system so that consumers can get actively associated with the recycling and reusing system. Improved material science would reduce footprints at the consumption and production points for biodegradable and renewable materials. Innovations from such trends embrace more than just addressing ecological considerations but also form new pathways for economic recovery and strengthen their importance in promoting the worldwide adoption of principles in the circular economy by technology.

Business model innovations like product-as-a-service are integral to the circular economy. Product-as-a-service models ensure that producers design for durability and recyclability because consumers will only lease rather than buy products (Ting et al. 2023). This goes a long way in reducing waste and, at the same time, instills a culture of sustainability among the consumers, who are motivated to return the product at the end of its lifecycle for reuse or recycling (Ting et al. 2023). However, issues are presented by the shift into the technology-driven circular economy. The company setups carry with them enormous costs, experts in managing the new role are scarce, and, most importantly, the companies are a form of resistance against the adoption of the new way of doing things over the conventional (Awan et al. 2021). This calls for investment in training and development, equipping employees with a new role of technology, and opening up avenues for innovative business models, a factor Saeed et al. point out in their 2023 research (Saeed et al. 2023).

Technological innovations are essential to achieving a circular economy to help businesses optimize resources, work toward waste elimination, and promote sustainability. It will dramatically streamline the operations of organizations using digital technologies, blockchain, and AI. Change is difficult, but if innovation opportunities are reduced with increased sustainability, then the principle needs to be integrated across the industrial sectors. This results in innovations through more available knowledge and science, leading to the escalating consciousness of making an environment greener. When a business house sees an opportunity in its enterprise that is made more favorable to the environment, lowering emissions of greenhouse gases, along with the material used significantly, it understands that embedding effective circular economy strategies inside is very necessary. Black and Decker drill-just one example of proof it supports the Internet of Things. This appliance would charge a consumer by consumption of time with a notice for replacement of components. This again demonstrates how sustainability is used in practical implementation (Awan et al. 2021).

Institutional factors are also responsible for consumer acceptance development of circular economy principles. For instance, the European Union (EU) policies for designing products and extending the lifetime of products have successfully shifted the focus of the consumer toward durability, reparability, and functionality (Alonso-Almeida et al. 2020). Towards the end of its life cycle, most parts of the product are recycled and reused as similar or smaller-sized products. Governments worldwide are aligning legal frameworks to foster circular economy transitions, setting the stage for a greener and more sustainable future.

1.5 Challenges in Adopting Industry 4.0 and 5.0 for Circular Goals

The adoption of Industry 4.0 and 5.0 technologies to achieve the goals of the circular economy means integrating complex systems like IoT, AI, robotics, and advanced analytics. However, companies face significant challenges, particularly in accessing technical expertise that can make this interconnected system work properly. It involves ensuring seamless integration across diverse platforms, legacy systems, and supply chain networks, often lacking interoperability to support circular practices. Organizations face several barriers, including high initial investment requirements, lack of skilled labor, and unwillingness to change from traditional practices (Alfarizi et al. 2023). Companies, therefore, should have training and development programs that focus on preparing employees with knowledge to use new technologies and adopt new business models (Jones and Wynn 2021). Laskurain-Iturbe et al. (2023) argues that the lack of knowledge and comprehension of the benefits of Industry 4.0 technology will be mitigated, hence diminishing opposition to smart manufacturing and circular economy frameworks.

Adopting Industry 4.0 and 5.0 technology requires substantial financial expenses for necessary infrastructure, machinery, and employee education and development. This would discourage small and medium-sized enterprises (SMEs) since their financial resources would not allow them to afford such enormous amounts. Businesses may be discouraged from maintaining their present financial constraints if they believe that returns for these technologies would never materialize in the near future. Industry 4.0 and 5.0 are data-driven processes, therefore gathering, storing, and processing significant amounts of information need to be systematized (Westphal and Seitz 2021). The challenge when it comes to this is that of security data security and against sensitive business information (Jawaid and Ahmed 2023; Kasu et al. 2022).

Cybersecurity threats, like as hacking and data breaches, often undermine credibility in the effective implementation of circular models. Business enterprises must have robust cybersecurity strategies to safeguard vulnerable data. They are required to adhere to the principles of the General Data Protection Regulation (GDPR) (Kasu et al. 2022). Business companies have to address the integration challenge of cybersecurity solutions in their operations. This includes advanced security technologies, the frequency conducting of risk assessments, and setting a culture toward cybersecurity awareness and actions in the workforce from throughout an organization (Gwebu and Barrows 2020). Smart manufacturing and circular practice depend on a competent digital-technologically savvy and sustainable practices-focused workforce.

However, not in many companies, owing to various reasons of incompetence, mainly deficits of technological or management competencies and weaknesses found by the organizations. Closing this skills gap calls for significant investment in education, training, and reskilling, with costs both in time and money spent. Cultural resistance within organizations also impedes the adoption of Industry 4.0 and 5.0. Some of the factors that might sometimes be a barrier to advancement include deeply rooted attitudes, a fear of the unknown, and a lack of awareness about the advantages of contemporary technology. These are just some of the things that can sometimes block progress. The construction industry is highly challenged in the implementation of digital technologies, lacks a digital culture, and is resistant to change (Aghimien et al. 2022). Such barriers may inhibit the complete potential of innovations intended to lead sustainable practices in pursuit of circular economy goals.

Organizational culture is a fundamental variable influencing employee attitudes about embracing technology. In the opinion of Alassaf et al. (2020), organizational culture has an enormous impact on readiness to adopt open innovation strategies, especially in adopting Industry 4.0 and 5.0 technologies in an organization. Employees are less likely to embrace new technologies because they may feel that the organization is not prepared for the changes that new technologies bring. They will be afraid of layoffs or the company is not ready for its employees to be ready and manage the change process. Talapatra and Gaine (2019) argue that frameworks of a culture of continuous improvement need to be developed to ensure innovative work environments. These frameworks create an environment that allows for change, reduces resistance to it and encourages employees to use new technologies.

Employees may view new processes as threatening their job security, and management may also be resistant (Yedalla 2025). All stakeholders must, therefore, be enlightened on the circular objectives this new technology will trigger, and that should change management processes for this purpose. The regulatory environment for Industry 4.0 and 5.0 technologies, including sustainability and circular economy issues, is changing in nature. From a business perspective, unclear, inconsistent, or inadequate local, national, and international policies may lead to uncertainty. Circular practices are more difficult for multinational corporations to adopt because of their challenges in complying with regional environmental regulations.

Supply chain complexity adds another layer of difficulty. Circularity requires strong coordination, but fragmented supplier standards and systems hinder traceability and transparency (Zils et al. 2025). In that sense, material recovery and recirculation will be adversely affected. While Industries 4.0 and 5.0 will focus on sustainable means, the initial level of increased energy consumption has originated from activities related to high-powered machinery and servers and their operation in sustaining data centers for services. Balancing such needs for energy with their environmental impact still forms a core to the success of embracing the circular economy.

Economic pressures from market demand fluctuations, resource scarcity, and competition from unsustainable practices are typical of companies pursuing circular economy practices through Industry 4.0 and 5.0. Innovative and alternative business models that are not always available and sometimes even inaccessible symbolize profitability and sustainability. Typically, standardized metrics and methodologies are absent in any measurement regarding the attainment of circular goals in the context of Industry 4.0 and 5.0. In that regard, these technologies lack clarity regarding benchmarks associated with the effectiveness of their application to achieve circular outcomes. Under such circumstances, businesses are faced with challenges in terms of how to define investments and efforts.

2 Conclusion

This chapter thus presents how the critical interaction of technological innovation interplays with the principles of the circular economy, which brings all these factors into creating the opportunity for a more sustainable future. The change from a linear economy into one closed-loop resource-efficient system is the transformation in terms of the analysis regarding the potential impact that Industry 4.0 and 5.0 technologies can place on any potential AI, blockchain, and IoT differences that will be able to make. The chapter also discusses how a core focus on automation and data-driven decision-making places Industry 4.0 in harmony with the human-centric way of innovation and sustainability that characterizes Industry 5.0. These technologies empower industries to minimize waste, provide better resource utilization, and build resilience to environmental and economic shocks. Thus, in this regard, circular economy practices are compatible with world sustainability initiatives and boost innovative business models that enhance long-term competitiveness.

This calls for strategic attention to the challenges to adopting such revolutionary technologies, including implementation costs, skill gaps, and resistance to change. So, they call for strategic attention. That being said, these are some of the barriers that need to be overcome by governments, industries, and academia through collaborative engagements that will make the ecosystem friendly to innovation and adaptation. This chapter presents the need for technology development integration in the circular economy practice to solve environmental issues and stimulate the sustainable development of society. Coordination, education, and training together with innovative approaches shall enable industries to use these technologies more effectively, bringing about the best possible sustainable future.

References

Acerbi F, Sassanelli C, Terzi S, Taisch M (2021) A systematic literature review on data and information required for circular manufacturing strategies adoption. Sustainability 13(4):2047. https://doi.org/10.3390/su13042047

Aghimien D, Ngcobo N, Aigbavboa C, Dixit S, Vatin NI, Kampani S, Khera GS (2022) Barriers to digital technology deployment in value management practice. Buildings 12(6):731. https://doi.org/10.3390/buildings12060731

Aguilar Esteva LC, Kasliwal A, Kinzler MS, Kim HC, Keoleian GA (2021) Circular economy framework for automobiles: Closing energy and material loops. J Ind Ecol 25(4):877–889. https://doi.org/10.1111/jiec.13088

Akkad MZ, Šebo J, Bányai T (2022) Investigation of the Industry 4.0 technologies adoption effect on circular economy. Sustain 14(19): 12815. https://doi.org/10.3390/su141912815

Akundi A, Euresti D, Luna S, Ankobiah W, Lopes A, Edinbarough I (2022) State of Industry 5.0—Analysis and identification of current research trends. Appl Syst Innov 5(1). https://doi.org/10.3390/asi5010027

Alassaf D, Dabić M, Shifrer D, Daim T (2020) The impact of open-border organization culture and employees' knowledge, attitudes, and rewards with regards to open innovation: an empirical study. J Knowl Manag 24(9):2273–2297. https://doi.org/10.1108/JKM-02-2020-0122

Alfarizi M, Hanum RK, Anggraeni DG, Qanita A, Al Hakim MR, Ngatindriatun N (2023) Accelerative capacity of keyresources Industry 4.0 in metropolitan culinary micro-small sector and green business sustainability impact. J Appl Bus Adm 7(2):186–200. https://doi.org/10.30871/jaba.v7i2.6166

Alonso-Almeida MM, Rodríguez-Antón JM, Bagur-Femenías L, Perramon J (2020) Sustainable development and circular economy: the role of institutional promotion on circular consumption and market competitiveness from a multistakeholder engagement approach. Bus Strateg Environ 29(6):2803–2814. https://doi.org/10.1002/bse.2544

Awan U, Sroufe R, Shahbaz M (2021) Industry 4.0 and the circular economy: A literature review and recommendations for future research. Bus Strat Environ 30(4):2038–2060. https://doi.org/10.1002/bse.2731

Batool H, Ye X, Wang T (2023) Studying the relationship between block chain technology and circular economy dimensions from production aspect and its association with organizational performance: A case study of pakistani firms. ABAC J 43(3). https://doi.org/10.59865/abacj.2023.29

Bhardwaj LK, Rath P, Jain H, Choudhury M (2025) Exploring the effects of e-waste on soil, water quality and human health. Discover Civ Eng 2(1):1–16. https://doi.org/10.1007/s44290-025-00167-2

Cahayani I, Fachurreza AM, Puspita AN (2023) Danone-Aqua circular economy performance in maximizing waste plastic value. JEJAK 16(1). https://doi.org/10.15294/jejak.v16i1.43476

Carayannis EG, Dezi L, Gregori G, Calo E (2022) Smart environments and techno-centric and human-centric innovations for Industry and society 5.0: A quintuple helix innovation system view towards smart, sustainable, and inclusive solutions. J Knowl Econ 13(2):926–955. https://doi.org/10.1007/s13132-021-00763-4

Charlier D, Fizaine F (2023) Decoupling gross domestic product and consumption of raw materials: a macro-panel analysis. Sustain Prod Consum 36:194–206. https://doi.org/10.1016/j.spc.2022.12.020

Chonsawat N, Sopadang A (2020) Defining SMEs' 4.0 readiness indicators. Appl Sci 10(24):8998. https://doi.org/10.3390/app10248998

Dana L-P, Salamzadeh A, Hadizadeh M, Heydari G, Shamsoddin S (2022) Urban entrepreneurship and sustainable businesses in smart cities: exploring the role of digital technologies. Sustain Technol Entrep 1(2):100016. https://doi.org/10.1016/j.stae.2022.100016

De Pascale A, Di Vita G, Giannetto C, Ioppolo G, Lanfranchi M, Limosani M, Szopik-Depczyńska K (2023) The circular economy implementation at the European Union level. Past, present and future. J Clean Prod 423:138658. https://doi.org/10.1016/j.jclepro.2023.138658

Ghaithan AM, Alshammakhi Y, Mohammed A, Mazher KM (2023) Integrated impact of circular economy, Industry 4.0, and lean manufacturing on sustainability performance of manufacturing firms. Int J Environ Res Public Health 20(6):5119. https://doi.org/10.3390/ijerph20065119

Greene M, Hobson K, Jaeger-Erben M (2024) Bringing the circular economy home–Insights from socio-technical perspectives on everyday consumption. Clean Responsible Consum 12:100157. http://doi.org/10.1016/j.clrc.2023.100157

Gwebu K, Barrows CW (2020) Data breaches in hospitality: is the industry different? J Hosp Tour Technol 11(3):511–527. https://doi.org/10.1108/JHTT-11-2019-0138

Hassan NM, Khan SAR, Ashraf MU, Sheikh AA (2023) Interconnection between the role of blockchain technologies, supply chain integration, and circular economy: A case of small and medium-sized enterprises in Pakistan. Sci Prog 106(3):1–22. https://doi.org/10.1177/00368504231186527

Henao-Hincapié LJ, Leyes M, Loeber-Vizcaíno GE, Cruz-Pérez A, Romero-Perdomo F, González-Curbelo MÁ (2024) Assessing consumer knowledge, attitudes, and adoption of circular economy practices in Colombia. Sustain Prod Consum 46:256–267. https://doi.org/10.1016/j.spc.2024.02.030

Hu Y, He X, Poustie M (2018) Can legislation promote a circular economy? A material flow-based evaluation of the circular degree of the Chinese economy. Sustainability 10(4):990. https://doi.org/10.3390/su10040990

Jakubelskas U, Skvarciany V (2023) Circular economy practices as a tool for sustainable development in the context of renewable energy: what are the opportunities for the EU? Oecon Copern 14(3):833–859. https://doi.org/10.24136/oc.2023.025

Jawaid SA, Ahmed, S (2023) The transformative economic impact of artificial intelligence. https://doi.org/10.20944/preprints202311.1384.v1

Jones P, Wynn MG (2021) The circular economy, resilience, and digital technology deployment in the mining and mineral industry. Int J Circ Econ Waste Manag 1(1):16–32. https://doi.org/10.4018/IJCEWM.2021010102

Kamalaldin A, Linde L, Sjödin D, Parida V (2020) Transforming provider-customer relationships in digital servitization: a relational view on digitalization. Ind Mark Manag 89:306–325. https://doi.org/10.1016/j.indmarman.2020.02.004

Kasu P, Hamandawana P, Chung T-S (2022) TPBF: Two-Phase Bloom-Filter-Based End-to-End data integrity verification framework for object-based big data transfer systems. Mathematics 10(9):1591. https://doi.org/10.3390/math10091591

Katrakazas P, Costantino M, Magnea F, Moore L, Ismail A, Bourithis E, Taşkın HB, Özen ZT, Sarı İA, Pissaridi K, Bachler J, Polic S, Pippione G, Paoletti R, di Falco R, Ferrario F (2021) An Equifinality energy management framework in terms of benchmarking practices and expectations: The EnerMan project outlook. Syst 10(1):2. https://doi.org/10.3390/systems10010002

Khajuria A, Atienza VA, Chavanich S, Henning W, Islam I, Kral U, Liu M, Liu X, Murthy IK, Oyedotun TDT, Verma P, Xu G, Zeng X, Li J (2022) Accelerating circular economy solutions to achieve the 2030 agenda for sustainable development goals. Circ Econ 1(1):100001. https://doi.org/10.1016/j.cec.2022.100001

Khan FA, Sheikh DAA, Zainab F (2024) The impact of SMEs capability for service innovation and its tactical green marketing on sustainable business performance. J Small Bus Strat 34(2):2024. https://doi.org/10.53703/001c.117659

Khan SAR, Ahmad Z, Sheikh AA, Yu Z (2023) Green technology adoption paving the way toward sustainable performance in circular economy: A case of Pakistani small and medium enterprises. Int J Innov Sci. https://doi.org/10.1108/IJIS-10-2022-0199

Khan SAR, Sheikh AA, Hassan NM, Yu Z (2024) Modeling the intricate association between sustainable service quality and supply chain performance: Moderating role of blockchain technology and environmental uncertainty. Sustain (Switz) 16(11). https://doi.org/10.3390/su16114808

Khan SAR, Tahir MS, Sheikh AA (2024) Sustainable performance in SMEs using big data analytics for closed-loop supply chains and reverse omnichannel. Heliyon 10(16). https://doi.org/10.1016/j.heliyon.2024.e36237

Khong I (2023) The circular economy's performance and the impact of digitalization. Int Trans Educ Technol 2(1):18–23. https://doi.org/10.33050/itee.v2i1.389

Knoth K, Fufa SM, Seilskjær E (2022) Barriers, success factors, and perspectives for the reuse of construction products in Norway. J Clean Prod 337:130494. https://doi.org/10.1016/j.jclepro.2022.130494

Larsen MSS, Lassen AH, Schou C (2023) Manufacturing innovation: a heuristic model of innovation processes for industry 4.0. Appl Syst Innov 6(6):98. https://doi.org/10.3390/asi6060098

Laskurain-Iturbe I, Arana-Landin G, Landeta-Manzano B, Jimenez-Redal R (2023) Assessing the uptake of Industry 4.0 technologies: Barriers to their adoption and impact on quality management aspects. Int J Qual & Reliab Manag 40(10):2420–2442. https://doi.org/10.1108/IJQRM-10-2022-0292

Mukherjee S, Nagariya R, Baral MM, Patel BS, Chittipaka V, Rao KS, Rao UVA (2023) Blockchain-based circular economy for achieving environmental sustainability in the Indian electronic MSMEs. Manag Environ Qual 34(4):997–1017. https://doi.org/10.1108/MEQ-03-2022-0045

Muriithi JK, Ngare IO (2023) Transitioning circular economy from policy to practice in Kenya. Front Sustain 4. https://doi.org/10.3389/frsus.2023.1190470

Onyeaka H, Tamasiga P, Nwauzoma UM, Miri T, Juliet UC, Nwaiwu O, Akinsemolu AA (2023) Using artificial intelligence to tackle food waste and enhance the circular economy: Maximising resource efficiency and minimising environmental impact: A review. Sustain 15(13):10482. https://doi.org/10.3390/su151310482

Özçatalbaş O (2023) An evaluation of the transition from linear economy to circular economy. In: Sustainable rural development perspective and global challenges. IntechOpen. https://doi.org/10.5772/intechopen.107980

Patalas-Maliszewska J, Kłos S (2019) An approach to supporting the selection of maintenance experts in the context of Industry 4.0. Appl Sci 9(9):1848. https://doi.org/10.3390/app9091848

Priyana IPO, Utami MAJP, Saputra UWE (2023) Blockchain technology for circular economy in plastic bank. Sinkron 7(2):637–646

Raja Santhi A, Muthuswamy P (2023) Industry 5.0 or industry 4.0S? Introduction to industry 4.0 and a peek into the prospective industry 5.0 technologies. Int J Interact Des Manuf 17(2):947–979. https://doi.org/10.1007/s12008-023-01217-8

Rajesh R, Kanakadhurga D, Prabaharan N (2022) Electronic waste: a critical assessment on the unimaginable growing pollutant, legislations and environmental impacts. Environ Chall 7:100507. http://doi.org/10.1016/j.envc.2022.100507

Rehman AU, AlFaify AY (2023) Evaluating industry 4.0 manufacturing configurations: an entropy-based grey relational analysis approach. Processes 11(11):3151. https://doi.org/10.3390/pr11113151

Rehman Khan SA, Ahmad Z, Sheikh AA, Yu Z (2022) Digital transformation, smart technologies, and eco-innovation are paving the way toward sustainable supply chain performance. Sci Prog 105(4):1–26. https://doi.org/10.1177/00368504221145648

Rejeb A, Appolloni A (2022) The nexus of industry 4.0 and circular procurement: a systematic literature review and research agenda. Sustainability 14(23):15633. https://doi.org/10.3390/su142315633

Rusmayadi G, Salawati U, Haslinah A, Judijanto L (2023) The effect of investment in green technology and renewable technology adoption on energy efficiency and carbon emissions reduction in indonesian manufacturing companies. West Sci Interdiscip Stud 1(11):1175–1183. https://doi.org/10.58812/wsis.v1i11.347

Saeed S, Arshad MY, Ahmed AS (2023) Advancing circular economy in industrial chemistry and environmental engineering: Principles, alignment with United Nations sustainable development goals, and pathways to implementation. Eur J Chem 14(3):414–428. https://doi.org/10.5155/eurjchem.14.3.414-428.2452

Sánchez-García E, Martínez-Falcó J, Marco-Lajara B, Manresa-Marhuenda E (2024) Revolutionizing the circular economy through new technologies: a new era of sustainable progress. Environ Technol Innov 33:103509. https://doi.org/10.1016/j.eti.2023.103509

Santos M, Rolo A, Matos D, Carvalho L (2023) The circular economy in corporate reporting: text mining of energy companies' management reports. Energies 16(15):5791. https://doi.org/10.3390/en16155791

Sehnem S, de Queiroz AAFSL, Pereira SCF, dos Santos Correia G, Kuzma E (2022) Circular economy and innovation: a look from the perspective of organizational capabilities. Bus Strateg Environ 31(1):236–250. https://doi.org/10.1002/bse.2884

Shadravan A, Parsaei HR (2023, March) Impacts of Industry 4.0 on smart manufacturing. Proceedings of the International Conference on Industrial Engineering and Operations Management. https://doi.org/10.46254/AN13.20230146

Shahzad U, Mohammed KS, Tiwari S, Nakonieczny J, Nesterowicz R (2023) Connectedness between geopolitical risk, financial instability indices and precious metals markets: novel findings from Russia Ukraine conflict perspective. Resour Policy 80:103190. https://doi.org/10.1016/j.resourpol.2022.103190

Sherif Z, Sarfraz S, Jolly M, Salonitis K (2023) Greening foundation industries: Shared processes and sustainable pathways. Sustain 15(19):14422. https://doi.org/10.3390/su151914422

Singh PK, Sarkar P (2023) An artificial neural network tool to support the decision making of designers for environmentally conscious product development. Expert Syst Appl 212:118679. https://doi.org/10.1016/j.eswa.2022.118679

Talapatra S, Gaine A (2019) Putting green lean six sigma framework into practice in a jute industry of Bangladesh: A case study. Am J Ind Bus Manag 09(12):2168–2189. https://doi.org/10.4236/ajibm.2019.912144

Ting LS, Zailani S, Sidek NZM, Shaharudin MR (2023) Motivators and barriers of circular economy business model adoption and its impact on sustainable production in Malaysia. Environ Dev Sustain 26(7):17551–17578. https://doi.org/10.1007/s10668-023-03350-6

Torbacki W (2021) A Hybrid MCDM Model Combining DANP and PROMETHEE II Methods for the assessment of cybersecurity in Industry 4.0. Sustain 13(16):8833. https://doi.org/10.3390/su13168833

Wang D, Yu A (2023) Supply chain resources and economic security based on artificial intelligence and blockchain multi-channel technology. Int J Inf Technol Syst Appr 16(3):1–15. https://doi.org/10.4018/IJITSA.322385

Westphal E, Seitz H (2021) Digital and decentralized management of patient data in healthcare using blockchain implementations. Front Blockchain 4. https://doi.org/10.3389/fbloc.2021.732112

Xiong Y, Guo H, Nor DDMM, Song A, Dai L (2023) Mineral resources depletion, environmental degradation, and exploitation of natural resources: COVID-19 aftereffects. Resour Policy 85:103907. https://doi.org/10.1016/j.resourpol.2023.103907

Yedalla J (2025) Building cyber-resilient smart cities: the role of AI and big data in urban security. Int J Sci Res 14(2):648–652. http://doi.org/10.21275/SR25210194541

Zhang Y, Hassan NM, Sheikh AA (2024) Unboxing the dilemma associated with online shopping and purchase behavior for remanufactured products: A smart strategy for waste management. J Environ Manag 351. https://doi.org/10.1016/j.jenvman.2023.119790

Zils M, Howard M, Hopkinson P (2025) Circular economy implementation in operations & supply chain management: building a pathway to business transformation. Prod Plan Control 36(4):501–520. http://doi.org/10.1080/09537287.2023.2280907

Insights into Eco-Product Designs and Eco-Business Model Strategies

Nadir Munir Hassan, Ibrahim Rashid Al Shamsi, Adnan Ahmed Sheikh, and Abdelheq Lachachi

Abstract The rapid industrialization of recent decades has driven significant economic growth and improved living standards. However, this development has often come at the expense of ecological sustainability, leading to severe resource depletion. Many industries have traditionally operated within an unsustainable "take-make-consume-dispose" economic framework. Compounding this challenge is the alarming rise in global waste production, projected to increase by an additional 70% by 2050 if current trends persist. In response, businesses increasingly adopt circular economy (CE) models by producing circular products as a sustainable alternative to the conventional linear paradigm. The circular economy facilitates a transformative shift, addressing the limitations of linear models and mitigating their adverse environmental impacts.

Keywords Circular Economy · Circular Product Design · Sustainability · Eco-Business Models

N. M. Hassan (✉)
Department of Business and Public Administration, Emerson University, Multan, Pakistan
e-mail: nadir.munir@eum.edu.pk

I. Al Shamsi · A. A. Sheikh · A. Lachachi
College of Business, University of Buraimi, Al Buraimi, Sultanate of Oman
e-mail: ibrahim.r@uob.edu.om

A. A. Sheikh
e-mail: adnan.a@uob.edu.om

A. Lachachi
e-mail: abdelheq.l@uob.edu.om

S. A. R. Khan et al. (eds.), *Circular Economy and Technological Innovation*, Industrial Ecology, https://doi.org/10.1007/978-981-96-5650-9_3

1 Insights into Eco-Product Designs & Eco-Business Innovative Strategies

With the unprecedented rise in environmental degradation, there has been an increased need for eco-product designs and sustainable business models. Therefore, the circular economy has emerged and has gained notable academic and professional attention across industries (Nudurupatiet al. 2022; Sohal et al. 2022). Conversely, along with the proponents of circular economy, there are critique studies that assert that CE is backed by a certain ideological base, with blurred boundaries and confusing theoretical formation, which is bound to face organizational challenges (Kirchherr et al. 2017). Meanwhile, as a concept, CE is focused on encouraging eco-friendliness, which deals with propagating environmental excellence, financial development, and social impartiality for future generations. Likewise, CE is an environmentally considerate operations management, which through "reduce, reuse and recycle," facilitates smart use of resources, lowering the pressure on resource utility. If implemented in true letter and spirit, CE can positively influence corporations' sustainable aspirations, letting them become even more environmentally friendly.

Furthermore, as has already been affirmed, to operate sustainably, firms are under immense burden from stakeholders to opt for sustainable production (Liu et al. 2021; Srhir et al. 2023). Hence, manufacturers in sustainable firms are forced to develop sustainable capabilities and adopt greener transformation, which isn't a simple change because it demands an overall sustainable shift in business processes, supply chains, and product designs (Bag et al. 2022; Kannan et al. 2022). The inability of manufacturers to develop their greener production capabilities brings them to the brink of multiple risks, including competitive disadvantage, diminishing reputation, environmental damage, and inability to capitalize on prevailing business opportunities. The shared argument clearly indicates the need for firms to deal in eco-friendly processes and products in assistance with sustainable operational formations (Buadit et al. 2023; Jafari et al. 2022; Quintana-García et al. 2021).

Similarly, with the ever-mounting pressure from practitioners and the government for a corporate sustainably creative road map, making it the central ingredient of a firm's strategic vision has become an inevitable reality (Bag et al. 2022). Consequently, firms across the globe have started to counter the misuse and exploitation of already diminishing resources. Several firms have opted for innovative programs, including sustainable, eco-friendly interactive formations with suppliers, within, and with the customers. Corporations have also adopted the guidelines concerning (reduction, recycling, and reuse), followed by related training initiatives for employees.

To be specific, Eco-innovation refers to the production, assimilation, or exploitation of a product, product, processes, or business tools that are unique to an organization, which, throughout the firm's life cycle, helps in reducing the environmental risks in comparison to alternative business processes. Eco-innovation, through eco-products and processes, converts the traditional manufacturing systems into a comparative circular system, which resultantly causes possibilities for society to relate with ever-changing environmental conditions and control resource depletion, along with causing opportunities for environment-friendly development and growth (Greco et al. 2023).

Literature has identified multiple forms of eco-innovation, including organizational, technical, and marketing-related innovation, Arundel and Kemp (2009). Additionally, the studies have categorized it as eco-innovation, eco-organizational, eco-process, and eco-product innovation (Klewitz and Hansen 2014). To be specific, Eco-product innovation deals with the formation of new or comparatively enhanced products in terms of features, materials, and technical aspects. For Example, eco-design can help firms improve products using organic material, with the ability to consume minimum energy. Eco-innovation also includes sustainable life-cycle analysis, eco-labeling, and eco-friendly packaging (Afum et al. 2020). As has been suggested by Klewitz and Hansen (2014), firms can achieve their sustainable aspirations and uplift their eco-efficiency, making products easy to reuse, decompose, and recycle. It's high time for firms operating across the globe, and specifically working in developing nations, to be mindful of their level of eco-innovation to reduce their harmful impact on the environment and enhance their role in the introduction of circular business models (Le and Ikram 2022).

Eco-process innovation involves the integration of novel components into a company's production systems and methodologies to manufacture eco-friendly products. Sustainable innovation primarily involves the implementation of new processes or the modification of existing ones to mitigate the detrimental environmental effects produced by companies (Huber 2008). Research indicates that eco-process innovation may encompass additive solutions, cleaner production technologies, or integration into industrial processes through output reclamation, production optimization, and input replacement.

Eco-organizational formations enhance corporate management processes through distinctive and sustainable methodologies in business activities. It pertains to the revitalization of organizational structures and activities, presenting a comparative formalized management framework as an environmental management system (Rennings et al. 2006). Eco-organizational design deals with sustainable product design, training, and learning tools, followed by environmental management teams to address sustainability concerns. The sustainable business models across firms also propagate the inculcation of the environment-friendly vision, stakeholder management, and employee engagement in sustainable activities (Singh et al. 2021). This largely means that firms focused on introducing eco-products must implement sustainable and eco-business models from the point of inception to the point of consumption. It largely will facilitate firms in reaping the benefits of being sustainable in the real sense (Chege et al. 2019). As suggested by Klewitz and Hansen (2014), eco-marketing also involves developing and promoting eco-products, along with managing its prompt distribution through eco-business models.

2 The Evolution from Linear to a Comparative Circular Economy; Reshaping Corporate-Operational Formation

Meanwhile, it's of great significance to unbox the phenomena of the circular economy compared to a comparative linear business model or formation. As explained above, the circular economy has gained reasonable attention from partitioners, researchers, corporations, and public corporations. Previously, the linear economy model was the centre of attraction, while CE has lately been considered an additional business model because of its positive impact on the environment. The phenomena of CE have reasonably been analysed by researchers across recent years, with most of them agreeing with the fact that it's a comparatively regenerative production and consumption model (Prieto-Sandoval et al. 2018). Moreover, it can't be termed an individual process involving firm, industry, and economic change. CE also facilitates and causes a sustainable shift in society's norms, values, attitudes, and behavior (Chizaryfard et al. 2021).

The Circular Economy is a comprehensive concept that addresses regenerative economic creation, focusing on efficient resource utilization to promote sustainable economic development (Kirchherr et al. 2017). It is recognized as a fundamental strategy for sustainable development, challenging the conventional linear economic model of source-manufacture-sell-use-dispose (Ellen MacArthur Foundation 2022). Despite the ongoing attention the circular economy (CE) has garnered from academics, industry, and society, less than 9% of the world economy is circular. Consequently, to facilitate and comprehend the transition from linear to circular economy, the industrial sector and its associated stakeholders play a pivotal role, ultimately determining the impact on the global environmental treasury (Bjørn et al. 2021).

Firms have lately understood the benefits and opportunities hidden within the CE concept. However, manufacturing firms, because of their lack of expertise, have largely remained unable to fully inculcate CE practices within and across their value chains (Aloini et al. 2021; Kumar and Basu 2023). CE also holds the potential to cause related, social, technological, and economic, social, technological, & institutional change that facilitates sustainable evolutions through the introduction of business model innovation and the introduction of governance-related rules and instruments (Jaeger and Upadhyay 2020; Lieder and Rashid 2016). Usually, the basic premise in which the CE economy is talked about contrasts with the Linear economy. Now, this transition between LE to CE is a bit technical in nature and demands that stakeholders be intellectually and technically equipped to generate the anticipated sustainable aspirations (Berry et al. 2024).

Therefore, it is important to unbox the phenomena at hand further to let readers, practitioners, and scholars understand and witness the stated transition. Unlike CE, LE is termed the economy that doesn't engage in the recycling process, from the point of origination to the point of consumption. LE is largely characterized through predetermined formulas, including "make-use-dispose, or take-make-use-dispose. In simple words, LE is labelled as a current economy, while CE is considered one of the business formations which managers must consider opting for. This means that firms must adopt thought processes and make operational shifts to facilitate the smooth transition from being the LE to a better and sustainable CE. While certain other studies have highlighted that an economy can't be labelled as CE or LE; rather, according to them, economies must be seen as a mix of both CE and LE in different proportions.

Yet, lately, CE is seen in contrast with the linear economic model, which states that resources at hand are large and can be disposed of once used to produce goods (Nowicki and Kafel 2021; Roberts et al. 2024). However, studies have reflected that, with such a linear model mindset, the world economy could lose around 3 to 6 trillion dollars by 2030 because of diminishing natural resources, followed by interrupted supply chains, resulting in price hikes (Lacy et al. 2015). Meanwhile, CE is very prevalent across political and business debates, which would possibly cause a paradigm industrial shift. CE has surfaced as an acknowledged business model for its evident role in conceptualizing sustainable business solutions for uplifting supply chain performances (Wasserbaur et al. 2022; Korhonen et al. 2018). Meanwhile, for a smooth transition from linear to a comparative circular and sustainable economy, legislative bodies, firms, and academics will have to facilitate the adoption and acceptance of circularity norms and be mindful of their role in generating sustainable business outcomes. This means that without the active engagement of all the potential stakeholders, CE might remain unable to operate at its full potential.

3 Transforming Customer Experience Through Eco-Friendly Products and Business Designs Within the Circular Economy

Firms have recently faced immense pressure from social organizations, practitioners, and consumers to implement sustainable business operations (Kostis and Kafka 2023). Likewise, the emergence of Technologies like AI, Blockchain, and others has blurred the line between customers and managers (Ta et al. 2022). Moreover, customers have a role in value co-creation and are regarded as the co-producers of the products and services in an environment-friendly manner (Andersén 2021). Therefore, it's observed that, in the contemporary global landscape, the interaction between consumer behavior and greener products/processes has been the major reason behind the paradigm shift in Favor of sustainability (Andersén 2021). Firms are supposed to simultaneously rely on both sustainable and customer orientations to provide customers with a competitive service experience, which in turn will help achieve sustainable corporate goals (Fader 2020). With the recent sensitization of customers, firms, and governments towards sustainable business practices, firms are mindful of being held accountable for the overall impact of their business practices on the global ecosystem. Therefore, firms consider keeping customers at the center of their corporate decisions for a better and flawless sustainable customer experience (Cain 2023).

Additionally, present-day managers are required to reset their strategic aspirations, with a larger focus on the environmental outcomes of their corporate actions. Meanwhile, in the given debate on setting environmental corporate policies, also demand from customers, to activiely engage in co-creating sustainable values (Signori et al. 2019). Such research will help integrate environmental, social, and economic corporate agendas. Similarly, there is a rising need for empirical investigations on integrating firms' sustainable strategic and operational priorities and customer orientation. Firms are made to redefine their scope in line with the needs of both customers and the environment to ensure lasting competitive advantage.

As already explained, Circular Economy (CE) is critical for firms' sustainable aspirations, which, by moving away from linear economic business models, focuses on reuse, remanufacturing, refurbishing, and recycling (Khan et al. 2024a, b; Zhang et al. 2024; Zhang et al. 2024). Meanwhile, researchers have also explored phenomena like socialization, which largely deals with providing customers with lasting services, with a larger emphasis on the circularity of the industrial ecosystems. Similarly, recent empirical investigations have asked for further studies to be conducted on the role of sericitization on overall firms' and industries' circularity (Palakshappa et al. 2024). Service orientation has inspired manufacturing firms to move beyond a product to a more service-centric orientation, which brings a notable change within the firm's business landscape. It helps firms develop their supply chains in a way that guides the entire life cycle of both products and services to provide customers with the solutions they need to their problems (Yang and Evans 2019).

Furthermore, as CE principles go beyond firms and operate at a much broader spectrum, the role and contribution of internal service-based strategies for firms in facilitating circular evolution can't be undermined. Through customer orientation, sustainable firms can further create value-generating streams (Tukker 2015), achieving and sustaining customer relationships for lasting competitive advantages (Spring and Araujo 2017). Therefore, through the circularity of the business, the basic principle of value creation goes beyond financial performance, engulfing environmental benefits for firms, customers, and other related stakeholders (Russell-Bennett et al. 2024). Furthermore, for system-wide, circular customer experience, firms are required to keep their entire supply chains aligned in order to offer circular service offerings.

At a comparative strategic front, meaningful corporate choices are required to be made at all stages of the value chain, starting from the sourcing, designing, and, ultimately, implementation of the circular service phenomena. Customers' expectations are spread across the supply chains, demanding an even more holistic, sustainable service experience (Kühlet al. 2020). To add to the customer-related experience within eco-friendly firms, remanufacturing and maintenance have been around, making up the value propositions of modern-day corporations. Yet, such a strategic, operational transition in Favor of circularity, both within and beyond, is an important avenue for future research. Furthermore, other studies have considered the role of customer engagement in effectively facilitating the transition of firms from LE models to improved CE business models (Tunn et al. 2021). It is, therefore, of great significance to collaborate with customers on all fronts in order to co-create value and digital solutions to customers' modern-day problems.

To this level, CE has been explored through multiple lenses, including economic, strategic, and operational, though there still is the need for further exploration of CE on customer-related experiences (Clube and Tennant 2020). Customers need to be involved and considered in all the business processes to provide them with the best value. Likewise, the role of customers in CE processes has not been sufficiently analyzed, giving rise to the need for empirical investigations to be conducted on the intersection of customers with that of the circular economy (Watling et al. 2018). Additionally, studies have highlighted the need to explore the attitudes and behaviors that customers might hold regarding the whole phenomena of circular economy, which might assist both society and the policymakers concerned (Stankevich 2017).

Meanwhile, both practitioners and researchers are mindful of the need to understand the concept of sustainable customer experience, which offers firms an opportunity to differentiate their product offerings, along with causing enhanced customer loyalty, positive word of mouth, increased cross-selling opportunities, reduced price sensitivity, and ignition of firm's growth chances through improved corporate reputation (Ferraresi and Schmitt 2018). Like all business processes, replacing LE and implementing CE aren't free of challenges, which must be looked into (Klink et al. 2024).

4 Challenges in Effective Implementation of Circular Economy Using Innovative Business Strategies

With so many benefits of the Circular economy being elaborated, it is important to understand that its smooth implementation isn't free of challenges (Wong et al. 2020). It requires deliberation, arbitration, and intentional management principles to be applied to counter challenges, standing on one's way toward successfully implementing the Circular Economy concept (Takacs 2023). While it's of great importance to conceptualize that environmental downturn seriously hinders sustainable aspirations of developing economies. The number of drivers and constraints (both internal and external) are considered to inflict an inverse impact on socio-economic and environmental corporate and national performance. Therefore, a circular economy conceptualizes a self-generating sequential line of actions to keep hold of products in all possible formations and involves reducing, recycling, and reusing (Jabbour et al. 2020).

Circular Economy (CE) is a closed-loop system that encompasses the "Resource-Product-Renewed Resource" framework (Brown 2018). Corporate entrepreneurship is typically implemented at several tiers within business operations to promote the regulated utilisation of resources in the quest for sustainable development. Circular Economy (CE) also advocates for the systematic refurbishing of resources, resulting in environmentally responsible disposal of unused outputs (Reike et al. 2023). Current research on Circular Economy (CE) has examined various dimensions, encompassing product design, innovative business models, reuse, remanufacturing, technology integration, carbon footprint mitigation, and alternative evaluation methodologies (Maher et al. 2023; Assi et al. 2020; Tiwari et al. 2024; Wang et al. 2019). Despite the advantages of Circular Economy (CE), it faces problems such as the lack of secure technology-driven production and consumption resources, which sometimes impede companies from implementing CE practices that necessitate innovative solutions. Additional research has indicated that cultural barriers influence the acceptance and implementation of Circular business models within specific geographical or organizational contexts (Marrucci et al. 2024). Research has underscored the necessity of fostering interest among contemporary corporations about the acceptance of change as a pivotal factor for adopting Circular Economy (CE). The literature offers an outline of emerging difficulties and their respective solutions to assist academicians and practitioners in adopting and implementing CE (Nudurupatiet al. 2022). Despite recognition in the literature, numerous poor nations and organisations continue to struggle with waste management and the implementation of Circular Economy practices for sustainable development (Wiebe et al. 2019).

Thus, the adoption of Circular Economy (CE) may differ due to diverse local dynamics, distinct challenges, and the availability of resources across firms (Kamal et al. 2024). An issue faced by certain SMEs is their skepticism over the ability of circular economy concepts to yield significant cost savings, favorable financial results, and sustained performance (Austin and Rahman 2022). Consequently, corporate aversion to circular economic concepts, whether from insufficient awareness or the absence of regulatory restrictions, constitutes a significant hurdle for CE (Zhang et al. 2023). The absence of synergy and collaboration between leadership and legislative bodies in formulating effective policies for the implementation of CE constitutes a significant obstacle to its progress.

Likewise, CE requires a certain level of corporate setup, which contains a sufficient level of technology being implemented, along with a corporate willingness to adopt such changes. While in the presence of the above-mentioned hindrances, there is always the possibility of slowing down the implementation of the phenomena of CE. Furthermore, firms' lack of financial well-being is another critical resource for firms interested in positively adopting CE principles across business processes (Paletta et al. 2019). Usually, owners of family-owned SMEs or managers with typical mindsets don't prefer pursuing CE because of the cost associated with its proper and system-wide execution. Such traditional firms, widely available across developing nations, run businesses with a mindset that introducing such sustainable changes isn't more than just an experiment and may not benefit their goal of generating financial performance (Mishra et al. 2022).

Additionally, government support can greatly assist in infrastructural development and ecological policymaking, and intensifying the corporate circular initiatives also facilitates the prompt implementation of CE principles (Zhu et al. 2022). Likewise, revamping the institutional, corporate formations, and financial structures is the basis for corporations to move beyond linear to circular setup (Margeta 2019).

Additionally, firms available with research subsidies from governments and other socio-economic contributors, those who take interest in collaborating with academia. Meanwhile, others believe that scientific research and a conducive circular regulatory framework positively impact setting a sustainable tone for SMEs operating across developing nations (Zhu et al. 2022). Such a support system guides SMEs in replacing their industrial inputs, processes, and commodities from linear to comparatively innovative and sustainable systems (García-Quevedo et al. 2020). Legislators must educate and facilitate firms to become even more sustainable and socially responsible. Meanwhile, there is always a cost associated with adopting stated new standards available for the smooth running of circular and eco-friendly systems (D'Agostin et al. 2020), therefore before being implemented all stakeholders must review and revise the systems, their viability, and their impact on the environment at large, before implementing them (Geng and Doberstein 2008).

Lastly, policymakers must consider that there is a need to sensitize society at large about the significance and utility of adopting sustainable practices, the benefits of recycling, and eco-friendly disposal techniques. However, it is understandable that a firm's inability to spend on advanced sustainable technologies is one of the notable constraints. This is also because of firms' apprehensions about consumers' willingness to accept such a technological shift in Favor of recycled products, processes, and associated costs (Neri et al. 2023; Sheng et al. 2019). Despite the limited consumer and societal understanding of the circular economy concept, there has been a recent shift and increase in consumer knowledge, taste, and preferences for environmental sustainability (D'Agostin et al. 2020). Firms, governments, and society must take advantage of such a change among the masses towards sustainability and facilitate the adoption of technologies and practices that will benefit both the corporate world and the environment at large.

5 Conclusion & Way Forward

Despite all the recent advancements and empirical investigations on CE and the impact of its related practices on eco-products and processes for sustainable corporate performance, it is yet to reach its full potential. Likewise, it is of great importance to notice that due to uncontrolled socially irresponsible corporate practices, the world at large is faced with unprecedented challenges. Likewise, irresponsible actions by both the public and corporations have brought the planet to a threshold point, which can also be labeled as a tipping point, which can significantly alter the environmental dynamics. Therefore, to sustain the spectrum of ecosystems, adopting circular sustainable practices is imperative. Similarly, other scholars have propagated that stakeholders have also shown interest in Favor of greener products and processes being adopted for a better environment. Hence, Circular economy-led eco-product designs and processes are the stand-out solutions for their holistic outlook (i.e., triple bottom line) toward the problem environment faced across the globe.

In the same way, it is important to understand that the transformation towards CE has largely emerged as a strategic priority for researchers, legislators, practitioners, firms, and customers, specifically within the developing part of the world. Additionally, there is an increased demand for academic studies to explore the potential impact of circular economic practices on the overall environment and corporations' sustainable performance. For this reason, it has been categorized CE practices in several dimensions, including eco-product and process design, as one of the significant parts. At the same time, eco-designs and processes remain considerate of the environment, from inception to the deployment of production processes, and continue to make sustainable output available to the end consumers.

Conversely, because of divided opinions on the outcomes of the interrelationship between Circular economy practices and their impact on the socio-economic-environmental landscape of the world and businesses, research interest in the given domain is still intact. Similarly, the findings of the recent empirical studies stand mixed and contradictory on multiple occasions, increasing researchers' interest in exploring the phenomena even further. In the same manner, recent study reflected a significant association between the stated variables, while others have observed the inverse association between circular economy and sustainable performance outcome. Similarly, the influx of CE practices across business processes adds to the financial strain within firms. In contrast, others have found the positive impact of CEPs on sustainable energy consumption across the supply chain operations. However, there has been another limitation: most studies on circular economic practices and their influx across corporations have mostly focused on their impact on economic and environmental performance, ignoring their social impact. This also reflects that the research output and scope largely remain fragmented and limited, presenting a research gap that needs further investigation. Therefore, one needs to be mindful of the fact that the future belongs to the Circular economy and its constituent operational formations, which need further empirical and practical exploration.

References

Afum E, Agyabeng-Mensah Y, Sun Z, Frimpong B, Kusi LY, Acquah ISK (2020) Exploring the link between green manufacturing, operational competitiveness, firm reputation and sustainable performance dimensions: a mediated approach. J Manuf Technol Manag 31(7):1417–1438

Aloini D, Dulmin R, Mininno V, Raugi M, Schito E, Testi D, Tucci M, Zerbino P (2021) A multi-objective methodology for evaluating the investment in building-integrated hybrid renewable energy systems. J Clean Prod 329:129780

Andersén J (2021) A relational natural-resource-based view on product innovation: the influence of green product innovation and green suppliers on differentiation advantage in small manufacturing firms. Technovation 104:102254

Arundel AV, Kemp R (2009) Measuring eco-innovation

Assi LN, Carter K, Deaver E, Ziehl P (2020) Review of availability of source materials for geopolymer/sustainable concrete. J Clean Prod 263:121477

Austin A, Rahman IU (2022) A triple helix of market failures: Financing the 3Rs of the circular economy in European SMEs. J Clean Prod 361:132284

Bag S, Pretorius JHC (2022) Relationships between industry 4.0, sustainable manufacturing and circular economy: Proposal of a research framework. Int J Organ Anal 30(4):864–898

Berry LL, Yadav MS, Hole MK (2024) Reclaiming healthcare's healing mission for a sustainable future. J Serv Res 27(1):6–27

Bjørn A, Lloyd SM, Brander M, Matthews HD (2022) Renewable energy certificates threaten the integrity of corporate science-based targets. Nat Clim Chang 12(6):539–546

Brown T (2018) Farmers, subalterns, and activists: Social politics of sustainable agriculture in India. Cambridge University Press

Buadit T, Ussawarujikulchai A, Suchiva K, Papong S, Ma HW, Rattanapan C (2023) Environmental impact of passenger car tire supply chain in Thailand using the life cycle assessment method. Sustain Prod Consum 37:156–168

Cain A (2023) A figurational approach to environmental sustainability in the context of sport. Front Sport Act Living 5:1302458

Chege SM, Wang D, Suntu SL, Bishoge OK (2019) Influence of technology transfer on performance and sustainability of standard gauge railway in developing countries. Technol Soc 56:79–92

Chizaryfard A, Trucco P, Nuur C (2021) The transformation to a circular economy: framing an evolutionary view. J Evol Econ 31:475–504

Clube RK, Tennant M (2020) The Circular Economy and human needs satisfaction: Promising the radical, delivering the familiar. Ecol Econ 177:106772

D'Agostin A, de Medeiros JF, Vidor G, Zulpo M, Moretto CF (2020) Drivers and barriers for the adoption of use-oriented product-service systems: A study with young consumers in medium and small cities. Sustain Prod Consum 21:92–103

García-Quevedo J, Jové-Llopis E, Martínez-Ros E (2020) Barriers to the circular economy in European small and medium-sized firms. Bus Strategy Environ 29(6):2450–2464

Geng Y, Doberstein B (2008) Developing the circular economy in China: Challenges and opportunities for achieving'leapfrog development'. Int J Sustain Dev & World Ecol 15(3):231–239

Greco S, Mercuri C, Cock BD, Schär R (2023) Arguing through best practice: The role of argumentation from example in activists' social media posts on sustainable fashion. Discourse Stud 25(4):530–548

Huber J (2008) Pioneer countries and the global diffusion of environmental innovations: Theses from the viewpoint of ecological modernisation theory. Glob Environ Chang 18(3):360–367

Jabbour CJC, Fiorini PDC, Ndubisi NO, Queiroz MM, Piato ÉL (2020) Digitally-enabled sustainable supply chains in the 21st century: A review and a research agenda. Sci Total Environ 725:138177

Jaeger B, Upadhyay A (2020) Understanding barriers to circular economy: cases from the manufacturing industry. J Enterp Inf Manag 33(4):729–745

Jafari M, Shafaie SZ, Abdollahi H, Entezari-Zarandi A (2022) Green recycling of spent Li-ion batteries by deep eutectic solvents (DESs): leaching mechanism and effect of ternary DES. J Environ Chem Eng 10(6):109014

Kamal M, Ali SS, Gupta S, Jalil SA, Ahmed A (2024) Enhancing social sustainability in textile supply chains using neutrosophic sets based fuzzy goal programming. J Ind Manag Optim 0–0

Kannan D, Shankar KM, Gholipour P (2022) Paving the way for a green transition through mitigation of green manufacturing challenges: A systematic literature review. J Clean Prod 368:132578

Khan SAR, Sheikh AA, Hassan NM, Yu Z (2024a) Modeling the intricate association between sustainable service quality and supply chain performance: Moderating role of blockchain technology and environmental uncertainty. Sustain 16(11):4808

Khan SAR, Tahir MS, Sheikh AA (2024) Sustainable performance in SMEs using big data analytics for closed-loop supply chains and reverse omnichannel. Heliyon 10(16)

Kirchherr J, Reike D, Hekkert M (2017) Conceptualizing the circular economy: An analysis of 114 definitions. Resour Conserv Recycl 127:221–232

Klewitz J, Hansen EG (2014) Sustainability-oriented innovation of SMEs: A systematic review. J Clean Prod 65:57–75

Klink J, Carneiro GS, Fonseca BCDD (2024) Bridging the gap between production and ecology: a multiregional input-output analysis of current Brazilian and Chinese productive and ecological relations. Brazil J Polit Econ 44(4):e243623

Korhonen J, Honkasalo A, Seppälä J (2018) Circular economy: The concept and its limitations. Ecol Econ 143:37–46

Kostis PC, Kafka KI (2023) Examining the interplay of climate change, cultural dynamics, and sustainable development: A global perspective. Sustain 15(18):13652

Kumar A, Basu R (2023) Do eco-labels trigger green product purchase intention among emerging market consumers? J Indian Bus Res 15(3):466–492

Lacy P, Rutqvist J, Lacy P, Rutqvist J (2015) The roots of the circular economy. Waste to Wealth: The Circular Economy Advantage, pp 19–23

Le TT, Ikram M (2022) Do sustainability innovation and firm competitiveness help improve firm performance? Evidence from the SME sector in vietnam. Sustain Prod Consum 29:588–599

Lieder M, Rashid A (2016) Towards circular economy implementation: a comprehensive review in context of manufacturing industry. J Clean Prod 115:36–51

Liu Y, Cruz-Morales P, Zargar A, Belcher MS, Pang B, Englund E, Dan Q, Yin K, Keasling JD (2021) Biofuels for a sustainable future. Cell 184(6):1636–1647

Maher J, Ashford T, Verdonck M, English E, Burkhart S (2023) Equipping nutrition graduates for the complex realities of practice: Using practitioner perspectives and experiences to inform authentic sustainability curriculum. J Hum Nutr Diet 36(4):1406–1416

Margeta J (2019) A review of sustainable septage management strategies on the islands in Croatia. Water Sci Technol 79(10):1833–1843

Marrucci L, Daddi T, Iraldo F (2024) Creating environmental performance indicators to assess corporate sustainability and reward employees. Ecol Ind 158:111489

Mishra R, Naik BKR, Raut RD, Paul SK (2022) Circular economy principles in community energy initiatives through stakeholder perspectives. Sustain Prod Consum 33:256–270

Neri A, Negri M, Cagno E, Kumar V, Garza-Reyes JA (2023) What digital-enabled dynamic capabilities support the circular economy? A multiple case study approach. Bus Strateg Environ 32(7):5083–5101

Nowicki P, Kafel P (2021) Circular economy aspects in official statements of selected polish organizations operating on the polish stock market. In: 2021 IEEE International Conference on Technology and Entrepreneurship (ICTE), Augest 2021, pp 1–6. IEEE

Nudurupati SS, Budhwar P, Pappu RP, Chowdhury S, Kondala M, Chakraborty A, Ghosh SK (2022) Transforming sustainability of Indian small and medium-sized enterprises through circular economy adoption. J Bus Res 149:250–269

Palakshappa N, Dodds S, Grant S (2024) Tension and paradox in women-oriented sustainable hybrid organizations: a duality of ethics. J Bus Ethics 190(2):327–346

Paletta A, Fava F, Ubertini F, Bastioli C, Gregori G, La Camera F, Douvan AR (2019) Universities, industries and sustainable development: Outcomes of the 2017 G7 environment ministerial meeting. Sustain Prod Consum 19:1–10

Prieto-Sandoval V, Jaca C, Ormazabal M (2018) Towards a consensus on the circular economy. J Clean Prod 179:605–615

Quintana-García C, Benavides-Chicón CG, Marchante-Lara M (2021) Does a green supply chain improve corporate reputation? Empirical evidence from European manufacturing sectors. Ind Market Manag 92:344–353

Reike D, Hekkert MP, Negro SO (2023) Understanding circular economy transitions: The case of circular textiles. Bus Strateg Environ 32(3):1032–1058

Rennings K, Ziegler A, Ankele K, Hoffmann E (2006) The influence of different characteristics of the EU environmental management and auditing scheme on technical environmental innovations and economic performance. Ecol Econ 57(1):45–59

Roberts L, Wang Y, Elamer AA (2024) Do Vice Chancellors' career horizon matter for university sustainability performance? The moderating role of soft information. Int J Financ & Econ

Russell-Bennett R, Rosenbaum MS, Fisk RP, Raciti MM (2024) SDG editorial: Improving life on planet earth–a call to action for service research to achieve the sustainable development goals (SDGs). J Serv Mark 38(2):145–152

Sheng G, Xie F, Gong S, Pan H (2019) The role of cultural values in green purchasing intention: empirical evidence from Chinese consumers. Int J Consum Stud 43(3):315–326

Signori P, Gozzo I, Flint DJ, Milfeld T, Satinover Nichols B (2019) Sustainable customer experience: Bridging theory and practice. The synergy of business theory and practice: Advancing the practical application of scholarly research, pp 131–174

Singh MP, Chakraborty A, Roy M, Tripathi A (2021) Developing SME sustainability disclosure index for Bombay Stock Exchange (BSE) listed manufacturing SMEs in India. Environ Dev Sustain 23:399–422

Sohal A, Nand AA, Goyal P, Bhattacharya A (2022) Developing a circular economy: An examination of SME's role in India. J Bus Res 142:435–447

Srhir S, Jaegler A, Montoya-Torres JR (2023) Introducing a framework toward sustainability goals in a supply chain 4.0 ecosystem. J Clean Prod 138111

Takacs A (2023) The positive effects of green technology investments on growth expectations. Technol Soc 75:102407

Tiwari S, Srivastava R (2024) Performance analysis of sustainable metaverse: A bibliometric analysis. Benchmarking: Int J

Tukker A (2015) Product services for a resource-efficient and circular economy–a review. J Cleaner Produc 97:76–9

Tunn VS, Van den Hende EA, Bocken NM, Schoormans JP (2021) Consumer adoption of access-based product-service systems: The influence of duration of use and type of product. Bus Strateg Environ 30(6):2796–2813

Wang C, Ghadimi P, Lim MK, Tseng ML (2019) A literature review of sustainable consumption and production: A comparative analysis in developed and developing economies. J Clean Prod 206:741–754

Wasserbaur R, Sakao T, Milios L (2022) Interactions of governmental policies and business models for a circular economy: A systematic literature review. J Clean Prod 337:130329

Wiebe KS, Harsdorff M, Montt G, Simas MS, Wood R (2019) Global circular economy scenario in a multiregional input–output framework. Environ Sci Technol 53(11):6362–6373

Wong CY, Wong CW, Boon-itt S (2020) Effects of green supply chain integration and green innovation on environmental and cost performance. Int J Prod Res 58(15):4589–4609

Yang M, Evans S (2019) Product-service system business model archetypes and sustainability. J Clean Prod 220:1156–1166

Zhang S, Anser MK, Peng MYP, Chen C (2023) Visualizing the sustainable development goals and natural resource utilization for green economic recovery after COVID-19 pandemic. Resour Policy 80:103182

Zhang Y, Hassan NM, Sheikh AA (2024) Unboxing the dilemma associated with online shopping and purchase behavior for remanufactured products: A smart strategy for waste management. J Environ Manage 351:119790

Zhu Z, Liu W, Ye S, Batista L (2022) Packaging design for the circular economy: A systematic review. Sustain Prod Consum 32:817–832

The Impact of Integration, Hyper Agility, and Resilience Capability on Agile Strategy: Leading Towards Firms' Sustainable Performance

Obaidullah Shah, Sherbaz Khan, and Adeel Shah

Abstract

Background The mounting challenges in global supply chains, intensified by pandemics, geopolitical strife, and environmental calamities, underscore the need for enhanced resilience mechanisms. Disruptions caused by government intervention and their implications require a scientific investigation in the context of the supply chain. To understand supply chain disruptions, this study explores the interplay between government efficiency and crucial dynamic attributes like supply chain hyper agility and resilience capability. Through this investigation, the researchers also aspire to explain the ramifications of government legislation on the effectiveness of SCM.

Materials and methods This study accumulated data from 385 participants in the Pakistani manufacturing sector, adopting a 95% confidence interval and a permissible error of 5%. Digital survey methodologies facilitated the gathering of responses, culminating in a substantial response rate of 85.5% for a total of 450 questionnaires. Participants were employees of major manufacturers in Pakistan who are presently in managerial positions in a supply chain.

Results The study investigates the mediatory role of the Leagile strategy in linking supply chain hyper agility (SCHA), supply chain resilience capability (RC), and supply chain integration (SCI) with Sustainable Performance. The role of Government Effectiveness is also studied. The impact of government effectiveness on Leagile is being investigated using the three independent variables (SCHA, RC, and

O. Shah · A. Shah (✉)
Department of Supply Chain Management, Institute of Business Management, Karachi, Pakistan
e-mail: adeel.shah@iobm.edu.pk

O. Shah
e-mail: obaidullah.shah@iobm.edu.pk

S. Khan
Department of Business Administration, Jinnah University for Women, Karachi, Pakistan
e-mail: analyzeus@gmail.com

S. A. R. Khan et al. (eds.), *Circular Economy and Technological Innovation*, Industrial Ecology, https://doi.org/10.1007/978-981-96-5650-9_4

SCI). Additionally, while Government Effectiveness demonstrates a nuanced relationship with the Leagile strategy, its direct impact on resilience capability suggests possible counter-intuitive associations with a negative beta of –0.165. All three constructs of SCHA, RC, and SCI were found to have a significant impact on Leagile Strategy, which then also had a significant impact on sustainable performance.

Conclusion This study explores new areas of supply chain capabilities to withstand disruptions, accentuating the government's pivotal role in harnessing hyperagility and reinforcing resilience capabilities during crises. An in-depth examination of the limitations presents avenues for future researchers to refine further and expand on the core findings. This study distinguishes itself by probing into the moderating effect of governmental efficacy in the nexus between supply chain adaptability and resilience.

Keywords Supply chain integration · Supply chain resilience · Hyperagility · Leagile Strategy · Sustainable performance · Government Effectiveness · COVID-19

1 Introduction

Supply Chain is a multidisciplinary field, enveloping all business aspects of an organization. The functional spread is Interscope in nature, with agility as a vital feature in today's era, which has transformed the supply chain into an organic entity that reacts to both internal and external stimuli. The stimuli could help increase the efficiency and performance of the chain created and could also derail and disrupt. Sustainable performance of organizations is a need of the present times. With climate change deteriorating immensely, the need to focus on supply chains' roles in achieving better sustainable performance is more desperate than it was ever before. The world has witnessed in the recent past that COVID-19, a globally disruptive event, became a reason for all business activities to halt until governments around the globe developed measures to bring matters close to former normality. Started to emerge in early 2020, the Coronavirus pandemic impacted 214 countries, with aviation, tourism, transport and manufacturing industries being the upfront victims of this pandemic's lockdown; moreover, the estimated figures by the Asian Development Bank state that cumulative economic losses due to COVID-19 would be around USD 5.8 to 8.8 trillion (Barai and Dhar 2024).

In the contemporary, evolving business environment, SCM presents many intricate challenges and promising avenues for enterprises. The tenets of integration, collaboration, and adaptability are often extolled as essential for the successful navigation of the supply chain environment, invariably influencing business performance and fostering a sustained competitive edge. As in the practical business realities of the world, disruptions are inevitable and preparing beforehand and staying resilient during crises are hallmarks of great supply chains. Events such as the globally impacting conflicts, natural disasters and pandemics have compelled businesses all over the world to restructure their approach and try and cover as many areas of risk as possible (Di Paola et al. 2023).

This research study provides insights for managers, especially those working in a manufacturing enterprise, to understand the factors that enhance supply chain resilience by providing an intermingling of applicable and observable constructs, namely supply chain internal integration, the transformative potential of Hyper-agility, and the moderating influence of governmental efficiency. This will assist the managers in preparing against any radical disruption they may face and expound beforehand on any major disruptive event that may impact their business flow of material, information, or funds. An efficient supply chain ensures that the resources, such as materials, are delivered timely, within estimated costs and as per the quality required (Akinsulire et al. 2024), and it is only possible if managers prepare against challenges before they appear or come close to their supply chain operations.

2 Background of the Topic

Like other domains of business, supply chains also faced similar disruptions in their upstream and downstream operations. Such disruptions are unavoidable in situations like a pandemic, any radical geopolitical changes such as Brexit, and particularly during a conflict. Supply chain uncertainties are elevated, and any major event that takes place during such situations impacts all supply chain operations in one way or another. Supply chains are not independent. They are dependent globally, locally, politically, environmentally, financially, and socially. Each stakeholder that is included plays its part, such as the government. It is imperious for global supply chains in the world now to not just possess technology and carefully drafted strategic action plans against risks but also rapidly implement decisions based on real-time data analytics to counter challenges (Patel 2023), such as timely communication with suppliers for securing raw materials in case of foreseen shortages in globally.

In a post-COVID world, one of many lessons learned by manufacturers and businesses all over the world includes investing in and developing resilience for their material supply chains in downstream and upstream channels. This can be highlighted by the works of Li et al. (2023), in which 1717 research articles based on supply chain resilience were analyzed, and the authors presented three core themes or capabilities that were found to be common in all the literature; these included interconnectivity, transformability and sharing. The authors described interconnection in supply chains as the strength of the connection between supply chain partners, the capability to sense the trends or any upcoming change that would impact the business or supply chains is described as transformability. The construct of sharing in the research work was described as the mutual use of resources, such as temporary employees from partners in supply chains, to counter timely surges in demand.

One of the insightful works among an abundance of literature on supply chain resilience was presented by Kähkönen et al. (2023). The authors analyzed supply chain resilience with dynamic capability views on the impact caused by disruptions from the COVID-19 pandemic. The study was based on medical equipment manufacturing companies in Italy and Finland. As medical equipment such as face masks was wanted with more than ever an increase in demand by retailers during COVID-19, it was discovered that three elements needed for manufacturers supply chain resilience included rearrangement of available resources, a rapid response ability and rapid decision-making capabilities. It was explained that rearranging or reconfiguring resources by organizations was instrumental in maintaining and developing supply chain resilience. The disruptions were classified as upstream and downstream; upstream disruptions included shortage or inconstancy in supply from the suppliers, and downstream disruptions during the COVID included changes in demand from the consumer's end.

Radical changes in the supply market (upstream) and from the consumer demand (downstream) in the supply chain are frequently termed "supply chain disruption." Supply chain (SC) disruption was described by Hamidu et al. (2023) as simply those circumstances that disturb the flow of supplies, money or resources and impair the organization's ability to satisfy customer demands. In their work, the authors explained that almost 70% of the organizations in the world face supply chain disruptions to any extent, and disruptions may be pertaining to supply, natural disasters or changes in the existing market landscape. The authors further elaborated their work on supply chain disruptions by culminating in the notion of Dynamic Capability. Dynamic capability is the utilization of resources in multiple advantageous manners, which enables organizations to move forward from the competition and sustain their position in case of a crisis.

Figure 1 highlights that the manufacturing industry was among the highly exposed sectors to material shortages in lieu of global disruptions. It shows a reply from a number of business managers who affirmed that they faced material shortages during the COVID-19 pandemic.

Supply chains in the world have and will always be a source of risks for organizations. Supply chain activities include interacting with external stakeholders and organizations, which includes passing on relevant information. Such suppliers work and operate in the marketplace and with other players in the industry. Burden to be agile for making the finished product available on shelves as trends began while being lean and having minimum waste to keep the costs as low as possible. More of a hybrid strategy with lean and agile efficiency notions, the Leagile strategy's adoption is positively influenced by the capacity of the enterprise, changing situations in its environment and the positive perception about the innovation as revealed by a study on Egyptian manufacturing firms (Hashem and Aboelmaged 2023).

In 2019, the COVID-19 pandemic left the world in an unprecedented situation that had a global impact so immense and rapid that it halted almost all economic and commercial activities in the world. As described in Fig. 2, the global economic growth indicator, the world's Gross Domestic Product (GDP), dropped into negative numbers also during the summit of COVID-19's impact. With such a prominent decrease in economic outlook, it was also during this period that supply chain weaknesses, integration, and resilience were most focused. A disruption of this magnitude, the effects of which are not yet completely submersed, does leave supply chain professionals

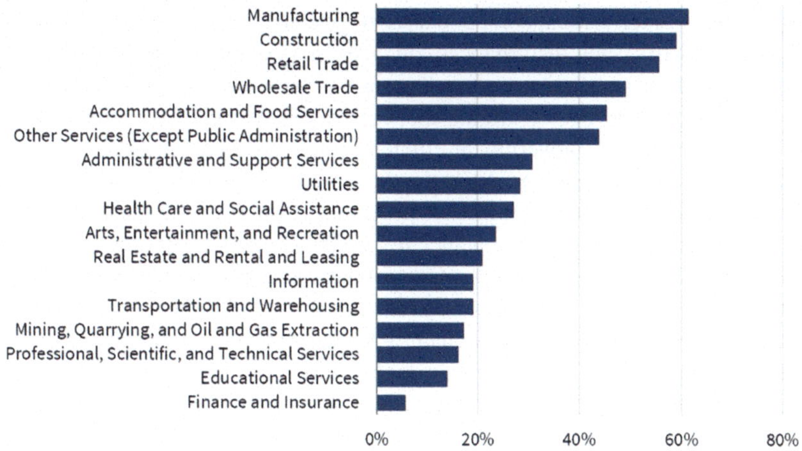

Fig. 1 Data from the United States Census Bureau highlights industries with the percentage of business managers who confirmed that their business faced material shortages during the COVID. (*Source* U.S Bureau of Census [2021])

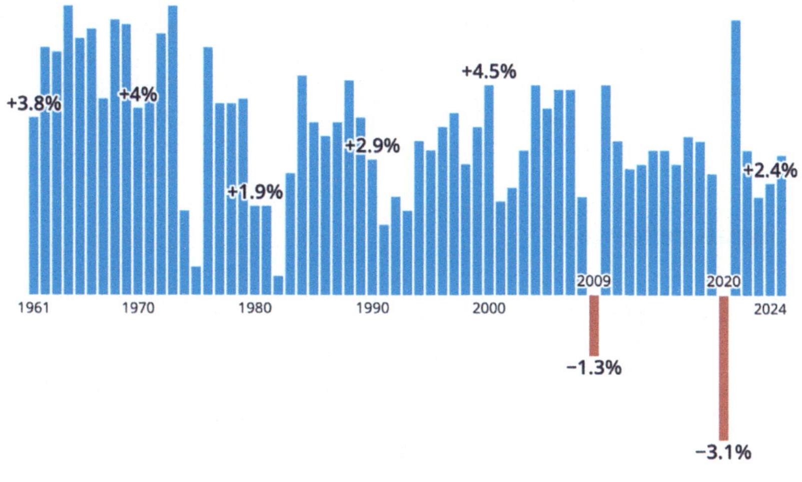

Fig. 2 Statistical figures for the global economy GDP growth. 2023 (*Source* The World Bank, Global Economic Prospects [])

eager to invest in their supply chain network resilience capabilities. Such radical disturbances in supply chains are likely to be present all year long; it is the capability to respond and recover quickly in an ever-changing environment that determines the very survival of such supply chains (Alvarenga and Oliveira 2023) and, ultimately, of the organizations.

The effects would be felt more keenly in industries producing high-value goods, where supply chains are typically long and spread out. Imagine a post-disruption world where a sudden critical component shortage causes production or assembly to grind to a standstill. Such disturbances can weaken a company's ability to function and lead to widespread economic repercussions. The main aim of this study is to provide empirical data demonstrating the interplay between supply chain internal integration, hyperagility, government efficiency, and sustainable advantage. Along with a combination of Lean and Agile practices with 'the Leagile strategy.' It aims to provide businesses with a comprehensive interpretation of the mechanisms and rationale by which these factors enhance resilience against disruptions. Along with other constructs, the inclusion of a construct for the role of government policies makes this study rather distinctive from several articles in the literature. The impact that government policies have on supply chains has not been studied comprehensively at present and requires more focus (Dubey et al. 2023).

The transformative potential of emergent digital platforms will impact supply chain resilience. Exploring technology is important to prepare against disruptions. Understanding technological limitations and the extent to which investing in technology can give supply chain managers leverage over competition is a crucial set of assessments. This is to say that since the majority of supply chain decisions are based on data-driven analytics, such as material requirement scheduling and demand forecasting being on the top of the list, technology is one of the contributing elements for supply chain resilience presently. A study based on Chinese manufacturers revealed that the role of technologies implemented or invented is enhanced as complexity or information is increased; the final results revealed that technology owned by organizations impacts a manufacturer's resilience (Cui et al. 2023).

3 Literature Review

3.1 Theory Development

This study involves theoretical development by integrating the Resource Based View (RBV) and Dynamic Capabilities (DC) theoretical notions. An introductory argument for the Resource-Based View can be presented for it to be the most widely applied theoretical lens for supply chain sustainability studies or for studying sustainable performance for business processes due to its notions enabling organizations to look 'inwards' within existing and owned resources for gaining competitive advantage over the others. RBV theory argues that organizational leadership can attain a competitive advantage over others by aligning and consuming their physical and non-physical resources, which lie within their organizational bounds; resources can be physical, its employees or stakeholders, and strong internal processes (Rodrigo 2024).

A Dynamic Capabilities theory can be introduced as one of the most handful theoretical lenses supporting research work for supply chain resilience. As iterated in the literature above, industrial dynamics for all organizations are always variable, a prime example of which was the radical change brought about by COVID-19. The DC theory can be defined as the manner, extent, and limit organizations in the world alter their resources, procedures, products and services to quickly change the dynamics of the environment they operate within; present literature divides DC theoretical framework into two domains, one is where organizations focus on procedures and to realign resources, this is also the domain the authors of this study tend to rely on, and the other domain of DC focuses on leadership capabilities and vision of the leader to bring the organization out from the crisis (Leso et al. 2024).

This unique combination enhances understanding of the consequences of Resilience Capability (RC) on long-term competitive advantage. The research utilized a variety of RBV and DC frameworks to explore the relationship between inherent organizational resources and their ability to adapt over time. It specifically focused on how these factors enhance resilience within the supply chain. The integration of RBV and DC has significantly contributed to our understanding of organizational supply chain capabilities. This research develops theoretical rigor by emphasizing that the significance of resources does not solely originate from their accessibility. The distinctive attributes that render them uncommon, precious, difficult to replicate, and irreplaceable are the factors that provide strategic significance in attaining competitive advantages. When examining RC from a distribution center standpoint, the research emphasizes the importance of adaptively restructuring accessed resources to address fluctuations.

The study also provides substantial insight by examining the impact of government regulations on SCM. Hence, we expand the breadth of firm-centric RVB and DC frameworks by integrating an external environmental dimension. This integration enhances the relevance of frameworks within a dynamic corporate landscape for the supply chain.

Dynamic Capabilities framework consists of a set of approaches, methods, and techniques by which organizations combine resources, reconfigure them, and exploit them in ways that enable them to achieve their objectives (Quayson et al. 2023). Quayson et al. (2023) also states that dynamic capabilities allow organizations to achieve their targets set out for the care and protection of the environment. One of the core notions for the RBV is that the resources under consideration must not be readily available and that they must not be easily imitated. The inclusion of the DC framework and RBV theory in this research work reiterates the same notion. With the integration of an increased-than-usual level of responsiveness (termed as hyper agility), the integration of supply chain resources, and its resilience, this research determines the effect of these three variables on a strategy that is a combination of lean and agile principles. Afterward, the effect of this strategy on an organization's long-term sustaining competitive advantage is observed.

This connects to the DC framework as the study explores the way or in which approach these three variables, which are an organization's internal resources (level of responsiveness, integration among processes, and resilience), contribute to Leagile's strategy and ultimately to developing a sustaining competitive advantage. Based on the DC framework, the study will determine and then recommend the set of approaches or measures that can be taken to combine, reconfigure, or exploit resources in a certain way to achieve the organization's objective, such as lower wastage and higher efficiencies. RBV's central notion is addressed as all three variables considered are internal resources or organizational capabilities. Such capabilities are built over years of learning curve and market exposure. The proposed study is particularly interested in integration, partnerships, and adaptability within the context of SCM, owing to their rarity and significance. Organizations must explore pertinent theories to sustain their competitive advantage amidst the current era of rapid technological advancements and increasing resilience (Khan et al. 2022).

3.2 Hyperagility and Leagile Strategy

The connection between supply chain hyper agility (SCHA) and Leagile strategy is about allocating the organization's resources in a way that allows it to readily adapt to external changes before others in the competition. Such resources can range from forecasting methodologies to a resilient distribution network. Work by Raj et al. (2023) highlighted the role of information processing and the way it impacts a supply chain's ability to react against changes in market conditions; the authors presented a model for SCHA and showed that the ability to process information impacts increased SCHA. This integration enables enterprises to enhance their efficiency and flexibility within a dynamic digital environment (Overby et al. 2006).

The first hypothesis (H1) tests the relation between SCHA and Leagile strategy. As demonstrated by Abdelilah et al. (2023), agile supply chain operations are not merely a product of applying lean manufacturing work processes only. There is a need for the integration of lean strategies with supply chain operations, harmoniously complementing each other to have a desired level of agile responsiveness to changes in the market. Combining a strategy based on lean and agile principles leads to digital adaptability, which enhances flexibility in operations (Overby et al. 2006).

Building further on H1, this study tests that the Leagile strategy acts as a mediator between SCHA and sustainable performance in its second hypothesis, H2. H2 is built on the notion that separately applying the principle of lean manufacturing or separately molding supply chains for agile adaptation does not garner long-term sustainable results. Any one of the ways, in their singularity, may produce results that are as per the standards and would fulfill all the benchmarks for performance, but this does not last long, and sustaining those standards does not happen for a long time, especially during disruptions. This is evident from a case presented by Raedemaecker (2020) in which a financial institution or a financial service provider struggled with their customer service; the organization had a traditional flow of work where a customer's complaints were bounced from one department to another. The company then integrated tools from lean and agile practices. With the lean approach, the company restructured the entire workflow by value mapping and establishing only a single point of contact for each function. For agility, the financial service is focused on establishing a team of individuals without a strictly defined flow of work. Such individuals were responsible for managing customer requests from beginning to end. As a result, the average time for resolving a concern decreased by a staggering 90%, and a 30% increase in customer positive ratings was observed.

The introduction of a new dimension is done to inculcate the impact of government policies on supply chains. Consequently, supply chains do not function in isolation, but regulatory policies greatly dampen or aggravate supply chain disruptions for organizations. The third hypothesis (H3) tests the notion that government regulations or interference has a significant impact on composing a robust, agile strategy. A study by Zaman et al. (2023) has provided a positive and impactful relation between government policies and their effect on supply chain activities, which would enhance translating the impact of SCHA measure for a strong Leagile strategy. The interdependence of technical advancement, strategic alignment, sustainability considerations, and government activities in contemporary society reflects organizational management's intricate and diverse nature. Considering this, the following hypotheses are proposed:

H1: SCHA has a significant impact on Leagile Strategy
H2: The relationship between SCHA and sustainable performance is significantly mediated by Leagile Strategy
H3: The relationship between SCHA and Leagile Strategy is significantly mediated by Government Effectiveness

3.3 Supply Chain Resilience and Leagile Strategy

Resilience in supply chain operations is about the ability to adjust and recover in case of any disruption or damage caused by disruptions in the external organizational environment. To achieve a resilient ability, business processes such as production, transportation, procurement, storage, and distribution must be aligned within the manufacturing organization and across supply chain partner organizations (Khan et al. 2022). It has been observed in previous studies that coherence within processes and partners across a supply chain is fundamental to producing optimal outcomes from lean practices applied (Prajogo et al. 2016; Yang et al. 2014).

H5 tests the notion that resilience capabilities impact sustainable performance for an organization contributing to Leagile's strategy. Hypothesis H6 investigates the impact of government policies on establishing the relationship between RC and Leagile Strategy. Ivanov (2022) studied resilience given three assets: safety stocks, data-based digital monitoring, and a contingency plan.

To sustain an organization's performance, it is fundamentally imperative to include the supply chain resilience or resilience capabilities (RC) of a supply chain in its strategy. Resilience, as indicated in the literature. Considering this, the following hypotheses are proposed:

H4: RC has a significant impact on Leagile Strategy
H5: Relationship between RC and sustainable performance is significantly mediated by Leagile Strategy

H6: Relationship between RC and Leagile Strategy is significantly mediated by government effectiveness

3.4 Supply Chain Integration and Leagile Strategy

The integration of SCM includes having supply chain partners, such as downstream distributors and suppliers in upstream operations, readily available to support when an organization is faced with disruptions. In such situations, it is imperative to have internal processes such as production, storage, and transportation be in line with supply chain partners. Any weakness within processes could cause the organization a significant financial loss in case of disruptions, such as in a situation of shortage of materials. Previous studies have supported that a strong integration between supply chain processes, internal and external, engenders increased implication of Leagile models, resulting in improved operational performance (Yang et al. 2014; Prajogo et al. 2016) Hypothesis H9 is composed to understand the impact of Government Effectiveness as a moderator for enhancing the impact of SCI on Leagile strategy.

According to Arkolakis et al. (2018) and Rajesh (2019), scholarly literature suggests that government regulations and policies substantially influence how enterprises handle and incorporate their supply chains. The potential influence of SCM integration on the adoption of the Leagile strategy is expected to be heightened within an environment where the government actively promotes innovation and collaboration. Ultimately, these ideas comprehensively explore the dynamic relationship between SCI, Leagile strategy, SSCP, and government efficiency. As mentioned above, the components establish a robust theoretical framework that lays the groundwork for forthcoming empirical investigations, comprehensively illustrating the interplay and impact of these elements within the contemporary corporate landscape.

H7: SCI has a significant impact on Leagile Strategy

H8: Leagile Strategy significantly mediates the relationship between SCI and sustainable performance

H9: Government effectiveness substantially moderates the relationship between SCI and Leagile Strategy

4 Theoretical Model

Figure 3 presents the study framework and the flow of impact for independent, moderating, mediating, and dependent variables.

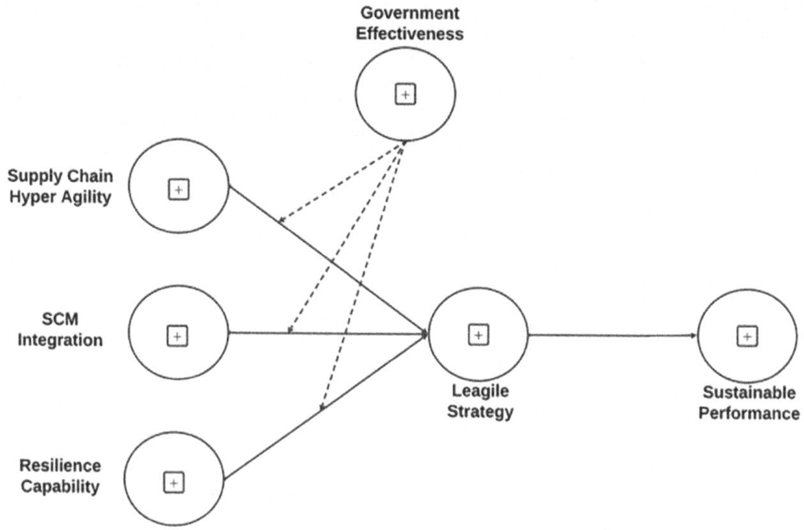

Fig. 3 Research Framework

5 Methodology

Shah et al. (2023a) designed a theoretical framework for empirical testing. They developed a theoretical framework known as RLS (Resource and Leagile Strategy). This model tested the organizational resources and capabilities that lead to better performance. Taking inspiration from the RLS model, the current study has developed its hypothesis and theoretical model to test the relationship between exogenous and endogenous constructs through Smart PLS. Figure 3 illustrates the research framework, and Table 1 provides definition of constructs.

The study aimed to have a sample size that would provide 95% confidence that the results were accurate within plus or minus 5% of the actual population value. Data were collected by distributing questionnaires via online platforms. The researchers distributed 450 questionnaires and received 385 completed questionnaires. As Fig. 3 shows, the researchers selected Resilience Capability (RC) as a stimulus because it creates uncertainty in an organization, implying that it is possible to measure how respondents' opinions are affected by the presence of this stimulus. Using RC as a stimulus, the researchers could better understand how individuals perceive and respond to uncertainty in SCM.

Variations in survey responses caused by the study instrument are a common source of methodological bias. Therefore, by strictly adhering to the established procedure, the study minimized the potential for prevalent methodological biases. The process involved developing a theoretical basis for the conceptual framework and modifying existing scales and measures. Using the updated dataset, we double-checked the questionnaire's validity and reliability. The first part of the questionnaire

Table 1 Construct and definitions used in theoretical model

Construct	Meaning	Citation
SC Hyperagility (SCHA)	A capability inspired by supply chain agility, which states that organizations proactively respond or improvise before others during supply chain disruptions for a limited or extended time	(Cohen and Kouvelis 2021; Müller et al. 2023; Raj et al. 2023)
SC Integration (SCI)	Capability refers to the synchronized collaboration between stakeholders (customer, supplier, and manufacturer) in the chain through strategies, practices, and processes to fulfill existential objectives	(Kim et al. 2022; Qi et al. 2017)
Resilience Capability (RC)	An organizational capability that makes a supply chain ready to learn, recover, and conserve operational continuity during a disruption	(Cotta et al. 2023; Gölgeci and Gligor 2022)
Leagile Strategy	A strategy combining lean and agile paradigms in the production ecosystem results in the creation of an information gateway known as a decoupling point	(Shah et al. 2023a)
Sustainable Performance	A performance based on a triple bottom line encompassing aspects of economics, environment, and social factors while satisfying and delivering the needs of customers or stakeholders through coordinated operations of an organization in the supply chain	(Shah et al. 2023b; Zhang et al. 2021)
Government Effectiveness	Tax relaxation, rental flexibilities, and soft loans for the general public provide government support for organizations	(Dubey et al. 2023; Ma et al. 2021)

relates to demographic data. It is measured on a nominal scale, as the data collected is categorical and cannot be measured on a numerical scale. The second part of the questionnaire relates to the main study and has six factors and 18 items. The six factors and 18 items are measured on a five-point rating scale, where one indicates strong disagreement, and five indicates strong agreement. So, the data collected here is ordinal, as it can be ranked in order from lowest to highest. However, the distance between each point on the scale is not equal.

6 Scales and Measurements

No constructs or measures were introduced; instead, existing concepts from previous research were used. Using established constructs and measures from earlier studies can be beneficial because it allows for easier comparison of results across studies and can increase the reliability and validity of a study's findings. However, it is essential to ensure that the constructs and measures used are appropriate in their number for the current study's research question and context (Table 2).

Table 2 Questionnaire development

Construct	References	Items
Hyperagility	Raj et al. (2023)	3
Government Effectiveness	Esfahbodi (2017); Kumar et al. (2020)	3
Supply Chain Integration (SCI)	Flynn et al. (2010)	3
Resilience Capability (RC)	El Baz and Ruel (2021) and Brandon-Jones et al. (2014)	3
Lcagile Strategy	Naylor et al. (1999); Oyombe et al. (2022)	3
Sustainable Performance	Saqib and Zhang (2021); Kwak et al. (2021)	3

7 Characteristics of the Respondents

The characteristics distribution of respondents is depicted in Table 3. The study had a sample size of 385 respondents, of whom 46.9% were female and 53.1% were male. The study found that 17.1% of respondents were in the age bracket of 21–30 years, while 82.9% were aged 31 and above, with the majority being above 50 years old. Regarding designation stratification, the data revealed that 45.5% of respondents were executives, 30.4% were managers, 15.2% were general managers, and 8.9% were CEOs of their organization. Such distribution based on demographic characteristics can help in the interpretation of the study's results and indicate how the findings may generalize to other populations.

Table 3 Profile of respondents

Characteristics	Percentage (%)
Gender	
Male	53.1
Female	46.9
Age	
20–30	17.1
31–above	82.9
Designation	
Executives	45.5
Managers	30.4
General Managers	15.2
CEOs	8.9

8 Results and Discussion

8.1 Model Fitness

Table 4 provides an overview of the measures of construct reliability and validity for the constructs examined in the study. Statistical measurements are engendered using Cronbach's Alpha, which gauges interrelation among constructs.

Composite Reliability (CR), an additional measure of internal consistency, incorporates the indicator loadings. The default assumption of equal loadings in Cronbach's Alpha is circumvented. The CR ratings for all constructs were above the threshold of 0.8, surpassing the commonly recognized minimum of 0.7. This indicates a robust consistency within the constructs. The AVE is a measure that quantifies the proportion of variance acquired by a construct from its indicators relative to the conflict captured due to measurement error. This measure assesses convergent validity. It is generally accepted that the AVE values should be equal to or greater than 0.5 to establish convergent validity. This criterion indicates that at least 50% of the variance in the indicators has been explained. All constructs examined in this study exhibited above-threshold AVE values, with the highest AVE values observed for Leagile Strategy and Sustainable Performance constructs.

These findings suggest that all the constructs exhibit strong convergent validity. The study's results indicate that the constructs under investigation, namely Hyperagility, Government Efficiency, Leagile Strategy, SC Integration, Resilience Capability, and Sustainable Performance, exhibit satisfactory internal consistency and convergent validity. Table 4 presents an overview of the reliability and validity of the primary constructs in the study, including Hyperagility, government efficiency, lean strategy, SCI, RC, and sustainable performance. Cronbach's Alpha, CR, and AVE were among the statistical methods employed to assess the internal consistency reliability and convergent validity of constructs in SEM. Table 5 below uses Heterotrait-monotrait ratio (HTMT) to assess discriminant validity.

The results indicate a robust internal consistency and convergent validity among the constructs under investigation: Hyperagility, government efficiency, Leagile strategy, integration, RC, and sustainable performance.

Table 4 Reliability of constructs

Construct reliability and validity	Cronbach's Alpha	Composite reliability	AVE
Hyperagility	0.778	0.857	0.601
Government Effectiveness	0.730	0.849	0.652
Leagile Strategy	0.777	0.870	0.691
SC Integration	0.733	0.846	0.647
RC	0.791	0.865	0.616
Sustainable Performance	0.781	0.872	0.694

Table 5 Heterotrait-monotrait ratio (HTMT)

Heterotrait-monotrait ratio (HTMT)	Values
Government Effectiveness < - > Hyperagility	0.845
Leagile Strategy < - > Hyperagility	0.972
Leagile Strategy < - > Government Effectiveness	0.921
SCI < - > Hyperagility	0.978
SCI < - > Government Effectiveness	0.935
SCI < - > Leagile Strategy	0.962
RC < - > Hyperagility	1.075
RC < - > Government Effectiveness	0.870
RC < - > Leagile Strategy	0.946
RC < - > SCI	0.920
Sustainable Performance < - > Hyperagility	0.902
Sustainable Performance < - > Government Effectiveness	0.873
Sustainable Performance < - > Leagile Strategy	0.849
Sustainable Performance < - > SCI	0.878
Sustainable Performance < - > RC	0.840

A widely used method for assessing discriminant validity within the SEM framework involves illustrating values derived from the Fornell-Larcker criterion, as in Table 6. As per the Fornell-Larcker criterion (Fornell and Larcker 1981), the implication is that the construct under consideration exhibits a higher degree of shared variance with its corresponding indicators (as evaluated by the square root of the AVE) than with any other construct inside the model. The diagonal elements of the table display the square roots of the AVEs for each construct. These values, ranging from the top left to the bottom right, all exceed 0.7 (Fornell et al. 1981), indicating satisfactory convergent validity. The diagonal elements, representing the correlations between different constructs, should have higher magnitudes than the off-diagonal elements inside the corresponding row and column.

One expressive instance is Hyperagility (SCHA), which exhibits a notable level of discriminant validity due to its square root AVE value of 0.775, surpassing its

Table 6 Fornell-larcker criterion

Fornell-Larcker criterion	DA	GE	Leagile Strategy	SCMI	SCR	SP
Hyperagility	0.775					
Government Effectiveness	0.639	0.808				
Leagile Strategy	0.769	0.702	0.831			
SCI	0.761	0.690	0.750	0.804		
RC	0.843	0.662	0.753	0.723	0.785	
Sustainable Performance	0.713	0.652	0.679	0.686	0.667	0.833

correlations with all other constructs (ranging from 0.639 to 0.843 in the first row). Several values deviate significantly from the normal distribution, with one notable example being the strong correlation observed between SCHA and RC, which is measured at 0.843. The Fornell-Larcker criterion is satisfied as the observed correlations, albeit indicating some degree of construct overlap, remain below the square roots of the AVE for the corresponding constructs (0.775 for DA and 0.785 for SCR). The Fornell-Larcker criterion posits that it is vital for all constructs to possess enough discriminant validity. While the HTMT satisfies the requirements for demonstrating discriminant validity, the identification of several substantial correlations between constructs suggests that the relationships between them should be further investigated in the future.

To assess the presence of multicollinearity among predictors, SEM employs Variance Inflation Factor (VIF) values, which are presented in Table 7. Multicollinearity refers to the occurrence of significant correlations among independent variables in a regression model, resulting in the conveyance of duplicate information. Consequently, the regression coefficients have the potential to exhibit instability and lack reliability. VIF values above 10 are suggestive of the presence of problematic multicollinearity in both regression analysis and SEM, as stated by researchers. According to O'Brien (2007), some academics advocate for a more conservative threshold, contending that VIF values above five may also indicate multicollinearity problems.

All the VIF values in Table 7 are the established threshold of 10, with the highest value at 2.120 observed for the variable SCR1. This suggests that multicollinearity among the predictors is not significant. The constructs of the model do not exhibit substantial levels of multicollinearity, even when applying the more stringent criterion of 5. The integration of SCM with government efficiency, exemplified by their respective VIF scores of precisely 1.000, is noteworthy. Given the assumption that these interaction terms, which have been constructed manually, are independent of other variables in the model, a VIF value of 1 indicates the absence of any collinearity. In summary, the VIF results suggest that the SEM model under consideration does not exhibit significant issues related to multicollinearity among the predictor variables. The VIF indicates that the SEM study will yield reliable and consistent estimates, as each predictor variable will contribute unique information rather than redundantly reiterating existing information.

Table 8 presents the VIF values for the inner model of a PLS-4 SEM analysis. The VIF values observed in this sample are below 10, a threshold commonly regarded as the minimum acceptable number. The interaction terms "Government Effectiveness x Hyperagility - > Leagile Strategy" and "Government Effectiveness x RC - > Leagile Strategy" have VIF values of 8.018 and 8.036, respectively. Although their score falls below the threshold of 10, it exceeds the more stringent criterion of 5. This observation suggests the presence of multicollinearity concerns that warrant additional investigation.

Nevertheless, none of the VIF values above the threshold of 5 10 indicates that severe multicollinearity is improbable. Researchers should exercise caution in their

Table 7 Collinearity statistics

Collinearity statistics	VIF
SCHA1	1.890
SCHA2	1.442
SCHA4	1.727
SCHA5	1.354
GE1	1.841
GE2	1.777
GE3	1.223
IS1	1.625
IS2	1.807
IS3	1.494
SA1	1.695
SA2	1.647
SA3	1.539
SCMI2	1.473
SCMI3	1.711
SCMI5	1.365
SCR1	2.120
SCR2	2.074
SCR3	1.466
SCR4	1.623
Government Effectiveness x SCI	1.000
Government Effectiveness x RC	1.000
Government Effectiveness x SCHA	1.000

Table 8 *VIF* Inner model

Inner model—List	VIF
Hyperagility - > Leagile Strategy	4.528
Government Effectiveness - > Leagile Strategy	2.257
Leagile Strategy - > Sustainable Performance	1.000
SCI - > Leagile Strategy	3.111
RC - > Leagile Strategy	4.116
Government Effectiveness x SCI - > Leagile Strategy	4.997
Government Effectiveness x Hyperagility - > Leagile Strategy	8.018
Government Effectiveness x RC - > Leagile Strategy	8.036

approach, primarily due to the potential presence of multicollinearity. This is particularly pertinent when incorporating the interactions between variables into their analyses. The higher VIF values observed may be attributed to the intrinsic nature of the interaction terms or suggest a significant overlap in variance between the interaction terms and other predictors. The VIF values seen in the internal model indicate that, on the whole, there is limited reason to be concerned about multicollinearity. However, it is worth noting that specific interaction terms may be contributing to potential issues. The provided findings fall within acceptable ranges. However, it is advisable to conduct further examinations to ensure the dependability of the model, particularly in cases where specific values closely approach the conservative threshold.

Table 9 evaluates a PLS-SEM (Partial Least Squares Structural Equation Modeling) prediction utility and precision model incorporating two separate constructs: Leagile Strategy and Sustainable Performance. The model's predictive accuracy can be assessed by utilizing the Q2predict values. A Q2 value greater than 0 is commonly used to demonstrate the predictive relevance of associated endogenous latent variables. The present research indicates the model's predictive utility for both the Leagile Strategy construct (0.692) and the Sustainable Performance construct (0.539). Furthermore, the model's predictive accuracy can be assessed using the Root Mean Square Error (RMSE) and the Mean Absolute Error (MAE). Smaller values of RMSE and MAE indicate improved prediction accuracy. The RMSE and MAE metrics for the Leagile Strategy exhibit values of 0.558 and 0.427, respectively (Table 9).

Conversely, Sustainable Performance demonstrates somewhat elevated values of 0.683 and 0.520, respectively. Based on the provided data, it can be observed that the model exhibits a slightly higher level of accuracy in forecasting the Leagile Strategy compared to its performance in predicting Sustainable Performance. Nevertheless, it is crucial to consider that the specific circumstances of the research and the standards set within the field of study significantly impact the understanding and evaluation of these metrics' level of acceptability or quality. However, conducting a comparative analysis with other research or established standards within this area could further enhance the comprehensiveness of the findings.

Table 9 Model fit—Q2

PLS-SEM	Q^2predict	RMSE	MAE
Leagile Strategy	0.692	0.558	0.427
Sustainable Performance	0.539	0.683	0.520

Table 10 Direct relationship

Path Model (Hypotheses)	Beta	SD	T Value	P value
Hyperagility - > Leagile Strategy	0.238	0.061	3.883	0.000
SCI - > Leagile Strategy	0.253	0.045	5.594	0.000
RC - > Leagile Strategy	0.230	0.056	4.133	0.000

8.2 Measurement Models

Table 10 showcases the outcomes derived from a PLS-SEM analysis. Focusing on the interconnections among the elements, the table serves as a valuable tool for validating specific hypotheses regarding the interrelationships among the various components of the model. The Beta (path coefficient) value indicates that the strength of the relationship between SCHA and the Leagile Strategy is 0.238. These findings suggest a positive correlation between the two constructs, wherein an increase of one unit in SCHA is associated with an additional 0.238 units of Leagile Strategy. The statistical significance of this association is denoted by a T-value of 3.883 and a standard deviation (SD) of 0.061.

To achieve statistical significance at the 5% level, T-values for studies in social sciences must exceed the critical value of 1.96. Based on the obtained T-value of 3.883 and the corresponding p-value of 0.000 (which is below the conventional significance threshold of 0.05), it can be concluded that there exists a statistically significant association between SCHA and Leagile Strategy. A correlation coefficient of 0.253 between SCI and Leagile Strategy suggests a favorable relationship. The T-value for the observed correlation is 5.594, indicating a substantial deviation from the null hypothesis. This value is significantly higher than the critical value of 1.96. Suggesting a statistically significant link. Additionally, the p-value for this association is 0.000, further supporting the conclusion of statistical significance. Finally, it is worth noting that the Beta coefficient, which measures the relationship between RC and Leagile Strategy, was calculated to be 0.230.

The obtained p-value of 0.000 suggests that the observed association is statistically significant. Additionally, the T-value of 4.133 is above the predetermined threshold, further supporting the significance of the link. The Beta values, ranging from 0.230 to 0.253, exhibit a possible level of relevance that falls within an intermediate range. Nevertheless, it is vital to comprehend these numerical values within the confines of the research investigation. In the study titled "A Primer on Partial Least Squares Structural Equation Modeling (PLS-SEM)", it is argued that the significance, relevance, and alignment of a route coefficient with earlier research and theoretical frameworks hold greater importance than the numerical value of the coefficient itself (Leguina 2015). The data analysis reveals that all links exhibit statistically significant positive route coefficients, supporting all three hypotheses examined in the SEM.

The PLS-SEM research offers valuable insights into the interconnections between various conceptualizations and their effects. The indirect relations are illustrated in Table 11. The Leagile Strategy is a substantial intermediary in multiple interactions, particularly between Hyperagility and Sustainable Performance, which is a noteworthy finding. The considerable association between agility and long-term performance (Beta $= 0.162$, $T = 3.704$, $p = 0.000$) highlights the importance of the approach in establishing a connection between the two variables. When considering Government Effectiveness as a mediating variable between Hyperagility and Leagile Strategy, an intriguing interaction effect emerges. The connection's significance, as indicated by a p-value of 0.071, is somewhat higher than the conventional threshold.

Nevertheless, the Beta value of 0.131 suggests that there is an association. Hair et al. (2017) posit that in the context of exploratory research, p-values that range up to 0.10 could be deemed acceptable, therefore serving as a plausible rationale for the borderline outcome.

Similarly, the Beta coefficient for the interaction effect between Government Effectiveness and SCI is 0.096, and the corresponding p-value of 0.057 indicates near statistical significance. The present observation of borderline significance aligns with the viewpoints about the appropriate utilization of p-value thresholds within specific research contexts. On the other hand, upon examining the variables of Government Effectiveness and RC, a moderation effect becomes apparent. Indicated by a negative Beta coefficient of 0.165 and a statistically significant p-value of 0.020. The study ultimately emphasizes the crucial role played by the Leagile Strategy in mediating the relationship between SCI and Sustainable Performance, as well as that between RC and Sustainable Performance. The Beta values of 0.172 and 0.157 demonstrate statistically significant associations, providing more evidence for the crucial mediating function of the Leagile Strategy. Upon synthesizing these findings, it becomes evident that certain relationships are clear and statistically significant, while others lack significance. For comprehensive conclusions, it is imperative to situate these findings within the broader context of the research subject and assess them in light of the existing body of literature.

Table 11 Indirect relationships

Path Model (Hypotheses)	Beta	SD	T value	P value
Hyperagility - > Leagile Strategy - > Sustainable Performance	0.162	0.044	3.704	0.000
Government Effectiveness x Hyperagility - > Leagile Strategy	0.131	0.072	1.807	0.071
Government Effectiveness x SCI - > Leagile Strategy	0.096	0.050	1.900	0.057
Government Effectiveness x RC - > Leagile Strategy	-0.165	0.071	2.329	0.020
SCI - > Leagile Strategy - > Sustainable Performance	0.172	0.033	5.279	0.000
RC - > Leagile Strategy - > Sustainable Performance	0.157	0.039	4.046	0.000

9 Discussion

The centrality of the Leagile Strategy in connecting various supply chain components to Sustainable Performance has long been presented in SCM research. However, its mediatory role, especially in emerging digital paradigms and the efficacy of governance mechanisms, has remained relatively under-explored. As discussed in this study, the results derived from the recent PLS-SEM analysis present a comprehensive view of interrelationships and their implications for the broader domain of supply chain strategy. One of the fundamental hypotheses, suggesting a significant relationship between Hyperagility and Leagile Strategy, is convincingly validated with a Beta value of 0.162 and a p-value of 0.00; this is related to the notion that hyperagility via technologies and digital coordination is significantly relevant in the literature (Christopher and Lee 2004). A beta value of 0.162 and an unequivocal p-value of 0.000 underline this assertion. The relevance of digital paradigms in shaping agile yet lean supply chain strategies has been emphasized in past literature (Christopher and Lee 2004). Results further elaborate that with a good Beta value of 0.162 being supported by a T-value of 3.704 and p-value of 0.000, it shows that a well-structured and well-composed Leagile strategy acts as a bridge for the optimal implication of applied supply chain agility measures for sustainable performance.

Results show that Government Effectiveness, with a p-value of 0.071, shows the construct's impact on the Leagile Strategy to be weak. A similar trend is observed for the relation between Government Effectiveness and SCI, and it can be observed that with a p-value of 0.057, the relation between these two variables and the tendency of Government Effectiveness to act as a moderating variable is not strong.

Based on these results, one might argue that higher government intervention or effectiveness might not always resonate with RC, at least in the context of shaping Leagile strategies. While this might seem counter-intuitive, considering the generally positive association between governance and business efficiencies, it opens avenues for further research. Perhaps it is time to delve deeper into which aspects of Government Effectiveness resonate with resilience and which might be counterproductive. In essence, this discussion, rooted in the empirical results of our study, not only validates several longstanding hypotheses but also nudges the domain towards newer, perhaps less-trodden research paths (Table 12).

10 Conclusion

In recent decades, manufacturers have witnessed several disruptive technologies and a global pandemic. Long-term supply chain disruptions have provided a resurgence in emphasizing, achieving, and maintaining the sustainable performance of organizations. Business landscapes are getting more and more disruptive from the depletion of resources and increased competition. In such dynamics, the agility, coherence and

Table 12 Hypotheses summary

Hypotheses	Hypotheses statements	Decision
H1	SCHA - > Leagile Strategy	Accepted
H7	SCI - > Leagile Strategy	Accepted
H4	RC - > Leagile Strategy	Accepted
H2	SCHA - > Leagile Strategy - > Sustainable Performance	Accepted
H3	Government Effectiveness x SCHA - > Leagile Strategy	Rejected
H9	Government Effectiveness x SCI - > Leagile Strategy	Rejected
H6	Govt Effectiveness x RC - > Leagile Strat	Rejected
H8	SCI - > Leagile Strategy - > Sustainable Perf	Accepted
H5	RC - > Leagile Strategy - > Sustainable Perf	Accepted

resilience in supply chains are fundamental for survival and for sustaining performance when other members of the industry are struggling. In this research, sustainable growth has been investigated to be impacted by a strategy composed of lean and agile principles. Such strategy is then backtracked to be originated by Hyperagility in supply chains, their integration among processes, and the extent to which they possess the ability to come back to their optimal functioning state. The addition of the government's role as a mediating factor is done to inculcate an external element. As all three independent variables are internal strengths of organizations, as highlighted by the RBV, the addition of the government's role injects an external element to present and investigate if the impact of external policies by authorities significantly contributes to or significantly hampers the composition of the Leagile strategy.

Findings presented that SCHA, SCI, and RC do impact the Leagile strategy significantly. The relationship between Leagile's strategy and sustainable performance was also found to be significant. The study hence presents the conclusion that the greater the supply chain ability, the more the ability to adjust and perform or improvise as the situation demands. This notion was elaborated comprehensively during the pandemic, which impacted almost all the world's supply chains. The pandemic altered the entire landscape of demand and supply operations, and organizations had to improvise and adjust to the high costs of storage and transportation to keep themselves above financial losses.

The findings of the second variable explain that the more complimenting operations are within a supply chain, the better the composition of the Leagile strategy would be. Leagile strategy and SCI connect on a fundamental level, and without harmony among supply chain operations, principles of Lean and Agile practices can not be composed into a strong strategy that could defend the organizational performance in the face of disruptions. SCI makes sure that all partners in a supply chain contribute at the right time and of the right magnitude, as expected by the situation at hand. A significant connection between SCI and the Leagile strategy shows that having all partners on board in a supply chain is crucial in the face of disruptions, such as in the case of shortages of material or a sudden drop in consumer demand for a product.

Results showing a significant relation between supply chain resilience (SCI) and Leagile strategy further elaborate on that, and the literature suggests that any strategy leading to sustainable performance is incomplete without a certain focus on supply chain resilience. Sustainable performance for organizations results from the application of Leagile's strategy and contribution to resilience measures, such as subcontracting operations, outsourcing services, and leveraging suppliers and distributors in times of crises, which is of vital importance.

For the variable of government effectiveness, the data analysis showed that no substantial connection is established in the formation or strengthening of the Leagile strategy, with government policies being a moderating variable. This is directed towards the fact that the role of government is not impactful either way for manufacturers in Pakistan. The government does not facilitate organizations in establishing sustainable performance for organizations in Pakistan. Further studies are needed to explore the reasons behind this un-impactful role.

However, the anticipated outcomes on the moderating impact of Government Effectiveness proved to be more intricate. The study's findings indicate that the government's efficiency level did not enhance the positive impacts of Hyperagility and SCI on the Leagile Strategy. As mentioned earlier, the results may be seen as substantiation of the notion that private-sector innovation has the potential to surpass government intervention and mitigate its influence in certain circumstances. The presence of a moderator, namely Government Effectiveness, reveals an unexpected adverse relationship between RC and Leagile Strategy, thus suggesting that specific governmental interventions may inadvertently diminish the advantages derived from RC. This discovery presents an opportunity for further exploration of the nuanced aspects of government interventions and their tangible impacts on SCM.

In summary, the results of this study enhance our understanding of the connections between integrated and resilient supply chain practices, sustainable performance outcomes, and digital efforts. The function of government is undeniably significant, but recent analysis suggests that its complexity surpasses previous assumptions. The acquisition of such expertise acquires greater significance due to the consistently changing corporate landscape. The anticipated outcomes of this research are poised to establish a foundation for subsequent investigations, consequently enriching the discourse about the advancement of sustainable and resilient supply chain tactics. This study significantly enhances the scholarly comprehension of dynamic capability theory by examining the potential enhancement of digital capabilities in RC through government intervention during crises. It addresses the existing gaps in macro and micro knowledge within management studies. In addition, it thoroughly evaluates its limitations and constraints, recognizing their potential to catalyze future academic inquiries.

10.1 Theoretical Implications

This project presented a unique combination of variables for an understanding of how resources such as agile capabilities, resilience strategies and approaches, and harmonious working of supply chain functions complement each other to sustain, maintain, and to some extent also elevate sustainable performance for organizations. One of the distinctive mediating variables that also adds a unique feature to the study is the role of government. The impact of government policies is studied as a mediating variable with all three independent ones. All of this contributes to theoretical development by presenting that the acquisition of resources as per the RBV notions is not enough to produce a long-lasting advantage for the organization. Other factors, such as the role of government policies with a strong Leagile strategy composed of organizational resources such as supply chain agility, resilience, and integration, are essential.

The study also provided a substantial theoretical contribution by examining the impact of government regulation on SCM. Expanding the breadth of the firm-centric RBV and DC frameworks, this research integrates an external environmental dimension for organizations. This integration enhances the applicability and relevance of these frameworks within a dynamic corporate landscape. Furthermore, the work contributed substantial insights to the theoretical discourse. The study ventured into empirical investigation by employing the RBV and DC frameworks within the specific context of SCM. The transition from theoretical abstraction to empirical grounding enhances the academic rigor of the research, bolstering the legitimacy of the findings and consequences. The strong interaction between the RBV and DC in RC and sustainable advantage makes this study a foundational contribution that can pave the way for future research. The research has made a significant theoretical contribution to strategic management and supply chain studies by providing detailed insights and establishing connections between theoretical concepts and real-world observations.

10.2 Practical Implications

The research emphasizes the substantial influence exercised by many supply chain participants, including producers, transporters, distributors, and retailers, on the ultimate outcomes attained by an enterprise. Based on the provided information:

- Industry professionals can devise strategies knowing that obtaining resources that are irreplaceable and can not be imitated easily will not merely sustain an organization against external competition and disruptions.
- Alignment of resources and capabilities (such as the ability to analyze market data trends and swiftly respond to disruptions, integrate stakeholders, and recover from low performance) with combined lean and agile practices is important for long-term sustainability.

- Integration of state-of-the-art SCM tools and advanced cloud platforms may be necessary to achieve excellence. These tools and platforms facilitate the rapid transmission of data and foster collaborative actions across organizations for better SCI.
- Government involvement or policies could weaken supply chain resilience and integration capabilities, resulting in weaker sustainability against disruptions in the ever-changing external market.

The data analyzed has presented the significance of aligning long-term goals and tactical objectives with key stakeholders throughout the supply chain. As mentioned above, the discoveries derived from the research hold potential value for organizations establishing and enhancing relationships with suppliers, consumers, and other significant collaborators.

Promoting a culture characterized by trustworthiness, mutual understanding, and consensus-based decision-making can improve RC and Hyperactivity. Regular performance audits and equitable allocation of risks and rewards are integral elements of this system.

Professionals in SCM decision-making need the expertise of individuals well-versed in academic and business domains to stay up to date on emerging theories, methods, and trends within this field of study to cultivate enduring innovation and establish a resilient strategic position in the digital era; this statement reiterates the significance of continuous intellectual pursuit and the exchange of ideas.

10.3 Limitations and Recommendations

The researchers acknowledge certain limitations and areas of inquiry that remain unexplored despite the rigorous approach employed in this work. It is imperative to remember that the assumptions underpinning the DC framework can be subjected to rigorous examination in the face of extraordinary circumstances, such as pandemics or significant disasters. The potential challenges that can compromise the reliability of assessments include subjective judgments and measurement errors. To enhance the breadth of understanding of operational dynamics and information systems, it is suggested that a more diverse approach be adopted, which may involve case studies. The study's generalizability is constrained due to its exclusive reliance on data acquired from the manufacturing sector of a single country. The study only concentrated on a single industry to mitigate the potential challenges arising from sector-specific biases.

10.4 Future Avenues

This study is concentrated on Pakistan's textile manufacturing industry. Academic investigators pertaining to Leagile Strategy or Sustainable Performance could look for further avenues in several other manufacturing industries, especially pharmaceutical, automobile and service sectors. In the future, the RC, SCI and SCHA can have an impact on resilience in supply chains with Artificial Intelligence (AI) as a mediator. The authors of this study would like to advise future researchers comprehensively on exploring the role of AI as a mediator or moderator for the Leagile Strategy. The reason is that AI has started to revolutionize many business operations in supply chains, and it is only a matter of time before AI becomes a regular part of supply chain processes, especially for information processing and data-driven decision-making. There exists a gap or undiscovered area in research for the exploration of AI in supply chain processes and in understanding its impact on sustainable performance for organizations around the world.

Appendix

Questionnaire

Respondents were asked to give their opinion on the constructs below on a Likert Scale ranging from point 1 to be for 'Strongly Disagree' opinion and point 5 for 'Strongly Agree' opinion. A 5-point Likert scale was applied to gather responses from the respondents.

Hyperagility (Raj et al. 2023)

- My organization operates under high internal time pressure to manufacture our products during highly uncertain situations
- My organization operates under high external time pressure to manufacture our products during highly uncertain situations
- My organization quickly prioritizes speed goals during highly uncertain market situations

Government Effectiveness (Esfahbodi et al. 2017; Kumar et al. (2020)

- National environmental regulations (such as waste emissions, cleaner production, etc.) have helped my organization adopt sustainable practices.
- Export countries' environmental regulations have motivated my organization to opt for sustainable practices.
- The government's efforts for resource-saving and conservation regulations have helped my organization to inculcate sustainable processes.

Supply Chain Integration (Flynn et al. 2010)

- The organization I am associated with can quickly respond to changes in market demand.
- The organization I am associated with has a good on-time delivery record for our customers.
- The organization I am associated with can quickly modify products to meet our major customer's requirements.

Resilience Capability (El-Baz and Ruel 2021; Brandon-Jones et al. 2014)

- In case of sudden demand fluctuation, material flow would be quickly restored by my organization
- It would not take long to recover normal operating performance under highly uncertain market situations
- Disruptions would be dealt with quickly by my organization in case of high uncertainty

Leagile Strategy (Naylor et al. 1999; Oyombe et al. 2022)

- My organization keeps a minimum inventory level to eliminate waste
- My organization operates using IT and market intelligence
- My organization quickly responds to changes in customer's requirements

Sustainable Performance (Saqib and Zhang 2021; Kwak et al. 2021)

- My organization uses environmentally friendly materials and components.
- My organization contributes towards improving the living conditions of the employees.
- My organization attempts to decrease the cost of energy consumption by sustainable practices.

References

Abdelilah B, El Korchi A, Amine Balambo M (2023) Agility as a combination of lean and supply chain integration: how to achieve a better performance. Int J Logist Res Appl 26(6):633–661. https://www.tandfonline.com/doi/pdf/10.1080/13675567.2021.1972949

Akinsulire AA, Idemudia C, Okwandu AC, Iwuanyanwu O (2024) Supply chain management and operational efficiency in affordable housing: an integrated review. Magna Sci Adv Res Rev 11(2):105–118. https://doi.org/10.30574/msarr.2024.11.2.0113

Alvarenga MZ, de Oliveira MPV, Oliveira T (2023) Let's talk about bad experiences instead of forgetting them: an empirical study on the importance of memory for supply chain disruption management. Int J Prod Econ 261:108872. https://doi.org/10.1016/j.ijpe.2023.108872

Arkolakis C, Costinot A, Donaldson D, Rodríguez-Clare A (2018) The elusive pro-competitive effects of trade. Rev Econ Stud 86(1):46–80. https://doi.org/10.1093/restud/rdx075

Barai MK, Dhar S (2024) COVID-19 pandemic: inflicted costs and some emerging global issues. Glob Bus Rev 25(3):812–831. https://journals.sagepub.com/doi/pdf/10.1177/0972150921991499

Brandon-Jones E, Squire B, Autry CW, Petersen KJ (2014) A contingent resource-based perspective of supply chain resilience and robustness. J Supply Chain Manag 50(3):55–73. https://doi.org/10.1111/jscm.12050

Christopher M, Lee H (2004) Mitigating supply chain risk through improved confidence. Int J Phys Distrib Logist Manag 34(5):388–396. https://doi.org/10.1108/09600030410545436

Cohen MA, Kouvelis P (2021) Revisit of AAA excellence of global value chains: Robustness, resilience, and realignment. Prod Oper Manag 30(3):633–643. https://doi.org/10.1111/poms.13305

Cotta D, Klink L, Alten T, Al Madhoon B (2023) How do supply chain managers perceive the relationship between resilience and sustainability practices? An exploratory study. Bus Strateg Environ 32(6):3737–3751. https://doi.org/10.1002/bse.3325

Cui L, Wu H, Wu L, Kumar A, Tan KH (2023) Investigating the relationship between digital technologies, supply chain integration and firm resilience in the context of COVID-19. Ann Oper Res 327(2):825–853. https://doi.org/10.1007/s10479-022-04735-y

de Raedemaecker S, Handscomb C, Jautelat S, Rodriguez M, Wienke L (2020) Lean management or agile? the right answer may be both. McKinsey & Company

Di Paola N, Cosimato S, Vona R (2023) Be resilient today to be sustainable tomorrow: different perspectives in global supply chains. J Clean Prod 386:135674. https://doi.org/10.1016/j.jclepro.2022.135674

Dubey R, Bryde DJ, Dwivedi YK, Graham G, Foropon C, Papadopoulos T (2023) Dynamic digital capabilities and supply chain resilience: The role of government effectiveness. Int J Prod Econ 258:108790. https://doi.org/10.1016/j.ijpe.2023.108790

El Baz J, Ruel S (2021) Can supply chain risk management practices mitigate the disruption impacts on supply chains' resilience and robustness? Evidence from an empirical survey in a COVID-19 outbreak era. Int J Prod Econ 233:107972. https://doi.org/10.1016/j.ijpe.2020.107972

Esfahbodi A, Zhang Y, Watson G, Zhang T (2017) Governance pressures and performance outcomes of sustainable supply chain management–An empirical analysis of UK manufacturing industry. J Clean Prod 155:66–78. https://doi.org/10.1016/j.jclepro.2016.07.098

Flynn BB, Huo B, Zhao X (2010) The impact of supply chain integration on performance: A contingency and configuration approach. J Oper Manag 28(1):58–71. https://doi.org/10.1016/j.jom.2009.06.001

Fornell C, Larcker DF (1981) Evaluating structural equation models with unobservable variables and measurement error. J Mark Res 18(1):39–50. https://doi.org/10.1177/002224378101800104

Gölgeci I, Gligor DM (2022) Guest editorial: Deepening the theoretical understanding of agility and resilience in global supply chains. Int J Phys Distrib Logist Manag 52(8):605–613. https://doi.org/10.1108/IJPDLM-09-2022-536

Hamidu Z, Boachie-Mensah FO, Issau K (2023) Supply chain resilience and performance of manufacturing firms: role of supply chain disruption. J Manuf Technol Manag 34(3):361–382. https://doi.org/10.1108/JMTM-08-2022-0307

Hashem G, Aboelmaged M (2023) Leagile manufacturing system adoption in an emerging economy: an examination of technological, organizational and environmental drivers. Benchmarking: Int J 30(10):4569–4600. https://doi.org/10.1108/BIJ-03-2022-0199

Hair J, Hollingsworth CL, Randolph AB, Chong AYL (2017) An updated and expanded assessment of PLS-SEM in information systems research. Ind Manag Data Syst 117(3):442–458. https://doi.org/10.1016/j.tre.2021.102290

Ivanov D (2022) Learn resilience: AURA (Active Usage of Resilience Assets) framework for post-COVID-19 supply chain management. The International Journal of Logistics Management 33(4):1196–1217. https://doi.org/10.1108/IJLM-11-2020-0448

Kähkönen AK, Evangelista P, Hallikas J, Immonen M, Lintukangas K (2023) COVID-19 as a trigger for dynamic capability development and supply chain resilience improvement. Int J Prod Res 61(8):2696–2715. https://doi.org/10.1080/00207543.2021.2009588

Khan MA, Ahmad SF, Irshad M (2022) Quantifying the mediating effect of resilience in supply chain: empirical evidence from oil and lubricant industry. J Dev Soc Sci 3(2):213–224. https://doi.org/10.47205/jdss.2022(3-II)21

Kim M, Lee G, Hwang Y, Kim TH, Kim DS (2022) Cost-benefit analysis of the integrated pharmaceutical supply chain information service after the establishment of the Korean Pharmaceutical Information Service. Front Pharmacol 13:925287. https://doi.org/10.3389/fphar.2022.925287

Kumar SU, Kumar DT, Christopher BP, Doss CGP (2020) The rise and impact of COVID-19 in India. Front Med 7:250. https://doi.org/10.1108/ITP-09-2018-0438

Kwak YH, Lee J (2021) Toward sustainable smart city: lessons from 20 years of Korean programs. IEEE Trans Eng Manage 70(2):740–754. https://doi.org/10.1109/TEM.2021.3060956

Leguina A (2015) A primer on partial least squares structural equation modeling (PLS-SEM). https://doi.org/10.1080/1743727X.2015.1005806

Leso BH, Cortimiglia MN, Ghezzi A, Minatogawa V (2024) Exploring digital transformation capability via a blended perspective of dynamic capabilities and digital maturity: a pattern matching approach. RMS 18(4):1149–1187. https://doi.org/10.1007/s11846-023-00692-3

Li D, Zhi B, Schoenherr T, Wang X (2023) Developing capabilities for supply chain resilience in a post-COVID world: a machine learning-based thematic analysis. IISE Trans. 55(12):1256–1276. https://www.tandfonline.com/doi/full/10.1080/24725854.2023.2176951

Ma S, He Y, Gu R, Li S (2021) Sustainable supply chain management considering technology investments and government intervention. Transp Res Part E Logistics Transp Rev 149, 102290. https://doi.org/10.1016/j.tre.2021.102290

Müller J, Hoberg K, Fransoo JC (2023) Realizing supply chain agility under time pressure: Ad hoc supply chains during the COVID-19 pandemic. J Oper Manag 69(3):426–449. https://doi.org/10.1002/joom.1210

Naylor JB, Naim MM, Berry D (1999) Leagility: Integrating the lean and agile manufacturing paradigms in the total supply chain. Int J Prod Econ 62(1–2):107–118. https://doi.org/10.1016/S0925-5273(98)00223-0

O'Brien RM (2007) A caution regarding rules of thumb for variance inflation factors. Qual Quant 41(5):673–690. https://doi.org/10.1007/s11135-006-9018-6

Overby E, Bharadwaj A, Sambamurthy V (2006) Enterprise agility and the enabling role of information technology. Eur J Inf Syst 15(2):120–131. https://doi.org/10.1057/palgrave.ejis.3000600

Oyombe GG, Awino ZB, Ogutu M, Njihia JM (2022) How leagile strategy and strategic partnership affect competitive advantage of construction supply chains. J Bus Strat Financ Manag 4(2):184. https://doi.org/10.12944/JBSFM.04.02.02

Patel KR (2023) Enhancing global supply chain resilience: Effective strategies for mitigating disruptions in an interconnected world. BULLET: J Multidisiplin Ilmu 2(1):257–264. https://journal.mediapublikasi.id/index.php/bullet/article/view/3482

Prajogo D, Oke A, Olhager J (2016) Supply chain processes: Linking supply logistics integration, supply performance, lean processes, and competitive performance. Int J Oper Prod Manag 36(2):220–238. https://doi.org/10.1108/IJOPM-03-2014-0129

Qi Y, Huo B, Wang Z, Yeung HYJ (2017) The impact of operations and supply chain strategies on integration and performance. Int J Prod Econ 185:162–174. https://doi.org/10.1016/j.ijpe.2016.12.028

Quayson M, Bai C, Sun L, Sarkis J (2023) Building blockchain-driven dynamic capabilities for developing circular supply chain: Rethinking the role of sensing, seizing, and reconfiguring. Bus Strateg Environ 32(7):4821–4840. https://doi.org/10.1002/bse.3395

Raj A, Sharma V, Shukla DM, Sharma P (2023) Advancing supply chain management from agility to hyperagility: a dynamic capability view. Ann Oper Res: 1–32. https://doi.org/10.1007/s10479-022-05158-5

Rajesh R (2019) Modeling the barriers of green supply chain practices: an Indian perspective. Int J Adv Manuf Technol 100(5–8):1493–1509. https://doi.org/10.1504/IJLSM.2010.033891

Rodrigo SP (2024) The role of social media in small and medium-sized restaurant businesses: a case study from Östersund, Sweden. https://miun.diva-portal.org/smash/record.jsf?pid=diva2%3A1834754&dswid=-6137

Saqib ZA, Zhang Q (2021) Impact of sustainable practices on sustainable performance: the moderating role of supply chain visibility. J Manuf Technol Manag 32(7):1421–1443. https://doi.org/10.1108/JMTM-10-2020-0403

Shah A, Rose C, Ibrahim A, Khan SAR, Tanveer M (2023a) A resource and leagile strategy in business operations for performance improvement. Decision Analytics Journal 7:100197. https://doi.org/10.1016/j.dajour.2023.100197

Shah A, Soomro MA, Zahid Piprani A, Yu Z, Tanveer M (2023b) Sustainable supply chain practices and blockchain technology in garment industry: An empirical study on sustainability aspect. J Strateg Manag. https://doi.org/10.1108/JSMA-04-2023-0080

The World Bank. Decent work & economic growth | SDG 8: Decent work & economic growth. Atlas of Sustainable Development Goals 2023. Accessed 17 Oct 2024. https://datatopics.worldbank.org/sdgatlas/goal-8-decent-work-and-economic-growth/?lang=en

Yang MGM, Hong P, Modi SB (2014) Impact of lean manufacturing and environmental management on business performance: An empirical study of manufacturing firms. Int J Prod Econ 129(2):251–261. https://doi.org/10.1016/j.ijpe.2010.10.017

Zaman SI, Khan S, Zaman SAA, Khan SA (2023) A grey decision-making trial and evaluation laboratory model for digital warehouse management in supply chain networks. Decis Anal J, 100293

Zhang X, Yu Y, Zhang N (2021) Sustainable supply chain management under big data: a bibliometric analysis. J Enterp Inf Manag 34(1):427–445. https://doi.org/10.1108/JEIM-12-2019-0381

Assessing Publication Trends in MIS, Economics, and Management: Exploring the Impact of Sustainable Practices, Circular Economy, and Digitalization

Muhammad Tanveer, Rehana Naheed, and Ikram Ul Haq

Abstract This bibliometric analysis examines the publishing growth and developing research trends in Management Information Systems (MIS), Economics, and Management over the course of 30 years. This research intends to elaborate on the research trends of the past 30 years in terms of highly cited articles, top authors, productive institutions, and top journals used for publications. The analysis shows that Wageningen University & Research is the most productive institution, with MIS Quarterly: Management Information Systems being the most often preferred journal for publication. Furthermore, co-occurrence of authors' used keywords analysis identifies keyword clusters such as information systems, innovation, and management, with emerging themes like sustainable practices, the circular economy, and digitalization. Future research trends indicate a shift towards narrower disciplines within economics, management, and MIS, such as sustainable practices, digital business, and economic policy. To analyze the publication growth and research trends within the disciplines of MIS, Economics, and Management. To identify the most influential articles, top authors, and productive institutions over the past 30 years. To explore the emerging themes of sustainable practices, circular economy, and digitalization in the context of these disciplines. Readers will gain insights into the historical and current publication trends in MIS, Economics, and Management. Scholars will be able to identify key institutions, authors, and journals contributing to these fields. Readers will understand the evolving research focus towards sustainability, digital transformation, and economic policies and how these trends impact future research.

M. Tanveer (✉)
College of Business, Imam Mohammad Ibn Saud Islamic University (IMSIU), Riyadh, Saudi Arabia
e-mail: mtnawaz@imamu.edu.sa

R. Naheed
Quaid-I-Azam School of Management Science, Quaid-I-Azam University Islamabad, Islamabad, Pakistan

I. U. Haq
College of Dentistry, Kingdom of Saudi Arabia, King Saud Bin Abdulaziz University for Health Sciences, Riyadh, Saudi Arabia

S. A. R. Khan et al. (eds.), *Circular Economy and Technological Innovation*, Industrial Ecology, https://doi.org/10.1007/978-981-96-5650-9_5

Keywords MIS · Sustainable Practices · Circular Economy · Digitalization · Management · Economics · Bibliometric Analysis

1 Introduction

Bibliometric analysis, a methodology, is the means to offer a broad, large-scale, summary of the huge number of scholarly literature. Through the quantitative analysis of the data that deals with the publication history, one can grasp the attributes and growth of the scientific productivity in a certain field of sustainable practices and circular economy (van Nunen et al. 2018). Bibliometric methods can be used to assess the research activities and the way of conducting the research of authors, journals, countries, and institutions (Rojas-Sánchez et al. 2023). Besides, they can be also employed to identify and measure the cooperation patterns among these people (Li and Zhao 2015). One can detect not only the authors and publications that have a significant influence but also the countries and institutions that publish in the field's foundational journals. The classification of categories assigned to the publications and the number of journals published on a certain subject can show the variety of research themes and the cross-disciplinary nature of a particular research domain. Bibliometric can be a tool to show the latest discoveries, trends, and the most popular subjects in a specified subject domain of study. Besides, the geographical and content-wise gaps are identified in a research area by using the bibliometric analysis technique (Gall et al. 2015). Further, bibliometric can be a great help in the decision-making process of the science. Its uses for academic positions are classified and the effectiveness of journals, nations, and institutions is judged over a wide scale. Besides, the funding agencies and the policymakers may use bibliometric findings to support the allocation of funds to the research (Ugolini et al. 2015).

The bibliometric enquiry is utilized for many reasons, for instance, to recognize the tendencies in the sustainable practices, performance of articles and periodicals, to identify the digitalization collaboration trends and research components, and to investigate the intellectual framework of a particular sphere in the scholarly published work (Donthu et al. 2021; Verma and Gustafsson 2020).

Bibliometrics is a significant area of information science, sustainable development, waste management with multiple applications. (e.g. Rafols et al. 2014; Fahimnia et al. 2015; Lin et al. 2016a, b; Metse et al. 2016; Tanveer et al. 2022). In the past few decades, bibliometric evaluation has grown more prevalent in sustainable development and business research (Donthu et al. 2021; Khan et al. 2021), and its acceptance can be characterised to the progress, accessibility, and availability of bibliometric software such as Leximancer, Gephi, VOSviewer, and scientific databases such as Elseiver's Scopus and Clarivate Analytics Web of Science, PubMed and the cross-disciplinary pollination of the bibliometric procedure from more significantly, the popularity of bibliometric evaluation in business research is not a passing trend, but rather a reflection of its practicality in dealing with broad amounts of scientific data and generating substantial effects on research.

Scientific study disciplines and publications are constantly evolving around the world. Understanding these publication trends through careful analysis is critical for assessing academic communities' intellectual pulse and determining future research orientations. The emergence of Management Information Technology in the last 20 years has had a profound impact on public, social, and personal spheres as well as our overall quality of life. It handles data and information—displayed in electronic, written, graphic design, or sound formats—by addressing communication, processing, storing, printing, and displaying in ways most convenient for users. This evolution, driven by advancements in communication and computer technologies, also aligns with the rise of sustainable practices, the circular economy, and digitalization, which are transforming how information systems operate, aiming for greater efficiency and sustainability (Mahmood et al. 2024; Butt et al. 2024).

Moreover, MIS, sustainable development, and circular economy provides an awareness of an organization's relative position and basic functioning forces. It facilitates the organization's control, planning, and successful execution of operational operations by giving decision-makers the accurate information they need (Mishra et al. 2015). Adding more to the publication growth; in economics, several Bibliometrics studies exist such as Coupe´ (2003), Scott and Mitias (1996) examined the leading economists and economics faculties that provide international rankings. Research has grown rapidly over the past few decades in all fields, including management and economics, on a global scale.

This study looks into the world of Bibliometrics, using quantitative approaches to investigate the publishing growth of three diverse but interconnected fields: MIS, Economics, Management, and sustainable development which hasn't been done before. Scholars and experts continue to enhance the MIS discipline by sharing their insights and experiences through scientific journals. Studying journals can identify trends and alterations affecting MIS theories, processes, and applications (Al-Kofahi et al. 2020; Özköse and Gencer 2017).

This study has been carried out to answer the following research questions:

RQ1: What are the top productive institutions?
RQ2: What are the top most frequently used journals for publications?
RQ3: What are the top keywords used by authors?
RQ4: What are the top authors and their affiliated institutions?

2 Literature Review

2.1 *Historical Perspective*

People have grasped the concept of management for thousands of years. Pindur et al. (1995) claimed that the backgrounds of basic management techniques may be traced to Middle Eastern priests who started keeping a written record of monetary transactions at least 3000 years before the birth of Christ. Around 400 BC, Socrates claimed that management was a distinct proficiency from practical capabilities and knowledge. Moreover, Frederick Herzberg's idea of worker motivation has made a noteworthy contribution to organization thinking about employee attitude (Peramatzis and Galanakis 2022). Herzberg (1959) contended that most of the motivating initiatives led by management, includes as better salaries, enhanced allowances, and more holidays duration, eventually unsuccessful because, while they reduced certain aspects of job frustration (what employees detested about their works), they did not escalate work satisfaction.

Management originated as a recognized discipline around the turn of the century. In Management, there are different approaches in different periods, the classical period lasted from the mid-nineteenth century to the early 1950s. During this time, three key techniques emerged: methodical management, social relations, and administration. Furthermore, Modern-day management techniques include analytical management, administrative comportment, structure theory, and the contingency outlook. Current techniques have changed at various levels since World War II, and have remained the cornerstone of contemporary management thought (Harrison et al. 2020).

2.2 *Conceptual Framework*

Management Information Systems (MIS) is a comparatively new academic discipline with a diverse historical perspective and legacy (Culnan and Swanson 1986; Tsai et al. 2022). MIS is a professional and practical subject that studies the managerial, strategic, and operational applications of information technology at various levels, including society, corporations, groups, and individuals. MIS consists of computer science, cognitive psychology, management, economics, operational research, organizational philosophy, and engineering theories, and continues to develop in collaboration with these fields (Tsai et al. 2022; Özköse et al. 2023).

Waston et al. (1991) define (MIS) as an organizational strategy of disseminating past, current, and anticipated information about to internal operations and external intelligence. Cocosila et al. (2011) conducted a scientometric analysis of MIS in three major categories; in global, regional, and national MIS conferences, it has found that the field is maturing in terms of collaborative research and scholarly output, with leading contributors focusing on a few academic meetings. Another bibliometric study carried out by Özköse et al. (2023) analyzed the 25,304 Scopus indexed articles on MIS and provided guidance for the future studies. According to Katerattanakul et al. (2006), management information system field combines of computer science, decision-making field, behavioral discipline, cognitive psychology, operations management, organizational theory, circular economy, and engineering. Moreover, since its establishment, MIS scholars have tracked the field's history, current, and future developments. Palvia et al. (2007) conducted research in the discipline that is evolving with a focus on laborious research methods including mathematical representations and laboratory trials. Another author Lin et al. (2016a, b) analyzed papers from the top ten journals on information systems and MIS in electronic business publications. The analysis has conducted from 1991 till 2014 was ten leading management and business journals. Bai and Li (2022) examined the publication output on e-commerce from 2001 to 2022 and pointed out the main research themes. They study described that in order to better serve clients, new technologies have been included into e-commerce.

Adding more to MIS, it provides structured information to management at all levels using data from internal and external sources. Ozkose and Gencer (2017) analyzed the field of MIS by bibliometric analysis. They were conducted through the Science Citation Index Expanded (SCI-E) and Social Science Index (SSCI). The understanding and identity creation of the MIS area requires evaluating information and investigating its intellectual foundation. Alfawareh et al. (2021) analyzed trends in MIS research from 2017 to 2021, comparing contributions from various nations and authors. The main highlights of their research were influential leading MIS publications sources, prolific authors, contributing countries, publications types, supporting research organizations, languages, and subject dispersion.

2.3 *Evaluation of Publication Growth*

Many Bibliometric analyses have been found in management under different domains, as Performance management addresses by Busi and Bititici (2006), this is a diversity of management areas and fields ranging from logistics to marketing to human resource management for being considered a central exercise in any organization. Scholars (Vernadat et. al 2013) have proposed a value-based and risk-based framework for performance measurement and management. Another domain is knowledge management, studies by scholars (Secundo et al. 2019; Secundo et al. 2019; Tanveer 2024). Circular economy and knowledge management has a crucial role in corporate economics and productivity (Drucker 1968), leading to several studies and activities focused on this topic. Environmental management is also another domain of management; Todua N. and Jashi C (2018) discussed the challenges of sustainable social development, including the importance of promoting healthy eating among people.

The last ten years following the global financial crisis of 2007–2009 have seen an increase in the usage of strategic management language in the banking sector, both among scholars and banking professionals. Furthermore, even if strategic management stresses both internal and external adaptation, it might be difficult to adjust to changes in the actual world in accordance with the markets that are dominant (Agarwal et al. 2009). Knowledge management was found to be the fundamental component of strategic management by researchers (Alani et al. 2018) who were examining the relationship between strategic orientation and product innovation.

Sustainability and risk management are added to the bibliometric analysis in the management area in order to further develop and get a deeper understanding of the significance of sustainability for each individual, company, and the economy as a whole. Increasingly, academics and professionals in the construction sector are paying attention to occupational health management. Adding more to health management and "Pilot Medical Examination Scheme for Construction Workers" in Hong Kong (Yi and Chan 2016), which are significant for qualifying and decreasing the occupational health threats.

Economics has the potential to be extremely vast; in fact, it has grown in scope during the last 200 years. The study of economics both at the individual and societal level (Krugman and Wells 2004). This study assists individuals in organizing their needs and requirements provided by the social norms, political circumstance, and decision-making processes of the community. Moreover, Economics focuses on the economy, coordination, scarcity, choice, and human behavior.

In economics, several studies have found on the economics domain that has Bibliometrics analysis. Additionally, the field of bibliometrics is a subject that extensively combines and intersects philology, information science, mathematics, and statistics in a particular field (Khan et al. 2023).

There is research in the domain of economic is digital economics; according to Ellison (2005), The digital economics literature has influenced various fields, including crime, public goods, economics, urban finances, labour capitals, development funds, health-care investments, mass media finances, public investment, and global assets. Bibliometrics has an extensive variety of applications in numerous fields, such as business and economics. Other writers have also highlighted the share of minor expenses for digital finance (e.g. Shapiro and Varian (1998), Borenstein and Saloner (2001). Another field of economics is behavioral economics; Birnberg and Ganguly (2012) discuss how individuals make decisions and impact others, including organizations, markets, and society. Behavioral Economics has led to new areas of study, including Behavioral Finance (Tomer 2007; Tanveer et al. 2022).

MIS and Economics are inseparably connected through a variety of channels, particularly the use of information technology to increase economic efficiency, decision-making processes, and overall production (Laudon and Laudon 2004). Similarly, the relationship between MIS and management is also critical, as MIS aids managerial decision-making, organizational control, and strategic planning processes (Laudon and Laudon 2020). In summary, fundamental literature and research themes are still lacking, this study is reviewing the past 30 years of bibliometric analysis in the field of Economics and Management along with MIS to evaluate the Publication Growth.

2.4 Summary of the Review of Relevant Literature

The importance of many viewpoints in research is becoming more widely acknowledged, especially in the fields of MIS, management and economics. Research highlights the significance of incorporating diverse cultural, geographical, and socio-economic contexts to enhance comprehension and relevance of theories. This pattern is in line with international campaigns that support fair and inclusive research methods. The literature review reveals that there is knowledge gap on the assessment of publication trends on MIS, economics and management. The present study will highlight the prominent bibliometric features of this topic to unveil a dynamic landscape characterized by publication activity globally. As these fields continue to evolve, scholars are poised to address new challenges and contribute to the body of knowledge in meaningful ways.

3 Research Methodology

This research has used a quantitative approach to carry out relevant results. A retrospective bibliometric was used on the Scopus database in the first week of 2024.

3.1 Sampling, Data Collection

A keyword of "Management Information System", OR "Management Information Systems" AND "Management" AND "Economic" OR "Economics" was inserted in the search box with Boolean Operator "AND" and "OR" the option of "TITLE-ABS-KEY" was selected.

To refine the types of document, the study selected only articles and reviews. Other documents conference proceedings, conference abstracts, editorials, book chapters, and book and book reviews were excluded. In the filter of language only "English" was selected, and the documents published in other languages were excluded. The time frame of 30 years from 1994 to 2023 was selected from the year filter. The dataset was downloaded in CSV (Comma Separated Value) files for the analysis in the VOSviewer database. Microsoft Excel was used for calculating the percentages. A total of 3090 documents were found and after utilizing the inclusion/exclusion criteria 1091 documents (articles and reviews) were selected for examination.

Remarkable progress was detected in the early 10 years (1994–2003) and about half of the articles ($n = 534$; 48.94%) were published. In the next 10 years (2004–2013), a bit slow progress was found and 28.78% ($n = 314$) of articles were published. The lowest number of publications were recorded ($n = 243$; 22.27%) during the last 10 years from 2014 to 2023. All the selected articles were cited 31,867 times with a mean ratio of 29.20 citations per article.

3.2 Research Model

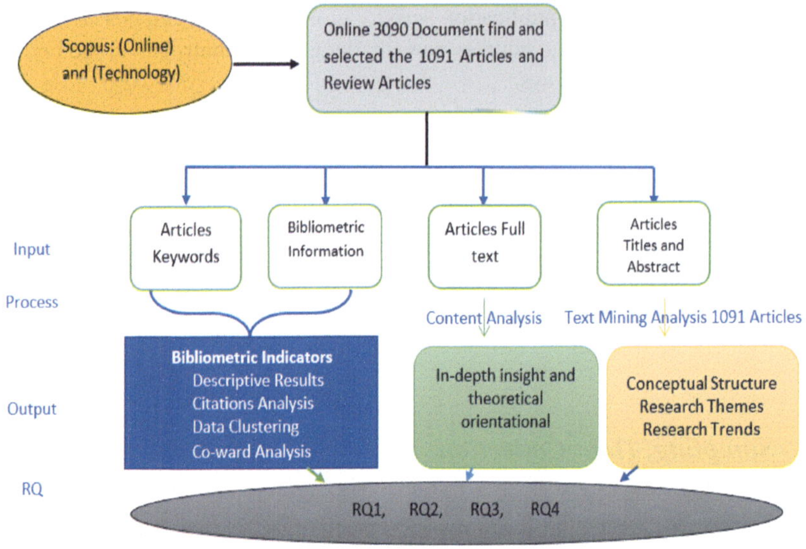

4 Data Analysis and Results Interpretation

Several analyses have been used to utilize the structure and development of this research. The following is the specific analysis of this present research. Bibliometrics is an important tool in scientific decision-making. It is commonly used to rank academic applicants and assess the success of journals, countries, and institutions. The findings can also be used to help policymakers and funding agencies in research funds allocation (Ugolini et al. 2015). Baker et al. (2020) describe a quantitative approach for managing large amounts of scientific literature maps, providing associations between articles, citations, journals, and citation networks, and predicting future research trends. VOS viewer software developed by van Eck and Waltman. Furthermore, to provide thorough insights into published papers about publishing growth of MIS, Economics & Management. Numerous bibliometric parameters have provided exhaustive facts and information. Citation analysis, network analysis, country-wise analysis, collaborative analysis, co-word & author, or institution-wise analysis has been used.

4.1 Article and Citation Analysis

Table 1 shows the publication growth in MIS, Economics, and Management in the past 30 years. The table indicates that the highest number of total articles is 361 in

Table 1 Article and Citation Analysis

Intervals	Total Articles	Total Citations	Citation Impact
1994–1998	316	5224	16.53
1999–2003	218	4591	21.06
2004–2008	202	14,224	70.42
2009–2013	112	4166	37.20
2014–2018	106	2267	21.39
2019–2023	137	1395	10.18

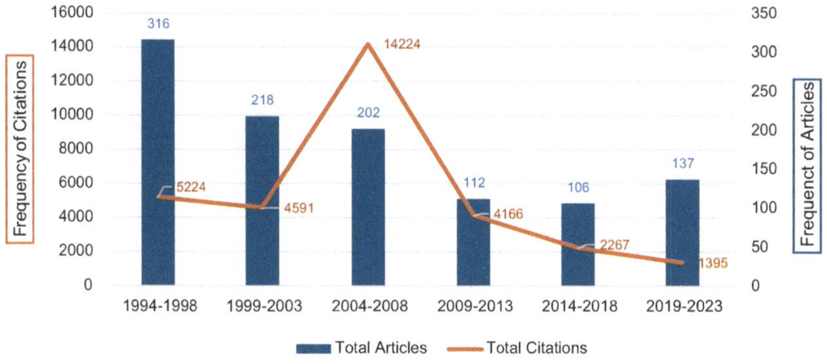

Fig. 1 Article and Citation Analysis

years 1994–1998. Whereas, the highest number of citations are from the year 2004 to 2008. The highest citation impact is also from the years 2004 to 2008. Figure 1 illustrates the graph from the year 1994 to 2023.

4.2 Analysis of Co-authorship Network by Country

Table 2 shows the publication growth in the top 20 countries in which the United States stands on top with a total 300 articles (27.49%) and these articles were cited 21,149 times with an average of 64.09 cites/article, followed by China, and the United Kingdom with 72 and 67 articles, respectively. The articles produced by South Korea have gained the highest citation impact (97 cites/article), followed by Hong Kong (85 cites/article) and the Netherlands (77 cites/article), among all the top 20 productive countries.

Figure 2 created by VOS viewer software shows a network co-authorship of 37 countries in which cluster one (9 Red Countries) United Kingdom, Canada, Bangladesh, South Africa, Ghana, Maldives, Tanzania, Malawi, and Norway. Cluster two (4 Green Countries) Germany, Greece, Italy, and Denmark. Cluster three (8 Blue countries) China, Hongkong, United Arab Emirates, India, Turkey, Sweden,

Table 2 Co-authorship network- country wise analysis

Serial No	Name of country	Total articles	Total citations	Citation impact
1	United States	330	21,149	64.09
2	China	72	1082	15.03
3	United Kingdom	67	1567	23.39
4	Germany	34	1249	36.74
5	Canada	32	1263	39.47
6	India	29	330	11.38
7	Taiwan	24	1100	45.83
8	Netherlands	21	1618	77.05
9	Australia	19	350	18.42
10	Italy	19	1002	52.74
11	Hong Kong	13	1105	85.00
12	Indonesia	13	101	7.77
13	France	12	534	44.50
14	Greece	12	562	46.83
15	South Africa	11	197	17.91
16	South Korea	11	1067	97.00
17	Spain	11	343	31.18
18	Portugal	10	237	23.70
19	Russian Federation	10	65	6.50
20	Sweden	10	520	52.00

and the Netherlands. Cluster four (4 Yellow countries) France, Spain, Portugal, and the Russian Federation. Cluster five (Indigo countries) are New Zealand, Australia, and Singapore. Cluster six (Orange countries) consists of the United States, Taiwan, and Switzerland, and others.

Table 3 contains the list of the 20 most productive institutions with their number of total articles, total citations, and citations impact. Wageningen University & Research, Netherlands stands on top with total of nine articles. Whereas, the "City University of Hong Kong", "New York University", and "University of Minnesota Twin Cities" are on second place with articles. While "University of Maryland, College Park" has the highest citation among all the institutions on the list. Moreover, the "University of Maryland, College Park" also has the highest number of citation impacts.

Table 3 demonstrates the utmost commonly used periodicals for publications in which the top-20 journals with articles, citations, and citation impact are presented (on the topic evaluating the Publication Growth in "Management Information System). The Journals mentioned in this table illustrate that articles published in MIS Quarterly Management Information System were highly cited with 7970 total citations numbers and information system research has total citations of 2153, and on the

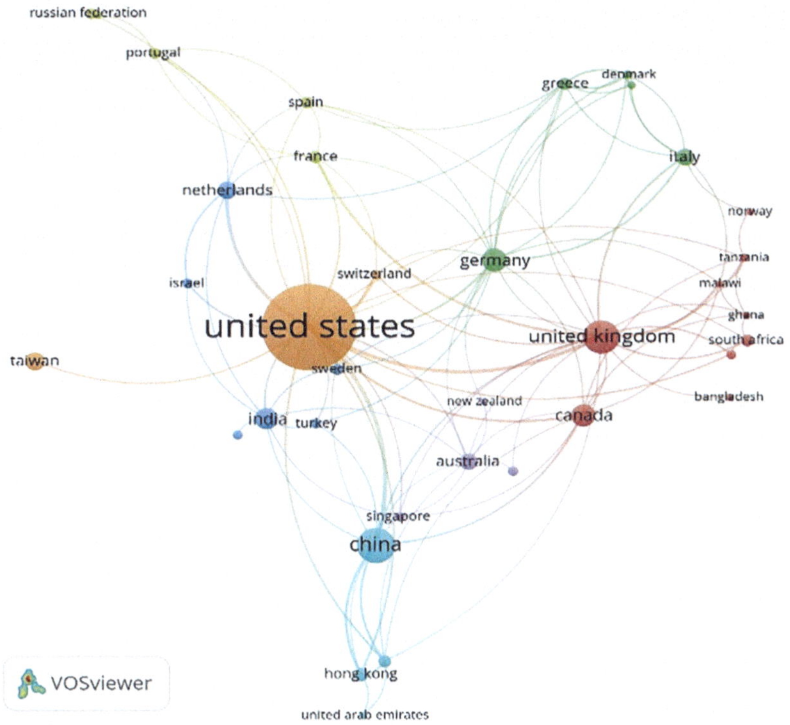

Fig. 2 Network of co-authorship by country

second number. Moreover, table 3 illustrates different ranges less to high in terms of total citations used by journals for publication. According to Reid and Chen (2007), if the article receives a greater number of citations, is considered as a highly cited article.

Table 4 shows the top 20 most cited articles. Author Wasko M.M.; Faraj S. has the highest number of citations (3857) in the journal MIS Quarterly: MIS. Author Davenport T.H. has the second-highest number of citations (2368) in Harvard Business Review. Similarly, the rest of the cited articles with authors' names and journals have been explained.

4.2.1 Co-word Exploration (Keyword Analysis)

Co-word exploration is predicated on the co-occurrence of terms that help in pinpointing research hotspots within a certain topic of study. Co-occurrence analysis states that a total of 2206 keywords have been used by authors.

Table 5 and Fig. 3 represent the co-occurrence of the top 20 keywords. Figure 2 created by VOS viewer software represents different clusters. Cluster 1 (4 Red

Table 3 Frequently Used Sources of Publications

Sr. No	Name of journal	Coverage span	Total articles	Total citations	Citation impact
1	Health Management Technology	1994–2009	34	25	0.74
2	Healthcare Informatics the Business Magazine for Information and Communication Systems	1994–2007	33	10	0.30
3	Health Data Management	1994–2014	29	7	0.24
4	MIS Quarterly Management Information Systems	1997–2021	24	7970	332.08
5	International Journal of Information Management	1994–2008	14	306	21.86
6	Journal of Management Information Systems	2003–2012	12	548	45.67
7	Information and Management	1994–2008	10	881	88.10
8	Management Science	1994–2023	10	853	85.30
9	Modern Healthcare	1994–2013	10	0	0.00
10	Infocare Information Strategies for Healthcare Networks	1995–1997	9	0	0.00
11	Materials Management in Health Care	1994–2007	9	0	0.00
12	Expert Systems With Applications	1994–2012	8	768	96.00
13	Information Systems Research	1994–2008	8	2153	269.13
14	International Journal of Technology Management	2000–2006	8	288	36.00
15	Computers and Electronics in Agriculture	1995–2022	7	378	54.00
16	Health Policy and Planning	2004–2018	7	218	31.14
17	International Journal of Production Economics	1994–2006	7	410	58.57
18	Journal of Digital Imaging	1998–2001	7	44	6.29
19	Manufacturing Computer Solutions	1996–2004	7	0	0.00
20	Proceedings of The Hawaii International Conference on System Sciences	2001	7	106	15.14

keywords) Information System, Innovation, e-business, and supply chain. Cluster 2 (5 Green keywords) Management, Strategy, Information System, Knowledge Management, and Management Information System. Cluster 3 (4 Blue keywords) Information technology, Information management, Evaluation, and MIS. Cluster 4 (2 Yellow keywords) management information system, geographical information system. Cluster (2 Indigo keywords) India and China.

Table 4 Top 20 highly cited articles

Sr. No	Authors	Title	Article type	Year	Journal	Total citation	Citation density by year
1	Wasko M.M.; Faraj S	Why should I share? Examining social capital and knowledge contribution in electronic networks of practice	Article	2005	MIS Quarterly: Management Information Systems	3815	200.79
2	Davenport T.H	Putting the enterprise into the enterprise system	Article	1998	Harvard business review	2368	91.08
3	Zhu K.; Kraemer K.L	Post-adoption variations in usage and value of e-business by organizations: Cross-country evidence from the retail industry	Review	2005	Information Systems Research	1142	60.11
4	Gans N.; Koole G.; Mandelbaum A	Telephone Call Centers: Tutorial, Review, and Research Prospects	Review	2003	Manufacturing and Service Operations Management	933	44.43
5	Melville N.P	Information systems innovation for environmental sustainability	Review	2010	MIS Quarterly: Management Information Systems	914	65.29
6	Santhanam R.; Hartono E	Issues in linking information technology capability to firm performance	Review	2003	MIS Quarterly: Management Information Systems	788	37.52
7	Podsakoff P.M.; Mackenzie S.B.; Bachrach D.G.; Podsakoff N.P	The influence of management journals in the 1980s and 1990s	Article	2005	Strategic Management Journal	593	31.21

(continued)

Table 4 (continued)

Sr. No	Authors	Title	Article type	Year	Journal	Total citation	Citation density by year
8	Piccoli G.; Ives B	Review: IT-dependent strategic initiatives and sustained competitive advantage: A review and synthesis of the literature	Article	2005	MIS Quarterly: Management Information Systems	532	28.00
9	Carmel E.; Agarwal R	Tactical approaches for alleviating distance in global software development	Article	2001	IEEE Software	523	22.74
10	Dao V.; Langella I.; Carbo J	From green to sustainability: Information Technology and an integrated sustainability framework	Article	2011	Journal of Strategic Information Systems	504	38.77
11	Wu W.-W	Choosing knowledge management strategies by using a combined ANP and DEMATEL approach	Article	2008	Expert Systems with Applications	470	29.38
12	Drummond M.F.; Schwartz J.S.; Jönsson B.; Luce B.R.; Neumann P.J.; Siebert U.; Sullivan S.D	Key principles for the improved conduct of health technology assessments for resource allocation decisions	Review	2008	International Journal of Technology Assessment in Health Care	343	21.44
13	Lee J.-N.; Miranda S.M.; Kim Y.-M	IT outsourcing strategies: Universalistic, contingency, and configurational explanations of success	Review	2004	Information Systems Research	335	16.75

(continued)

Table 4 (continued)

Sr. No	Authors	Title	Article type	Year	Journal	Total citation	Citation density by year
14	Dinev T.; Xu H.; Smith J.H.; Hart P	Information privacy and correlates: An empirical attempt to bridge and distinguish privacyrelated concepts	Article	2013	European Journal of Information Systems	298	27.09
15	Castelletti A.; Pianosi F.; Soncini-Sessa R	Integration, participation and optimal control in water resources planning and management	Article	2008	Applied Mathematics and Computation	286	17.88
16	Bjørnson F.O.; Dingsøyr T	Knowledge management in software engineering: A systematic review of studied concepts, findings and research methods used	Review	2008	Information and Software Technology	256	16.00
17	Levina N	Collaborating on multiparty information systems development projects: A collective reflection-in-action view	Article	2005	Information Systems Research	251	13.21
18	Cherbakov L.; Galambos G.; Harishankar R.; Kalyana S.; Rackham G	Impact of service orientation at the business level	Article	2005	IBM Systems Journal	251	13.21

(continued)

Table 4 (continued)

Sr. No	Authors	Title	Article type	Year	Journal	Total citation	Citation density by year
19	Nam K.; Rajagopalan S.; Rao H.R.; Chaudhury A	A Two-Level Investigation of Information Systems	Article	1996	Communications of the ACM	246	8.79
20	Sørensen C.G.; Fountas S.; Nash E.; Pesonen L.; Bochtis D.; Pedersen S.M.; Basso B.; Blackmore S.B	Conceptual model of a future farm management information system	Article	2010	Computers and Electronics in Agriculture	230	16.43

Table 5 Keyword analysis

Serial No	Keyword	Occurrences
1	Management Information Systems	36
2	Information Systems	22
3	Management Information System	21
4	Knowledge Management	17
5	Information Technology	16
6	MIS	13
7	Decision Support System	10
8	Sustainability	9
9	Supply Chain	9
10	Information System	9
11	Management	8
12	Information Management	8
13	Strategy	7
14	Innovation	7
15	Geographic Information System	7
16	China	7
17	India	5
18	Evaluation	5
19	e-Business	5
20	Developing Countries	5

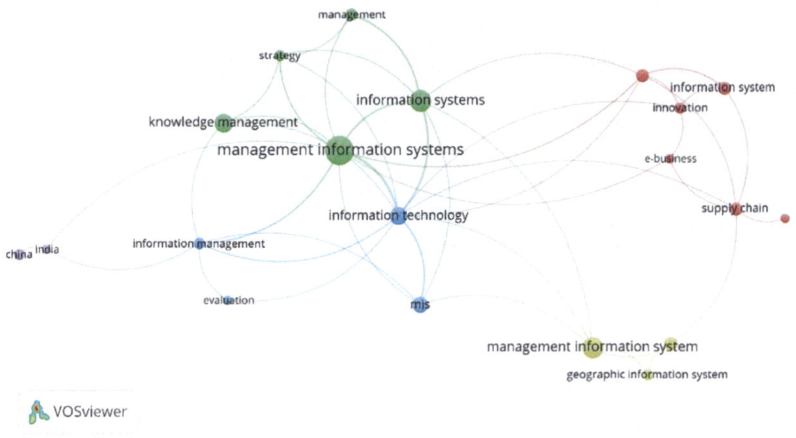

Fig. 3 Keyword analysis

4.2.2 Authors and Institution-Wise Analysis

Table 6 illustrates 20 authors and their affiliation with universities, their total articles, total citations and citation impact. Huirne, R B M is on top with 5 articles. While Dijkhuizen, A.A. Kauffman, R.J., Verstegen, J.A.A.M. are on second place with 4 articles. Fountas, Spyros has the highest number of total citations and citation impact.

5 Discussion

Organizations may have to make prompt decisions in the absence of appropriate evidence. This condition can put strain on decision-making process that are subject to rapid change and increased risk. In this scenario, information has emerged as a significant component and resource in organizational management, particularly in strategic decision-making processes. Holsapple (2008) underlined that understanding the identity creation of any specific field is achievable by evaluating the field's knowledge and investigating its intellectual foundation. Bibliometric studies are crucial for defining a particular topic and determining a researcher's expertise. These studies allow managers to learn about the latest developments within the scientific community as well as other scholars who have established a reputation for themselves (Yu et al. 2022. Managers and researchers can learn about publication trends in specific domains, including debate themes with statistical characteristics (Alfawareh et al. 2021). The findings of bibliometric studies aid in making correct decisions to minimize the occurrence of risk.

The current section answers all the research questions to provide all gathered information from the conducted bibliometrics analysis. RQ1 What are the top productive institutions? Table 3 offers a list of the top 20 most productive institutions that

Table 6 Authors and institution wise analysis

Sr #	Author's name	Affiliation	Total articles	Total citations	Citation impact
1	Huirne, R.B.M	Wageningen University & Research, Netherland	5	97	19.40
2	Dijkhuizen, A.A	Wageningen University & Research, Netherland	4	84	21.00
3	Kauffman, R.J	Singapore Management University, Singapore	4	343	85.75
4	Verstegen, J.A.A.M	Wageningen University & Research, Netherland	4	84	21.00
5	Briggs, Bill	Keck School of Medicine of USC, Los Angeles, United States	3	5	1.67
6	Elliott, Jaques	Requisite Organization International Institute, United States	3	0	0.00
7	Fadum, Ole	Fadum Enterprises, Inc, United States	3	0	0.00
8	Fountas, Spyros	Agriculture University of Athens, Greece	3	347	115.67
9	Gillespie, Greg	Information Technology & Security Audit at Global Payments	3	0	0.00
10	Goedert, Joseph	News Editor, Health Data Management magazine	3	0	0.00
11	Gurbaxani, Vijay	University of California, United States	3	73	24.33
12	Marietti, Charlene	McGraw-Hill-Healthcare Information Group, United States	3	0	0.00
13	Morrissey, John P	University of Plymouth, United Kingdom	3	0	0.00
14	Pedersen, Søren Marcus	KøbenhavnsUniversitet, Copenhagen, Denmark	3	296	98.67
15	Rebelo, Emilia Malcata	Universidade do Porto, Porto, Portugal	3	25	8.33
16	Shaw, Monica	Carabiner Communications, Atlanta, United States	3	5	1.67
17	Smith, H.L	Pacific University, United States	3	11	3.67
18	Waymack, P	Phoenix Services Managed Care Consulting, Ltd. United States	3	0	0.00
19	Zeng, Saixing X	Shanghai Jiao Tong University, Shanghai, China	2	212	106.00
20	Wohlgemuth, Volker	Fachhochschule für Technik und Wirtschaft Berlin, Berlin, Germany	2	112	56.00

also use collaborative analysis. With the amount of total publications, citations, and impact Wageningen University & Research in the Netherlands leads with nine papers. "City University of Hong Kong", "New York University", and the "University of Minnesota Twin Cities" are in second position for articles. The "University of Maryland, College Park", has the most citations of any institution on the list. Furthermore, the "University of Maryland, College Park" has the uppermost amount of citations.

Table 4 illustrates the answer of RQ 2; the top most frequently used journal for publications. Total articles, citations, and citation effect are shown (on the topic "Evaluating Publication Growth in Management Information System"). The journals indicated in this table show that articles published in MIS Quarterly Management Information System were highly cited, with 7970 total citations, and information system research had 2153 total citations, ranking second. Furthermore, Table 4 shows a wide variety of total citations employed by journals for publication. According to Reid and Chen (2007), articles with a higher number of citations are deemed highly referenced. Table 4 lists the top 20 most-cited articles. Author Wasko M.M.; Faraj S. has the most citations (3857) in the journal MIS Quarterly: Management Information Systems. Davenport T.H. is the author with the second highest amount of citations (2368) in Harvard Business Review. Similarly, the remaining cited publications have been described, along with the author's name and journal.

Adding more to the conclusion, RQ 3 indicates about top keywords used by authors. Figure 3 illustrates Co-word analysis also known as keyword analysis. The analysis reveals that authors utilized a total of 2206 keywords. Table 6 and Fig. 3 show the co-occurrence of the top 20 terms. Figure 2, developed by VOS viewer software, depicts various clusters. Cluster 1 (4 red keywords) includes information systems, innovation, e-business, and supply chain. Cluster 2 (5 green keywords): Management, Strategy, Information System, Knowledge Management, and Management Information System. Cluster 3 (4 blue keywords) includes information technology, information management, evaluation, and misinformation. Cluster 4 (2 Yellow keywords) includes management and geographical information systems. India and China form a cluster with two Indigo keywords. Figure 4 depicts a bar graph from most used to least used keywords. Finally, the RQ 4 illustrates the top authors and their affiliated institutions. Table 6 shows 20 writers and their university affiliations, as well as their total number of works, citations, and impact. Huirne, R B M leads with five articles. While Dijkhuizen, A.A. Kauffman, R.J., and Verstegen, J.A.A.M. are in second place with four articles. Fountas, Spyros has the highest number of total citations and citation impact. Hence, this research will help future scholars learn more about bibliometric analysis in this field.

The study's vital outcomes demonstrate the research scenario on MIS, economics, and technology and the findings can support the scholars, practitioners, and policymakers to understand the correlation of these three interlinked themes. Every bibliometric study has some limitations, firstly, the dataset of publications was acquired from the Elsevier's Scopus database by using a specific search strategy. It might be a chance that some important studies may have been overlooked in our navigation process. We chose the research published only in the English language. Future

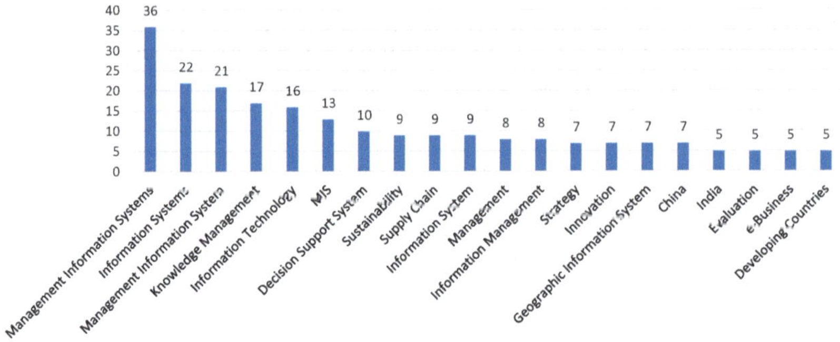

Fig. 4 Bar graph of keywords ranked from most used to least used

studies can include the dataset from the Web of Science and add the other languages to broaden the publication graph.

Following could be future research trends in publication growth. Fields could be narrower in economics, management, and MIS fields of different years, like Sustainable Economics and Management Practices, digital business, economic policies, and advanced discipline.

6 Conclusion

The study illustrated that research progress in MIS, Economics, and Management has observed fluctuation. The findings provide worldwide scenarios on the targeted themes and figure out parameters that have had a significant impact. The utmost number of articles (29%) were published in the first interval (1994–1998) but the articles distributed in the third interval (2004–2008) were found most influential based on citation impact. The United States surpassed the rest of the world in research productivity while Wageningen University & Research, Netherlands emerged as the most productive institution. Among the top 20 most frequently used journals, top-three belonged to the healthcare sector. It indicates the importance of MIS, economics, and management in biomedical setup. About half of the citations (47%) gained by the top-20 highly cited articles and *Management Information System, Information System* and *Knowledge Management* were found the most preferred areas of research. Hence, the findings of the current paper is anticipated to serve as benchmark for the forthcoming studies.

7 Future Research

The findings of this study provide a foundation for future research trajectories in Management Information Systems (MIS), Economics, and Management, with several emerging themes poised to influence these fields. A notable future direction is the integration of sustainable practices into MIS and management strategies, which will become increasingly important as organizations strive for environmental responsibility and operational efficiency. Additionally, the concept of the circular economy is likely to reshape traditional economic models, encouraging research on resource optimization, waste reduction, and sustainable growth. The ongoing digitalization of industries will also continue to transform the landscape, offering new opportunities for research on the intersection of technology, business, and economic policy. These areas are expected to generate significant interest and innovation, serving as critical focus points for scholars and practitioners alike in the coming years.

Implications

This study emphasizes the importance of incorporating sustainable practices within the fields of MIS, Economics, and Management. Organizations can leverage the insights from this research to develop strategies that not only enhance operational efficiency but also promote environmental stewardship. Furthermore, the findings regarding the circular economy advocate for a paradigm shift in how resources are utilized and waste is managed, suggesting that future research should explore innovative models that prioritize sustainability.

Conclusion

In summary, the evolving landscape of MIS, Economics, and Management presents numerous opportunities for future research. By focusing on sustainable practices, the circular economy, and the impact of digitalization, scholars and practitioners can contribute to the advancement of these disciplines while addressing pressing global challenges. The findings of this study serve as a stepping stone for further exploration in these vital areas.

References

Alfawareh FS (2021) A bibliometric analysis of published articles on management information systems (MIS). Information and Knowledge Management 11(4):142–149

Al-Kofahi, MK, Hassan H, Mohamad R, Intan TP, Com M (2020) Information systems success model: a review of literature. Int J Innov, Creat Chang 12(8)

Ates A, Garengo P, Cocca P, Bititci U (2013) The development of SME managerial practice for effective performance management. J Small Bus Enterp Dev 20(1):28–54

Backhouse RE, Medema SG (2009) Retrospectives: on the definition of economics. Journal of Economic Perspectives 23(1):221–233

Bai Y, Li H (2022) Mapping the evolution of e-commerce research through co-word analysis: 2001–2020. Electron Commer Res Appl 55:101190

Butt JM, Tanveer M, Alqahtani MS, Khan MF, Khan ZU (2024) Buying environmentally sustainable products: the role of materialism and product comparison in purchasing behavior. Uncertain Supply Chain Manag 13(1). https://doi.org/10.5267/j.uscm.2024.7.005

Cocosila M, Serenko A, Turel O (2011) Exploring the management information systems discipline: a scientometric study of ICIS. PACIS and ASAC. Scientometrics 87(1):1–16

Culnan MJ, Swanson, EB (1986) Research in management information systems, 1980–1984: points of work and reference. Mis Quarterly 289–302

Donthu N, Kumar S, Mukherjee D, Pandey N, Lim WM (2021) How to conduct a bibliometric analysis: An overview and guidelines. J Bus Res 133:285–296. https://doi.org/10.1016/j.jbusres.2021.04.070

Fahimnia B, Sarkis J, Davarzani H (2015) Green supply chain management: a review and bibliometric analysis. Int J Prod Econ 162:101–114

Gall M, Nguyen KH, Cutter SL (2015) Integrated research on disaster risk: is it really integrated? Int J Disaster Risk Reduct 12:255–267. https://www.sciencedirect.com/science/article/pii/S2212420915000138

Harrison RL, Reilly TM, Creswell JW (2020) Methodological rigor in mixed methods: an application in management studies. J Mixed Methods Res 14(4):473–495

Holsapple CW (2008) The pulse of multiparticipant systems. J Organ Comput Electron Commer 18(4):333–343

Khan KI, Nasir A, Saleem S (2021) Bibliometric analysis of post covid-19 management strategies and policies in hospitality and tourism. Front Psychol 12:769760

Khan SAR, Yu A, Ridwan IL, Irshad AR, Ponce P, Tanveer M (2023) Energy efficiency, carbon neutrality and technological innovation: a strategic move towards green economy. Economic Research Ekonomska Istraživanja 36(2):2140306. https://doi.org/10.1080/1331677X.2022.2140306

Laudon KC, Laudon JP (2004) Management information systems: managing the digital firm. Pearson Education

Li W, Zhao Y (2015) Bibliometric analysis of global environmental assessment research in a 20-year period. Environ Impact Assess Rev 50:158–166

Lin AJ, Hsu CL, Chiang CH (2016a) Bibliometric study of electronic commerce research in information systems & MIS journals. Scientometrics 109:1455–1476

Lin HF, Su JQ, Higgins A (2016b) How dynamic capabilities affect adoption of management innovations. J Bus Res 69(2):862–876

Mahmood H, Irshad, AuR, Tanveer M (2024) Do innovation and renewable energy transition play their role in environmental sustainability in Western Europe? Humlties Soc Sci Commun 11(1):22. https://doi.org/10.1057/s41599-023-02539-4

Metse AP, Wiggers JH, Wye PM, Wolfenden L, Prochaska JJ, Stockings, EA, ... Bowman JA (2016) Smoking and mental illness: a bibliometric analysis of research output over time. Nicotine & Tob Res, ntw249

Mishra L, Kendhe R, Bhalerao J (2015) Review on management information systems (MIS) and its role in decision making. Int J Sci Res Publ 5(10):1–5

Özköse H, Gencer CT (2017) Bibliometric analysis and mapping of management information systems field. Gazi University Journal of Science 30(4):356–371

Özköse H, Ozyurt O, Ayaz A (2023) Management information systems research: a topic modeling based bibliometric analysis. Journal of Computer Information Systems 63(5):1166–1182

Palvia P, Pinjani P, Sibley EH (2007) A profile of information systems research published in Information & Management. Information & Management 44(1):1–11

Peramatzis G, Galanakis M (2022) Herzberg's motivation theory in workplace. Psychology 12(12):971–978

Pindur W, Rogers SE, Suk Kim P (1995) The history of management: a global perspective. J Manag Hist 1(1):59–77

Rafols I, Hopkins MM, Hoekman J, Siepel J, O'Hare A, Perianes-Rodríguez A, Nightingale P (2014) Big Pharma, little science?: A bibliometric perspective on Big Pharma's R&D decline. Technol Forecast Soc Chang 81:22–38

Rojas-Sánchez MA, Palos-Sánchez PR, Folgado-Fernández JA (2023) Systematic literature review and bibliometric analysis on virtual reality and education. Educ Inf Technol 28(1):155–192. https://doi.org/10.1007/s10639-022-11167-5

Secundo G, Ndou V, Del Vecchio P, De Pascale G (2019) Knowledge management in entrepreneurial universities: a structured literature review and avenue for future research agenda. Manag Decis 57(12):3226–3257

Tanveer M (2024) Cracking the code: The influence of personality traits on knowledge management culture and sharing behavior. Uncertain Supply Chain Management 12(4):2547–2558

Tanveer M, Khan SAR, Umar M, Yu Z, Sajid MJ, Haq IU (2022) Waste management and green technology: Future trends in circular economy leading towards environmental sustainability. Environ Sci Pollut Res 29(60):80161–80178. https://doi.org/10.1007/s11356-022-23238-8

Tsai CH, Zdravkovic J, Stirna J (2022) Modeling digital business ecosystems: a systematic literature review. Complex Systems Informatics and Modeling Quarterly 30:1–30

Ugolini D, Bonassi S, Cristaudo A, Leoncini G, Ratto GB, Neri M (2015) Temporal trend, geographic distribution, and publication quality in asbestos research. Environ Sci Pollut Res 22(9):6957–6967. https://doi.org/10.1007/s11356-014-3925-1

Van Nunen K, Li J, Reniers G, Ponnet K (2018) Bibliometric analysis of safety culture research. Saf Sci 108:248–258

Verma S, Gustafsson A (2020) Investigating the emerging COVID-19 research trends in the field of business and management: a bibliometric analysis approach. J Bus Res 118:253–261

Vernadat F, Shah L, Etienne A, Siadat A (2013) VR-PMS: a new approach for performance measurement and management of industrial systems. Int J Prod Res 51(23–24):7420–7438

Yi W, Chan A (2016) Health profile of construction workers in Hong Kong. Int J Environ Res Public Health 13(12):1232

Yu Z, Waqas M, Tabish M, Tanveer M, Haq IU, Khan SAR (2022) Sustainable supply chain management and green technologies: a bibliometric review of literature. Environ Sci Pollut Res 29(39):58454–58470

Sustainability Practices Across Industries and Regions

Circular Economy and Commitment of Asian, South American, and Middle Eastern Higher Education Institutions to Sustainability Agenda

Ilya Bystrov, Mohamed Wahish Hashim, and Sonia Umair

Abstract Higher education serves as a foundation for sustainability and the circular economy. In this way, the commitment of higher education institutions (HEIs) to the sustainability agenda defines the future success of these concepts when university graduates complete their studies, join the workforce, and begin to implement what they have learned in the daily operations of companies and organizations. The current study attempts to characterize such commitment through a comparative analysis of the strategic statements of HEIs belonging to ASEAN (Association of South East Asian Nations), GCC (Gulf Cooperation Council), and MERCOSUR (Southern Common Market). The research aligns institutional missions, visions, goals, and values with the Sustainable Development Goals (SDGs) formulated by the United Nations (UN) through content analysis. The study is based on the sample of 197 HEIs representing the given regional associations. Similar research from 2020–2021 also enables the tracking of change dynamics. The research reveals that in 27%, 45%, and 38% of cases, the strategic statements of ASEAN, GCC, and MERCOSUR HEIs align with at least one SDG. SDGs 3, 13, 14, and 16 are mostly overlooked by the studied institutions. In all studied regions, SDGs 4, 8, and 9 are the primary focus of the HEIs. The overall growth of commitment to sustainability agenda for ASEAN and GCC institutions within 2020–2024 is positive.

I. Bystrov (✉) · M. W. Hashim
University of Buraimi, Al Buraimi, Oman
e-mail: ilya.b@uob.edu.om

M. W. Hashim
e-mail: mohamed.w@uob.edu.om

S. Umair
Dhofar University, Salalah, Oman
e-mail: swaqas@du.edu.om

S. A. R. Khan et al. (eds.), *Circular Economy and Technological Innovation*, Industrial Ecology, https://doi.org/10.1007/978-981-96-5650-9_6

1 Introduction

Circular economy (CE) is a multifaceted concept. If we look at the relevant publications, we will be surprised to discover that dozens, if not hundreds, of authors interpret this term in different ways (Kirchherr et al. 2017). The common ground can also be found in the idea of improved usage of resources, even though it is still widely debated what and how should be improved (Velenturf and Purnell 2021). There is still confusion regarding the meaning of the CE term, even decades after the moment it was introduced (Nobre and Tavares 2021). Recent publications suggest that the focus of CE extends beyond the preservation of materials to include economic growth (Nikolaou et al. 2021), the social dimension (Valencia et al. 2023), and the maximization of material value (Reike et al. 2018). A review of 200 definitions, coded through core principles, aims, and enablers ranging from waste minimization, overall resource efficiency, increased product lifespan, design that enables recyclability, and closed-loop systems to economic and social resilience, constitutes the most comprehensive recent attempt to define the essence of the CE (Kirchherr et al. 2023).

From a different perspective, the United Nations formulated the well-known and widely accepted Sustainable Development Goals (SDGs) to address the same challenges. For instance, SDG 6, SDG 7, and SDG 12 target clean water, clean energy, and responsibility in production and consumption, respectively. Still, it should be mentioned that sustainability itself as a concept has been criticized for being vague and not free from internal contradictions (Hickel 2019; Ward et al. 2016). In a broad sense, the relationship between the concept of sustainability and the circular economy can be characterized as complimentary, with the latter serving as an operationalization (Ghisellini et al. 2016; Murray et al. 2017) or applicational approach to bring sustainability principles closer to reality.

We would like to emphasize that multiple research publications trace a deep connection between sustainability and circular economy, as the next section of this chapter shows. At the same time, worldwide higher education systems not only equip specialists with the necessary skills and knowledge for their future careers but also foster a deep philosophical understanding that underpins both sustainability and circular economy. The greater the commitment of higher education institutions to the sustainability agenda, the more prepared their graduates will be to tackle the new challenges of transforming circular economy concepts into reality.

1.1 Objective

This chapter's objective is to measure commitment to the sustainability agenda of HEIs across the countries of three associations located in Asia, the Middle East, and South America.

1.2 Chapter Learning Outcomes

After reading this chapter, the reader will be able to:

1. Explain the relationship between circular economy and sustainability concepts.
2. Compare the overall commitment to sustainability principles of HEIs belonging to ASEAN, GCC, and MERCOSUR.

The structure of this chapter includes an Introduction, Literature Review, Methodology, Results and Discussion, and Conclusion and Recommendation sections. The introduction section provides the background as well as learning and research objectives. The literature review section contains a brief discussion of the recent studies that focus on sustainability and circular economy concepts and reviews the role of higher education as a prerequisite for their realization. The methodology section describes the approach we used to meet the research objective, while the results and discussion section contains the results of the study and interpretation of the findings. The last section of the study—the conclusion and recommendations—underlines the key findings of the research and basic recommendations to the university-level decision-makers.

2 Literature Review

2.1 Relationship Between Sustainability and Circular Economy Concepts

Sustainability is considered as a foundational concept for the circular economy. Both concepts emphasize the significance of efficiency in resource usage, beginning with waste minimization and reusability and culminating in designs that promote longer product lifespans and closed-loop systems, as well as economic and social development. Below, we briefly characterize these links.

A significant number of publications share a common focus of interest in both concepts towards resource efficiency. The Sustainable Development Goals 6, 11, and 13 encompass the provision of clean water and sanitation, the promotion of sustainability in cities and communities, and the promotion of responsible production and consumption, which aims to optimize the use of natural resources. The concept of circular economy supports this by advocating recycling, repeated usage, and regeneration (Gao et al. 2024; Kumareswaran et al. 2024; Onyeaka et al. 2023).

In a similar way, minimization of waste is at the center of attention for both concepts. While sustainability calls for less generation of waste, the circular economy operationalizes it through repeated use of materials for different purposes or through restoration and reusage (Klemeš et al. 2021; Sundaram et al. 2024; Voudrias 2023; Wani et al. 2023). This approach peaks in methods that enable extending the lifespan of products and design them in such a way that their recyclability at the end of the lifecycle and extended material circularity are ensured (Güngör 2024; Mesa 2023; Pauer et al. 2020).

Both sustainability and circular economy concepts devote significant attention to issues related to renewable energy and the reduction of carbon emissions. SDGs 7 and 13 address the availability of affordable and clean energy and climate action, respectively, in the context of sustainability (Alnaqbi and Alami 2023; Jabeen et al. 2020; Lee et al. 2023). The circular economy concept tackles the issue by lowering emissions linked to raw material extraction, utilizing superior manufacturing techniques, and enhancing waste management through more efficient resource utilization (Jakubelskas and Skvarciany 2023; Kristia and Rabbi 2023; Mutezo and Mulopo 2021).

Biodiversity is the less obvious and direct link between sustainability and circular economy concepts. SDGs 14 and 15, which focus on life below water and life on land, respectively, express sustainability's aim to protect ecosystems and biodiversity (Krauss 2022; Lehmann 2023; Zhang et al. 2023). In turn, the circular economy indirectly contributes to this goal by reducing the need for resource extraction, thereby minimizing negative environmental effects such as habitat destruction and biodiversity loss (Junge et al. 2023; Ruokamo et al. 2023; Stephenson and Damerell 2022).

Economic and social development is the final, yet no less significant, dimension where sustainability and circular economy concepts intersect. Aspiration toward long-term economic, environmental, and social resilience is the core essence of sustainability (e.g., SDG 1, 8, and 9). The circular economy facilitates such resilience through the development and application of approaches that attempt to decouple economic growth and resource consumption (Agarwala 2023; Baldassarre and Calabretta 2024; Lei et al. 2021), prioritize localized production and consumption that benefit the local communities and that are more adaptable to change (Grèzes-Bürcher and Grèzes 2023; Pusz et al. 2024).

2.2 *Higher Education as a Prerequisite for Implementation of Sustainability and Circular Economy Principles*

As we share the understanding that the concept of circular economy represents the instrumentalization of the idea of sustainability, the commitment of higher educational institutions to sustainability plays a crucial role in supporting the implementation of circular economy principles. The same notion is supported by other researchers who either consider the universities as transformational engines in achieving sustainability through SDGs (Cuesta-Claros et al. 2022; Purcell et al. 2019) or criticize them for insufficient efforts in this field (Stein 2024).

Integrating sustainability-related topics, assignments, case studies, field trips, and even entire courses into curricula not only raises learners' awareness of the problems and social impacts of the traditional linear economy but also equips them with the knowledge of potential solutions suggested by sustainability principles and the circular economy approaches. We witness this process unfolding across all continents, impacting nearly every study field, from business, IT, and engineering to sports education and healthcare (Abd-Elwahed and Al-Bahi 2021; Álvarez-Nieto et al. 2022; Angelaki et al. 2024; Bor et al. 2023; Moreno-Luna et al. 2021). Despite the imperfections and ongoing challenges, it's clear that efforts are underway (Arefin et al. 2021; Duarte et al. 2023; Mair and Druckman 2023).

The equally important task of higher education is to assist learners in the elaboration of critical thinking, problem-solving, and innovation skills that they will use further in their careers to answer the challenges for the benefit of companies and organizations that employ them (Fang and O'Toole 2023; Heldal et al. 2024; Killion et al. 2022; Purnomo et al. 2022). If successful, the new graduates will possess skills such as eco-design, green engineering, sustainable supply chain management, and, more broadly, the development of business models that align with the principles of the circular economy.

Education that incorporates learning materials and assessments related to sustainability also influences values and reshapes behaviors in learners (Danaher et al. 2021; Fekih Zguir et al. 2021; Ni et al. 2024; Rajabifard et al. 2021). This implies that learners, upon graduation, will prioritize solutions that align more closely with sustainability in their professional lives and adopt more sustainable practices in their personal lives. These practices may include reducing waste, reusing products and materials, and supporting recycling efforts.

Given everything we've discussed above, it's clear that education plays a crucial role in laying the groundwork for the advancement of sustainability as a principle and the circular economy as a means of implementing it.

3 Methodology

We selected qualitative methods, specifically content analysis, to meet the research goal of the study. We selected 10 higher education institutions from each of the three regions—GCC, ASEAN, and MERCOSUR—for comparative analysis, excluding Laos and Uruguay. The online representation of Laos' higher education institutions is inadequate; either the institution's website is absent, it lacks a section detailing the institution's mission, vision, values, and goals, or it lacks an English version. Consequently, we excluded Laos entirely from our analysis. The search for higher educational institutions in Uruguay allowed us to identify only seven institutions for analysis. Consequently, we chose 197 institutions for our analysis, dividing them as Table 1 shows.

We conducted the analysis in three consecutive stages, in the same way as it was done in our previous research (Bystrov and Panigrahi 2021):

Table 1 Sample summary

Association/Country	Number of selected HEIs
ASEAN, including	**90**
Brunei	10
Cambodia	10
Indonesia	10
Myanmar	10
Malaysia	10
Philippines	10
Singapore	10
Thailand	10
Vietnam	10
GCC, including	**60**
Bahrain	10
Kuwait	10
Oman	10
Qatar	10
Saudi Arabia	10
United Arab Emirates	10
MERCOSUR, including	**47**
Argentina	10
Bolivia	10
Brazil	10
Paraguay	10
Uruguay	7

Stage 1: We studied the mission and vision statements of the selected 197 HEIs for terms that could demonstrate the institution's relationship to the sustainability agenda.

Stage 2: We analyzed secondary strategic documents to map their content to the SDGs. HEIs' values, strategic goals, and objectives were studied, and the most common terms that relate these statements to SDGs were identified.

Stage 3: We compared the obtained results to our observations from the same sample of GCC and ASEAN institutions in 2020–2021. The MERCOSUR universities were not part of the earlier study.

For the purposes of the study, we used the same sample of GCC and ASEAN educational institutions as in earlier research (Magd and Bystrov 2021). This enabled us to trace the dynamics of certain aspects of the studied matter.

4 Results and Discussion

Most of the higher education institutions of the GCC region made their key strategic documents public. We were able to locate vision and mission statements, as well as goals and/or values, on the websites of 59 HEIs out of 60 selected for the GCC region, representing more than 98%. Similar to that, ASEAN HEIs also make these documents publicly available—86 out of 90 selected institutions, or more than 95%. All of the selected institutions had bilingual sites, which significantly eased access to the required documents. Institutions from the MERCOSUR region demonstrated lesser openness. Firstly, most institutional websites were in the local language (Spanish or Portuguese), which seriously limited access to the required documents and statements. Secondly, the proportion of institutions that did not make the key strategic statements available is relatively higher—9 out of 57 selected institutions, or more than 15%.

The first stage of the analysis supposed overall evaluation of HEIs' commitment to sustainability agenda by identification of references to it through usage of terms like "sustainability," "sustainable," "sustainable development," or similar in mission and vision statements. The average for the three regions showed that 49 out of 197 selected institutions (or 24.9%) had such a reference. The highest results were demonstrated by GCC institutions, where the reference to sustainability reached 30% (18 out of 60 institutions in absolute numbers), while ASEAN (21 institutions out of 90) and MERCOSUR (10 institutions out of 47) HEIs were below the average with 23.3% and 21.3%, respectively.

We also compared the level of commitment measured by the frequency of referencing sustainability-related terms in the mission and vision statements with the previous data (collected in the end of 2020) for GCC and ASEAN institutions. Both regions demonstrated a noticeable increase in the number of HEIs, whose key strategic statements are sustainability-aligned. For the ASEAN and GCC regions, the share and absolute number of such institutions were 15% (or 14 out of 90 HEIs) and 11% (or 7 cases of 60), respectively. In this way, over a period of four years, the number of HEIs that at least declared their involvement in the sustainability agenda increased by two times in the GCC region and by 30% in the ASEAN region. This is particularly significant because both the earlier and current study used the same sample of institutions.

It needs to be noticed that in case an institution didn't have such a reference but its website contained a separate section dedicated to sustainability, then we considered such a case as a positive reference. Overall, similar cases amounted to 6 for both the GCC and ASEAN regions, but none for the MERCOSUR region.

On the next stage, we extended our analysis of mission and vision statements by adding a review of institutional goals or objectives, values, and similar second-tier strategic documents. Table 2 presents the results of mapping the content of these statements to 17 SDGs.

The mapping exercise revealed that institutions representing all three studied regions completely ignored certain sustainable development goals, which were

Table 2 Mapping the content of strategic-level statements to SDGs

Sustainable development goal	ASEAN	GCC	MERCOSUR
SDG 1: No Poverty			✔
SDG 2: No Hunger		✔	
SDG 3: Good Health and Well-being			
SDG 4: Quality Education	✔	✔	✔
SDG 5: Gender Equality		✔	
SDG 6: Clean Water and Sanitation	✔	✔	✔
SDG 7: Affordable and Clean Energy	✔	✔	✔
SDG 8: Decent Work and Economic Growth	✔	✔	✔
SDG 9: Industry, Innovation and Infrastructure	✔	✔	✔
SDG 10: Reduced Inequalities	✔	✔	✔
SDG 11: Sustainable Cities and Communities	✔	✔	✔
SDG 12: Responsible Consumption and Production	✔	✔	✔
SDG 13: Climate Action			
SDG 14: Life Below Water			
SDG 15: Life on Land	✔		
SDG 16: Peace, Justice and Strong Institutions			
SDG 17: Partnerships for the Goals		✔	

related to climate, water life, peace and justice. Surprisingly, HEIs in all regions also failed to prioritize the sustainable development goal that pertained to health and well-being. Overall, institutions of the GCC region demonstrated alignment with the highest number of SDGs (11 out of 17), followed by ASEAN and MERCOSUR (both demonstrated alignment with 9 SDGs). Compared to a similar study four years ago, GCC and ASEAN institutions have significantly improved their dedication to the sustainability agenda. Previously, the strategic statements of GCC institutions aligned with only three SDGs, whereas ASEAN institutions aligned with seven SDGs.

Table 3 below provides a brief summary of how all strategic statements were aligned with the SDGs. If an institution had a dedicated sustainability section on its website, we also used its contents for the analysis.

As shown in Table 3, the HEIs' attention was focused on SDG4, SDG8, and SDG9, which targeted accessibility to inclusive education, economic development in general, and activities related to innovation, infrastructure, and industry. In most cases, the number of institutions in all three regions aligned with these SDGs was higher than 10%, with the highest alignment result of 30% with SDG8 in the GCC region and the lowest of 8.5% with the same SDG in the MERCOSUR region. It's important to note that, in addition to the previously mentioned SDGs, GCC institutions also demonstrated a 10% alignment with SDG7, which addresses clean and

Table 3 Alignment of institutional mission/vison statements, goals/objectives and values with SDGs

Sustainable development goal	ASEAN	GCC	MERCOSUR
SDG 1: No Poverty	No alignment	No alignment	1.5% (1 out of 57 institutions)
SDG 2: No Hunger	No alignment	1.5% (1 out of 60 institutions)	No alignment
SDG 3: Good Health and Well-being	No alignment	No alignment	No alignment
SDG 4: Quality Education	20% (18 out of 90 institutions)	15% (9 out of 60 institutions)	12% (7 out of 57 institutions)
SDG 5: Gender Equality	No alignment	3.5% (2 out of 60 institutions)	No alignment
SDG 6: Clean Water and Sanitation	2% (2 out of 90 institutions)	5% (3 out of 60 institutions)	3.5% (2 out of 57 institutions)
SDG 7: Affordable and Clean Energy	2% (2 out of 90 institutions)	10% (6 out of 60 institutions)	5% (3 out of 57 institutions)
SDG 8: Decent Work and Economic Growth	12% (11 out of 90 institutions)	30% (18 out of 60 institutions)	8.5% (5 out of 57 institutions)
SDG 9: Industry, Innovation and Infrastructure	14.5% (13 out of 90 institutions)	28.5% (17 out of 60 institutions)	23% (13 out of 57 institutions)
SDG 10: Reduced Inequalities	2% (2 out of 90 institutions)	3.5% (2 out of 60 institutions)	7% (4 out of 57 institutions)
SDG 11: Sustainable Cities and Communities	6.5% (6 out of 90 institutions)	3.5% (2 out of 60 institutions)	1.5% (1 out of 57 institutions)
SDG 12: Responsible Consumption and Production	1% (1 out of 90 institutions)	1.5% (1 out of 60 institutions)	3.5% (2 out of 57 institutions)
SDG 13: Climate Action	No alignment	No alignment	No alignment
SDG 14: Life Below Water	No alignment	No alignment	No alignment
SDG 15: Life on Land	1% (1 out of 90 institutions)	No alignment	No alignment
SDG 16: Peace, Justice and Strong Institutions	No alignment	No alignment	No alignment
SDG 17: Partnerships for the Goals	No alignment	1.5% (1 out of 60 institutions)	No alignment

affordable energy. Overall, the GCC's institutions demonstrated the highest alignment results, while the MERCOSUR institutions showed the lowest, with ASEAN HEIs demonstrating the medium comparative level of alignment.

Table 4 presents a selection of terms used by HEIs in their strategic statements, which enables us to align these statements with specific SDGs.

As shown in Table 4, the strategic statements have a stronger alignment with most of the SDGs and a relatively weaker alignment with some of them. In this way, the variety of terms that higher education institutions use to indicate alignment with SDG 4 encompasses nearly all topics addressed by this SDG, including inclusivity, access to education for diverse social groups, etc. The choice of terms indicates alignment with SDGs 1, 2, 5, 6, 7, 10, 12, and 15, bringing us directly to the concept of sustainability. As an example of the relatively weaker alignment, we can name SDG 8. In the latter case, the universities prefer to use more general terms related to economic development and employment opportunities. The same applies to SDG 9.

Since our study utilizes the same sample of HEIs, we can compare the alignment results from now to the end of 2020 and the beginning of 2021. Table 5 provides the comparison results.

Overall, in the year-to-year comparison, we observe an increase in the number of HEIs, whose strategic statements can be aligned with SDGs, in both the GCC and ASEAN, from 16 to 27 in the first case and from 21 to 27 in the second case. Despite the equal number of such institutions in 2024, the differences in the size of the regional sample (60 for GCC and 100 for ASEAN) result in the current number representing an astonishing half of all sampled universities (45%), compared to 30% in ASEAN. In both cases, there is a growing commitment to the sustainability agenda, but the GCC is demonstrating a significantly faster pace of growth. In 38% of cases, the strategic statements of MERCOSUR institutions align at least with one SDG, placing them in a middle position.

Our observations are mostly coherent with the research results of other studies. Firstly, a recent study (Menon and Suresh 2022) named institutional commitment as one of key enablers that facilitate education for sustainable development. Similar attempts to evaluate the commitment of HEIs to sustainability principles through content analysis have already been conducted. For example, a relatively recent study that focused on Portuguese universities and their strategic documents with the goal to assess implementation of sustainability principles in the local educational sector (Farinha et al. 2019). An earlier study attempted to conduct a similar evaluation of US universities (Casarejos et al. 2017). Despite the positive evaluation of their sustainability implementation, some aspects, like the amount of waste generated, greenhouse gas emissions, and the efficiency of water use, still need improvement. These observations fit well with our results, which demonstrate the relatively lower alignment of HEIs' strategic documents with SDGs focusing on responsible consumption and production, climate action, and water resources.

In a similar vein, numerous studies confirm our observation that universities prioritize SDGs related to quality education, the availability of decent work, economic growth, innovation, and infrastructure. One such study (Gamage et al. 2022) identifies the economic dimension of sustainable development as the primary area of

Table 4 Terms that were used to align strategic statements with SDGs

Sustainable development goal	ASEAN	GCC	MERCOSUR
SDG 1: No Poverty	No alignment	No alignment	"improving the quality of life"
SDG 2: No Hunger	No alignment	"importance of food sustainability"	No alignment
SDG 3: Good Health and Well-being	No alignment	No alignment	No alignment
SDG 4: Quality Education	"sustainable education ecosystem" "students of all backgrounds and diverse cultures" "university for all people" "…particularly for the socially disadvantaged" "inclusive … and sustainable technological university"	"the University welcomes students … from all ethnic, geographical, cultural and religious backgrounds" "sustainability as part of … teaching"	"to be inclusive university" "Inclusion, diversity and equity"
SDG 5: Gender Equality	No alignment	"to create next generation of female leaders" "we champion inclusivity, diversity and equity"	No alignment
SDG 6: Clean Water and Sanitation	"focus on resource efficiency"	"use of water and energy follows three guidelines—reduce, re-use, recycle"	"resource-saving"
SDG 7: Affordable and Clean Energy	"enhancing its energy usage through an Energy Supply Strategy Framework"	"use of water and energy follows three guidelines—reduce, re-use, recycle"	"responsible use of energy"
SDG 8: Decent Work and Economic Growth	"sustainable economy" "economic and social development"	"supporting sustainable growth of the country" "economic and social development" "economic development"	"economic sustainability"

(continued)

Table 4 (continued)

Sustainable development goal	ASEAN	GCC	MERCOSUR
SDG 9: Industry, Innovation and Infrastructure	"impact innovation"	"innovative research … that yield sustainable impact" "build science and knowledge society" "innovation"	"research and technology"
SDG 10: Reduced Inequalities	" reduce inequality"	"support to learners to avoid any inequalities"	"… improve the quality of life, especially of the most disadvantaged"
SDG 11: Sustainable Cities and Communities	"Improve the quality of life of … communities" "towards sustainable society" "shape … society sustainably" "sustainable and inclusive development of the country" "… sustainable services for … glocal communities" "distinctive character for sustainable societies"	"… meets the needs of society in order to achieve sustainable development."	"to benefit the local community"
SDG 12: Responsible Consumption and Production	"using less, not creating more"	"reduce, re-use, recycle"	"to promote care for the environment"
SDG 13: Climate Action	No alignment	No alignment	No alignment
SDG 14: Life Below Water	No alignment	No alignment	No alignment
SDG 15: Life on Land	"support environmental and forestry-related field"	No alignment	No alignment
SDG 16: Peace, Justice and Strong Institutions	No alignment	No alignment	No alignment

(continued)

Table 4 (continued)

Sustainable development goal	ASEAN	GCC	MERCOSUR
SDG 17: Partnerships for the Goals	No alignment	"collaborates with local and global entities"	No alignment
Alignment with multiple SDGs	"… focuses its efforts on resource efficiency—using less, not creating more" "… encompasses … environmental health"	"sustainable human, social, economic, and environmental development" "preserving and protecting our natural resources" "fair and sustainable world" "Consider the impact … on the environment" "Integrate and balance the economic, social and environmental spheres to meet current and future needs" "To contribute to the environmental, societal and economic sustainable development"	"Sustainability and socio-environmental responsibility" "Environmental responsibility" "Institution committed to the environment, aware of the conservation of natural resources" "to promote care for the environment"

progress. Another study (Mawonde and Togo 2019) concludes that a university can make the greatest contribution in SDG 4, which pertains to education, but it can also contribute in other areas. A recent case study, which focused on a university in Thailand (Nelles et al. 2022), revealed "stagnant" progress towards the realization of SDG 2, a finding that aligns well with our results, indicating minimal alignment with this SDG.

In addition, some studies' conclusions may contradict our own observations or warrant further debate. For example, a recent systematic literature review (Ocaña-Zuñiga et al. 2023) that focuses on the implementation of SDGs in HEIs notes that the majority of related studies originate from Europe, while research generation in developing countries is minimal. Even though this observation is correct, it does not reflect the level of commitment of developing countries' HEIs to sustainability but, rather, can be evidence of financial challenges that authors from such countries have if they attempt to publish in high-reputation indexed journals. Another example is a publication that describes a case of a Philippines-based university (Bustamante and Viloria 2021) that demonstrates a solid commitment in advancing not only SDG 4, 8, and 10, which matches our observations, but SDGs 16 and 17 as well. Our results indicate a lack of alignment between the ASEAN HEIs and the latter two SDGs. The

Table 5 Summary of frequency dynamics of SDG mapping

Country	Number of HEIs with positive mapping to at least 1 SDG, 2021	Number of HEIs with positive mapping to at least 1 SDG, 2024
ASEAN		
Brunei	3	2
Cambodia	1	2
Indonesia	4	4
Myanmar	2	0
Malaysia	1	5
Philippines	4	5
Singapore	0	0
Thailand	2	6
Vietnam	4	3
GCC		
Bahrain	3	6
Kuwait	3	3
Oman	1	5
Qatar	4	4
Saudi Arabia	3	3
United Arab Emirates	2	6
MERCOSUR		
Argentina	Not measured	2
Bolivia	Not measured	2
Brazil	Not measured	7
Paraguay	Not measured	6
Uruguay	Not measured	1

Note: The term "not measured" refers to our previous study (Magd and Bystrov 2021), which only analyzed institutions in the GCC and ASEAN

small size of the country-level samples can explain such a discrepancy. However, we draw our conclusions not for individual countries but for the entire region. At the ASEAN level, we used a sample size of 90, and while some institutions may align with these SDGs, their overall contribution on the regional level remains minimal.

5 Conclusion and Recommendations

In conclusion, we would like to highlight the following observations and findings of this study:

- HEIs in all observed regions primarily focus on SDGs 4, 8, and 9, which address education, economic development, research, and infrastructure.
- The GCC institutions have demonstrated the highest alignment results with the sustainability agenda.
- The overall commitment of GCC and ASEAN HEIs to sustainability agenda is growing.
- GCC institutions have shown the fastest growth, outperforming their ASEAN counterparts within the four-year period.
- HEIs of the MERCOSUS also show good level of commitment to the sustainability agenda, which allows to place them between the other two observed regions.

Having positively evaluated the commitment of HEIs to the sustainability agenda across all three studied regional associations, we still propose the following recommendations:

- Institutions should pay more attention to the transparency and disclosure of strategic-level statements. When an institution's website lacks these statements or is only available in one language, it negatively impacts the institution's reputation.
- The strategic-level statements completely overlook some SDGs, which could be addressed in the next revision cycle.
- Being committed to the sustainability agenda in the key strategic statements is a good starting point. However, the ultimate results are achieved when this commitment defines the efforts on the operational level.

Further studies could focus on delving deeper into a country-specific analysis, incorporating other regional associations into the analysis, or transitioning from the strategic to the operational level and conducting case studies on how operational plans, teaching and learning processes, and programs reflect strategic alignment with the sustainability agenda.

References

Abd-Elwahed MS, Al-Bahi AM (2021) Sustainability awareness in engineering curriculum through a proposed teaching and assessment framework. Int J Technol des Educ 31(3):633–651. https://doi.org/10.1007/s10798-020-09567-0

Agarwala N (2023) Promoting circular economy in the shipping industry. J Int MaritE Saf, Environ Aff, Shipp 7(4):2276984. https://doi.org/10.1080/25725084.2023.2276984

Alnaqbi SA, Alami AH (2023) Sustainability and renewable energy in the UAE: a case study of Sharjah. Energies 16(20):7034. https://doi.org/10.3390/en16207034

Álvarez-Nieto C, Richardson J, Navarro-Perán MÁ, Tutticci N, Huss N, Elf M, Anåker A, Aronsson J, Baid H, López-Medina IM (2022) Nursing students' attitudes towards climate change and sustainability: a cross-sectional multisite study. Nurse Educ Today 108:105185. https://doi.org/10.1016/j.nedt.2021.105185

Angelaki ME, Bersimis F, Karvounidis T, Douligeris C (2024) Towards more sustainable higher education institutions: implementing the sustainable development goals and embedding sustainability into the information and computer technology curricula. Educ Inf Technol 29(4):5079–5113. https://doi.org/10.1007/s10639-023-12025-8

Arefin MdA, Nabi MdN, Sadeque S, Gudimetla P (2021) Incorporating sustainability in engineering curriculum: a study of the Australian universities. Int J Sustain High Educ 22(3):576–598. https://doi.org/10.1108/IJSHE-07-2020-0271

Baldassarre B, Calabretta G (2024) Why circular business models fail and what to do about it: a preliminary framework and lessons learned from a case in the European Union (Eu). Circular Economy and Sustainability 4(1):123–148. https://doi.org/10.1007/s43615-023-00279-w

Bor Ö, Tosun B, Eler S, Eler N (2023) Sport academics' awareness and knowledge of sustainability in higher education in Türkiye. Sustainability 15(8):6527. https://doi.org/10.3390/su15086527

Bustamante CB, Viloria R (2021) Extent of sustainability practices in San Beda University: the basis for action plan formulation. Bedan Res J 6(1):171–195. https://doi.org/10.58870/berj.v6i1.26

Bystrov I, Panigrahi S (2021) Commitment of higher education institutions to sustainability agenda: evidences from GCC countries. J Contemp Issues Bus GovMent 27(02). https://doi.org/10.47750/cibg.2021.27.02.438

Casarejos F, Gustavson LM, Frota MN (2017) Higher education institutions in the United States: commitment and coherency to sustainability vis-à-vis dimensions of the institutional environment. J Clean Prod 159:74–84. https://doi.org/10.1016/j.jclepro.2017.05.034

Cuesta-Claros A, Malekpour S, Raven R, Kestin T (2022) Understanding the roles of universities for sustainable development transformations: a framing analysis of university models. Sustain Dev 30(4):525–538. https://doi.org/10.1002/sd.2247

Danaher M, Wu J, Hewson M (2021) Sustainability: a regional australian experience of educating secondary geography teachers. Educ Sci 11(3):126. https://doi.org/10.3390/educsci11030126

Duarte M, Caeiro SS, Farinha CS, Moreira A, Santos-Reis M, Rigueiro C, Simão J (2023) Integration of sustainability in the curricula of public higher education institutions in Portugal: do strategic plans and self-report align? Int J Sustain High Educ 24(9):299–317. https://doi.org/10.1108/IJSHE-01-2023-0001

Fang J, O'Toole J (2023) Embedding sustainable development goals (SDGs) in an undergraduate business capstone subject using an experiential learning approach: a qualitative analysis. Int J Manag Educ 21(1):100749. https://doi.org/10.1016/j.ijme.2022.100749

Farinha C, Caeiro S, Azeiteiro U (2019) Sustainability strategies in Portuguese higher education institutions: commitments and practices from internal insights. Sustainability 11(11):3227. https://doi.org/10.3390/su11113227

Fekih Zguir M, Dubis S, Koç M (2021) Embedding Education for Sustainable Development (ESD) and SDGs values in curriculum: a comparative review on Qatar, Singapore and New Zealand. J Clean Prod 319:128534. https://doi.org/10.1016/j.jclepro.2021.128534

Gamage KAA, Munguia N, Velazquez L (2022) Happy sustainability: a future quest for more sustainable universities. Soc Sci 11(1):24. https://doi.org/10.3390/socsci11010024

Gao JQ, Li D, Qiao GH, Jia QR, Li SR, Gao HL (2024) Circular economy strategies in supply chains, enhancing resource efficiency and sustainable development goals. Environ Sci Pollut Res 31(6):8751–8767. https://doi.org/10.1007/s11356-023-31551-z

Ghisellini P, Cialani C, Ulgiati S (2016) A review on circular economy: the expected transition to a balanced interplay of environmental and economic systems. J Clean Prod 114:11–32. https://doi.org/10.1016/j.jclepro.2015.09.007

Grèzes-Bürcher S, Grèzes V (2023) Designing a sustainable, circular culinary system. Circ Econ Sustain. https://doi.org/10.1007/s43615-023-00295-w

Güngör B (2024) Circular economy business model framework considering product sustainability. In: Bragança L, Cvetkovska M, Askar R, Ungureanu V (eds) Creating a roadmap towards circularity in the built environment, Springer Nature Switzerland. pp 305–315. https://doi.org/10.1007/978-3-031-45980-1_25

Heldal R, Nguyen N-T, Moreira A, Lago P, Duboc L, Betz S, Coroamă VC, Penzenstadler B, Porras J, Capilla R, Brooks I, Oyedeji S, Venters CC (2024) Sustainability competencies and skills in software engineering: an industry perspective. J Syst Softw 211:111978. https://doi.org/10.1016/j.jss.2024.111978

Hickel J (2019) The contradiction of the sustainable development goals: growth versus ecology on a finite planet. Sustain Dev 27(5):873–884. https://doi.org/10.1002/sd.1947
Jabeen S, Malik S, Khan S, Khan N, Qureshi MI, Saad MSM (2020) A comparative systematic literature review and bibliometric analysis on sustainability of renewable energy sources. Int J Energy Econ Policy 11(1):270–280. https://doi.org/10.32479/ijeep.10759
Jakubelskas U, Skvarciany V (2023) Circular economy practices as a tool for sustainable development in the context of renewable energy: what are the opportunities for the EU? Oecon Copernic 14(3):833–859. https://doi.org/10.24136/oc.2023.025
Junge L, Adam N, Morris JC, Guenther E (2023) Building a biodiversity-positive circular economy: the potential of recycling using industrial symbiosis. Circ Econ Sustain 3(4):2037–2060. https://doi.org/10.1007/s43615-023-00259-0
Killion AK, Ostrow Michel J, Hawes JK (2022) Toward identifying sustainability leadership competencies: insights from mapping a graduate sustainability education curriculum. Sustainability 14(10):5811. https://doi.org/10.3390/su14105811
Kirchherr J, Reike D, Hekkert M (2017) Conceptualizing the circular economy: an analysis of 114 definitions. Resour Conserv Recycl 127:221–232. https://doi.org/10.1016/j.resconrec.2017.09.005
Kirchherr J, Yang N-HN, Schulze-Spüntrup F, Heerink MJ, Hartley K (2023) Conceptualizing the circular economy (revisited): an analysis of 221 definitions. Resour Conserv Recycl 194:107001. https://doi.org/10.1016/j.resconrec.2023.107001
Klemeš JJ, Fan YV, Jiang P (2021) Plastics: friends or foes? the circularity and plastic waste footprint. Energy Sources, Part A: Recover, Util, Environ Eff 43(13):1549–1565. https://doi.org/10.1080/15567036.2020.1801906
Krauss JE (2022) Unpacking SDG 15, its targets and indicators: tracing ideas of conservation. Globalizations 19(8):1179–1194. https://doi.org/10.1080/14747731.2022.2035480
Kristia K, Rabbi MF (2023) Exploring the synergy of renewable energy in the circular economy framework: a bibliometric study. Sustainability 15(17):13165. https://doi.org/10.3390/su151713165
Kumareswaran K, Ranasinghe S, Jayasinghe GY, Dassanayake KB (2024) Systematic review on liquid organic waste (LOW) characteristics, processing technologies, and their potential applications: towards circular economy and resource efficiency. J Clean Prod 447:141286. https://doi.org/10.1016/j.jclepro.2024.141286
Lee C-C, Zhang J, Hou S (2023) The impact of regional renewable energy development on environmental sustainability in China. Resour Policy 80:103245. https://doi.org/10.1016/j.resourpol.2022.103245
Lehmann I (2023) Inspiration from the Kunming-Montreal global biodiversity framework for SDG 15. Int Environ AgreemS: Polit, Law Econ 23(2):207–214. https://doi.org/10.1007/s10784-023-09608-8
Lei H, Li L, Yang W, Bian Y, Li C-Q (2021) An analytical review on application of life cycle assessment in circular economy for built environment. J Build Eng 44:103374. https://doi.org/10.1016/j.jobe.2021.103374
Magd H, Bystrov I (2021) Commitment of higher educational institutions to sustainability agenda: comparative study of GCC and ASEAN. Glob Bus Manag Res: Int J 13(3):Article 3
Mair S, Druckman A (2023) Assessing the suitability of sustainability frameworks for embedding sustainability in higher education curricula: pragmatism versus transformation. Int J Sustain High Educ 24(9):318–334. https://doi.org/10.1108/IJSHE-08-2020-0315
Mawonde A, Togo M (2019) Implementation of SDGs at the University of South Africa. Int J Sustain High Educ 20(5):932–950. https://doi.org/10.1108/IJSHE-04-2019-0156
Menon S, Suresh M (2022) Modelling the enablers of sustainability in higher education institutions. J Model Manag 17(2):405–439. https://doi.org/10.1108/JM2-07-2019-0169
Mesa JA (2023) Developing a material selection index based on circularity: a multiple lifecycle approach. Resour Conserv Recycl 199:107240. https://doi.org/10.1016/j.resconrec.2023.107240

Moreno-Luna L, Robina-Ramírez R, Sánchez-Oro M, Serrano JC (2021) Drivers for sustainability awareness development in tourism curricula: the case of Spanish universities. Land 10(9):939. https://doi.org/10.3390/land10090939

Murray A, Skene K, Haynes K (2017) The circular economy: an interdisciplinary exploration of the concept and application in a global context. J Bus Ethics 140(3):369–380. https://doi.org/10.1007/s10551-015-2693-2

Mutezo G, Mulopo J (2021) A review of Africa's transition from fossil fuels to renewable energy using circular economy principles. Renew Sustain Energy Rev 137:110609. https://doi.org/10.1016/j.rser.2020.110609

Nelles W, Visetnoi S, Middleton C, Orn-in T (2022) Higher education institutions, SDG2 and agri-food sustainability: lessons from Chulalongkorn university and Thailand. Environ Dev Sustain 24(9):10975–10996. https://doi.org/10.1007/s10668-021-01892-1

Ni L, Fayaz Ahmad S, Alsanie G, Lan N, Irshad M, Bin Saeed RH, Bani Ahmad A, Khan Y (2024) Investigating the role of green curriculum in shaping pro-environmental behaviors and environmental values orientation for sustainability. Int J Sustain High Educ. https://doi.org/10.1108/IJSHE-05-2023-0207

Nikolaou IE, Jones N, Stefanakis A (2021) Circular economy and sustainability: the past, the present and the future directions. Circ Econ Sustain 1(1):1–20. https://doi.org/10.1007/s43615-021-00030-3

Nobre GC, Tavares E (2021) The quest for a circular economy final definition: a scientific perspective. J Clean Prod 314:127973. https://doi.org/10.1016/j.jclepro.2021.127973

Ocaña-Zuñiga CL, Tineo M, Fernandez-Zarate FH, Quiñones-Huatangari L, Huaccha-Castillo AE, Morales-Rojas E, Miguel-Miguel HW (2023) Implementing the sustainable development goals in university higher education: a systematic review. Int J Sustain Dev Plan 18(6):1769–1776. https://doi.org/10.18280/ijsdp.180612

Onyeaka H, Tamasiga P, Nwauzoma UM, Miri T, Juliet UC, Nwaiwu O, Akinsemolu AA (2023) Using artificial intelligence to tackle food waste and enhance the circular economy: maximising resource efficiency and minimising environmental impact: a review. Sustainability 15(13):10482. https://doi.org/10.3390/su151310482

Pauer E, Tacker M, Gabriel V, Krauter V (2020) Sustainability of flexible multilayer packaging: environmental impacts and recyclability of packaging for bacon in block. Cleaner Environmental Systems 1:100001. https://doi.org/10.1016/j.cesys.2020.100001

Purcell WM, Henriksen H, Spengler JD (2019) Universities as the engine of transformational sustainability toward delivering the sustainable development goals: "living labs" for sustainability. Int J Sustain High Educ 20(8):1343–1357. https://doi.org/10.1108/IJSHE-02-2019-0103

Purnomo AR, Yulianto B, Mahdiannur MA, Subekti H (2022) Embedding sustainable development goals to support curriculum merdeka using projects in biotechnology. Int J Learn, Teach Educ Res 22(1):406–433. https://doi.org/10.26803/ijlter.22.1.23

Pusz M, Jonas AEG, Deutz P (2024) Knitting circular ties: empowering networks for the social enterprise-led local development of an integrative circular economy. Circ Econ Sustain 4(1):201–232. https://doi.org/10.1007/s43615-023-00271-4

Rajabifard A, Kahalimoghadam M, Lumantarna E, Herath N, Hui FKP, Assarkhaniki Z (2021) Applying SDGs as a systematic approach for incorporating sustainability in higher education. Int J Sustain High Educ 22(6):1266–1284. https://doi.org/10.1108/IJSHE-10-2020-0418

Reike D, Vermeulen WJV, Witjes S (2018) The circular economy: new or refurbished as CE 3.0?—exploring controversies in the conceptualization of the circular economy through a focus on history and resource value retention options. Resour Conserv Recycl 135:246–264. https://doi.org/10.1016/j.resconrec.2017.08.027

Ruokamo E, Savolainen H, Seppälä J, Sironen S, Räisänen M, Auvinen A-P (2023) Exploring the potential of circular economy to mitigate pressures on biodiversity. Glob Environ Chang 78:102625. https://doi.org/10.1016/j.gloenvcha.2022.102625

Stein S (2024) Universities confronting climate change: beyond sustainable development and solutionism. High Educ 87(1):165–183. https://doi.org/10.1007/s10734-023-00999-w

Stephenson PJ, Damerell A (2022) Bioeconomy and circular economy approaches need to enhance the focus on biodiversity to achieve sustainability. Sustainability 14(17):10643. https://doi.org/10.3390/su141710643

Sundaram T, Govindarajan RK, Vinayagam S, Krishnan V, Nagarajan S, Gnanasekaran GR, Baek K-H, Rajamani Sekar SK (2024) Advancements in biosurfactant production using agro-industrial waste for industrial and environmental applications. Front Microbiol 15:1357302. https://doi.org/10.3389/fmicb.2024.1357302

Valencia M, Bocken N, Loaiza C, De Jaeger S (2023) The social contribution of the circular economy. J Clean Prod 408:137082. https://doi.org/10.1016/j.jclepro.2023.137082

Velenturf APM, Purnell P (2021) Principles for a sustainable circular economy. Sustain Prod Consum 27:1437–1457. https://doi.org/10.1016/j.spc.2021.02.018

Voudrias EA (2023) Management of COVID-19 healthcare waste based on the circular economy hierarchy: a critical review. Waste Manag & Res: J Sustain Circ Econ 0734242X231198424. https://doi.org/10.1177/0734242X231198424

Wani NR, Rather RA, Farooq A, Padder SA, Baba TR, Sharma S, Mubarak NM, Khan AH, Singh P, Ara S (2023) New insights in food security and environmental sustainability through waste food management. Environ Sci Pollut Res 31(12):17835–17857. https://doi.org/10.1007/s11356-023-26462-y

Ward JD, Sutton PC, Werner AD, Costanza R, Mohr SH, Simmons CT (2016) Is decoupling GDP growth from environmental impact possible? PLoS ONE 11(10):e0164733. https://doi.org/10.1371/journal.pone.0164733

Zhang Y, Li Y, Liu J (2023) Global decadal assessment of life below water and on land. iScience 26(4):106420. https://doi.org/10.1016/j.isci.2023.106420

The Complex Nexus of Military Spending, Economic Growth, Energy Consumption and Environmental Sustainability: Insights from India and China

Muhammad Sibt e Ali, Nitu Maurya, and Laeeq Razzak Janjua

Abstract The balance between economic prosperity and environmental sustainability has become critical for emerging economies like China and India. As the majority of world community confronts the simultaneous problems of resource depletion and climate change. Contributing to the rapid economic growth in both countries is rapid industrialization, urbanization, militarization, and increasing energy consumption. However, this growth is similarly encumbered with a considerable ecological cost, especially in terms of unsustainable use of resources and enhanced greenhouse gas emissions. This chapter attempts to investigate the impact of some key macroeconomic variables such as economic growth, energy consumption, FD, military spending, oil consumption, and TO on environmental degradation in China and India on environmental sustainability. This study investigates the long-term and short-term relationship between these variables and environmental outcomes by using an ARDL model, for the period 1983 to 2023. The comparative analysis underlines differences in how the coal-based economy of China and India's growing momentum for renewable energy got highlighted regarding influencing the relationship of drivers at the macroeconomic level with CO_2 emissions. The outcome of this research aim to provide insights that can guide policy development, ensuring that economic and environmental objectives are better aligned to achieve sustainable development goals in both countries.

Keywords CO_2 emissions · Macroeconomic variables · Environmental sustainability · Economic growth · Energy consumption · FD · Military spending · TO · ARDL model · Sustainable development

M. Sibt e Ali
Business School Zhengzhou University, Henan, China

N. Maurya
IILM University, Greater Noida, Uttar Pradesh, India

L. R. Janjua (✉)
WSB University, Dąbrowa Górnicza, Poland
e-mail: laeeq.janjua@wsb.edu.pl

S. A. R. Khan et al. (eds.), *Circular Economy and Technological Innovation*, Industrial Ecology, https://doi.org/10.1007/978-981-96-5650-9_7

Abbreviations

TO	Trade openness
FD	Financial development
FDI	Foreign direct investment
ME	Military expenditure
APEC	Asia Pacific Economic Cooperation
CO_2	Carbon dioxide
EN	Energy Consumption
FO	financial openness
RE	Random Effect
FE	Fixed effect
PMG	Pool mean group
FMOLS	Fully modified Ordinary least square
GHG	Green house gases
S-SEA	South and Southeast Asian
FF	fossil fuel

1 Introduction

The World Conference on Environment and Development (WCED) (1987) defined sustainable development as "development that satisfies present needs without undermining the ability of future generations to fulfill their own needs." Ekins and Medhurst (2006) argued that the 'development' component of sustainable development signifies fulfilling human needs and enhancing quality of life, while the 'sustainability' component denotes the capacity to preserve this in the future. The long-term objective of sustainable development is to synchronize investments, strategies, and goals that relate to society and the environment. Burford et al. (2013) described sustainable development as a multidimensional phenomenon, promoting social and environmental protection within the framework of cultural, religious, and institutional values. The three pillars of sustainable development are economic viability, social equity, and environmental stewardship, and according to Teodorescu (2012), each must be given equal consideration to enhance sustainability.

Environmental sustainability is a critical and essential pillar of sustainable development, as sustainability cannot be achieved without environmental protection and safety (Tan and Kwek 2016). Greenhouse gas emissions, especially CO_2, pose a significant threat to environmental sustainability. Carbon emissions account for over 60% of the greenhouse effect globally (Repo et al. 2011), and the world is facing both climate change and resource depletion crises, which complicate the balance between economic growth and environmental preservation (Zhang et al. 2022). On the other hand these challenges are particularly prominent in fast-growing countries like China and India, which are experiencing rapid economic growth spurred by industrialization, urbanization, and increased energy consumption. However, such developments come with considerable environmental costs, especially due to rising CO_2 emissions and unsustainable resource use (Wang and Azam 2024). China and India, as the world's largest energy consumers and CO_2 emitters (Ahmed et al. 2021), face unique challenges in balancing economic growth with environmental responsibility. While both countries experience substantial industrial growth and trade openness, their economic structures, energy dependencies, and policy priorities differ (Pata and Caglar 2021; Wenlong et al. 2023). China's reliance on coal and large-scale industrialization (Wen 2021) contrasts with India's growing investment in renewable energy (Behuria 2020) and its diversified economic sectors. Both countries, however, face international pressure to reduce their environmental impact, especially within the context of global climate agreements like the Paris Agreement.

In addition to economic and energy considerations, military strength in India and China is prominent in Asia (Laksmana and Chong 2023), with both countries holding significant military assets (see Fig. 1). The high number of military assets necessitates substantial oil consumption, further impacting the environment (Khan et al. 2023). Wang and Zhang (2023) explored renewable energy and economic growth's roles in environmental sustainability within emerging economies. They found a strong correlation between renewable energy policies and environmental improvements, emphasizing the need for adaptive policy changes in rapidly industrializing countries like China and India. Lee and Ho (2022) conducted a comparative analysis of China and India, focusing on how distinct energy policies, especially China's coal dependency and India's shift to renewables, impact their environmental challenges differently.

Military expenditure bears high environmental costs, especially in developing countries like India and China. Shafique and Shaikh (2023) conducted an across-country analysis, which highlighted that the higher the military expenditure, the

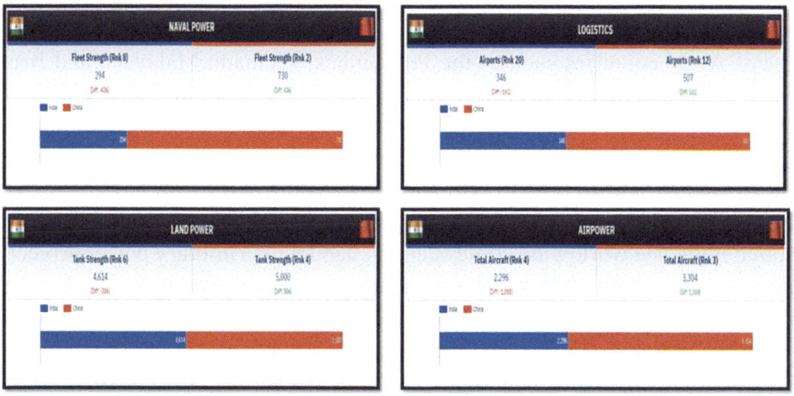

Fig. 1 Miliatry and logistics comparision between India and China. *Source* Global fire power [access on 15–09-2024]

higher is the level of environmental degradation due to resource-intensive operation of military functions. In another related work, Chang and Sun (2023) using data from China and India, & endorse that military investment heightens environmental stresses, thus showing that both countries face challenges in meeting their defense needs to their environmental priorities. Other determinants of environmental quality included trade openness and FDI. Likeiwse, Zafar and Hussain (2022) indicated that economic openness without regulatory frameworks can lead to deterioration in environmental quality. Li and Zhou (2024) extended this view further by focusing on the BRICS countries including China and India and found that TO and FDI can facilitate sustainable growth provided adequate environmental regulations are used within the country.

Furthermore on the other hand, the impact of renewable energy on carbon emissions has become an essential area of study. Kumar and Singh (2023) assessed India's renewable energy policies and found that they have had a positive effect on carbon reduction, underlining India's commitment to sustainability. Lin and Liu (2022) analyzed renewable energy adoption in China and India, highlighting that while renewable energy reduces emissions, the scale and speed of adoption significantly affect environmental outcomes.

India and China are among the most populous nations and have been growing their economies at very fast rates. Coupled with their economic growth, both countries have continuously invested high resources in the development and maintenance of their military capabilities over the years (Wang and Zhang 2023). Geopolitical issues, regional rivalry, border issues, historical tensions, and the desire to gain global power status are some of the various factors that determine why India and China incur high military spending (Lee and Ho 2022). China is becoming an economic and military power, and its military spending mirrors its aspirations on the arena of international relations (Chang and Sun 2023). Modernization in the sphere of military affairs is dictated by ambitions: to ensure interests and gains by all means and to control disputed territories, establishing oneself as a regional power in the Asia–Pacific (Shafique and Shaikh 2023). The main reason for increasing military spending in China is its claims to the South China Sea. China has a territorial dispute with most Southeast Asian countries such as the Philippines, Vietnam, Malaysia, and Brunei over several islands and maritime rights in the region (Li and Zhou 2024). The South China Sea is a resource-rich area that comprises one of the most important sea lanes in the world; this draws a motivational reason why China would invest in a modern capable military, especially the navy (Wang and Zhang 2023). As such, the Belt and Road Initiative (BRI) of infrastructure investments in extending China's economic influence worldwide comes hand in hand with a military power projection requirement in securing its overseas interests (Kumar and Singh 2023). The more internationalized the economy becomes, the more military expenditure is required to secure the sea lanes, trade routes, and investments abroad (Chang and Sun 2023).

India's military spending also reflects its regional security imperatives and aspiration to become a major global player (Zafar and Hussain 2022). Its borders with China and Pakistan, both neighbors, are disputed; the threats emanating from these two neighbors have been a driver of its defense spending (Lee and Ho 2022). India and China have a long-standing dispute over borders, most notably in the Ladakh region, and clashes between the two militaries have taken place. The Sino-Indian War of 1962 had long-term effects on Indian defense policy, and recent years have shown further escalation of tensions along the border, as seen in the Galwan Valley clash in 2020 (Shafique and Shaikh 2023). Intrinsic to China's military modernization is the pressure it places on India to keep increasing its capabilities to defend its territorial integrity (Wang and Zhang 2023). One of the main causes for high military expenditure by both India and China is their disputed border, extending over 3,500 km. Despite several negotiations, these differences are yet to be resolved, and the Line of Actual Control (LAC) remains a flashpoint (Chang and Sun 2023).

Indeed, there was a serious escalation in the form of a clash that occurred in Galwan Valley in 2020, with fatalities on both sides. Since then, the border has been volatile; military infrastructure includes roads and airbases built up by both countries (Kumar and Singh 2023). Another critical factor behind China's rising military expenditure is its rapid military modernization, shifting from a reliance on ground-based forces to a technologically advanced force capable of power projection beyond its borders (Li and Zhou 2024). India has also prioritized modernization to keep pace with its regional rivals and ensure the armed forces are prepared for future challenges (Wang and Zhang 2023). Accordingly, geopolitical concerns, regional competition, border disputes, military modernization, and domestic political considerations play their role in having the two armies maintain such high expenditures. (Lee and Ho 2022). Military strength is an inseparable ingredient in safeguarding territorial integrity, and effectively exercising influence in international relations. For this reason, both countries have continuously maintained high military expenditure. A trend indicative of regional stability risks and further escalation in case of conflict. (Shafique and Shaikh 2023).

This study focuses on understanding the interplay between key macroeconomic variables such as economic growth, energy consumption, FD, military spending, oil consumption, TO and their environmental impacts in China and India. These variables have been selected because they are some of the key drivers of economic growth and may affect, either directly or indirectly, the level of environmental degradation in a country. For instance, increased energy use, industrial output, and ownership could generate more carbon gas. On the other hand, an increased level of FD may exacerbate or mitigate the environmental harm depending on the nature of investments. The ARDL approach is conducted in order to study the long-run and short-run influences of crucial macroeconomic determinants like energy consumption, economic growth, TO, FD, and military spending on environmental degradation in China and India, using time series data for 1983–2023.

Lastly, the findings will offer insights into how economic and environmental policies can be better aligned to achieve sustainable development goals in both countries thus India and China.

2 Literature Review

The association between macroeconomic variables and environmental degradation, particularly in relation to CO_2, has been explored extensively in literature. This review synthesizes key findings from multiple studies, highlighting the influence of variables such as FD, ME, TO, EN, and economic growth on environmental outcomes (see appendix 1 for abberiviations). The research spans various geographic regions, from Asia to the Middle East, and employs different econometric models to capture the dynamic relationships between these variables.

A. **Financial development and environmental sustainability**

The mixed effects of the financial development on environmental outcomes remain a central focus of recent studies. Usman and Hammar (2021) indicate that FD enhances environmental quality by funding sustainable technologies in APEC countries. Conversely, on the other hand Liu and Song (2020) show that FD exacerbates CO_2 emissions in China, especially in regions with high industrial activities., Wu and Zhang (2022) endorse in their study concerning BRICS countries, showed that FD contributes to reducing CO_2 when investments are oriented toward clean energy technologies; it, therefore, shows that the structure and focus of financial development are really critical in determining environmental outcomes. Further, Jamil et al. (2021a) identified that in G-20 countries, FD combined with renewable energy investments has positive implications in terms of CO_2 reduction. In contrast, Mohammed Saud et al. (2019) established that in Venezuela, FD has the complete opposite effect in that it reduced environmental degradation due to the use of more sustainable energy sources. Koengkan (2018) also found that in MERCOSUR countries, FD-driven economic expansion has both short—and long-term effects on increasing CO_2 emissions due to industrial growth, which was confirmed by Qin et al. (2023) in a study of Latin American countries.

B. **Military Expenditure (ME) and Environmental sustainability**

Military expenditure (ME) has significant environmental implications, as the energy-intensive nature of military activities contributes to CO_2 emissions. Solarin et al. (2017) analyzed ME in Ghana and found that it increases CO_2 emissions by shifting resources toward energy-heavy sectors. More recently, Erdogan et al. (2022a) examined the Mediterranean region, revealing that increased defense spending correlates with environmental degradation, especially in economically stronger nations with higher ME budgets. Shafique and Shaikh (2023) expanded on this through a global study, indicating that high military spending correlates with ecological footprints, especially in countries balancing defense and sustainability objectives. Similarly, Chang and Sun (2023) found that in China and India, military investments exert additional environmental pressures as these countries expand defense budgets to meet regional security demands. This aligns with Al-Mulali and Sab's (2012) "treadmill of destruction" concept, where heightened military spending drives energy demand and complicates environmental policy implementation. Military expenditure is critical factor influencing environmental degradation. Solarin et al. (2017) investigated the pollution haven hypothesis (PHH) in Ghana, showing that military spending can exacerbate CO_2 emissions by diverting resources toward energy-intensive sectors, such as defense and manufacturing. This is supported by the findings of Erdogan et al. (2022a), who analyzed military expenditure in Mediterranean countries and found that higher defense budgets are associated with increased environmental degradation, particularly in developed nations. In a more specific context, Ahmed et al. (2020) examined Pakistan and revealed that military spending, alongside economic growth, contributes significantly to the country's ecological footprint. This study echoed earlier research by Al-Mulali and Sab (2012), who demonstrated that in 19 selected countries, military expenditures exacerbate CO_2 emissions, pointing to a "treadmill of destruction" in countries with high defense spending.

C. **Trade Openness (TO), Globalization, and Environmental sustainability**

Trade openness (TO) affects environmental quality in diverse ways, influenced by a country's income level and regulatory standards. The Pollution Haven Hypothesis suggests that low-income countries, which often lack stringent environmental regulations, attract industries that increase CO_2 emissions (Ayadi 2020). In a recent study on One Belt One Road (OBOR) countries, Saud et al. (2020) showed that economic activities tied to trade openness raise environmental costs due to industrial expansion, though high-income countries can mitigate emissions with advanced technologies (Akadiri et al. 2019). Supporting this, Zafar and Hussain (2022) highlighted the importance of regulatory frameworks in managing environmental impacts related to trade and FDI. Liobikienė and Butkus (2018) examined NAFTA countries and found that TO initially worsens environmental quality but eventually improves it as income levels and regulatory capacities increase. More recently, Li and Zhou (2024) focused on BRICS nations, including India and China, finding that TO and FDI support sustainable growth only when supported by robust environmental policies. The impact of TO and globalization on environmental quality has been a focal point in the literature. Saud et al. (2020) examined the role of globalization in the One Belt One Road (OBOR) initiative countries, revealing that TO, combined with FD, has significant implications for CO_2 emissions. Their findings suggest that while trade can facilitate economic growth, it also leads to greater environmental degradation due to increased industrial activities. This conclusion is reinforced by Akadiri et al. (2019), who examined the interplay between energy consumption, TO, and carbon emissions across multiple countries. Their work emphasizes that without stringent environmental regulations, trade liberalization can lead to higher CO_2 emissions—a finding consistent with the pollution haven hypothesis explored by Ayadi (2020) in West African economies. TO is considered an important determinant affecting environmental and carbon emissions. TO affects the environment in three ways: technology effect, scale effect, and composition effect (Shahzad et al. 2017). In the technology effect, technology improves when trade activities increase and carbon emissions start decreasing. In scale effect, if free trade activities enhance, then trade output and trade volume also increases, and as a result, it starts to affect the environment deleteriously. In the composition effect, low-income countries prefer to invest in those industries; making the environment more polluted (Bakhsh et al. 2017b).

On the other hand, (Ayadi 2020) explained the pollution haven hypothesis and factor endowment hypothesis to clarify the relationships between TO and Co_2 emissions. In the pollution haven hypothesis, developing countries with a low level of income are interested in producing pollutant goods which become the cause of the increase in Co_2 emissions. Furthermore, due to the absence of environmental safety policies, developing countries turn into a haven for multinational companies that are taking advantage by planting their factories into these low-level income countries, making the environment harmful. According to the factor, the endowment hypothesis develops that countries that prefer to produce clean goods without affecting nature can benefit from free trade compared to developing countries. Furthermore, Rodrik (2018) said that free trade was formulated after World War II, and gradually the concept turned into a theory. However, theory started to use in practice, and in the 1980s, it became easy to access communication and transportation means at a low cost. Likewise, Murshed (2020) claimed that due to the increase in TO activities, fuel utilization also increased in transportation and energy production.

Liobikienė and Butkus (2018) studied the impact of the North American Free Trade Agreement on the climate. The comparative advantage analysis was preceded by the panel data of Canada, the United States of America, and Mexico during the years 1980–1991. The result showed that climate conditions became unfavorable as trade and economic activities happened, but after the increase in income per capita, the environmental pollution decreased. On the other hand, Dasgupta and De Cian (2018) investigated the impact of TO on the environment. Scale, composition, and technological effects were analyzed by taking panel data of high-level countries from 1971–1996 and low-level countries from 1980–1996. The results indicated that trade liberalization impacts the environment at both high level and low-level countries. Some countries' TO significantly affected climate change, while others showed a more negligible effect on atmosphere alteration.

D. **Energy Consumption (EN) and environmental Susustaibility**

Non-renewable energy consumption, especially fossil fuels like oil and coal, directly correlates with increased CO_2 emissions. Zafar et al. (2021) examined top remittance-receiving countries, highlighting that fossil fuel consumption is a major driver of environmental degradation. Behera and Dash (2017) observed similar patterns in the South and Southeast Asia (S-SEA) regions. Meanwhile, renewable energy adoption may offset emissions, but reliance on fossil fuels often reduces the potential impact of renewables (Menon 2019a). Kumar and Singh (2023) studied India's renewable energy policies, noting that the shift towards renewable sources positively affects carbon reduction, which aligns with the national sustainability goals. Lin and Liu (2022) examined China and India, revealing that while renewable energy deployment helps reduce emissions, the varying scale and pace of implementation influence environmental outcomes across regions. Energy consumption, particularly from non-renewable sources, remains a central driver of CO_2 emissions. Zafar et al. (2021) conducted an extensive study on top remittance-receiving countries and found that EN, especially oil and coal, directly correlates with increased CO_2 emissions. This relationship has been echoed by several studies, including Behera and Dash (2017), who analyzed the S-SEA region and demonstrated that economic growth, driven by FF consumption, intensifies environmental degradation. Similarly, Menon (2019b) found that in India, TO and EN have aggravated CO_2 emissions, underlining the environmental cost of rapid industrialization.

E. **Economic Growth and Environmental sustainability**

The EKC hypothesis posits that economic growth initially leads to environmental degradation but later results in lower pollution levels once income thresholds are met. Özokcu and Özdemir (2017) confirmed this in Turkey, where economic growth beyond a specific income level was linked to reduced CO_2 emissions. In contrast, Bakhsh et al. (2017a) found that in Pakistan, economic growth continually worsens environmental quality, challenging the EKC. More broadly, Bildirici and Gökmenoğlu (2017) showed a long-run positive relationship between growth and CO_2 emissions in South Africa. Addressing regional contrasts, a 2022 study by Rahman and Lin (2022) on Asian countries emphasized that EKC's applicability varies, with countries like China and India experiencing continued emissions growth despite economic expansion. The Energy Kuznets Curve (EKC) hypothesis, which posits that economic growth initially worsens environmental quality but eventually leads to improvements, has been tested in multiple studies. For instance, Özokcu and Özdemir (2017) confirmed the EKC hypothesis in Turkey, showing that beyond a certain income threshold, economic prosperity leads to reduced CO_2 emissions. However, the applicability of the EKC hypothesis varies across countries and regions, as demonstrated by Bakhsh et al. (2017a) in Pakistan, where economic prosperity continues to exacerbate environmental degradation without the anticipated decline in emissions.

Studies underscore that FD, ME, TO, EN, and economic growth exhibit complex relationships with environmental degradation, often shaped by regional factors and economic structure. Financial development and military expenditure show dual effects; they can benefit environmental quality if aligned with sustainability goals but can also drive CO_2 emissions when unchecked. Recent research, including Wu and Zhang (2022), recommends tailored policy approaches, with specific emphasis on promoting renewable energy in fossil fuel-dependent regions. In addition, countries with high ME should explore balancing defense needs with environmental goals to mitigate ecological impacts. There remains a critical need for standardized models and consistent cross-regional studies to clarify these relationships further, especially in emerging economies with varying regulatory frameworks.

3 Research Framework and Objective of Study

The existing literature provides a comprehensive understanding of the dynamic relationships between FD, military spending, TO, energy consumption, and environmental degradation across different regions. On one hand, there is great potential for FD and technological innovation to reduce environmental damage; on the other hand, high levels of military expenditure and non-renewable energy consumption pose a challenge. Indeed, the variance in findings across regions shows how complex these relationships are and also calls for policy approaches which need to be specific for each country to achieve its economic objectives in tandem with environmental ones. There exists a variation from one region to another concerning the extent to which these macroeconomic variables determine the ecological degradation. For example, Rahman et al. (2020) demonstrated that in Bangladesh, factors such as foreign direct investment (FDI) and electricity consumption have a substantial impact on CO_2 emissions, a trend similar to the findings in Ghana (Kwakwa 2022) and Pakistan (Malik et al. 2020). These studies underscore the need for region-specific policies to manage the trade-offs between economic growth and environmental sustainability. Given below are the objectives of the study aligned with rsearch framework (see Fig. 2).

I. To analyze the impact of key macroeconomic variables—such as economic growth, energy consumption, FD, military spending, oil consumption, and TO—on environmental degradation, specifically focusing on CO_2 emissions.
II. To examine both long-run and short-run relationships between CO_2 emissions and the aforementioned macroeconomic variables, identifying how these factors influence environmental outcomes over different time horizons.
III. To conduct a comparative analysis of these relationships in the context of China and India, investigating how variations in their economic structures, energy use patterns, and policy approaches affect environmental sustainability.

Based on the research objective and framework give Eq. 1 will be empirically analysed,

$$CO_{2t} = \beta_0 + \alpha_1 EN_t + \alpha_2 Y_t + \alpha_3 FD_t + \alpha_4 MS_t + \alpha_5 TO_t + \alpha_6 COC_t + £_t \quad (1)$$

In Eq. 1, CO_2 refer to Carbon Dioxide Emission, EN refer to Energy Consumption, Y refer to Economic Growth, FD refer to financial development, ME refer to Military

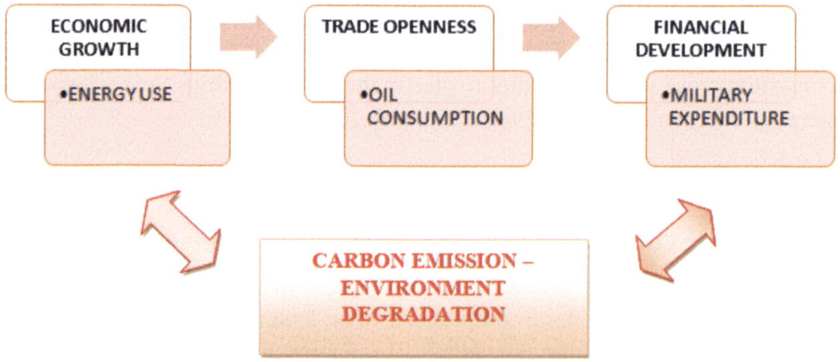

Fig. 2 Research framework *Source* Author's own

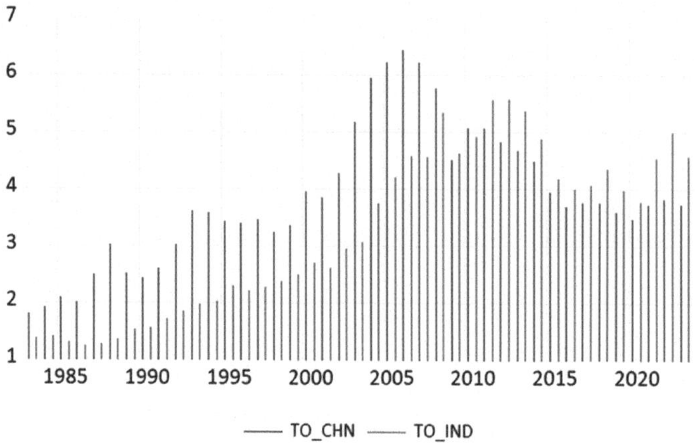

Fig. 3 Trade openness

Spendings, TO refer to Trade openness and COC refer to Oil Consumption. Similarly £ is Error term and t represent time series data set. The variables utilized in this model vary based on the units of measurement. Normalizing and transforming the data of the variables into a consistent measuring system is, therefore, essential for resolving this issue. For this reason, the natural log has been used to circumvent any issues with the time series data of any of the model's variables.

$$\begin{aligned} \mathrm{LnCO}_{2\mathrm{t}} = \beta_0 + \alpha_1 \mathrm{LnEC}_\mathrm{t} + \alpha_2 \mathrm{LnY}_\mathrm{t} + \alpha_3 \mathrm{LnFD}_\mathrm{t} + \alpha_4 \mathrm{LnMS}_\mathrm{t} \\ + \alpha_5 \mathrm{LnTO}_\mathrm{t} + \alpha_6 \mathrm{LnCOC}_\mathrm{t} + £_\mathrm{t} \end{aligned} \tag{2}$$

Here, 'LnEN_t is the log form of energy consumption, LnY_t is the log form of economic growth (Y), LnFD_t is the log form of FD (FD), LnME_t is the log form of Military spending, LnTO_t is the log form of TO, LnCO_2 is the log form of carbon dioxide emission ($CO_{2)}$ and LnOC_t is the log form of Oil consumption"; while t represents that data is time series, beta (β) and alpha (α) show the parameters which require to estimate and £ denotes error term. Furthermore, see Figs. 1, 2, 3, 4, 5, 6,7, 8, and Fig. 9 which indicate the trends of used variable in the research.

3.1 *Descriptive Statistics and Correlation*

It is used to describe the features of the data of the population or sample. Mean, median, and mode are included in central tendency measures while standard deviation are used to measure the variability of data. Descriptive statistics of China and India are given in the Tables 1a and 1b.

Furthermore, Tables 2a and 2b represent collelation analysis of all the used variable in the research, connection among the endogenous and exogenous variables

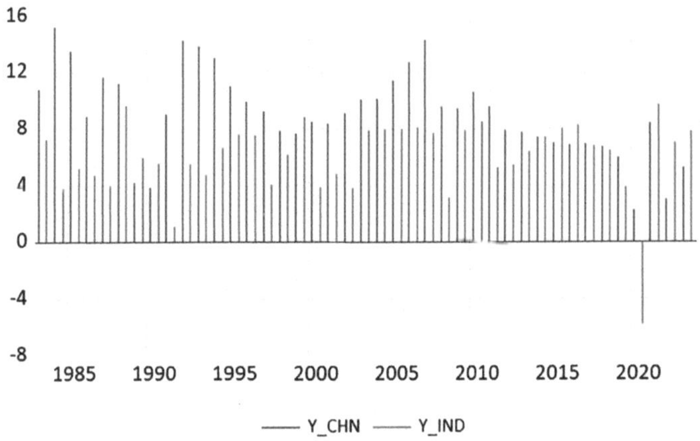

Fig. 4 Economic growth

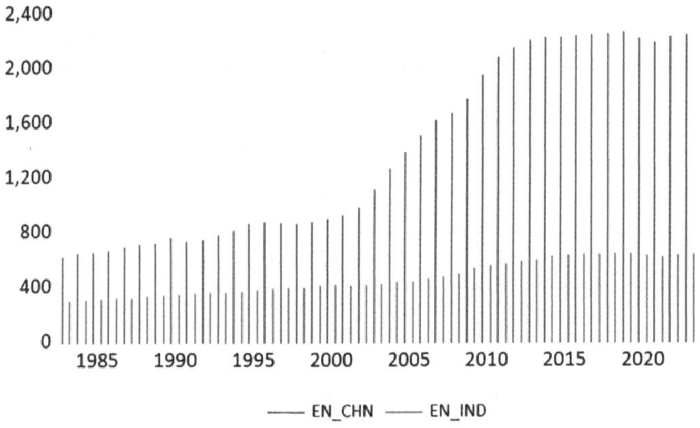

Fig. 5 Energy consumption

does not suggest the presence of multicollineraity as all the correlation coefficient is less then 0.80.

3.2 Empirical Analysis

3.2.1 Unit Root

In time series analysis, it is essential to determine whether the data is stationary at the level. If the data is not stationary at the level, it indicates the presence of a unit root in the data. Furthermore, to assess whether the data is stationary at the

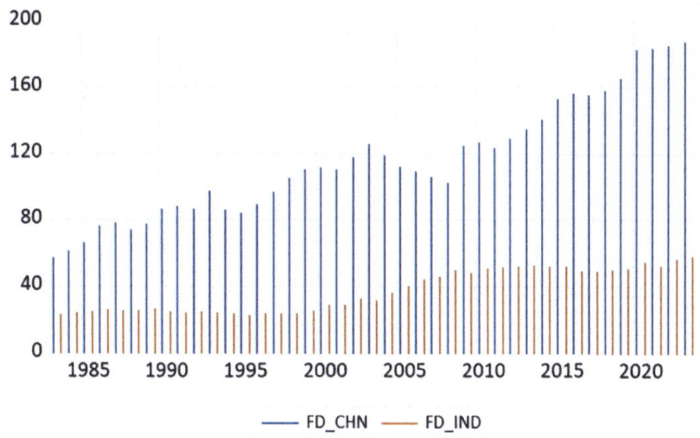

Fig. 6 Financial development

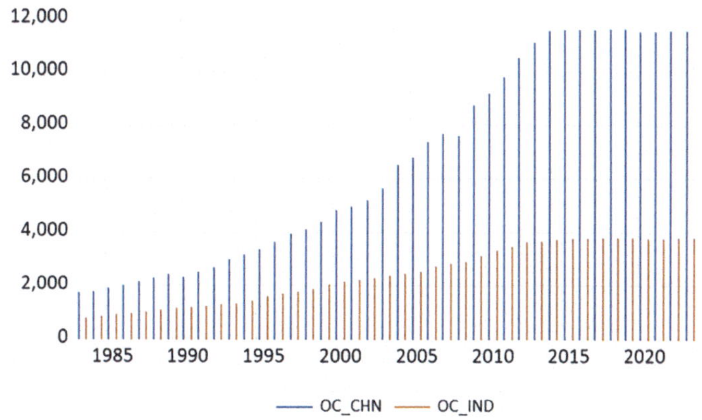

Fig. 7 Oil consumption

level, the Augmented Dickey-Fuller and Phillips-Perron tests are used to ascertain the stationary level among the variables (see Eq. 3); nonetheless, time series data demonstrates non-stationary characteristics. This analysis will lead us toward the next level of our analysis."

$$\Delta y_t = \gamma y_{t-1} + \sum_{i=1}^{p} \beta_i \Delta y_{t-i} + u_t \tag{3}$$

In both test, if the probability values of variables are greater than 0.05 then it indicates that unit root is present in data and further allow us to determine the order of integration of variables, see Tables 3a and 3b.

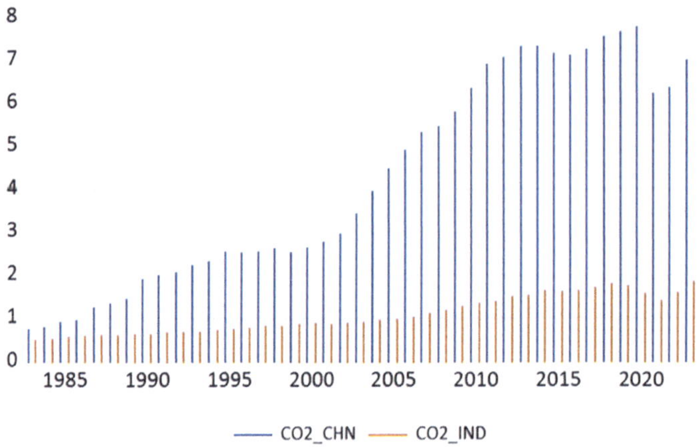

Fig. 8 Carbon emission

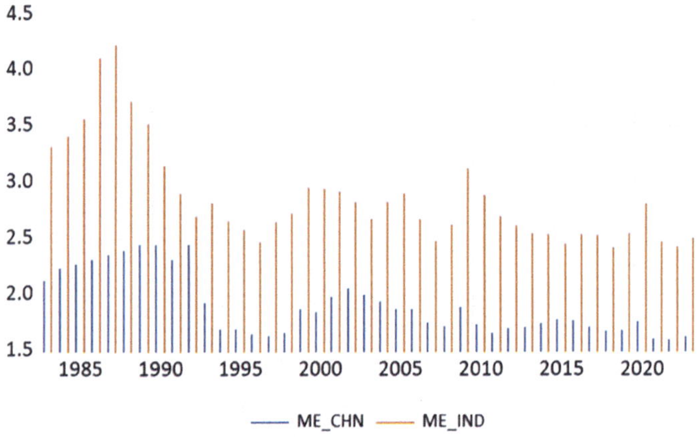

Fig. 9 Miliarty expenditure

Table 1a. Summary statistics China

China					
Variable	Mean	Median	Std Dev	Maximum	Minimum
$lnCO_2$_CN	1.496	1.294	0.437	2.122	0.900
lnEN_CN	7.027	6.802	0.491	7.211	6.393
lnFD_CN	4.623	4.670	0.320	5.211	3.982
lnY_CN	2.283	2.326	0.323	2.784	1.208
lnME_CN	1.122	1.047	0.161	1.538	0.966
lnOC_CN	8.448	8.479	0.697	9.360	7.415
lnTO_CN	3.566	3.607	0.387	4.181	2.596

Table 1b. Summary statistics India

India					
Variable	Mean	Median	Std Dev	Maximum	Minimum
$lnCO_2$_IND	0.672	0.6365	0.417	1.091	0.371
lnEN_IND	6.074	6.033	0.270	6.498	5.660
lnFD_IND	3.520	3.378	0.339	4.029	3.069
lnY_IND	1.819	1.971	0.702	2.363	-2.110
lnME_IND	1.359	1.340	0.106	1.654	1.232
lnOC_IND	7.544	7.662	0.571	8.239	6.467
lnTO_IND	3.324	3.295	0.491	4.039	2.581

Table 2a. Correlation analysis—China

Variable	$lnCO_2$_CN	lnEN_CN	lnFD_CN	lnY_CN	lnMS_CN	lnCOC_CN	lnTO_CN
$lnCO_2$_CN	1						
lnEN_CN	0.798	1					
lnFD_CN	0.789	0.792	1				
lnY_CN	−0.238	−0.268	−0.327	1			
lnME_CN	−0.725	−0.725	−0.787	0.041	1		
lnOC_CN	0.795	0.797	0.7458	−0.258	−0.778	1	
lnTO_CN	0.724	0.713	0.743	0.162	−0.769	0.781	1

Table 2b. Correlation analysis—India

Variable	$lnCO_2$_IND	lnEN_IND	lnFD_IND	lnY_IND	lnMS_IND	lnCOC_IND	lnTO_IND
$lnCO_2$_IND	1						
lnEN_IND	0.778	1					
lnFD_IND	0.735	0.738	1				
lnY_IND	−0.122	0.118	−0.110	1			
lnME_IND	−0.660	−0.682	−0.522	−0.083	1		
lnOC_IND	0.7585	0.778	0.803	−0.051	−0.719	1	
lnTO_IND	0.789	0.693	0.798	0.020	−0.743	0.7458	1

Table 3a. Unit root analysis—China

Variable	Augmented Dickey-Fuller		Phillips-Perron	
	Trend and Intercept		Trend and Intercept	
	At level	At 1st Different	At level	At 1st Different
$lnCO_2$_CN	−0.22 (0.9842)	−8.478(0.006)***	−0.797(0.785)	−4.192(0.010)***
lnEN_CN	−0.541(0.976)	−8.269(0.007)***	−1.255(0.915)	−8.163(0.000)***
lnFD_CN	−2.348(0.403)	−4.217(0.010)***	−1.678(0.695)	−4.217(0.010)***
lnY_CN	−6.923(0.001)***	−8.076(0.000)***	−8.382(0.004)***	−17.794(0.000)***
lnME_CN	−2.157(0.300)	−5.323(0.005)***	−2.974(0.347)	−5.263(0.007)***
lnOC_CN	−2.367(0.300)	−4.314(0.005)***	−2.476(0.349)	−5.223(0.007)***
lnTO_CN	−2.447(0.400)	−3.854(0.007)***	−1.256(0.699)	−4.583(0.008)***

CN—refer to china
*** indicat level of significance at 5%

Table 3b. Unit root analysis—India

Variable	Augmented Dickey-Fuller		Phillips-Perron	
	Trend and Intercept		Trend and Intercept	
	At level	At 1st Different	At level	At 1st Different
$lnCO_2$_IND	−0.693 (0.9842)	−7.238(0.000)***	−0.896(0.914)	−4.192(0.010)***
lnEN_IND	−0.475(0.976)	−6.129(0.000)***	−1.147(0.936)	−8.473(0.000)***
lnFD_IND	−3.471(0.403)	−3.367(0.020)***	−1.778(0.647)	−4.697(0.010)***
lnY_IND	−4.473(0.001)***	−8.253(0.000)***	−8.296(0.026)***	−9.994(0.000)***
lnME_IND	−1.637(0.300)	−5.698(0.008)***	−2.412(0.698)	−5.269(0.007)***
lnOC_IND	−3.127(0.300)	−5.366(0.004)***	−2.473(0.338)	−5.478(0.007)***
lnTO_IND	−3.567(0.560)	−2.794(0.023)**	−3.636(0.749)	−5.113(0.002)***

IND—refer to India
*** indicat level of significance at 5%

3.2.2 ARDL (Auto Regressive Distributed Lag)

To estimate Eq. 1, we used the ARDL method proposed by Pesaran et al. (2001) due to the fact the all variable are stationry at I(0) and I(1). To analyze the long-run relationship, the following ARDL model is estimated, represented by Eq. 4"

$$\Delta CO_{2t}\gamma_0 + \sum_{k=1}^{m}\gamma_{1k}\Delta CO_{2t-k} + \sum_{k=1}^{m}\gamma_{2k}\Delta EN_{t-k} + \sum_{k=1}^{m}\gamma_{3k}\Delta Y_{t-k} + \sum_{k=1}^{m}\gamma_{4k}\Delta FD_{t-k}$$
$$+ \sum_{k=1}^{m}\gamma_{5k}\Delta MS_{t-k} + \sum_{k=1}^{m}\gamma_{6k}\Delta TO_{t-k} + \sum_{k=1}^{m}\gamma_{7k}\Delta COC_{t-k} + \Psi_1 CO_{2t-1} + \Psi_2 EN_{t-1}$$
$$+\Psi_3 Y_{t-1} + \Psi_4 FD_{t-1} + \Psi_5 MS_{t-1} + \Psi_6 TO_{t-1} + \Psi_7 COC_{t-1} + \mu_t \quad (4)$$

The ARDL approach has several benefits. First, selecting the right lags is the key to ARDL's ability to resolve endogeneity-related problems (Pesaran et al. 1999). In addition, by minimizing potential autocorrelation issues, the ARDL estimate provides both long-run and short-run components. Engle and Granger (1987) also provide an equation for cointegration analysis; however, unlike ARDL estimation, their estimate fails to address endogeneity and serial correlation problems. To check long term association among the variable, we perform Wald-test which hypothesize Ho: $\beta 1 = \beta 2 = \beta 3 = \beta 4$ indicating no cointegration, against Ha: $\beta 1 \neq \beta 2 \neq \beta 3 \neq \beta 4$. Furthermore, we also compare F-statistics value with the lower and upper bound critical value at 1%, 2.5%,5%, and 10% by Pesaran et al. al. (2001), if F statistics value is greater than the upper bound, we will reject Ho of no cointegration relations and vice versa.

Table 4a. presents the estimated bound value for China, F-statistics, which is 6.334 greater than the upper bound and lower bound, thus which indicate the existence of long-term association among the variables.

Table 4b. presents the estimated bound value for India, F-statistics, which is 5.033 greater than the upper bound and lower bound, thus which indicate the existence of long-term association among the variables.

Table 4a. Bound test estimation-China

Bound test (china) (1,3,1,1,2,0,3)			
Test Statistics	*Significance*	*I(0)*	*I(1)*
F-Statistics = 6.334, $K = 6$	10%	1.99	2.94
	5%	2.27	3.28
	2.5%	2.55	3.61
	1%	2.88	3.99

Table 4b. Bound test estimation—India

Bound test (India) (1,3,0,1,3,3,3)			
Test Statistics	*Significance*	*I(0)*	*I(1)*
F-Statistics = 5.033, $K = 6$	10%	1.99	2.94
	5%	2.27	3.28
	2.5%	2.55	3.61
	1%	2.88	3.99

Table 5a. Long-run estimations—China dependent variable—CO_2

Variable	Coefficient	t-statistics	Probability
lnEN_CN	0.776	9.376	0.000***
lnFD_CN	−0.100	−1.397	0.174
lnY_CN	0.114	2.362	0.026**
lnME_CN	0,319	2.910	0.007***
lnCOC_CN	0.177	1.855	0.075*
lnTO_CN	0.001	0.049	0.978
Constant_CN	−5.617	16.071	0.000***

Table 5b. Long-run estimations—India-dependent variable—CO_2

Variable	Coefficient	t-statistics	Probability
lnEN_IND	1.035	10.705	0.000***
lnFD_IND	0.106	1.865	0.079*
lnY_IND	0.003	−0.291	0.774
lnME_IND	−0.117	−1.662	0.114
lnOC_IND	0.117	2.262	0.037**
lnTO_IND	−0.094	−1.715	0.094
Constant_IND	−3.227	7.261	0.000***

There is long term association exists among the variable. Therefore the next level of our model estimation is analyzed short and long-run dynamics. Tables 5a and 5b, shows the long-run, whereas Tables 6a and 6b shows short-run estimations of ARDL.

3.2.3 Results and Discssion

The study offers insights into empirical linkage between military spending, oil consumption and carbon emission. Tables 5a and 5b, shows the long run association between the endogenous and exogenous variables. Results shows that, 1 unit increase in energy consumption causes 0.776% of carbon emission in China. Similar positive association also appeared in India. However, in case of India, energy consumption causes 1.33% more carbon emission then China; thus more harmfull for the envionrment. Similar findings are also suggested by previous authors such as Janjua (2021), Rahman et al. (2017) and Ridzuan (2019). Furthermore, in short run the there is also positive association eciting for both countries see Table 8. In case of economic growth, for China economic growth appeard to be harmfull for envionrment thus causing more carbon emission both in long-run and short-run. 1% increase in economic growth causes 0.11% in long-run and 0.023% in short-run carbon emission at 5% level of signaificance. On the other hand, economic growth also causes carbon emission for Indian but only in short-run. 1 unit increases in economic growth causes 0.013% of carbon emission see Table 6b. The positive association between

Table 6a. Short-run estimations—China (dependent variable: CO_2)

Variable	Coefficient	t-statistics	Probability
ΔlnEN_CN	0.414	5.935	0.000***
ΔlnEN_CN(−1)	0.352	4.698	0.002***
ΔlnFD_CN	0.019	0.485	0.635
ΔlnFD_CN(−1)	−0.022	−0.536	0.586
ΔlnY_CN	0.023	2.618	0.016**
ΔlnY_CN(−1)	−0.055	−3.369	0.000***
ΔlnMS_CN	0.097	1.719	0.1000*
ΔlnMS_CN(−1)	−0.089	−1.236	0.082*
ΔlnCOC_CN	0.229	0.056	0.006***
ΔlnCOC_CN(−1)	0.176	2.897	0.008***
ΔlnTO_CN	0.934	8.506	0.569
ΔlnTO_CN(−1)	−0.286	−6.369	0.223
ECT(−1)_CN	*−0.934*	*−8.506*	*0.000****

*Note**** Indicate level of significance at 1%, ** Indicate level of significance at 5%,* Indicate level of significance at 10%

Table 6b. Short-run estimations—India (dependent variable: CO_2)

Variable	Coefficient	t-statistics	Probability
ΔlnEN_IND	1.217	6.530	0.000***
ΔlnEN_IND(−1)	−0.233	−1.205	0.244
ΔlnFD_IND	0.239	0.185	0.056*
ΔlnFD_IND(−1)	0.022	0.256	0.695
ΔlnY_IND	0.013	4.436	0.004***
ΔlnY_IND(−1)	0.256	3.695	0.006***
ΔlnMS_IND	0.010	0.216	0.831
ΔlnMS_IND(−1)	0.057	1.006	0.328
ΔlnCOC_IND	0.618	5.718	0.000***
ΔlnCOC_IND(1)	0.028	2.567	0.020**
ΔlnTO_IND	0.013	0.027	0.635
ΔlnTO_IND(−1)	0.115	3.385	0.003***
ECT(−1)_IND	*−0.984*	*−7.366*	*0.000****

*Note**** Indicate level of significance at 1%, ** Indicate level of significance at 5%,* Indicate level of significance at 10%

economic growth and carbon emission are also affirmed by previous studies such as, Sharma et al. (2019), Zafar et al. (2021), Jamil et al. (2021b), Rahaman et al. (2022) and Batool et al. (2022). Military spending appeared to be harmful for envionrment in case of China both in long-run and short-run. 1 unit increases in military spending causes 0.139% in long-run and 0.097% in short-run of carbon emission at 1% and

10% level of significane respectively. Which indicate the spending done by Chinese government as military expenditure damaging the envionrment by cause more carbon emission. These findings also supported by previous studies such as Erdogan et al. (2022b). Likewise, energy consumption, oil consumption also significantly causes carbon emission in the China and the India in long-run and short-run. For China, 1 unit increases in oil consumption causes 0.177% in long-run and 0.229% in short-run of carbon emission at 10% and 1% level of significane respectively. On the other hand,, 1 unit increases in oil consumption causes 0.117% in long-run and 0.618% in short-run of carbon emission at 5% and 1% level of significane respectively for the India. The findings suggest that, in both countries oil consumption appeard to be harmfull for envionrment which might be due to high number of transportation vechiles on the roads; thus they are consume more fossil fuels in shap of oil. The positive association between oil consumption and carbon emission also mentioned by previous empirical stydies such as He et al. (2005) and Khan et al. (2019). FD also appeared to be major cause of air pollution however only in case of the India. According to Tables 7 and 8, 1 unit increase in FD via domestic credit to private sector causes 0.106% in long-run and 0.239% in short-run of carbon emission at 10% level of significance, which indicate that the credit by financial institution are not using in environmental friendly sector thus causing more airpollution. Similar findings also mentioned by (Saud et al. 2020; Usman and Hammar 2021; Liu and Song 2020).

Moreover, ECM (−1) is also negative and significant; thus, the system has 93.4% for the China and 98.4% for the India, speed of adjustment toward the equilibrium as mention by (Ridzuan et al. 2018).

After estimating ARDL bound test, Long & short-Run dynamics, major diagnostic tests are performed see Table 7. The diagnostic tests include the Jarque–Bera Normality test, the Lagrange multiplier test of residual serial correlation, and the Breusch-Pagan-Godfry test of heteroscedasticity. All three of these tests have a significance level of $P > 0.05$. Please see Table 6, which details all of the diagnostic tests performed on the estimated model after estimating. Additionally, our model meets the stability criterion for both the CUSUM and CUSUMSQ graphs, which are used to visually analyze the model's stability. The CUSUM and CUSUMSQ lines are all within the 5% significance threshold, as you can see Fig. 10 for the China and for the India Fig. 11 respectively.

Table 7 Post estimation diagnostic test

TEST	CHINA	INDIA
Serial Correlation	5.236 (0.785)	3.582 (0.167)
Normality	2.784 (0.855)	1.455 (0.685)
Heteroscedasticity	11.022 (0.414)	13.014 (0.114)
CUSUM	Stable	Stable
CUSUMSQ	Stable	Stable

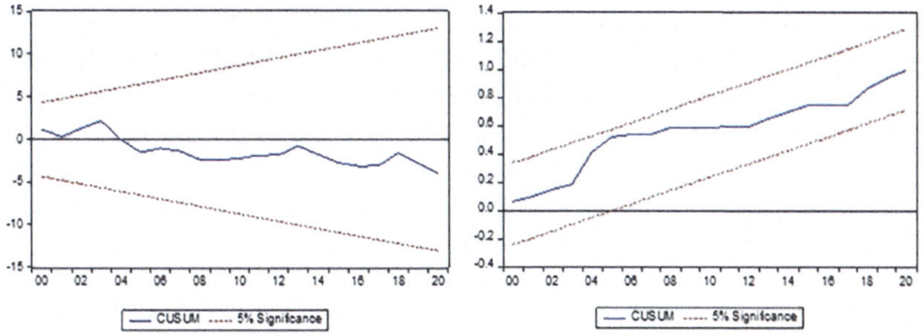

Fig. 10 Cusum and CusumSQ (China)

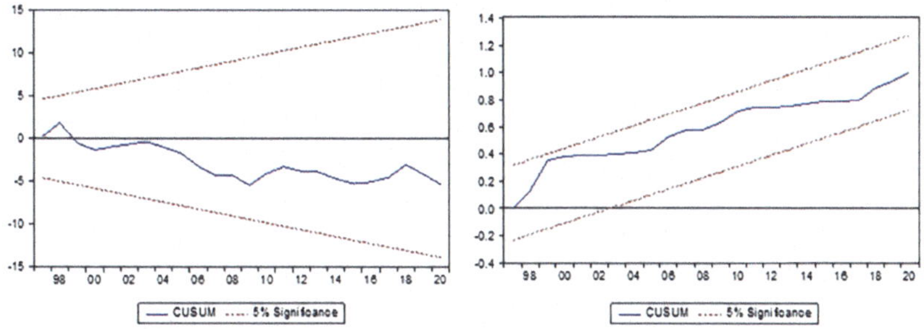

Fig. 11 Cusum and CusumSQ (India)

4 Discussion

The findings of this chapter add weight to the complex relationship between economic growth, energy consumption, military expenditure, financial development, trade openness, and environmental degradation in China and India. Both these emerging economies show a similar trend of facing environmental challenges due to extensive reliance on fossil fuels, heavy industrial activities, and high military spending. Precisely, the results from the ARDL indicate that military expenditure significantly influences the positive output of CO_2 emission in both countries and reflects the extent of environmental cost from continued defense-related activities. In China, it could be much stronger since wide-ranging infrastructure for the military is usually involved in environmentally sensitive areas, thus exacerbating CO_2 emissions and causing long-term damage to the environment. Furthermore, other specific factors contributing to environmental degradation in both countries are energy consumption. Energy consumption in India and China greatly relies on coal and oil thus on fossil fuels, and these are the major sources of the currently soaring CO_2 emissions. It tallies with findings in other literature that fossil fuel dependence contributes directly to environmental degradation. Going to renewable energy sources, such as solar, wind, and hydro, requires a drastic change in policies and major investments. Considering a fact, the two countries did launch the installation of renewable projects, but it is still not scaled up compared to its growing consumption of non-renewable energy sources. Financial development is very mixed in its impact. On one hand, it can support green projects, promote the use of greener technologies through mechanisms such as green bonds or environmentally-oriented investments. On the other hand, however, the data shows that absent regulatory steps, FD generally results in higher industrial activities and energy use, which tend to increase environmental degradation. It also portrays dual effects of trade openness, which turns out to be positive when regulatory standards are in place and enforced that help reduce pollution, whereas negative when strong environmental policy is lacking. Estimations show that the researchers hint at the fact that in countries like China and India, because of the attraction of noxious industries in their countries without stringent environmental safeguards, trade openness results in higher CO_2 emissions.

The heavy military expenditure aggravates the environmental problems of both countries. Military activities in environmentally sensitive areas like the Himalayas lead to deforestation and habitat loss, besides heavy emissions due to machinery and road and other infrastructure-building activities. Moreover, the maintenance and testing of nuclear capabilities pose serious environmental and health hazards, with the emission of toxic elements; further, hazardous waste from military arsenals is extremely expensive to deal with. These environmental challenges are a loud call for confidence-building measures and regional security frameworks that might ease the pressure on heavy military spending along contentious borders.

5 Conclusion

The findings of this chapter highlight the urgent need for realigning China and India's macroeconomic priorities to align with sustainable development goals. Military expenditure, energy consumption, and industrialization are vital for economic growth and security but are the very things that bring about unprecedented environmental degradation. Policymakers must work on a twin-track approach: one that addresses immediate environmental risks and another that lays down the foundation for longer-term sustainability. In the case of shared environmental degradation, less reliance on fossil fuels, investments in renewable energy, carbon pricing mechanisms, and green finance will imply that great strides are taken by both countries. Furthermore, CBMs and regional cooperation will help address security concerns with minimal sacrifice environmentally.

6 Implications

6.1 *Theoretical Implications*

Conclusively, this chapter has added to the literature of the Environmental Kuznets Curve hypothesis by proposing the inefficiency of economic growth to work as a sole indicator for reducing environmental degradation. This study confirms that economic growth can first enhance environmental stress and then is unable to achieve a "turning point" due to continued reliance on fossil fuel and high military spending. The findings give reasons for the inclusion of green financial development strategies in economic development policy, among other sustainable policies, rather than growth itself acting as a panacea to environmental damage.

6.2 *Practical Implications*

Concretely, the findings of this comparative analysis call for immediate policy measures by the governments of China and India to pursue a rapid reduction of dependence on fossil fuel energy, improvements in energy efficiency, and the adoption of pricing mechanisms for carbon. Green finance is equally important to enable financial institutions to help finance projects that contribute to environmental sustainability. Moreover, regional CBMs would scale down the military tensions and might enable both the sides to allocate the military funds towards sustainable development initiatives. A more balanced approach to economic and defense policies between China and India could bring in a key environmental benefit by way of reducing CO_2 emissions, improving air quality, and fortifying the resilience against climate change.

6.3 *Limitations and Future Research*

This study based on the ARDL model, for the period 1983–2023, affects the predictive capability of this study for developments beyond 2023, especially because both countries are likely to change their policy direction in light of environmental issues. Future studies can employ more complex models such as the SEM model, which would represent the multi-dimensional effects of these variables. Additionally, although this study applies to China and India, the cross-country comparisons that might be made with other developing countries could provide broader details into regional heterogeneity in the nexus between economy and environment.Future studies could also analyze the role of emerging technologies, such as carbon capture and storage (CCS), and their potential in mitigating the adverse environmental impacts of economic growth. Finally, research exploring the impact of public awareness initiatives and policy acceptance on environmental outcomes would provide a more holistic understanding of sustainable development efforts in emerging economies.

Appendix—1

Data Source and Units

"Energy consumption (EN) is measured from a kg of oil equivalent per capita; percentage of change in annual economic growth proxy for economic growth; FD is measured through domestic credit to the private sector as a percentage of the gross domestic product; TO is measured from import plus exports as a percentage of gross domestic. Data are extracted from WDI (World Bank Development Indicator) over the period 1983 to 2023".

Mercosur—The Southern Common Market, commonly known by Spanish abbreviation—Mercosur—Listed countries are Argentina, Brazil, Paraguay, Uruguay, Venezuela, Bolivia, Chile, Colombia, Ecuador, Guyana, Peru and Surinam.

References

Ahmed Z, Ahmad M, Murshed M, Vaseer AI, Kirikkaleli D (2021) The trade-off between energy consumption, economic growth, militarization, and CO_2 emissions: does the treadmill of destruction exist in the modern world? Environ Sci Pollut Res 29(12):18063–18076. https://doi.org/10.1007/s11356-021-17068-3

Ahmed Z, Zafar MW, Mansoor S (2020) Analyzing the linkage between military spending, economic growth, and ecological footprint in Pakistan: evidence from cointegration and bootstrap causality. Environ Sci Pollut Res 27(33):41551–41567. https://doi.org/10.1007/s11356-020-10076-9

Akadiri SS, Bekun FV, Sarkodie SA (2019) Contemporaneous interaction between energy consumption, economic growth, and environmental sustainability in South Africa: what drives what? Sci Total Environ 686:468–475

Al-Mulali U, Sab CNBC (2012) The impact of energy consumption and CO_2 emission on the economic and FD in 19 selected countries. Renew Sustain Energy Rev 16(7):4365–4369

Ayadi FS (2020) Trade openness and environmental degradation: the pollution haven hypothesis revisited. Int J Environ Stud 77(3):474–488

Bakhsh K, Rose S, Ali MF, Ahmad N, Shahbaz M (2017a) Economic growth, CO_2 emissions, renewable waste and FDI relation in Pakistan: new evidence from 3SLS. J Environ Manage 196:627–632

Bakhsh K, Yasmeen R, Ali M (2017b) Nexus between economic growth and environmental degradation: evidence from Pakistan. Environ Sci Pollut Res 24(36):27832–27847

Batool Z, Raza SMF, Ali S, Abidin SZU (2022) ICT, renewable energy, financial development, and CO_2 emissions in developing countries of East and South Asia. Environ Sci Pollut Res 1–11.

Behera SR, Dash DP (2017) The effect of urbanization, energy consumption, and foreign direct investment on CO_2 in the SSEA (South and Southeast Asian) region. Renew Sustain Energy Rev 70:96–106

Behuria P (2020) The politics of late late development in renewable energy sectors: dependency and contradictory tensions in India's national solar mission. World Dev 126:104726
Bildirici M, Gökmenoğlu SM (2017) Environmental degradation, renewable energy, and economic growth: evidence from the BRICS countries. Energy 135:183–191
Burford G, Hoover E, Velasco I, Janoušková S, Jimenez A, Piggot G, Podger D, Harder MK (2013) Bringing the "missing pillar" into sustainable development goals: towards intersubjective values-based indicators. Sustainability 5(7):3035–3059
Chang Y, Sun X (2023) Military spending and its environmental implications: insights from China and India. J Environ Policy & Plan 25(1):54–67
Dasgupta S, De Cian E (2018) The influence of institutions, governance, and public opinion on the environment: synthesized findings from applied econometrics studies. Energy Res Soc Sci 43:77–95
Ekins P, Medhurst J (2006) The European structural funds and sustainable development: a methodology and indicator framework for evaluation. Evaluation 12(4):474–495
Erdogan S, Cetin M, Okumus I (2022a) Military expenditure and environmental degradation in the Mediterranean region. Environ Sci Pollut Res 29(3):22958–22967
Erdogan S, Gedikli A, Çevik Eİ, Öncü MA (2022b) Does military expenditure impact environmental sustainability in developed Mediterranean countries? Environ Sci Pollut Res 29:31612–31630. https://doi.org/10.1007/s11356-021-18226-3
He P, Sun Y, Zhang Y, Li T (2020) COVID–19's impact on stock prices across different sectors—an event study based on the Chinese stock market. Emerg Mark Financ Trade 56(10):2198–2212
He W, Abbas Q, Alharthi M, Mohsin M, Hanif I, Vo XV, Taghizadeh-Hesary F (2020) Integration of renewable hydrogen in light-duty vehicle: nexus between energy security and low carbon emission resources. Int J Hydrogen Energy 45(51):27958–27968
He K, Huo H, Zhang Q, He D, An F, Wang M, Walsh MP (2005) Oil consumption and CO2 emissions in China's road transport: current status, future trends, and policy implications. Energy Policy 33(12):1499–1507
Jamil K, Liu D, Gul RF, Hussain Z, Mohsin M, Qin G, Khan FU (2021a) Do remittance and renewable energy affect CO_2 emissions? Empirical evidence from selected G-20 countries. Energy & Environ 33(5):0958305X211029636
Jamil S, Salman M, Khan Z (2021b) Role of financial development and renewable energy in mitigating carbon emissions: evidence from G-20 countries. Renewable Energy 173:678–686
Janjua LR (2021) Financial flows and environmental degradation: empirical evidence from Algeria using auto regressive distributed lag estimation (ARDL). Int J Circ Econ Waste Manag (IJCEWM) 1(2):1–15
Khan A, Sun C, Xu Z, Liu Y (2023) Geopolitical risk, economic uncertainty, and militarization: significant agents of energy consumption and environmental quality. Environ Impact Assess Rev 102:107166
Khan I, Khan N, Yaqub A, Sabir M (2019) An empirical investigation of the determinants of CO_2 emissions: evidence from Pakistan. Environ Sci Pollut Res 26(9):9099–9112
Koengkan M (2018) The impact of economic growth and financial development on environmental degradation: evidence from Mercosur countries. Environ Sci Pollut Res 25(3):2889–2896
Kumar S, Singh P (2023) India's renewable energy policy and its impact on carbon emissions: a step toward sustainability. Energy Policy 169:113128
Kwakwa PA (2022) The effect of industrialization, militarization, and government expenditure on CO_2 in Ghana. Environ Sci Pollut Res 29(56):85229–85242. https://doi.org/10.1007/s11356-022-21187-w
Laksmana EA, Chong B (2023) Introduction: partnership or polarization? Southeast Asian security between India and China. Contemp Southeast Asia: J Int Strat Aff 45(2):145–165
Lee J, Ho T (2022) Comparative analysis of energy policies in China and India and their effects on environmental sustainability. Energy Environ Res 12(2):45–59
Li X, Zhou L (2024) Trade openness, FDI, and environmental sustainability in BRICS nations: the moderating role of policy frameworks. J Clean Prod 289:125732

Lin M, Liu Q (2022) Renewable energy adoption and CO_2 emissions in China and India: a comparative study. Environmental Development 41:100673

Liobikienė G, Butkus M (2018) The challenges and opportunities of climate change policy under different stages of economic development. Sci Total Environ 642:999–1007

Liu H, Song Y (2020) FD and carbon emissions in China since the recent world financial crisis: evidence from a spatial-temporal analysis and a spatial Durbin model. Sci Total Environ 715:136771

Malik MY, Latif K, Khan Z, Butt HD, Hussain M, Nadeem MA (2020) Symmetric and asymmetric impact of oil price, FDI and economic growth on carbon emission in Pakistan: evidence from ARDL and non-linear ARDL approach. Sci Total Environ 138421

Menon N (2019a) Economic growth, renewable energy, and CO_2 emissions in India: the dynamic nexus. Energy Policy 131:211–219

Menon P (2019b) An Indian story on carbon emission, energy consumption, trade openness, and financial development. J Public Aff 19(4):e1953

Mohammed Saud MA, Guo P, Haq IU, Pan G, Khan A (2019) Do government expenditure and financial development impede environmental degradation in Venezuela? PloS One 14(1):e0210255

Murshed M (2020) An empirical analysis of the non-linear impacts of ICT trade openness on renewable energy transition, energy efficiency, clean cooking fuel access and environmental sustainability in South Asia. Environ Sci Pollut Res 27(29):36254–36281

Özokcu S, Özdemir Ö (2017) Economic growth, energy, and environmental Kuznets curve. Renew Sustain Energy Rev 72:639–647

Pata U, Caglar M (2021) Economic structure, trade openness, and environmental degradation: evidence from BRICS countries. Ecol Econ 180:106860

Pesaran MH, Shin Y, Smith RP (1999) Pooled mean group estimation of dynamic heterogeneous panels. J Am Stat Assoc 94(446):621–634

Pesaran MH, Shin Y, Smith RJ (2001) Bounds testing approaches to the analysis of level relationships. J Appl Econom 16(3):289–326

Qin Q, Yu Y, Liu Y, Zhou J, Chen X (2023) Industrial agglomeration and energy efficiency: a new perspective from market integration. Energy Policy 183:113793

Rahaman M, Hossain M, Chen S (2022) The impact of foreign direct investment, tourism, electricity consumption, and economic development on CO_2 emissions in Bangladesh. Environ Sci Pollut Res 1–15

Rahman KM, Melville L, Fulford D, Huq SI (2017) Greenhouse gas mitigation capacity of a small scale rural biogas plant calculations for Bangladesh through a general life cycle assessment. Waste Manage Res 35(10):1023–1033

Rahman MM, Hosan S, Karmaker SC, Chapman AJ, Saha BB (2020) The effect of remittance on energy consumption: panel cointegration and dynamic causality analysis for South Asian countries. Energy 119684

Rahman M, Lin C (2022) Revisiting the environmental Kuznets curve hypothesis in Asian countries: the role of urbanization, trade, and renewable energy. J Environ Manage 302:113966

Repo A, Tuomi M, Liski J (2011) Indirect CO_2 from producing bioenergy from forest harvest residues. Gcb Bioenergy 3(2):107–115

Ridzuan AR (2019) The impact of corruption on environmental quality in the developing countries of ASEAN-3: the application of the bound test. 670216917

Ridzuan AR, Ismail NA, Hamat AFC (2018) Foreign direct investment and trade openness: do they lead to sustainable development in Malaysia?. Editorial Board, 81

Rodrik D (2018) What do trade agreements really do? J Econ Perspect 32(2):73–90

Saud S, Chen S, Haseeb A (2020) The role of FD and globalization in the environment: accounting ecological footprint indicators for selected one-belt-one-road initiative countries. J Clean Prod 250:119518

Shafique M, Shaikh A (2023) Military expenditure and environmental degradation: a global analysis. Def Peace Econ 34(2):138–152

Shahzad SJH, Kumar RR, Zakaria M, Hurr M (2017) Carbon emission, energy consumption, trade openness and financial development in Pakistan: a revisit. Renew Sustain Energy Rev 70:185–192

Sharma K, Bhattarai B, Ahmed S (2019) Aid, growth, remittances and carbon emissions in Nepal. Energy J 40(1):129–142

Solarin SA, Sahu BK, Bekun FV (2017) Military expenditure and environmental degradation in Ghana: evidence from ARDL approach. Environ Sci Pollut Res 24:13078–13092

Tan YS, Kwek LJ (2016) Environmental sustainability and sustainable development. In: 50 years of environment: Singapore's journey towards environmental sustainability, pp. 247–264.

Teodorescu AM (2012) Links between the pillars of sustainable development. Annals of the University of Craiova, Economic Sciences Series, p 1

Usman A, Hammar N (2021) Financial development and its role in environmental degradation mitigation through technological innovation. Energy 233:121058

Wang J, Azam W (2024) Natural resource scarcity, fossil fuel energy consumption, and total greenhouse gas emissions in top emitting countries. Geosci Front 15(2):101757

Wang X, Zhang Y (2023) The role of renewable energy and economic growth in environmental sustainability: evidence from emerging economies. J Environ Manage 324:116097. https://doi.org/10.1016/j.jenvman.2023.116097

Wenlong Z, Tien NH, Sibghatullah A, Asih D, Soelton M, Ramli Y (2023) Impact of energy efficiency, technology innovation, institutional quality, and trade openness on greenhouse gas emissions in ten Asian economies. Environ Sci Pollut Res 30(15):43024–43039

Wen Y (2021) China's industrial revolution: a new perspective. China Econ Rev 69:101671

Wu H, Zhang Q (2022) Financial development, environmental regulation, and CO_2 emissions in emerging economies: evidence from BRICS. J Environ Econ Manag 111:102582

Zafar MW, Saleem MM, Destek MA, Caglar AE (2021) The dynamic linkage between remittances, export diversification, education, renewable energy consumption, economic growth, and CO_2 emissions in top remittance-receiving countries. Sustain Dev

Zafar S, Hussain H (2022) Trade openness, foreign direct investment, and environmental quality: a meta-analysis. Environ Res Lett 17(5):055008

Zhang H, Shao Y, Han X, Chang HL (2022) A road towards ecological development in China: the nexus between green investment, natural resources, green technology innovation, and economic growth. Resour Policy 77:102746

A Multivariate Analysis of Economic Growth, Energy Consumption, and Carbon Emissions in Highly Mountainous Economies: An Empirical Evidence

Amjad Mahmood, Yasir Habib, Shahzad Ahmad Khan, and Sajjad Nawaz Khan

Abstract Energy consumption, economic growth, and environmental degradation have interconnected impacts that have risen to the forefront of public policy discussions in highly mountainous economies (HME). This study exploits a panel vector autoregression (PVAR) and system-GMM approach to research the bond across economic growth, energy consumption, and carbon emissions of HME countries from 1971 to 2020. A multivariate model was used to establish key relationships with policy implications. The findings of this study indicate that countries' environmental performance levels are enhanced by economic growth and energy consumption patterns. The long-run estimators' findings suggest that carbon emissions are caused by energy consumption and that the relationship is positive. Economic growth and carbon emissions were negatively correlated. Carbon emissions negatively affect population density and natural resource depletion. The results of the Panel Granger Causality test revealed a mutual causal relationship between economic growth and energy consumption. However, GDP was found to causally affect carbon emissions in only one direction. In countries with significant mountainous regions, the impulse response function demonstrated the presence of an environmental Kuznets curve. Hence, based on the analysis of the dynamic interplay between energy consumption,

A. Mahmood (✉)
School of Management, Air University, Islamabad, Pakistan
e-mail: amjadmehmod@outlook.com

Y. Habib
UNITEN Business School (UBS), Institute of Energy Policy and Research (IEPRe), Universiti Tenaga Nasional, Kajang, Selangor, Malaysia
e-mail: yasir.habib@uniten.edu.my

S. A. Khan
College of Business, University of Buraimi, Al Buraimi, Oman
e-mail: shahzad@uob.edu.om

S. N. Khan
Department of Commerce and Economics, Emerson University, Multan, Pakistan
e-mail: Sajjad.nawaz@eum.edu.pk

S. A. R. Khan et al. (eds.), *Circular Economy and Technological Innovation*, Industrial Ecology, https://doi.org/10.1007/978-981-96-5650-9_8

economic growth, and levels of environmental degradation across nations, it becomes evident that coexistence plays a vital role in achieving sustainable development rather than pursuing trade-offs.

Keywords Environmental degradation · Energy consumption · Natural resource depletion · Highly mountainous economies

1 Introduction

Over the past few decades, climate change has been the most prominent and thought-provoking environmental issue. Climate change is the most earth-shaking threat to sustainable development (Destek and Sarkodie 2019; Fletcher et al. 2024). The world economy has grown immensely owing to rapid urbanization and industrialization (Dong et al. 2018). The World Bank (2020f) ascertained that the world's Gross Domestic Product (GDP) had grown significantly (by roughly three-fold) with an average annual growth rate of 3.01%, from $19.983 trillion US $ (constant 2010 US dollars) in 1971 to $84.91 trillion US $ (constant 2010 US dollars) in 2020. Simultaneously, the global urban population has multiplied by 2.5, averaging 30 percent, from 1.382 billion in 1970 to 4.359 billion in 2020 (World Bank 2020f). One of the implications of such economic development and population growth is a significant increase in worldwide energy consumption.

This integrative framework allows for an increased understanding of the complex interactions between energy consumption, economic growth, CO_2 emissions, population density, trade openness, and natural resource depletion. This framework can be used to develop strategies for decarbonizing the economy and transitioning to a low-CO2 future. It can also be used to inform policymakers and stakeholders regarding the trade-offs involved when making decisions related to energy and climate change. As one of the most challenging environmental problems, climate change has piqued the interest of governments, international organizations, and academics. According to the Kaya identity, economic growth, population expansion, energy intensity consumption, and CO_2 emissions contribute to global warming (Kaya and Yokobori 1998). For their part, scientists and policymakers have blamed rapid economic expansion and a rise in fossil fuel use as the primary reason for the high Emission of CO_2 (Andreoni and Galmarini 2016; Aşici 2013; Sohag et al. 2015; Sultana et al. 2023; Yusuf 2023). According to current estimates, the total cost of combating climate change is comparable to 5% of the annual GDP, which has now declined and, in the future, to a 20% loss if quick actions are not taken (Stern 2008). Hence, reducing energy demand is necessary to mitigate CO_2 emissions. Conversely, it is also a fact that reducing Emission of CO_2 is said to have macroeconomic costs (Fan et al. 2010; González-Álvarez and Montañés 2023). The exponential growth of conventional sectors has caused significant social and environmental concerns due to the excessive exploitation of natural resources and pollution (Khan et al. 2023a). To mitigate the Emission of CO_2, reducing the consumption of energy may negatively affect economic growth because it is an integral part of the production process (Hunter et al. 2023).

Consequently, there are two primary lines of empirical research. The validity has been tested empirically as part of the first line of research on environmental sustainability and economic growth. According to the EKC, environmental quality initially deteriorates as income rises and eventually improves (Grossman et al. 1995). Economic growth will initially lead to an increase in CO_2 emissions, but this increase will gradually decrease with time. China and India are the most CO_2 emitters, but on the other hand, these countries have the most emerging and developing economies. This is mainly because different countries have different strategies and policies for promoting economic growth. In some countries, economic growth has been achieved without any regard for environmental protection, whereas in others, environmental concerns have been considered. Hence, the relationship between economic growth and environmental decline may not always be straightforward.

Some studies suggest that pollution negatively influences economic growth, while others find that pollution can have a positive effect. This contradiction is likely due to the varying contexts in which pollution and economic growth are studied (Ahmad et al. 2017; Al-Mulali et al. 2013; Awewomom et al. 2024). Another line of empirical research focuses on the connection between energy consumption and economic growth. Kraft and Kraft (1978) were the first to conduct this research. Policymakers need to know the effects of their decisions on energy consumption, CO_2 emissions, and economic growth to make the most effective policies. By examining the relationships between these three factors, they can better understand the implications of their decisions. Therefore, some experts have proposed that these two lines of research should be examined together (Soytas et al. 2009). A more precise understanding of the relationship between energy consumption and CO_2 emissions might help reconcile the conflicting effects of economic, energy, and environmental conservation initiatives. Owing to their interdependence, energy consumption, economic growth, and CO_2 emissions must be evaluated within a unified framework to avoid misspecification. Despite the significant attention given to both economic growth and environmental effects, few empirical studies have integrated these two areas of research to investigate causal relationships. Therefore, there is a paucity of empirical data supporting the idea that environmental damage and economic growth are associated. Several studies have observed a Granger causation relationship between economic growth and environmental degradation (Adebayo et al. 2024; Soytas et al. 2009). The objective of this study was to address the gaps in current knowledge using a multivariate approach. This study aims to address the gaps in the existing knowledge by employing a multivariate approach that considers trade openness. Trade openness has substantial effects on energy consumption, economic growth, and CO_2 emissions (Ghani 2012; Shahbaz et al. 2014; Q. Wang et al. 2023). First, it provides a detailed analysis of the relationship between economic growth and energy utilization in a developing economy. Second, it examined the effects of energy sources on CO_2 emissions. Finally, this study provides evidence for the importance of energy conservation policies. This study makes three distinct contributions to the literature, which is unique among empirical studies. First, this study used the panel vector autoregression (PVAR) method to evaluate the relationship between energy consumption, economic growth, and CO_2 emissions.

Using the system-generalized method of moments (system-GMM) - estimator, this advanced econometric approach estimates the interactions between variables and simultaneously tests Granger causality. Because it addresses the problem of endogeneity in the data, this cutting-edge econometric approach ensures that the findings are robust, accurate, and consistent. By examining the variance decomposition and impulse response functions, it is feasible to forecast the impact of an economic development shock on CO_2 emissions and energy consumption in both short and long terms. To the best of our knowledge, this is the first study to use Highly Mountainous Economies (Pakistan, China, India, Nepal, and Bangladesh) as samples to analyze the causal links among economic growth, energy consumption, CO_2 emissions, population density, trade openness, and natural resource depletion. This study selected a sample of five HME countries for several reasons. First, these nations collectively possess a substantial amount of the world's natural resources, including 1.82% of proven crude oil reserves (measured in billion barrels) and dry natural gas production totaling 294.5 billion cubic feet, accounting for approximately three-quarters of coal production (in thousands of tons).

Additionally, they represent 20.67% of global oil consumption measured in thousand barrels per day, with a significant land area covering up to almost 10%. Second, their population is equivalent to almost half (41.36%) globally, contributing about one-fourth (27.89%) of the world's GDP, as well as household consumption comprising seventy-four percent (74%). Third, these nations made an appreciable contribution to CO_2 emissions, registering nearly 38% on record for the HME countries alone in 2019. Given the information mentioned above, research on the empirical connections among CO_2 emissions, urbanization, industrialization, energy use, and trade openness is necessary. Such research may enable decision-makers to develop long-term and short-term plans to reduce CO_2 emissions and ensure the sustainable use of natural resources.

In academic discourse, there is consensus on the notable relationships among carbon emissions, energy consumption, and economic growth. However, due to variations in the timeframes and methodologies used in research studies, the findings have not been consistently aligned across the board. Further advancements are required to address these discrepancies. Most existing studies focus on individual countries or regions as their research subjects rather than targeting the main actors responsible for greenhouse gas emissions. Additionally, earlier investigations have predominantly concentrated on non-renewable or fossil energy sources when examining this field over a decade ago. The increasing prevalence of renewable energy necessitates an examination of the relationships between different forms of energy, economic growth, and carbon emissions. In light of this, our study analyzes panel data to identify the top five greenhouse-gas-emitting countries. We explore the connections and underlying mechanisms linking energy consumption, economic growth, and carbon emissions through empirical analysis. This discovery is innovative and has not been discussed previously in the current body of research.

The remainder of this paper is organized as follows. The literature review is presented in Part 2, and the methods and results are summarized in Sects. 3 and 4, with subsections. Finally, we conclude with a discussion of the implications and policy recommendations, based on the findings presented in Sect. 4.

2 Literature Review

A systemic perspective on the relationship among energy consumption, economic growth, and CO_2 emissions could yield valuable policy implications and address potential misspecification issues. The negative correlation between energy usage and economic development is a fact, alongside the positive association between economic growth and CO_2 release. Therefore, understanding the relationship among energy consumption, CO_2 emissions, and economic growth is important for developing policies that promote sustainable economic growth. Several researchers have suggested that these two distinct branches of research are inextricably linked and should be investigated jointly to circumvent problems that are inherently associated with each of them. One of the criticisms that has been leveled at the EKC (Environmental Kuznets Curve) research is the contention that a rise in money does not invariably result in an improvement in environmental quality since pollutant emissions, specifically Emission of CO_2, rise linearly with income (Fodha and Zaghdoud 2010). According to Raihan and Tuspekova (2022), studies examining the connection between energy utilization and economic development but ignoring the effects of Emissions of CO_2 make a negligible contribution to the existing body of research.

Because energy consumption directly affects pollution levels, an integrated strategy is required. Economic growth has long-term causal impacts that contribute to rising pollution levels and energy consumption in France. Co-integration and vector error-correction modeling techniques were used by Ang (2017) to investigate the interconnections between emissions of pollutants, energy consumption, and output in France during the time period from 1960 to 2000.This study demonstrated a one-way causation between energy use and production growth in the short term. Using Johansen co-integration, VECM, and ARDL approaches, Shareef et al. (1996) followed up on the work of Ang (2007) to examine the relationship among electricity consumption, CO_2 emissions, energy consumption, and economic growth in Bangladesh.

Research shows that there is a significant relationship between economic growth and energy consumption over an extended period. However, it should be noted that no direct cause-and-effect link has been definitively established. Mirza and Kanwal (2017) found a bidirectional causative link between Pakistan's economic growth and the Emission of CO_2 from 1971 to 2009.

As part of Soytas et al. (2009) investigation, income, CO_2 emission, and energy consumption were studied for their connection to environmental impacts in the USA. The model's results, which also consider labor and gross fixed capital formation, show that income does not directly contribute to the long-run Emission of CO_2.

The results of a Turkish expansion of the Soytas and Sari (2009) study showed that the Emission of CO_2 Granger has a direct, powerful effect on the consumption of energy, but not vice versa. In their academic study, Menyah (2010) and Ghani (2012) investigated the extended-term causal correlation among South African economic growth, energy consumption, and pollutant emissions over four decades from 1965 to 2006. The study employed the ARDL bound test methodology, revealing a robust positive association between these two variables. Furthermore, through an adapted Granger causality assessment approach, the authors identified a unidirectional causal relationship between economic growth rates, energy consumption patterns, and both pollutant and greenhouse gas emissions in South Africa.

Chopra et al. (2022) employed the Canonical Co-integration Regression methodology to explore the extent to which CO_2 emissions have contributed to impeding economic progress in Latin American and Caribbean countries during the period spanning from 1980 until 2008 and what role consumption of energy played in driving that growth. According to the findings, 60% of the countries show positive long-run connections among economic growth, energy consumption, and CO_2 emissions, whereas 40% have diversified results. Khan et al. (2023b) indicate that the link between sustainable firm performance and corporate social responsibility is influenced by green capability. Omri (2013) discovered a link among the emission of CO_2, energy consumption, and economic growth through simultaneous equation models for 14 MENA countries from 1990 to 2011. The research findings demonstrate a strong correlation between energy consumption and economic development. Furthermore, the study revealed that there is a one-way causal relationship between energy consumption and CO_2 emissions, while economic growth has two-way causality with CO_2 emissions within the region.

Salahuddin and Gow (2014) discovered a noteworthy and favorable correlation between energy consumption, CO_2 emission, and economic growth in GCC countries. Their research indicated that increasing CO_2 levels does not necessarily result in economic prosperity. The study also reveals a Granger causal relationship between energy usage and CO_2 emissions, with causation flowing one way from economic expansion to energy consumption. In addition to other factors, population growth has emerged as a significant driver of increased CO_2 emission. A growing population requires higher energy consumption for power generation, industrial activities, and transportation, resulting in elevated levels of emissions from fossil fuels (J. Wang and Azam, 2024). It is worth noting that young individuals have the potential to emit up to 20 times more greenhouse gases than their adult counterparts. However, adopting environmentally friendly practices such as reducing car usage, implementing recycling programs, and utilizing energy-efficient appliances and lighting can help mitigate these emissions effectively according to a study by Murtaugh and Schlax (2009). Hence, when analyzing the relationship between CO_2 emissions, growth, and energy consumption, population density should be considered a key component.

Moreover, trade and exports are linked to energy use and, thus, to CO_2 emissions. For instance, altered patterns in agricultural production can affect trade. Furthermore, the rise in manufacturing and transportation activities linked to commerce can have consequences on energy consumption and climate change. Danish et al.

(2023) found that the increase in natural resource rent leads to CO_2 emission, indicating that overreliance on such rent disrupts ecological sustainability in the US. Dingru et al. (2023) study, among others, indicated that urbanization and trade openness impacted Sub-Sahara Africa's energy use. Kharrazi et al. (2013) raise a query regarding the notion that increased sustainability can be solely equated with reducing overall resource consumption within a system. Given this, the analysis of the relationship among carbon emissions, growth, and energy consumption still needs to consider exports or trade as a key component. The HME nations have experienced remarkable economic progress over the past few decades. Unfortunately, this rapid development has contributed to a significant loss of natural resources, hastening the emergence of environmental problems.

While the relationship among natural resources, energy, economic growth, and the environment has been extensively studied at the regional and national levels, only a few studies have drawn global attention. The regional differences in natural resource depletion, energy consumption, urbanization, industrialization, trade openness, and CO_2 emissions should not be disregarded. This study investigated the correlation between natural resource depletion, economic development, energy utilization, trade liberalization, CO_2 emissions, urbanization, and industrialization across five HME economies from to 1971–2020. This study sought to address the gaps identified in the literature on this topic. We use several causality tests, including the panel unit root test, co-integration test, and Granger causality test, to examine cross-sectional dependence in the panel units. Our study differs from earlier studies on this topic in two key ways. First, unlike previous literature on this topic, our estimation technique considers cross-sectional dependence between nations. Second, we introduced natural resource depletion into our CO_2 emission and energy use models, an aspect overlooked in previous research. This inclusion holds significant implications for policy formulation and analysis within HME nations, particularly for mitigating CO_2 emissions by fostering sustainable practices regarding natural resource consumption. This study has significant implications for policymakers, as it offers the potential to shape comprehensive economic, trade, population, and energy policies that foster sustainable growth in these countries. By implementing energy conservation measures in these nations without compromising economic growth (provided there is no causal relationship between energy use and GDP growth), environmental quality can be improved. Alternatively, if exports or economic expansion augment CO_2 emissions through a causal relationship, prioritizing the abandonment of traditional notions of economic growth or adopting energy-efficient technologies for production becomes crucial. If Granger's high population density contributes to CO_2 emissions, effective legislation should be implemented to promote population development, town reorganization, and decentralization.

2.1 Economic Growth and Emission of CO_2

The relationship between economic growth and CO_2 emissions has undergone extensive empirical analysis for more than two decades and it has been found that there is a link between the two. The Environmental Kuznets Curve (EKC) hypothesis, which has been advanced in certain published publications, contends that a curvilinear relationship exists between the level of CO_2 emissions and economic growth, referred to as an inverted U-shape. For instance, studies by Jahanger et al. (2023) provided evidence for the EKC hypothesis, which suggests that economic expansion initially worsens environmental quality before it improves when growth levels up. This is in contrast to Jiang et al. (2022) findings, which indicated that Emission of CO_2 rose together with economic expansion. According to Agboola et al. (2021) Emission of CO_2 begin to fall once the economy reaches a particular income level. However, the results of Akbostancı et al. (2009) did not support the EKC hypothesis' tenets. Income and carbon emissions were found to be positively and adversely correlated in low- and high-income nations, respectively, by Martínez-Zarzoso and Bengochea-Morancho (2004).

A Research on sustainable development and climate change in sub-Saharan Africa was conducted by Joseph and Wood (2010) in which he employed the panel co-integration approach to demonstrate the strong positive relationship between climatic change and growth. Nevertheless, Zubair et al. (2020) discovered opposing findings when examining Nigeria's economic development and environmental issues. Their research revealed a nonlinear correlation between environmental harm and economic expansion, demonstrating an N-shaped pattern. They advocated the adoption of strong environmental protection policies regardless of the nation's income level. Carbon emissions and GDP have a positive relationship, according to Agboola et al. (2021) They added that compared to other energy sources, electricity produced minimal pollution. The EKC hypothesis, however, was confirmed by Ozturk and Acaravci's (2013) research as being true for the economy of Turkish. Hamdi and Sbia (2014) found indications of the Environmental Kuznets Curve (EKC) theory in their examination of carbon dioxide emissions, energy consumption, and actual output within a collection of Gulf Cooperation Council (GCC) nations over an extended period. In a different study, Muftau et al. (2014) used the cointegration technique to examine the relationship between the Emission of CO_2 and GDP for West African countries and discovered a long-run equilibrium relationship. According to Rahman and Kashem's (2017) study on the correlation between energy use, carbon emissions, and industrial growth in Bangladesh, a direct relationship was found between industrial output and CO_2 emissions over short- and long-term periods.

Rahman's (2019) research also unveiled a uni-directional causal link between GDP levels and CO_2 emissions for eleven heavily populated Asian countries. S. Zhang et al. (2022a) have developed a model for multi-objective optimization to tackle potential conflicts in policies relating to GDP growth, reduction of carbon emissions, energy conservation, and employment levels within China's economic sectors. Furthermore, it was discovered that a prolonged N-shaped connection exists between income status and CO_2 emissions in West Africa, which discredits the validity of EKC theory. In Tunisia, Mbarek et al. (2017) likewise discovered both immediate and long-term effects of economic expansion on Emission of CO_2. Saidi and Hammami (2015) examine the relationship between energy consumption, CO_2 emissions, and economic growth in 58 countries. Based on their empirical analysis, they found evidence that higher levels of CO_2 emissions had a negative impact on economic growth.

2.2 *Economic Growth and Trade Openness*

The relationship between trade openness and economic growth is crucial to consider when devising effective trade policies. In earlier studies, theoretical models have been developed to explain how trade openness affects economic growth. Bouoiyour (2003) investigated the relationship between Morocco's economic expansion and its trade openness. According to these findings, long-term causality is absent. Imports and exports rose, raising the GDP in the short term. According to Calderon et al. (2004), trade openness favors growth in wealthy nations, but does not impact growth in developing nations. Freund and Bolaky (2008) discovered a favorable effect of trade openness on per capita income using cross-country data from 126 nations. In addition, their findings indicated that whereas rigid economies did not see a rise in living standards due to increasing trade, more flexible economies did.

In contrast, Sarkar (2008) discovered through a time-series analysis study that trade openness had a detrimental impact on India's economic growth. The trade-GDP ratio was employed in the study as a proxy for openness. According to Chang et al. (2009), if complementary policies are implemented, the relationship between growth and openness would be significantly strengthened. Over the sample period of 1960–2000, Ersoy and Ulas (2013) investigated the correlation between economic growth over a prolonged period and open trade policies. The findings show that numerous characteristics connected to trade openness have a long-term, significant, and favorable relationship with economic growth. Rahman et al. (2017) research on significant developed and emerging nations discovered a reciprocal association between economic growth and trade openness. Rahman and Mamun (2016) conducted a separate study in Australia and arrived at the same conclusion. In their analysis, Eris and Ulasan (2013) failed to establish a correlation between trade liberalization and sustained economic progress. The effects of trade openness on the economic growth of Southeast European nations were examined by Fetahi-Vehapi et al. (2015). The research conducted by Rahman et al. (2020) revealed that the impact of trade openness on economic growth was favorable but contingent upon factors such as initial per capita income and other variables. Conversely, no significant correlation between these two parameters was identified without considering the abovementioned conditions. This finding is consistent with earlier research conducted by Taher (2020) which also showed a positive correlation between economic growth and trade openness. Musila and Yiheyis (2015) also looked at how trade openness affected investment levels and Kenya's pace of economic growth. According to their findings, a shift in trade openness impacts economic growth over the long term through its interaction with an increase in physical capital.

2.3 *Economic Growth and Population Density*

Population density was viewed as an exogenous variable in many prior research that looked at how population density affects agricultural production (Benin, 2006; Gebremedhin et al. 2006; Jansen et al. 2006; Warren, 2023). An academic demonstration conducted by Carlino et al. (2007) revealed that patent intensity positively correlates with employment density. According to their findings, a city with twice the employment density of another would experience a 20 percent increase in patent intensity. This finding suggests that higher levels of employment concentration can lead to increased innovation and technological advancement. S. Zhang et al. (2022b) findings demonstrate positive synergies and trade-offs when considering multiple objectives. They found synergy between efforts to minimize air pollutant emissions and identified a trade-off in minimizing energy consumption while maximizing employment opportunities.

According to Ciccone and Hall (1996), the availability of a wide range of intermediate goods can result in increased production yields owing to density. Additionally, they contend that density might lead to rising output returns. The creation of infrastructure was found to benefit from population density, as noted by Raupach et al. (2010) and Frederiksen (1981). Rahman's (2017) academic investigation into 11 Asian nations revealed a reciprocal relationship between Gross Domestic Product and population density. Furthermore, his research highlights the constructive impact of population expansion on economic advancement. This phenomenon was also confirmed by Musah et al.'s (2021) empirical study, which uncovered that government intervention may be crucial in harnessing population growth to promote knowledge-based economic development. The empirical findings of the above research show little agreement in the literature regarding the relationships between growth and CO_2 emissions, growth and trade openness, and growth and population density. The main causes of these discrepancies include country or regional variability in terms of economic development rates, energy consumption patterns, commerce and trade volume patterns, and population density. Hence, research focusing on particular nations or regions is essential to reduce ongoing disagreement in the literature. This new study will make a substantial contribution to the literature because it is based on the unique characteristics of South Asian countries.

3 Data and Methodology

This study covers 1971 to 2020 and includes five countries: Pakistan, China, India, Nepal, and Bangladesh. The consumption of energy (ECM) was estimated using kilograms of oil equivalent per capita. The GDP per capita was used to represent economic growth (EG), with CO_2 emissions measured in metric tons per capita. Trade (exports and imports) measures trade openness as a percentage of the GDP. We also used trade openness (percentage of GDP), natural resource depletion (percentage of GNI), and population density (people per sq. km of land area) as control variables. Further details regarding the variables.

The measurement trends are presented in Table 1 and Fig. 1.

This study employed the panel vector auto-regression (PVAR) technique. By combining the traditional VAR methodology, which assumes that the variables of

Table 1 The description of variables

Variable name	Variable code (symbols)	Unit of measurement	Source
Emission of CO_2	CO_2	Metric tons (per capita)	IEA
Energy consumption	ECM	Kg of oil equivalent (per capita)	World Bank (2020b)
Gross domestic product	GDP	Constant 2015 US$ (per capita)	World Bank (2020c)
Population density	POPD	People per sq. km of land area	World Bank (2020d)
Trade openness	TOP	Trade (% of GDP)	World Bank (2020e)
Natural resources depletion	NRD	% Of GNI	World Bank (2020a)

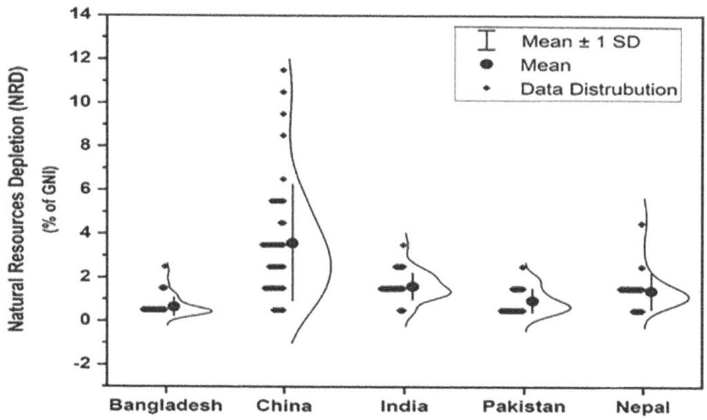

Fig. 1 Data trends of NRD in highly mountainous economies from 1971 to 2020. (*Source* Author's drawing)

the entire system are endogenous, with panel data analysis, which considers unobserved individual heterogeneity, PVAR offers the advantages of both approaches. The empirical model for economic growth (EG) Gross Domestic Product (GDP), consumption of energy (ECM), CO_2 emissions, and the control variables population density (POPD), trade openness (TOP), and natural resource depletion (NRD) are given in Eq. 1 considering the first-order PVAR, and the optimal lag for the model is selected as indicated by Andrews and Lu (2001). Therefore, the panel VAR for the first order is as follows:

$$Z_{it} = \eta_i + \Psi(I)Z_{it-1} + \upsilon_i + \Phi_t + \varepsilon_{it} \tag{1}$$

where i denotes the number of the countries ($i = 1,2.....5$), t indicates the time (from 1971 to 2020), Z_{it} is consumption of energy (EC) (ECM), economic growth (EG) (GDP), CO_2 dioxide emissions (CO_2) and the control variables population density (POPD), trade openness (TOP) and natural resource depletion (NRD), $\Psi(I)$ is the lag operator, v is an individual-specific effect, θ is the fixed time effect, and ε is the stochastic error term.

To remove the country-specific effect, estimate the following Eq. 2

$$\Delta Z_{it} = \Delta\eta_i + \Psi(I)\Delta Z_{it-1} + \Delta\upsilon_i + \Delta\Phi_t + \Delta\varepsilon_{it} \tag{2}$$

where Δ is the difference operator.

In contrast to conventional vector autoregressions, the system generalized method of moments (GMM) panel VAR expands the estimation period and enhances the precision and reliability of the findings. To obtain accurate and consistent estimates and overcome the weakness of the first difference, a system-generalized method of moments (System-GMM) is used.

This study calculated the orthogonal impulse response function (OIRF) to measure the reaction between endogenous variables. The expression for this computational function is as follows:

$$OIRF(S, C) = \frac{\vartheta y_{i,t+s}}{\vartheta(\eta_{i,t})_c} \tag{3}$$

In expression (3), $y_{i,t}$ is the endogenous variable, S is the shock number to C-th component $\eta_{i,t}$ (Figs. 2, 3, 4, 5 and 6).

4 Results and Discussion

This study analyzes the interconnectedness among economic growth, carbon emissions, and energy consumption in economies characterized by mountainous terrain. In Table 2, descriptive statistics disclose the average CO_2 emissions of 0.9568 kt CO_2 with maximum and minimum values of 7.5572 and 0.0162 kt of CO_2, respectively.

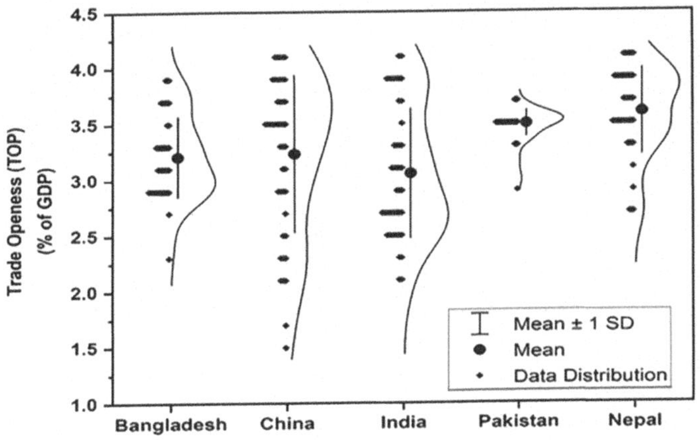

Fig. 2 Data distribution of TOP in highly mountainous economies from 1971 to 2020. (*Source* Author's drawing)

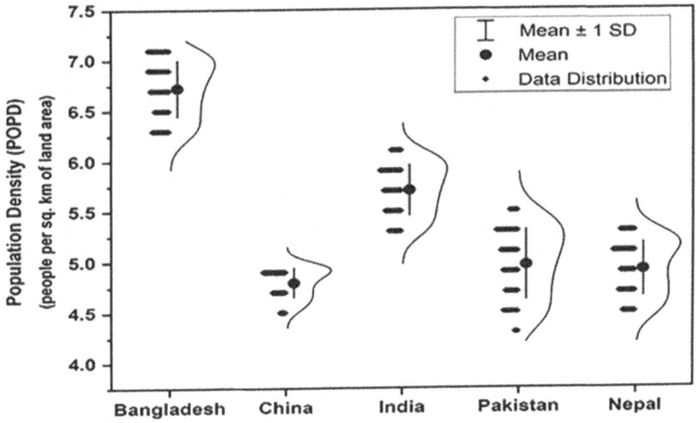

Fig. 3 Distribution of POPD in highly mountainous economies from 1971 to 2020. (*Source* Author's drawing)

The average urban population level was 5.4206, with the maximum value approaching 7.1104. The Pearson correlation results in Table 2 validate that CO_2 emissions are positively correlated with ECM, GDP, TOP, and NRD.

Note * denotes statistical significance at 10% level. (Panel data for 1971–2020).

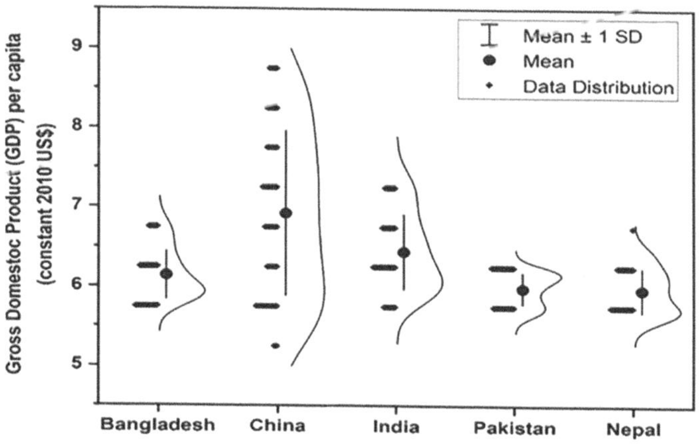

Fig. 4 Spatial distribution of GDP in highly mountainous economies from 1971 to 2020. (*Source* Author's drawing)

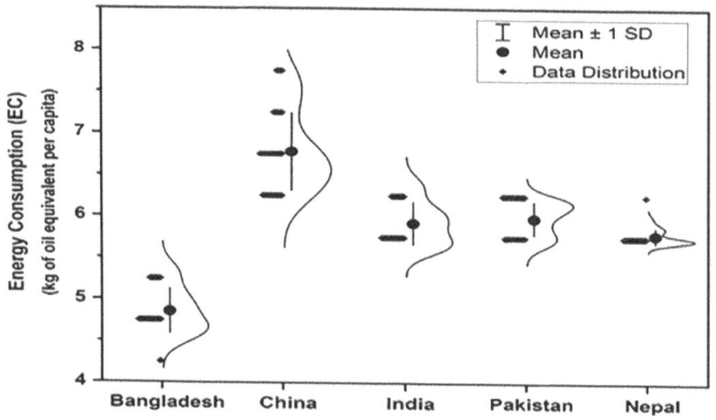

Fig. 5 Distribution of EC in highly mountainous economies from 1971 to 2020. (*Source* Author's drawing)

5 System-GMM PVAR Causality Results

The causal associations between economic growth, carbon emissions, and energy consumption are shown in Table 3, along with other control variables.

This study used the system-generalized moment PVAR method, forecast error variance decomposition, and impulse response functions to present the empirical results. Table 3 indicates the causal links among economic growth, trade openness, population density, carbon emissions, natural resource depletion, and energy consumption at the HME level. The findings in Table 3 suggest that the detrimental effects of CO_2 emissions on the GDP cannot be overlooked. This highlights the pressing need to address and mitigate carbon dioxide emissions to safeguard

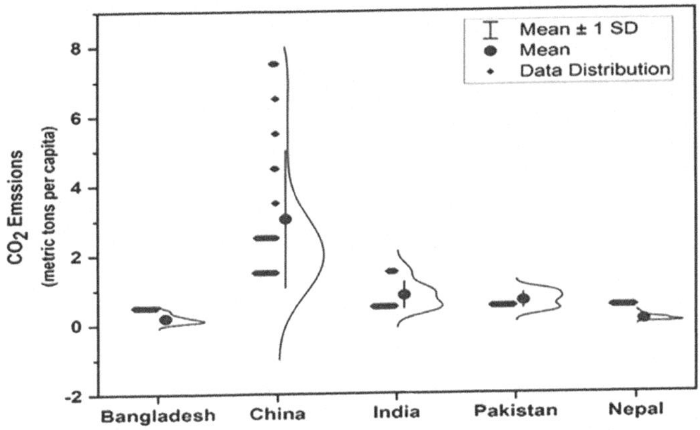

Fig. 6 Distribution pattern of CO_2 emissions in highly mountainous economies from 1971 to 2020. (*Source* Author's drawing)

economic growth and development. The data reveal a clear correlation between high levels of greenhouse gas emissions, such as CO_2, and negative consequences on GDP. The analysis suggests a direct correlation between rising air pollution levels and a decline in economic growth. This poses a significant threat to the economy and underscores the critical role that carbon emissions play in contributing to poor air quality across HMEs. The source of this degradation is predominantly industrial activities, which have severe consequences for public health and overall social well-being. These findings are consistent with previous studies conducted by Halimahton et al. (2012) indicating that without urgent intervention measures such as strict regulations on emissions or alternative energy sources being introduced.

Further deterioration may occur at an alarming rate, exposing the potential for future development of these nations. Zhang et al. (2023) suggested that to address environmental concerns effectively, policies should not only focus on promoting the advancement of renewable energy but also prioritize enhancing the implementation of carbon storage and utilization technologies. Some expert suggests that an increase in economic growth would not lead to increased energy consumption, contrary to previous studies by Saidi and Hammami (2015). The results revealed a clear cause-and-effect correlation between energy consumption and carbon emissions. Specifically, for every 1% increase in carbon emissions, there is an associated 3.287% increase in energy consumption. Several academics believed that energy consumption destroys ecosystems (H. Liu et al. 2023; López-Menéndez et al. 2014; Uddin et al. 2024). This has led to a higher proportion of non-renewable energy in the overall energy mix (Jebabli et al. 2023; Tong et al. 2020). Using coal, crude oil, and natural gas as energy sources is a non-renewable resource that pollutes the environment. These empirical findings are in line with Xia et al. (2022)

In contrast, research has revealed a negative correlation between economic growth and carbon emission. Specifically, for every 1% increase in economic growth, carbon emissions decreased by 0.004%. This finding emphasizes that, although increased

Table 2. Summary of descriptive statistics and correlation analysis

Variables	Mean	Std. Dev	Min	Max	CO_2	ECM	GDP	POPD	TOP	NRD
CO_2	0.9568	1.4019	0.0162	7.5572	1					
ECM	6.8907	2.2386	4.4497	12.0215	0.1444*	1				
GDP	6.2922	0.6518	5.4715	8.7174	0.8563*	−0.0045	1			
POPD	5.4206	0.7736	4.3493	7.1104	−0.2455*	−0.4369*	0.0872	1		
TOP	3.3169	0.5091	1.5935	4.1663	0.2578*	0.2604*	0.5289*	0.0127	1	
NRD	1.6375	1.6572	0.1212	11.4108	0.4076*	−0.0317	0.1929*	−0.3223*	−0.0973	1

Table 3 Results from the dynamic panel SYS-GMM models

Independent variables	Dependent variables					
	dCO_2	dECM	dGDP	dPOPD	dTOP	dNRD
dCO_2		3.287***	−0.412**	−5.629***	0.108**	−0.015***
		[0.000]	[0.017]	[0.000]	[0.034]	[0.001]
dECM-1	−0.066**		−0.188***	-0.545*	0.012	−0.004***
	[0.020]		[0.000]	[0.097]	[0.260]	[0.000]
dGDP-1	−0.004*	0.819***		−1.204***	0.090***	−0.007***
	[0.070]	[0.000]		[0.002]	[0.000]	[0.000]
dPOPD-1	−0.001***	−0.001	0.001		0.011	0.021
	[0.007]	[0.281]	[0.722]		[0.873]	[0.109]
dTOP-1	−0.801***	1.464***	−0.957***	−1.648		−0.007*
	[0.000]	[0.000]	[0.000]	[0.140]		[0.055]
dNRD-1	−4.312***	11.195***	3.068***	8.138	0.253	
	[0.000]	[0.000]	[0.001]	[0.191]	[0.256]	

Note ***, **,* mean significance levels at the 1%, 5% and 10%

income has positive effects on the environment, it does not fully compensate for the detrimental impact of economic growth on carbon emissions. It can be concluded from this finding that economic growth decreases the degradation of the environment, in line with empirical results identified by Asici (2013), Pao et al. (2011), Erdogan (2024), Tamazian et al. (2009) and Liu et al. (2017).

Furthermore, energy consumption hinders economic progress, as is evident from its negative relationship - an increase of 1% in energy usage leads to a decline of up to 1.88% in economic growth rates. This correlation illustrates excessive and inefficient utilization at the HME level, resulting in unfavorable effects on income levels. Menyah and Wolde-Rufael's (2010) research sports this stance regarding how energy consumption adversely impacts GDP advancement.

Moreover, there is an inverse relationship between the CO_2 emissions and energy consumption. A 1% increase in carbon emissions leads to a 0.66% drop in energy consumption, contradicting the positive effect observed by Apergis and Payne (2014a). The findings suggest that trade openness has a positive effect on energy consumption but negatively impacts economic growth and carbon emissions. Specifically, a 1% increase in trade openness decreased economic growth by 0.957% and carbon emissions by 0.801%. Additionally, the study revealed a positive relationship between CO_2 emissions and trade openness, with every 1% increase in CO_2 emissions leading to a 0.108% increase in trade openness.

Carbon emissions negatively affect population density and natural resource depletion. The results show that population density and natural resource depletion decrease by 5.629% and 0.015%, respectively, when carbon emissions increase by 1%. The correlation between economic growth and population density is crucial because it highlights the complex nature of human migration patterns. The increasing level of economic development results in an upsurge in individual income, which consequently leads to people's inclination towards urban areas where they can access better facilities and amenities. This trend also perpetuates due to the increase in family members resulting from higher incomes compared to those earning less. This connection emphasizes that socioeconomic factors play a critical role in shaping demographic shifts within society.

6 Forecast Error Variance Decomposition

This section provides the forecast error variance decomposition for economies with high mountainous terrains. Within a 10-year horizon, CO_2 emissions account for 0.4058% of the variance in consumption of energy (ECM), while they account for 0.3323% of the variance in CO_2 emissions (Table 4).

7 Impulse Response Analysis

Based on Monte Carlo simulations, this section provides response functions and 95% confidence interval bands. Using orthogonalized VAR residuals, we can isolate an economic growth (EG) shock from the consumption of energy (ECM) and CO_2 emission responses. Figure 1 illustrates how the consumption of energy (ECM) initially declines in response to a positive shock to economic growth (EG), but then gradually rises and stabilizes in the long run.

PVAR satisfies the stability conditions based on the stability graph. Consequently, the VAR model is stable when all given values are within the unit circle. Concerning the PVAR model stability and good forecasting and policy suggestions, the roots of the companion matrix show that there are many given values in the unit circle (Fig. 7).

8 Stability Graph

PVAR meets the stability conditions based on stability graphs. In the VAR model, all the companion matrices must be strictly less than one for the model to be stable (Abrigo and Love, 2016; Lütkepohl, 2005). Therefore, the VAR model is stable if all eigenvalues fall within the unit circle. A good indication of the stability of the PVAR models is that the eigenvalues for the HME parameters lie within the unit circle, indicating that the models can provide reliable forecasts and recommendations to policymakers (Fig. 8).

Table 4 Forecast-error variance decomposition

Forecast horizon		Impulse variable					
		dCO_2	dECM	dGDP	dPOPD	dTOP	dNRD
dCO_2							
0		0	0	0	0	0	0
1		1	0	0	0	0	0
2		0.6871	0.2954	0.0067	0.0001	0.0050	0.0057
3		0.6702	0.2889	0.0274	0.0010	0.0057	0.0068
4		0.6594	0.2948	0.0286	0.0020	0.0081	0.0070
5		0.6544	0.2980	0.0292	0.0026	0.0083	0.0076
6		0.6539	0.2973	0.0300	0.0029	0.0084	0.0075
7		0.6527	0.2981	0.0300	0.0032	0.0084	0.0076
8		0.6522	0.2982	0.0300	0.0036	0.0084	0.0076
9		0.6519	0.2980	0.0300	0.0041	0.0084	0.0076
10		0.6516	0.2979	0.0300	0.0045	0.0084	0.0076
decm							
0		0	0	0	0	0	0
1		0.4914	0.5086	0	0	0	0
2		0.4088	0.5616	0.0219	0.0000	0.0006	0.0072
3		0.4118	0.5404	0.0374	0.0002	0.0032	0.0071
4		0.4073	0.5431	0.0367	0.0003	0.0049	0.0077
5		0.4059	0.5432	0.0377	0.0003	0.0049	0.0079
6		0.4061	0.5425	0.0380	0.0003	0.0051	0.0079
7		0.4059	0.5427	0.0380	0.0003	0.0051	0.0079
8		0.4058	0.5427	0.0381	0.0003	0.0051	0.0080
9		0.4058	0.5427	0.0381	0.0003	0.0051	0.0080
10		0.4058	0.5427	0.0381	0.0003	0.0051	0.0080
dgdp							
0		0	0	0	0	0	0
1		0.2092	0.0100	0.7809	0	0	0
2		0.3624	0.1796	0.4158	0.0005	0.0316	0.0101
3		0.3192	0.2638	0.3702	0.0006	0.0306	0.0157
4		0.3252	0.2561	0.3706	0.0016	0.0311	0.0154
5		0.3238	0.2635	0.3626	0.0024	0.0319	0.0157
6		0.3228	0.2641	0.3624	0.0030	0.0318	0.0159
7		0.3230	0.2642	0.3618	0.0033	0.0318	0.0158
8		0.3227	0.2647	0.3612	0.0037	0.0318	0.0158
9		0.3225	0.2647	0.3610	0.0042	0.0318	0.0158
10		0.3223	0.2645	0.3608	0.0047	0.0318	0.0158

(continued)

Table 4 (continued)

Forecast horizon		Impulse variable					
		dCO_2	dECM	dGDP	dPOPD	dTOP	dNRD
dpopd							
0		0	0	0	0	0	0
1		0.0137	0.0219	0.0224	0.9420	0	0
2		0.0117	0.0257	0.0192	0.9425	0.0000	0.0009
3		0.0138	0.0492	0.0160	0.9201	0.0001	0.0008
4		0.0129	0.0616	0.0130	0.9118	0.0000	0.0006
5		0.0114	0.0649	0.0111	0.9119	0.0001	0.0006
6		0.0105	0.0656	0.0100	0.9132	0.0001	0.0007
7		0.0100	0.0665	0.0093	0.9134	0.0001	0.0007
8		0.0097	0.0676	0.0088	0.9131	0.0001	0.0007
9		0.0095	0.0687	0.0084	0.9127	0.0001	0.0007
10		0.0093	0.0694	0.0080	0.9126	0.0001	0.0007
dnrd							
0		0	0	0	0	0	0
1		0.1175	0.0010	0.0282	0.0068	0.0176	0.8289
2		0.1315	0.1027	0.0339	0.0059	0.0164	0.7097
3		0.1329	0.1124	0.0335	0.0062	0.0162	0.6988
4		0.1327	0.1133	0.0339	0.0066	0.0162	0.6974
5		0.1329	0.1133	0.0339	0.0070	0.0162	0.6967
6		0.1328	0.1133	0.0339	0.0074	0.0162	0.6963
7		0.1328	0.1133	0.0340	0.0077	0.0162	0.6960
8		0.1328	0.1134	0.0340	0.0080	0.0162	0.6957
9		0.1327	0.1134	0.0339	0.0084	0.0162	0.6954
10		0.1327	0.1134	0.0339	0.0087	0.0162	0.6952

9 Robustness Check

Tables 4 and 5 show the results of estimating all three models using the Augmented Mean Group (AMG) and Panel Granger Causality. Aligning with the system GMM are the findings of the AMG and Panel Granger Causality. These significant findings confirm the validity of the conclusions drawn from this study, indicating their applicability in policy.

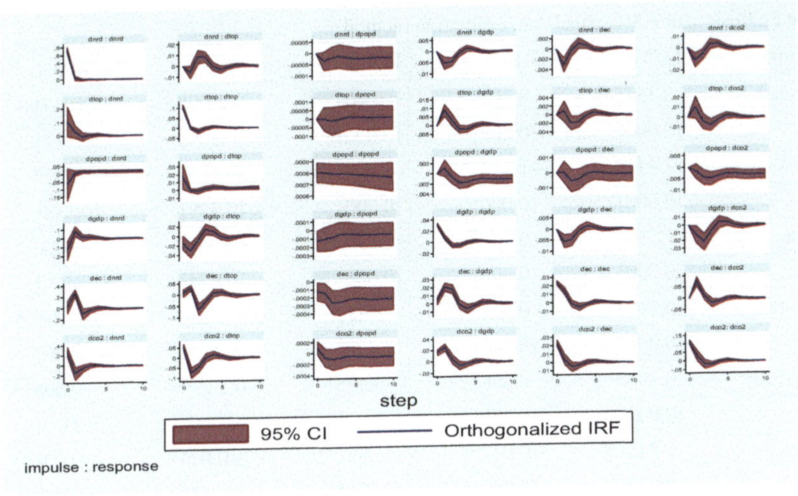

Fig. 7 Impulse response functions. (*Source* Author's drawing)

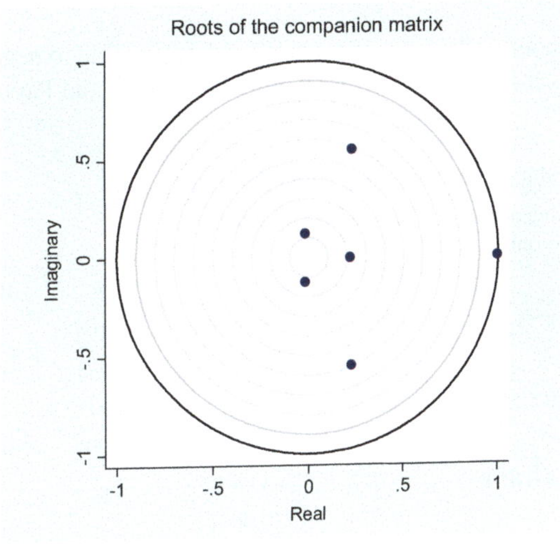

Fig. 8 HME stability graph. (*Source* Author's drawing)

10 Panel Granger Causality Results

Lastly, we carry out a panel Granger causality test to further understand the interconnectedness of the variables.

From Table 6, a complementary relationship appears between economic growth and energy consumption, as evidenced by the bidirectional relationship between GDP and ECM. A policy aimed at optimizing a country's consumption of energy efficiency

Table 5 Results of AMG panel data estimation method

Countries	ECM	GDP	POPD	TOP	NRD
Bangladesh	0.337***	0.108***	−0.407***	−0.008	−0.004
	[0.000]	[0.000]	[0.000]	[0.369]	[0.312]
China	3.445***	−1.122***	−25.741***	−0.112	−0.017
	[0.000]	[0.000]	[0.000]	[0.329]	[0.114]
India	1.756***	0.000***	−0.906***	0.015	−0.006
	[0.000]	[0.998]	[0.058]	[0.624]	[0.409]
Pakistan	0.391***	0.611***	−1.827***	−0.120***	0.031***
	[0.000]	[0.000]	[0.000]	[0.000]	[0.000]
Nepal	0.298***	0.346***	−0.575***	0.105***	−0.008**
	[0.003]	[0.000]	[0.000]	[0.000]	[0.020]
Panel	1.245**	−0.012*	−5.891**	−0.024*	−0.001**
	[0.043]	[0.069]	[0.036]	[0.065]	[0.046]

Note *, **, and *** denote statistical significance at the 0.10, 0.05 and 0.01 levels respectively. The figures are in parentheses [.] are the prob-values

under such circumstances would not be able to negatively affect real income as long as it enhances energy efficiency (Apergis and Payne, 2014b).

Table 6 Panel granger causality results

Independent variables	Dependent variables					
	dCO_2	dECM	dGDP	dPOPD	dTOP	dNRD
dCO_2		71.694***	5.719**	14.046***	4.474**	10.398***
		[0.000]	[0.017]	[0.000]	[0.034]	[0.001]
dECM-1	5.397**		17.961***	2.762*	1.270	15.962***
	[0.020]		[0.000]	[0.097]	[0.260]	[0.000]
dGDP-1	0.027	64.640***		9.900***	32.858***	13.495***
	[0.870]	[0.000]		[0.002]	[0.000]	[0.000]
dPOPD-1	7.304***	1.161	0.126		0.026	2.573
	[0.007]	[0.281]	[0.722]		[0.873]	[0.109]
dTOP-1	39.300***	53.778***	15.071***	2.177		3.675*
	[0.000]	[0.000]	[0.000]	[0.140]		[0.055]
dNRD-1	67.788***	93.107***	11.626***	1.711	1.290	
	[0.000]	[0.000]	[0.001]	[0.191]	[0.256]	

Note *, **, and *** denote statistical significance at the 0.10, 0.05 and 0.01 levels, respectively. The figures are in parentheses [.] are the prob-values

In addition, energy consumption, population density, trade openness, and natural resource depletion bi-directionally cause carbon emissions, whereas unidirectional causality extends from GDP to carbon emissions in highly mountainous economies.

11 Conclusions

Economic growth, the environment, and the relationship between economic growth and energy consumption have been studied extensively in academic literature over the years. In this study, we employed a dynamic causal relationship between economic growth, CO_2 emissions, and energy consumption for the first time. This approach allows us to analyze the interconnectedness of these factors in a new and comprehensive way. Panel data from five nations from 1971 to 2020 were used in this study. The study's policy implications are as follows. Empirical evidence shows a two-way correlation between energy consumption and economic growth, but that energy consumption negatively affects economic growth. The correlation between the Emission of CO_2 and GDP growth is uni-directional. CO_2 emissions negatively impact economic growth. Consumption of energy and CO_2 emissions are positively correlated.

The macroeconomic costs of environmental and energy conservation programs aimed at reducing CO_2 emissions have been highlighted in this study. As a result of the findings, as energy consumption and CO_2 emissions are not directly related, we believe that structural measures should be implemented to ensure robust economic growth because CO_2 emissions contribute to economic growth, and actions aimed at reducing them on the HME levels will likely restrain future growth.

12 Policy Implications

Governments in highly mountainous economies (HMEs) should implement more stringent regulations targeting emission-intensive sectors. The introduction of carbon pricing mechanisms, such as carbon taxes or cap-and-trade systems, could provide incentives for businesses to adopt cleaner technologies, thereby reducing CO_2 emissions without compromising economic growth. Policymakers should prioritize initiatives that promote the transition from non-renewable energy sources to renewable alternatives, including wind, solar, and hydropower. By establishing ambitious renewable energy targets and offering incentives such as tax credits for renewable energy projects, governments can reduce their dependence on fossil fuels, ultimately leading to a decrease in CO_2 emissions. Given that CO_2 emissions remain a critical challenge, investment in Carbon Capture and Storage technology could provide a pathway to mitigate the environmental impact of fossil fuel consumption. By subsidizing research and development in Carbon Capture and Storage, governments could facilitate the deployment of these technologies, enabling industries to reduce their carbon footprint rather than relying on extensive growth models focused on increasing output. Governments should promote intensive growth models that emphasize efficiency, productivity, and sustainability. This shift prioritizes long-term economic stability and environmental sustainability, supporting a balanced approach to development. Across sectors, including industry, agriculture, and transportation, this approach can foster innovation in energy conservation and environmental protection. Collaborations between government and private sectors can facilitate technological advancements that reduce emissions and promote sustainability. By adopting these strategies, policymakers can work towards sustainable economic growth while minimizing the adverse environmental impacts associated with energy consumption and CO_2 emissions. These recommendations support a transition towards more environmentally sustainable economies, particularly for HMEs, aligning with global climate goals and enhancing resilience against environmental degradation.

13 Limitations and Future Directions

The limitations of this study include several potential avenues for future research, and the study's focus on Highly Mountainous Economies (HMEs) may restrict the generalizability of the findings to other regions. Subsequent investigations should encompass diverse geographical areas to enhance their broader applicability. The panel estimation methodology employed in this study does not consider unique country-specific factors. Future research could use cross-country comparisons within HMEs, categorizing nations by economic development or energy dependency. Factors such as institutional quality and human capital were not considered in this study. Future investigations should explore how these variables influence sustainable development. The current study did not differentiate between renewable and non-renewable energy sources. Subsequent research can examine their distinct effects on sustainability. A more comprehensive time-series analysis could reveal short-term trends and capture the impact of policy changes and economic shifts. These research directions would enhance the robustness and relevance of the findings across diverse contexts.

References

Abrigo MRM, Love I (2016) Estimation of panel vector autoregression in Stata. Stata J 16(3):778–804. https://doi.org/10.1177/1536867X1601600314

Adebayo TS, Alola AA, Ullah S, Abbas S (2024) The growth impacts of agriculture value-added, energy utilization, and environmental degradation in Pakistan: Causality in continuous wavelet transform approach. Nat Res Forum 48(2):343–363. https://doi.org/10.1111/1477-8947.12306

Agboola MO, Bekun FV, Joshua U (2021) Pathway to environmental sustainability: Nexus between economic growth, energy consumption, CO_2 emission, oil rent and total natural resources rent in Saudi Arabia. Resour Policy 74:102380. https://doi.org/10.1016/j.resourpol.2021.102380

Ahmad S, Lavin A, Purdy S, Neurocomputing Z (2017) Unsupervised real-time anomaly detection for streaming data. Elsevier. https://www.sciencedirect.com/science/article/pii/S0925231217309864

Akbostancı E, Türüt-Aşık S, Tunç Gİ (2009) The relationship between income and environment in Turkey: Is there an environmental Kuznets curve? Energy Policy 37(3):861–867. https://doi.org/10.1016/j.enpol.2008.09.088

Al-Mulali U, Fereidouni HG, Lee JY, Sab CN (2013) Exploring the relationship between urbanization, energy consumption, and CO_2 emission in MENA countries. Elsevier

Anastacio JA (2017) Economic growth, CO_2 emissions and electric consumption: Is there an environmental Kuznets curve? An empirical study for North America countries. Dergipark.Org.Tr 7(2):65–71

Andreoni V, Galmarini S (2016) Drivers in CO_2 emissions variation: A decomposition analysis for 33 world countries. Energy 103:27–37

Andrews D, Econometrics, BL-J (2001) Consistent model and moment selection procedures for GMM estimation with application to dynamic panel data models. Elsevier 101: 123–164.

Apergis N, Payne JE (2014a) Renewable energy, output, carbon dioxide emissions, and oil prices: evidence from South America. Energy Sources, Part B: Economics, Planning, and Policy 10(3):281–287. https://doi.org/10.1080/15567249.2013.853713

Apergis N, Payne JE (2014b) Renewable Energy, Output, Carbon Dioxide Emissions, and Oil Prices: Evidence from South America. Energy Sources, Part B: Econ, Plan, Policy 10(3):281–287. https://doi.org/10.1080/15567249.2013.853713

Aşici AA (2013) Economic growth and its impact on environment: A panel data analysis. Ecol Ind 24:324–333. https://doi.org/10.1016/J.ECOLIND.2012.06.019

Awewomom J, Dzeble F, Takyi YD, Ashie WB, Ettey ENYO, Afua PE, Sackey LNA, Opoku F, Akoto, O (2024) Addressing global environmental pollution using environmental control techniques: a focus on environmental policy and preventive environmental management. Discov Environ 2(1):1–20. https://doi.org/10.1007/S44274-024-00033-5

Benin S (2006) Policies and programs affecting land management practices, input use, and productivity in the highlands of Amhara Region, Ethiopia. Strat Sustain Land Manag East Afr Highl, 217–256.

Bouoiyour, J (2003) Trade and GDP growth in Morocco: short-run or long-run causality? Revista Brasileira de Economia de Empresas 3(2).

Calderon CA, Servén L (2004) The effects of infrastructure development on growth and income distribution. Available at SSRN 625277.

Carlino GA, Chatterjee S, Hunt RM (2007) Urban density and the rate of invention. J Urban Econ 61(3):389–419

Chang C, Glover GH (2009) Relationship between respiration, end-tidal CO_2, and BOLD signals in resting-state fMRI. Neuroimage 47(4):1381–1393

Chopra R, Magazzino C, Shah MI, Sharma GD, Rao A, Shahzad U (2022) The role of renewable energy and natural resources for sustainable agriculture in ASEAN countries: Do carbon emissions and deforestation affect agriculture productivity? Resour Policy 76:102578. https://doi.org/10.1016/j.resourpol.2022.102578

Danish Ulucak R, Baloch MA (2023) An empirical approach to the nexus between natural resources and environmental pollution: Do economic policy and environmental-related technologies make any difference? Resources Policy, 81, 103361. https://doi.org/10.1016/j.resourpol.2023.103361

Destek MA, Sarkodie SA (2019) Investigation of environmental Kuznets curve for ecological footprint: The role of energy and financial development. Sci Total Environ 650:2483–2489. https://doi.org/10.1016/j.scitotenv.2018.10.017

Dingru L, Onifade ST, Ramzan M, AL-Faryan MAS (2023) Environmental perspectives on the impacts of trade and natural resources on renewable energy utilization in Sub-Sahara Africa: Accounting for FDI, income, and urbanization trends. Resources Policy, 80, 103204. https://doi.org/10.1016/j.resourpol.2022.103204

Dong K, Hochman G, Zhang Y, Sun R, Li H, Liao H (2018) CO_2 emissions, economic and population growth, and renewable energy: Empirical evidence across regions. Energy Economics 75:180–192. https://doi.org/10.1016/j.eneco.2018.08.017

Erdogan S (2024) Linking green fiscal policy, energy, economic growth, population dynamics, and environmental degradation: Empirical evidence from Germany. Energy Policy 189:114110. https://doi.org/10.1016/J.ENPOL.2024.114110

Eriş MN, Ulaşan B (2013) Trade openness and economic growth: Bayesian model averaging estimate of cross-country growth regressions. Econ Model 33:867–883

Ersoy E, Ulas U (2013) Energy consumption and stock market relationship: Evidence from turkey. International Journal of Energy Economics and Policy 3(4):34–40

Fan Z, Wang K, Wei T, Yan J, Song L, Carbon BS (2010) An environmentally friendly and efficient route for the reduction of graphene oxide by aluminum powder. Elsevier

Fetahi-Vehapi M, Sadiku L, Petkovski M (2015) Empirical analysis of the effects of trade openness on economic growth: An evidence for South East European countries. Procedia Economics and Finance 19:17–26

Fletcher C, Ripple WJ, Newsome T, Barnard P, Beamer K, Behl A, Bowen J, Cooney M, Crist E, Field C, Hiser, K, Karl, DM, King DA., Mann ME, McGregor DP, Mora C, Oreskes N, Wilson M (2024) Earth at risk: an urgent call to end the age of destruction and forge a just and sustainable future. PNAS Nexus 3(4). https://doi.org/10.1093/PNASNEXUS/PGAE106

Fodha M, Zaghdoud O (2010) Economic growth and pollutant emissions in Tunisia: An empirical analysis of the environmental Kuznets curve. Energy Policy 38(2):1150–1156. https://doi.org/10.1016/J.ENPOL.2009.11.002

Freund C, Bolaky B (2008) Trade, regulations, and income. J Dev Econ 87(2):309–321

Gebremedhin B, Hoekstra D, Tegegne A (2006) Commercialization of Ethiopian agriculture: extension service from input supplier to knowledge broker and facilitator. International Livestock Research Institute

Ghani GM (2012) Does trade liberalization effect energy consumption? Energy Policy 43:285–290. https://doi.org/10.1016/j.enpol.2012.01.005

González-Álvarez MA, Montañés A (2023) CO_2 emissions, energy consumption, and economic growth: Determining the stability of the 3E relationship. Econ Model 121:106195. https://doi.org/10.1016/J.ECONMOD.2023.106195

Grossman G, Economics AKT (1995) Economic growth and the environment. Academic.Oup.Com.

Halimahton B, Elsadig MA, Mizan H (2012) The impact of CO_2 on economic growth in Asian 8. Procedia Soc Behav Sci 35(2012):389–397

Hall RE, Jones CI (1996) The productivity of nations. National Bureau of Economic Research Cambridge, Mass., USA

Hunter N, Walsh B, Delgado Ramos, GC, Greenwalt J, Roberts D, Oke C, Nielsen D, Slotow R (2023) Cities and climate change science after Edmonton: Knowledge, people, and organisations' influence and outreach. Curr Res Environ Sustain 6:100231. https://doi.org/10.1016/j.crsust.2023.100231

Jahanger A, Hossain MR, Usman M, Onwe JC (2023) Recent scenario and nexus between natural resource dependence, energy use and pollution cycles in BRICS region: Does the mediating role of human capital exist? Resour Policy 81:103382

Jansen HGP, Rodriguez A, Damon A, Pender J, Chenier J, Schipper R (2006) Determinants of income-earning strategies and adoption of conservation practices in hillside communities in rural Honduras. Agric Syst 88(1):92–110

Jebabli I, Lahiani A, Mefteh-Wali S (2023) Quantile connectedness between CO_2 emissions and economic growth in G7 countries. Resour Policy 81:103348. https://doi.org/10.1016/J.RESOURPOL.2023.103348

Jiang Q, Rahman ZU, Zhang X, Guo Z, Xie Q (2022) An assessment of the impact of natural resources, energy, institutional quality, and financial development on CO_2 emissions: Evidence from the B&R nations. Resour Policy 76:102716. https://doi.org/10.1016/j.resourpol.2022.102716

Joseph S, Wood A (2010) Assessment of positive functioning in clinical psychology: Theoretical and practical issues. Clin Psychol Rev 30(7):830–838. https://doi.org/10.1016/j.cpr.2010.01.002

Kashem MA, Rahman MM (2019) CO_2 emissions and development indicators: a causality analysis for Bangladesh. Environmental Processes 6:433–455

Kaya Y, Yokobori K (1998) Environment, energy and economy: Strategies for sustainability

Khan SAR, Ahmad Z, Sheikh AA, Yu Z (2023a) Green technology adoption paving the way toward sustainable performance in circular economy: a case of Pakistani small and medium enterprises. Int J Innov Sci, Ahead-Of-Print(ahead-of-print). https://doi.org/10.1108/IJIS-10-2022-0199

Khan SAR, Sheikh AA, Ahmad Z (2023b) Developing the interconnection between green employee behavior, tax avoidance, green capability, and sustainable performance of SMEs through corporate social responsibility. J Clean Prod 419:138236. https://doi.org/10.1016/j.jclepro.2023.138236

Kharrazi A, Rovenskaya E, Fath BD, Yarime M, Kraines S (2013) Quantifying the sustainability of economic resource networks: an ecological information-based approach. Ecol Econ 90:177–186. https://doi.org/10.1016/j.ecolecon.2013.03.018

Kraft K (1978) On the relationship between energy and GNP. JSTOR

Liu X, Zhang S, Bae J (2017) The nexus of renewable energy-agriculture-environment in BRICS. Appl Energy 204:489–496. https://doi.org/10.1016/J.APENERGY.2017.07.077

Liu H, Wong WK, The Cong P, Nassani AA, Haffar M, Abu-Rumman A (2023) Linkage among Urbanization, energy Consumption, economic growth and carbon Emissions. Panel data analysis for China using ARDL model. Fuel 332:126122. https://doi.org/10.1016/J.FUEL.2022.126122

Looney R, Frederiksen P (1981) The regional impact of infrastructure investment in Mexico. Reg Stud 15(4):285–296

López-Menéndez AJ, Pérez R, Moreno B (2014) Environmental costs and renewable energy: re-visiting the Environmental Kuznets Curve. J Environ Manage 145:368–373. https://doi.org/10.1016/J.JENVMAN.2014.07.017

Lütkepohl H (2005) New introduction to multiple time series analysis. New Introd Mult Time Ser Anal, 1–764. https://doi.org/10.1007/978-3-540-27752-1/COVER

Martínez-Zarzoso I, Bengochea-Morancho A (2004) Pooled mean group estimation of an environmental Kuznets curve for CO_2. Econ Lett 82(1):121–126. https://doi.org/10.1016/j.econlet.2003.07.008

Menyah K, Wolde-Rufael Y (2010) Energy consumption, pollutant emissions and economic growth in South Africa. Energy Economics 32(6):1374–1382. https://doi.org/10.1016/J.ENECO.2010.08.002

Mirza F, Kanwal A (2017) Energy consumption, carbon emissions and economic growth in Pakistan: Dynamic causality analysis. Elsevier

Muftau O, Iyoboyi M, Ademola AS (2014) An empirical analysis of the relationship between CO_2 emission and economic growth in West Africa. American Journal of Economics 4(1):1–17

Murtaugh PA, Schlax MG (2009) Reproduction and the carbon legacies of individuals. Glob Environ Chang 19(1):14–20. https://doi.org/10.1016/j.gloenvcha.2008.10.007

Musah M, Owusu-Akomeah M, Boateng, F, Iddris F, Mensah IA, Antwi SK, Agyemang JK (2021) Long-run equilibrium relationship between energy consumption and CO_2 emissions: a dynamic heterogeneous analysis on North Africa. Environ Sci Pollut Res 1–18.

Musila JW, Yiheyis Z (2015) The impact of trade openness on growth: The case of Kenya. Journal of Policy Modeling 37(2):342–354

Omri A (2013) CO_2 emissions, energy consumption and economic growth nexus in MENA countries: Evidence from simultaneous equations models. Energy Economics 40:657–664. https://doi.org/10.1016/J.ENECO.2013.09.003

Ozturk I, Acaravci A (2013) The long-run and causal analysis of energy, growth, openness and financial development on carbon emissions in Turkey. Energy Economics 36:262–267. https://doi.org/10.1016/j.eneco.2012.08.025

Pao HT, Yu HC, Yang YH (2011) Modeling the CO_2 emissions, energy use, and economic growth in Russia. Energy 36(8):5094–5100. https://doi.org/10.1016/J.ENERGY.2011.06.004

Ang JB (2007) CO_2 emissions, energy consumption, and output in France. Elsevier. https://doi.org/10.1016/j.enpol.2007.03.032

Rahman MM, Kashem MA (2017) Carbon emissions, energy consumption and industrial growth in Bangladesh: Empirical evidence from ARDL cointegration and Granger causality analysis. Energy Policy 110:600–608

Rahman MM, Mamun SAK (2016) Energy use, international trade and economic growth nexus in Australia: new evidence from an extended growth model. Renew Sustain Energy Rev 64:806–816

Rahman MM, Saidi K, Mbarek MB (2020) Economic growth in South Asia: the role of CO_2 emissions, population density and trade openness. Heliyon 6(5):e03903. https://doi.org/10.1016/j.heliyon.2020.e03903

Raihan A, Tuspekova A (2022) Role of economic growth, renewable energy, and technological innovation to achieve environmental sustainability in Kazakhstan. Curr Res Environ Sustain 4:100165. https://doi.org/10.1016/j.crsust.2022.100165

Raupach MR, Rayner PJ, Paget M (2010) Regional variations in spatial structure of nightlights, population density and fossil-fuel CO_2 emissions. Energy Policy 38(9):4756–4764. https://doi.org/10.1016/j.enpol.2009.08.021

Saidi K, Hammami S (2015) The impact of CO_2 emissions and economic growth on energy consumption in 58 countries. Energy Rep 1:62–70

Saidi K, Mbarek MB (2017) The impact of income, trade, urbanization, and financial development on CO_2 emissions in 19 emerging economies. Environ Sci Pollut Res 24:12748–12757

Salahuddin M, Gow J (2014) Economic growth, energy consumption and CO_2 emissions in Gulf Cooperation Council countries. Energy 73:44–58. https://doi.org/10.1016/J.ENERGY.2014.05.054

Sarkar D (2008) Multivariate data visualization with R. Use R

Sbia R, Shahbaz M, Hamdi H (2014) A contribution of foreign direct investment, clean energy, trade openness, carbon emissions and economic growth to energy demand in UAE. Econ Model 36:191–197. https://doi.org/10.1016/j.econmod.2013.09.047

Shahbaz M, Sbia R, Hamdi H, Ozturk I (2014) Economic growth, electricity consumption, urbanization and environmental degradation relationship in United Arab Emirates. Elsevier. https://www.sciencedirect.com/science/article/pii/S1470160X14002246

Shareef F, Sheikh M, Paradigms MJ (1996) Urbanization and Environmental Kuznets Curve in Pakistan: a Cointegration Analysis. Researchgate.Net. https://doi.org/10.24312/paradigms110205

Sohag K, Begum RA, Abdullah SMS, Jaafar M (2015) Dynamics of energy use, technological innovation, economic growth and trade openness in Malaysia. Energy 90:1497–1507

Soytas and economics, R S.-E., 2009, undefined, Sari, R., Economics, B. E.-E., 2007, undefined, Apergis, N., & Payne, J. E., 2009Apergis N, Payne JE (2009) Energy consumption and economic growth in Central America: Evidence from a panel cointegration and error correction model. Elsevier 31(2):211–216. https://doi.org/10.1016/J.ENECO.2008.09.002

Stern N (2008) The economics of climate change. American Economic Review 98(2):1–37. https://doi.org/10.1257/AER.98.2.1

Sultana T, Hossain MS, Voumik LC, Raihan A (2023) Does globalization escalate the carbon emissions? Empirical evidence from selected next-11 countries. Energy Rep 10:86–98. https://doi.org/10.1016/J.EGYR.2023.06.020

Taher H (2020) Financial development and economic growth impact on the environmental degradation in Lebanon. Int J Energy Econ Policy

Tamazian A, Chousa JP, Vadlamannati KC (2009) Does higher economic and financial development lead to environmental degradation: Evidence from BRIC countries. Energy Policy 37(1):246–253. https://doi.org/10.1016/J.ENPOL.2008.08.025

Tong T, Ortiz J, Xu C, Li F (2020) Economic growth, energy consumption, and carbon dioxide emissions in the E7 countries: A bootstrap ARDL bound test. Energy, Sustainability and Society 10(1):1–17. https://doi.org/10.1186/S13705-020-00253-6/FIGURES/2

Uddin H, Ahammed S, Rana MM, Majumder SC (2024) Investigating the relationship between environmental quality and tourism industry in Thailand. Environ Dev Sustain 26(5):12339–12365. https://doi.org/10.1007/S10668-023-03801-0/METRICS

Wang J, Azam W (2024) Natural resource scarcity, fossil fuel energy consumption, and total greenhouse gas emissions in top emitting countries. Geosci Front 15(2):101757. https://doi.org/10.1016/J.GSF.2023.101757

Wang Q, Li C, Li R (2023) How does renewable energy consumption and trade openness affect economic growth and carbon emissions? International evidence of 122 countries. Energy & Environ. https://doi.org/10.1177/0958305X231169010

Warren F (2023) Population density, urbanisation and agricultural mechanisation in modern Ghana. Rev Dev Econ 27(3):1605–1629. https://doi.org/10.1111/RODE.13007

World Bank (2020a) Adjusted savings: natural resources depletion (% of GNI) | Data. https://data.worldbank.org/indicator/NY.ADJ.DRES.GN.ZS

World Bank (2020b) Energy use (kg of oil equivalent per capita) | Data. https://data.worldbank.org/indicator/EG.USE.PCAP.KG.OE

World Bank (2020c) GDP (constant 2015 US$) | Data. https://data.worldbank.org/indicator/NY.GDP.MKTP.KD

World Bank (2020d) Population density (people per sq. km of land area) | Data. https://data.worldbank.org/indicator/EN.POP.DNST

World Bank (2020e) Trade (% of GDP) | Data. https://data.worldbank.org/indicator/NE.TRD.GNFS.ZS

World Bank (2020f) World Development Indicators | DataBank. World Bank

Xia W, Apergis N, Bashir MF, Ghosh S, Doğan B, Shahzad U (2022) Investigating the role of globalization, and energy consumption for environmental externalities: empirical evidence from developed and developing economies. Renewable Energy 183:219–228

Yusuf A (2023) Dynamic effects of energy consumption, economic growth, international trade and urbanization on environmental degradation in Nigeria. Energ Strat Rev 50:101228. https://doi.org/10.1016/J.ESR.2023.101228

Zhang Z, Yu Y, Kharrazi A (2023) Unstable decoupling of CO_2 emissions from sectoral economic growth calls for decarbonization policies based on multi-perspective accounting: a case study of Zhejiang. China. Environmental Science and Pollution Research 30(20):57503–57517. https://doi.org/10.1007/s11356-023-26513-4

Zhang S, Yu Y, Kharrazi A, Ren H, Ma T (2022a). How can structural change contribute to concurrent sustainability policy targets on GDP, emissions, energy, and employment in China? Energy 256:124614. https://doi.org/10.1016/j.energy.2022.124614

Zhang S, Yu Y, Kharrazi A, Ren H, Ma T (2022b) Quantifying the synergy and trade-offs among economy–energy–environment–social targets: a perspective of industrial restructuring. J Environ Manag 316:115285. https://doi.org/10.1016/j.jenvman.2022.115285

Zubair AO, Abdul Samad A-R, Dankumo, AM (2020) Does gross domestic income, trade integration, FDI inflows, GDP, and capital reduces CO_2 emissions? An empirical evidence from Nigeria. Curr Res Environ Sustain 2:100009. https://doi.org/10.1016/j.crsust.2020.100009

Environmental Kuznets Curve in Pacific Nations: Ict and Renewable Dynamics

Muhammad Sibt-e-Ali, Laeeq Razzak Janjua, Syed Muhammad Faraz Raza, and Kashif Javed

Abstract Information and Communications Technology has become the main driver for growth generation in the economies of East Asia and the Pacific. Besides, the uneven distribution of ICT along with renewable energy, resource rents, and urbanization threatens environmental sustainability. The study collected data from 1990 to 2023 of ten East Asia and Pacific developing economies. The main findings advantages to the study by achieving the EKC hypothesis. Based on panel FMOLS & DOLS estimation the findings economic growth enhances CO2 emission and squared term growth reduces CO2 emission; therefore, the inverted U shape of EKC has been ascertained in the long run. A pure form of energy, renewable energy reduces CO_2 emissions and mitigates environmental deterioration, while resource rents weaken environmental sustainability. Moreover, urbanization and ICT deteriorate environmental sustainability by surging CO_2 emissions. The overall findings showed the devastating influences of indicators that hurt environmental sustainability. Policy-makers should revitalize the natural resources and utilization of renewable energies for a clean environment. The distribution of natural resources in a more sustainable way and the tapping of deeper renewable resources is needed for urbanization. Along with that, ICT infrastructure development based on an innovative instructional ICT approach and green ICT should be implemented for environmental efficiency.

Keywords Technology · EKC · Economic properity · Urban population · Renewable energy rsources

M. Sibt-e-Ali
School of Business, Zhengzhou University, ZhengzhouHenan Province 450001, China

L. R. Janjua (✉)
WSB University, Dąbrowa Górnicza, Poland
e-mail: laeeq.janjua@wsb.edu.pl

S. M. F. Raza
School of Economics and Management, Wuhan University, Wuhan, China

K. Javed
School of Law, Zhengzhou University, Zhengzhou, China

S. A. R. Khan et al. (eds.), *Circular Economy and Technological Innovation*, Industrial Ecology, https://doi.org/10.1007/978-981-96-5650-9_9

1 Introduction

Over the last few decades, ICT has been one of the most recognized technological advancements, and its uses have been increased around the World. According to the Global Information Technology Report 2020 under the Network Readiness Index 2020, the digital transformation reflects technology and people, influencing the economy and environment. However, ICT is the digital revolution and introducing new business models to drive economic growth (World Economic Forum 2020). Information and communication technology is the backbone and essential element of the global economy in modern times (Voronkova et al. 2023). ICT benefits in socio-economic and increases the living standard of society (Danish et al. 2018). According to OECD, ICT has changed the economic structure of the world's economy by the increasingly global supply chain and economic prosperity (Del Baldo 2023; Iram et al. 2024). In terms of Asia and the Pacific, the growth in ICT is incredible, and some of East Asia and Pacific economies are the top performers of ICT growth. In this regard, Malaysia, Thailand, China, Mongolia, and the Philippines are the leading performer of ICT growth from East Asia and the Pacific region and ranked amongst the top 15 in the region (International Telecommunication Union ICT Development Index 2017).

ICT is one of the most influential indicators that affect the environmental conditions of the world economies. Though ICT is the best indicator to control the environmental issues, in contrary, uplifting ICT use is a major cause of high green energy demand and deterioration of environmental sustainability (ES). The contribution of ICT to global carbon emissions is extremely high (Wang et al. 2024; Ulucak and Khan 2020). ICT has direct and indirect influences on the environment. However, from East Asia and Pacific points of view, ICT is cheaply available, increasing its consumption and directly influencing environmental efficiency. However, the ICT also escalates the energy demand and indirectly affects the environmental conditions of East Asia and the Pacific region. ICT is expected to control CO_2 emissions in Asia; conversely, it is also likely to increase emissions of ICT sectors (Global e-Sustainability Initiative 2020). Further, it is admitted fact regarding its accessible approach. The advancement in the ICT sector in East Asia and the Pacific region scopes its consequence for long-term sustainability in East Asia and Pacific economies. It will be interesting to see whether the increase in its consumption degrade the environment or the advancement and its sustainable approach meets the environmental standards.

Urbanization is a positive sign for a country's social development and a symbol of human society. Urban attractiveness contributes to economic well-being by opening up the path for tourists, foreign investors, and the environment. Urban areas are essential for economic growth because the world's urban areas generate 70% of GDP. According to UN stats, urbanization increased 50% globally and is expected to growth 67% in the future. The world energy resources used in the urbanization process are mostly non-renewable resources i.e. oil, coal, and natural gas, and about 72%. On the other hand, 70% of energy is generated from renewables for urbanization (World Bank 2020a, b). Though, it is common and expected that urbanized cities emit

CO_2 while consuming non-renewable energy and mitigate ES. In contrast, renewable energy consumption (RENE) areas are less polluted and maintain ES. In East Asia and the Pacific, countries have faced challenges in renewable energy production and consumption, and environmental issues are extremely crucial. However, most cities are in urban process, and environmental pressure can increase due to the abundance of resource consumption. Regarding reducing global warming, a conference was conducted on climate change by the UN Environment programs in 2019 (UN 2019). It is evident that the East Asian leading economy China has overcome the environmental pressure following sustainable urban process, efficient natural resource and renewables consumption, and with the help of technological advancement (Fang et al. 2021). So, it will be interesting to see how these indicators will react to the environment of developing East Asian and Pacific economies.

The emerging East Asian and Pacific economies follow modern trends i.e. ICT, renewable energy, urbanization, natural resource rents to preserve environmental cleanliness. However, the problem is that these developing economies have serious concerns over their economic situation, which demands economic progression. While, the high abundance of these indicators will undoubtedly deteriorate the environment, which itself is a great threat to their prosperity. In this regard, the study will significantly measure the ES in East Asia and Pacific developing economies by following the best possible combination of economic growth with its squared effects, ICT, renewable energy, urbanization, natural resource rents. However, the study has some objectives which demand to achieve. The first goal of this analysis is to observe the squared influence of EGR on CO_2 emissions and possible confirmation of inverted U shape EKC for East Asia and Pacific developing economies. The second objective is to examine the role of ICT and urbanization for ES. However, it is also one objective to measure the renewable energy influence on secretions of carbon dioxide. Though, these countries have been non-renewable abundant for a long time. So, it will be interesting that how renewable adaptation will manage environmental sustainability in selected economies. Furthermore, we can't deny the importance of natural resource rents because East Asia and Pacific developing nations are resource-abundant. It will be interesting to measure whether these resource rents are sustainable and efficient to manage environmental sustainability.

ICT technologies are important in the effective integration and management of dispersed renewable energy sources, such as solar, wind, and hydroelectric power (Kothari et al. 2021). Renewable energy generation is inherently variable, with production depending on natural conditions-sunlight and wind patterns. On the other hand, ICT solutions, such as smart grids and predictive analytics, help balance these out and stabilize supply and demand (Panda and Das 2021). Smart grids make use of advanced sensors, real-time data collection, and communication systems to monitor and control energy flows (Dileep 2020).It will be able to integrate renewable energies easily into the already existing grids and maintain stability and reliability within the same. Moreover, solar panels and wind turbines can generate more power at a given time, which smart grids can store or redistribute efficiently (Khalid 2024). Additionally, ICT enables real-time monitoring of renewable energy installations, hence the rapid identification and resolution of issues for maximum output.

Likewise, big data and AI are transforming the renewable energy sector (Li et al. 2023). AI algorithms analyze vast amounts of data to predict energy production and consumption patterns. For example, predictive maintenance systems use AI to identify potential faults in wind turbines or solar panels before they occur, reducing downtime and increasing efficiency (Farrar et al. 2023). Big data is also instrumental in optimizing energy consumption through weather patterns, energy market analysis, and users' behaviour. Similarly, solar energy systems will change according to the amount of sunlight expected using the forecast (Krishnan et al. 2023). In addition, wind farms adjust the position of the turbines based on the given real-time data to result in maximum efficiency. Renewable systems will thus be reliable and cheap, leveraging such insights. Energy storage is a critical part of renewable energy systems, and ICT contributes significantly to this advancement (Sayed et al. 2023). Technologies such as battery management systems depend on ICT for monitoring and control of energy storage devices; these systems ensure efficiency in the charging and discharging and long-term storage of renewable energy (Earthineni and Rao 2023). In addition, ICT enables peer-to-peer energy trading and decentralized distribution. Block chain technology, a subset of ICT, develops transparent and secure platforms over which users can trade excess energy (Wang and Guo 2024). That approach stimulates community-based renewable energy projects and democratizes access to clean energy (Ikevuje et al. 2023). ICT enhances energy efficiency by availing to the user in real time the amount of energy consumed. Smart meters and mobile applications enable consumers to track and manage their energy usage, thereby creating a platform that encourages people to save energy. Furthermore, it reduces costs for individuals and contributes to the greater good of reducing carbon emissions. Likewise, ICT allows for VPPs, which pool the resources of distributed energy sources, such as rooftop solar panels and small-scale wind turbines, into one integrated entity (Aghamolaei and Fallahpour 2023). VPPs use ICT in order to optimize energy generation and distribution, further enhancing grid resilience and sustainability. ICT also plays a very key role in driving innovation and informing energy policy (Ibekwe et al. 2024). Advanced modelling and simulation tools help policymakers to evaluate the impact of renewable energy projects and design effective strategies. ICT-enabled platforms facilitate collaboration among stakeholders, including governments, private companies, and research institutions, thereby accelerating the adoption of renewable energy technologies.

However, the chapter structure is as follows: This existing section introduces the indicators, their significance, problems, and objectives. After this, Sect. 2 review the literature following three sub-sections and the research gap addressed in this research. Section 3 contains the data and variables, constructs the theoretical and econometric models, and provides the methodology approaches. Further, Sect. 4 interpret and discuss the results with economic reasons, while Sect. 5 concludes the paper with implications, limitations, and future directions.

2 Literature Review

2.1 ICT on Environmental Sustainability

Information and communication technology is a noticeable factor for economic well-being (Bilan et al. 2023). Rehman et al. (2023) explored the influence of ICT, institutional quality, energy consumption and EGR on environment within the EKC framework in ASEAN countries using data from 1990 to 2018. Furthermore, the study examines how the ecological footprint is affected by the interplay between ICT and institutional quality. To verify cross-section reliance, stationarity, and cointegration among parameters, they used Westerlund's cointegration tests, cross-section unit root, and cross-section dependency in the econometric analysis. For both short- and long-term estimation, they also used the PMG approach. The PMG estimates display that by reducing the ecological impact, ICT and institutional quality improve the environment. Furthermore, environmental degradation is also moderated by the joint effects of ICT and institutional quality. Additionally, when EGR and energy use rise, so does the ecological impact. Besides, the findings also prove the EKC theory within ASEAN nations. The findings advocates that ICT innovation and diffusion or improvement in the institutional quality framework can achieve the sustainable development goal of ES. However, the environment is the most concerning subject, usually ignored. The environment-friendly intensity of ICT can be favorable for economic well-being and the environment. There is some evidence of past studies which can be helpful to give an idea about the influence of ICT on the environment of different economies. Zhang and Liu (2015) elaborated that ICT significantly reduces CO_2 secretions in the central and eastern regions while inconsequential in China's western region. In the panel evidence of the OECD, ICT has not mitigated carbon dioxide emissions, and resultantly the increased CO2 secretions deteriorated the environment (Salahuddin et al. 2016). However, Danish et al. (2019) explored that ICT expressively mitigate CO_2 emissions in economies with high and middle income levels. Further, EKC theory was proven in all income groups countries. Asongu et al. (2019) elaborated that the ICT effects have diminished the CO_2 emissions in Sub-Saharan African economies. In another evidence of Sub-Saharan African economies, ICT has deteriorated the environmental quality. In contrast, the squared of EGR has mitigated CO_2 emissions and proven the EKC theory in Sub-Saharan African nations (Avom et al. 2020). In Latin American and Caribbean regions, the improvement in globalization and ICT has lessened carbon secretions and led to environmental sustainability, while economic growth and urbanization are opposed (Ahmed et al. 2021). In some large panel evidence, ICT has reduced carbon dioxide emissions, and the usage of ICT brings into being environmentally friendly for low income economies. In comparison, it hurts the ES in economies with middle and high per capita income (N'dri et al. 2021; Alatas 2021). In some shreds of evidence, ICT contribute to CO_2 secretions, while the efficiency and structure of information and communication investments mitigate CO_2 emissions (Lahouel et al. 2021; Wang et al. 2021).

2.2 ICT, Economic Growth and Renewable Energy on Environmental Sustainability

Haldar et al. (2023) used data for 16 emerging economies from 2000 to 2018 to validate the claim that ICT, internet use, and technical innovation in particular bring about structural changes that serve as a catalyst for economic growth. They have looked into how the EGR is affected by ICT, innovation, electricity consumption, and RENE. The results show that ICT promotes EGR monotonically while it also improves the impact of financial development on growth. ICT, however, has been shown to amplify the detrimental consequences of trade on EGR. An income-level analysis was conducted using both conditional and unconditional panel quantile estimators to capture these heterogeneities among these economies. Their findings demonstrate that internet use considerably boosts growth in the lower and middle income quantiles; innovation has a significant negative impact on growth, with the exception of the highest income quantile; and electricity consumption has a positive growth effect that is verified across all quantiles. TO succeed ecologically sustainable EGR, these findings imply that expanding internet connectivity may have a network effect and enhance these emerging economies' capital markets in addition to boosting the production of renewable electricity.

ICT and economic growth efforts are for economic wellbeing, while the environmental factor is mainly ignored by these factors usually when it comes to economic wellbeing. However, renewable energy is the aspect that generally assists in maintaining environmental sustainability without compromising economic wellbeing. There are some shreds of evidence of previous researches to reach us the consequences of the influences of ICT, EGR, and RENE on the environment. Al-Mulali et al. (2016) revealed that reneawable form of energy is noteworthy in reducing CO_2 emissions in South Asia, East Asia and the Pacific, Western Europe, and the Americas. Though, the square rate of growth has the validation of EKC of inverted U shape in all regions except the Sub-Saharan African region. Some evidence shows that renewables are foremost in the mitigation of CO_2 emissions and confirm the EKC theory (Danish et al. 2017; Dong et al. 2018; Sinha and Shahbaz 2018; Yao et al. 2019). Hanif et al. (2019) elaborated that the desired level of EGR has moderated carbon secretions and ascertained the EKC theory in developing Asian economies. Carbon secretions are alleviated by renewable energy in western and eastern Chinese regions. However, the square growth rate has mitigated CO_2 secretions only in the east of China and formed an inverted U EKC (Chen et al. 2019). Following more shreds of evidence, renewable energy is weak in reducing carbon emissions in MENA economies (Charfeddine and Kahia 2019), while renewable energy contributes to environmental betterment in BRIICS economies (Cheng et al. 2019). Moreover, RENE is found foremost in diminishing CO_2 emissions and leading to environmental sustainability in top CO_2 emitting countries and European economies. The squared level of growth has reduced CO_2 and formed an inverted U shape of EKC in European and top CO_2 emitting economies (Altintas and Kassouri 2020). Atsu et al. (2021) investigated that the upsurge in ICT contributed to CO_2 emissions and triggered environmental degradation in South Africa. At the same time, sustainable RENE has mitigated CO_2 emissions in South Africa. In evidence of ten topmost carbon dioxide emitters, ICT took its part to reduce carbon dioxide emissions while renewable energy turned out to be environmentally favorable. However, economic growth and natural gas resources have raised carbon dioxide emissions (Azam et al. 2021). In ASEAN, ICT with innovative clean technology policies and renewable energy has mitigated CO_2 emissions. However, EGR positively contributed to CO_2 emissions and squared EGR has convergence to the sustainable route and proven the EKC approach in ASEAN (Haini 2021). Evidence from World's leading ten pollutant economies, financial development and renewable energy have placed their role on maintaining environmental sustainability, while ICT's vital contribution in improving environmental quality is established (Caglar et al. 2021).

2.3 Urbanization and Resource Rents on Environmental Sustainability

Urbanization and natural resource rents (NRR) are undoubtedly the foremost factors for economic well-being and influence the environment. The urbanization process and rents income from natural resources contribute to economic growth, and sustainable outcomes contribute to environmental betterment. Similarly, inefficiency leads to environmental issues i.e. air pollution, which deteriorates environmental sustainability. Some previous studies have discussed the effects of urbanization and NRR on environmental conditions. Likewise, Rehman et al. (2024) investigated the effect of coal and oil rents, urban agglomeration, and EGR on quality of environment in Pakistan by employing annual data from 1971 to 2019. The asymmetric ARDL model was used in a study for data estimation. Natural resources significantly affect environmental quality. The economic progress also faces a severe effect, and through the analysis, the urban agglomeration affects the quality of ecology adversely through positive and negative shocks. Moreover, the results of oil rents were negative and positive towards carbonization whereas the coal rents harmed the environmental inclusion. Danish et al. (2019) evident that NRR contribute to ES in Russia, whereas environmental deterioration in South Africa. There is an inverted U shape of EKC with the help of natural resources proven in all countries except India. In the case of China, urbanization and resource rents have deteriorated the environment. However, in African economies, urbanization still failed to uphold environmental sustainability, while natural resource rents mitigate CO_2 releases and contribute to environmental sustainability (Ahmed et al. 2020; Asongu et al. 2020). In the evidence of panel countries, Khan et al. (2021) found that resources have full control over reducing the ecological footprint and improving the environment. While urbanization contrasts with natural resources and degrades the environment of manufacturing economies. Pata (2018) examined that urbanization with economic growth has massively enhanced Turkey's discharges of carbon dioxide. However, the squared growth level has gained massive appreciation in reducing CO_2 secretions and ascertaining the EKC approach. In the case of China's urban and non-urban zones, urbanization leads to environmental sustainability. However, environmental betterment is much more substantial in non-urban zones than in urban areas of China (Zheng et al. 2020). In Saudi Arabia, the consequences are opposed to China's urban and non-urban zones and shown an upsurge in CO_2 emissions because of urbanization, which hurts the environmental quality (Mahmood et al. 2020). In some evidence of China, Huo et al. (2021) found that environmental degradation increases due to urbanization in Chinese provinces. However, some cities, such as Shandong, have maintained environmental sustainability following sustainable urbanization, even in the presence of environmental pressure, which has been occurred due to inefficient NRR (Fang et al. 2021). In Southwest China, urbanization has gained environmental improvement, which is low in proportion as compared to increased urbanization (Lei et al. 2021). In the case of Bangladesh and Northeast Asian nations, CO_2 secretions have been exaggerated by urbanization which has worsened the environment (Rahman and Alam 2021; Liu et al. 2021).

The previous studies reviewed in this research have significantly studied the effect of EGR, ICT, RENE, NRR, and urbanization on the environmental conditions of concerned economies. Moreover, a significant number of findings have shown the existence of the EKC hypothesis, which we eagerly desire to prove Inverted U shape. However, still, some shortcomings addressed the research gap, which will be covered in this research. The literature review presented in this research has covered economies following Asia, Africa, ASEAN, BRICS, BRIICS, Europe, Latin American and Caribbean, MENA, Sub-Saharan Africa, large panels of developed and developing economies, and regional levels studies. However, this study has focused on the developing countries of East Asia and the Pacific following their income level, which has been rarely looked over in the literature. Further, this research has a unique grouping of variables to measure their influences on the environment and identify the EKC hypothesis, which is hardly proven with this combination and in the context of East Asia and the Pacific.

3 Data, Model and Methodology

3.1 Data, Variables, and Sources

The data to examine the influences of ICT, RENE, and urbanization on CO_2 emissions is taken from 1990 to 2023. Most East Asia and Pacific countries started strategic changes, the industrial revolution, technological advancement, resource-based economic structures, and urbanization during 1980 to 1990. However, the data is collected following the availability of balanced panel data, which starts from 1990 and ends in 2023. In this regard, Table 1 lists ten developing economies of East Asia and the Pacific region. The selection of country is consists of the availability of data, and World Development Indicators is taken as the data source. Further, the choice of countries is based on their developing status of lower middle and upper middle income levels. Moreover, the developing countries are selected following advanced tools such as advancement in ICT, RENE, urbanization growth, and CO_2 emissions. However, Table 1 illustrates the selection of countries, variables, their description, measuring units, and sources.

The data of selected variables are from World Bank, WDI (2023). https://databank.worldbank.org/source/world-development-indicators#advancedDownloadOptions

Table 1 Ten developing countries, variables' description and sources

East Asia and Pacific developing countries			
Lower middle-Income-Level	Cambodia, Indonesia, Mongolia, Myanmar, Philippines, Solomon Islands, Vietnam		
Upper middle-Income-Level	China, Malaysia, Thailand		
Variables	Description	Units	Sources
$LECO_2$	Carbon dioxide (CO_2) emissions are the proxy of environmental degradation	Metric tons per capita	World Bank, World Development Indicators (WDI) 2023
LEGR	Economic growth is an improvement in inflation-adjusted market value of economic goods-services in a particular time and taken as GDP per capita growth	Annual %	
$LEGR^2$	Squared term of Economic growth indicates its doubled effect for inverted U shape hypothesis, taken as (GDP per capita growth)^2	(annual %)^2	
LRENE	Renewable energy consumption is a clean form of energy and source for naturally replenishing resources	% of total final energy consumption	
LNRR	Natural resource rents are the rent income generated from the consumption of natural resources. East Asia and Pacific economies are resource-abundant nations and collect high returns from abundant resources. However, it is taken as Total natural resources rents	% of GDP	
LURG	Urbanization is a process of making an area more urban, taken as Urban population growth	Annual %	
LICT	ICT is the infrastructure to enable modern computing such as telecommunication, taken as Fixed telephone subscriptions	Per 100 people	

Note Countries' income level and region are from the World Bank List of Economies (2020)

3.2 Theoretical and Econometric Models

Kuznets Curve was first developed to curve the income level and inequality by Simon Kuznets (Kuznets 1955). However, the EKC was established to curve the income per capita and environmental degradation following U shape and inverted U shape of the EKC hypothesis. It is a fact that the nations at the initial level focus on economic progression. At the same time, less emphasis on environmental conditions deteriorates the environment and indications to U shape of EKC, refer as scale effect. After that, the economies further progress to achieve an economic growth level at which there is some concern for the environment. Though, this level can be achieved by emphasizing industrialization, termed as a composite effect. However, to get the desired level of economic progression, the policymakers follow the technique effect. In this effect, the theory suggests admiring sustainable resources, clean forms of energy such as renewable energy, and technological advancement to accomplish the anticipated level of EGR and environmental sustainability. So, following the technique effect, it is anticipated to get the desired EGR level, which the squared term of EGR can indicate, helps mitigate the carbon emissions and hold the inverted U-shape of EKC (Grossman and Krueger 1995). This research has followed the model of EKC hypothesis theory and is expected to prove the U and inverted U shape of EKC. However, the study focuses on acquiring environmental sustainability by adopting economic growth and its squared term, renewable energy, ICT, urbanization, and resource rents. Though, it can be possible to assume the inverted U shape of EKC in East Asia and Pacific developing economies.

The econometric model for the desired purpose is based on the following studies of Al-Mulali et al. (2016), Salahuddin et al. (2016), Danish et al. (2019), Chen et al. (2019) and Liu et al. (2021). The functional form in the first step to defining the association between the dependent variable and independent variables and the empirical model's econometric equation for estimation are given below:

$$ECO_2 = f\left(EGR, EGR^2, RENE, NRR, URG, ICT\right) \tag{1}$$

The above functional form equation defines the dependent variable ECO_2 as CO_2 emissions, which is the function of independent variables and is influenced by these indicators. The independent variables EGR and EGR^2 represent the economic growth and squared term of growth, respectively. However, RENE as renewable energy, NRR as natural resource rents, URG, and ICT indicates the growth of urbanization and information and communication technology. The logarithmic form econometric equation is as follow:

$$\begin{aligned} LECO_{2it} = {} & \beta_0 + \beta_1 LEGR_{it} + \beta_2 LEGR_{it}^2 + \beta_3 NRENE_{it} \\ & + \beta_4 LNRR_{it} + \beta_5 LURG_{it} + \beta_6 LICT_{it} + \mu_i \end{aligned} \tag{2}$$

Here, logarithmic form econometric Eq. (2) indicate the intercept and slope with β_0 and $\beta_{1\ldots0.6,}$ respectively. Further, *it* displays *i* as selected ten countries and *t* respect to time, while the term of error with μ_i.

3.3 Methodology Approach

The methodology approach has some steps, while descriptive statistics summarize selected indicators' statistical worth in the starting phase. After that, the next step involves some stationary econometric testing for order of integration among variables. The unit root tests are LLC (Levin et al. 2002), IPS (Im et al. 2003), and ADF and PP fisher type (Maddala and Wu 1999). Further, the study applies some critical tests such as Breusch Pagan LM, Pesaran scaled LM, Bias-corrected scaled LM, and Pesaran CD tests for the purposes of heterogeneity, serial correlation, unbiased and consistent estimates, and cross-section dependence (CSD) between variables (Breusch and Pagan 1980; Pesaran 2004, 2007). Pesaran CSD test consists of the H_o (no dependence of crosssections among variables) and alternative hypothesis (dependence of crosssections among variables), while expected the approval of null hypothesis for cointegration process.

$$CD = ((TN(N-1))/2)^{1/2}? \tag{3}$$

Equation (3) of the CD test illustrates time-dimensions and crosssections correspondingly by T and N. Whereas, for cross-sectional residuals, P/ specifies the coefficients of pair-wise correlation.

In the next step, cointegration testing first consists of Pedroni cointegration, which indicates cointegration between the model's indicators. This test follows within dimension and between dimension common and individual AR coefficients. The common AR coefficients of within dimension are panel statistics of v, rho, PP, and ADF. Whereas, between dimension individual AR coefficients are group statistics of rho, PP, and ADF (Pedroni 1999, 2004). In addition, Kao cointegration applies to assessing Pedroni cointegration outcomes and robustness by following t-statistic and probability of ADF (Kao 1999). However, the equation for Pedroni and Kao cointegration testing is settled below:

$$\begin{aligned} LECO_{2it} = {} & \beta_i + \rho_{it} + \beta_{1i}LEGR_{it} + \beta_{2i}LEGR^2_{it} + \beta_{3i}LRENE_{it} \\ & + \beta_{4i}LNRR_{it} + \beta_{5i}LURG_{it} + \beta_{6i}LICT_{it} + \varepsilon_{it} \end{aligned} \tag{4}$$

Above Eq. (4) specifies countries with time dimensions by *it*, whereas intercept, slope, and deterministic trends by β_i, $\beta_{i=1\ldots0.6}$ and ρ_{it}, correspondingly. Further, the cointegration test follows the null hypothesis, directs to no indication of cointegration, and designates by $\rho_i = 1$. At the same time, the alternative hypothesis is opposed to the null premise and follows within dimension ($\rho_i = \rho < 1$) and between dimension ($\rho_i < 1$).

Moreover, it is obligatory the long run existence with cointegration in the model to endorse the long run relationship between variables. In this regard, residual term equation is settled below;

$$\varepsilon_{it} = \rho_i \varepsilon_{it-1} + \mu_{it} \tag{5}$$

After that, Johansen Fisher cointegration applies to indicate cointegration in the model succeeding trace and eigen values (Maddala and Wu 1999). This unrestricted cointegration rank test consists of hypothesized CE's equations starting from none to almost 6. It is assumed that at least one CE hypothesized equation should reject the H_o to prove cointegration amongst variables and the possibility of long-run existence, which can be conceivable by the significant trace and eigen values.

Nevertheless, Panel Fully Modified Ordinary Least Square (P-FMOLS) (Pedroni 2000, 2001) and Dynamic Ordinary Least Square (P-DOLS) (Kao and Chiang 2000a, b) applies to inspect the dependent and independent variables' association in the long run. These estimates provide an unbiased and free from error estimation. However, P-FMOLS are efficient and precise long-term estimators, fulfill the shortcomings of simple OLS, and remove biased endogeneity and serial correlation. The P-FMOLS equation for long-run estimation is as follows:

$$\hat{\beta}_{FML} = \left[\sum_{i-1}^{N}\sum_{t-1}^{T}(X_{it} - \overline{X_i})(X_{it} - \overline{X_i})'\right]^{-1}\left[\sum_{i-1}^{N}\left(\sum_{t-1}^{T}(X_{it} - \overline{X_i})\hat{\Upsilon}_{\mathrm{it}}^{+} - \mathrm{T}\,\hat{\theta}_{\varepsilon u}^{+}\right)\right] \tag{6}$$

P-FMOLS' Eq. (6) denotes time and crosssection dimensions by T and N, while specific means by $\overline{X_i}$. Further, endogeneity series correction specifies by $\hat{\Upsilon}_{\mathrm{it}}^{+}$ with respect to i countries and t time. Moreover, $T\,\hat{\theta}_{\varepsilon u}^{+}$ is correction term in time and correct the serial correlation in ε and μ error terms.

Nevertheless, P-DOLS consists of crosssection lags to overcome the problem of serial correlation and to correct endogeneity series. In this study, P-DOLS applies to acquire error-free and biasedness corrected long-term estimation. Though, the Panel-DOLS estimation equation is settled below:

$$\hat{\beta}_{DOL} = \left(\sum_{i-1}^{N}\sum_{t-1}^{T}\tilde{Y}_{it}\,\tilde{Y}_{it'}\right)^{-1}\left(\sum_{i-1}^{N}\sum_{t-1}^{T}\tilde{Y}_{it}\tilde{Y}\tilde{Z}_{it'}\right) \tag{7}$$

In P-DOLS' Eq. (7), $\tilde{Y}_{it'}$ indicates the vector of regressors. However, the study purposes of examining the effect of EGR, squared term growth, RENE, resource rents, urbanization growth, and ICT on CO_2 emissions in the long run following P-FMOLS and P-DOLS.

4 Results and Discussion

This section discusses the results, stats with the confirmation of the statistical worth of the model, and is discussed in a descriptive statistical summary. After this, there are some diagnostic tests to check the heterogeneity, serial correlation, biased corrected scales, and cross-section dependency. Further, different unit root tests have shown the stationary level of the variables to decide the direction for long run estimation, which leads to FMOLS and DOLS. Before this, cointegration tests are applied to exist cointegration and long run existence among variables.

In Table 2, a descriptive statistical summary shows that all variables have moderate variations from their mean point. The significant jarque–bera values suggest that the model is statistically appropriate while indicating the data normality. However, skewness values show that all the variables are positively skewed and positively direct to their mean points. Further, kurtosis shows that $LECO_2$, $LEGR^2$, LNRR, and LICT are leptokurtic and have large potential outliers with a thin tail and high peakedness. Following LEGR, LRENE, and LURG, which are platykurtic and have the small potential of outliers with less peakedness. This summary suggests that the empirical model is strongly permitted by statistical terms and leads to further estimation.

After the statistical worth and data normality approval, Table 3 has some diagnostic tests to identify the cross-section dependence, serial correlation, heterogeneity, and biasness scale. The study has applied Breusch Pagan LM, Pesaran scaled LM, Bias-corrected scaled LM, and Pesaran CD tests for the purposes (Breusch and Pagan 1980; Pesaran 2007). Table 3 indicates that variables such as $LECO_2$, LEGR, $LEGR^2$, LRENE, LNRR, LURG, and LICT don't have heterogeneity and serial correlation problems, as proven by Breusch Pagan LM and Pesaran scaled LM tests. At the same time, the biased corrected LM scale indicates unbiased and consistent estimates. However, the Pesaran CD test has rejected the alternative hypothesis and accepts the null premise of no CSD among variables.

Table 4 illustrates the results of LLC (Levin et al. 2002), IPS (Im et al. 2003), ADF and PP fisher type (Maddala and Wu 1999) unit root tests which have shown the variables' integration order. The results are generated by the intercept and trend values of unit roots tests following I(0) and I(1) orders. The selected variables of the study such as $LECO_2$, LEGR, $LEGR^2$, LRENE, LNRR, LURG, and LICT are insignificant at the level I(0), while significant at the first difference I(1), indicate that all variables have the same stationary level at the first difference I(1) in all unit root tests (LLC, IPS, ADF, and PP fisher types). The integration order at the first difference among variables decides the cointegration estimation, and the direction for long run estimation leads to P-FMOLS and P-DOLS. The results of LLC, IPS, ADF, and PP fisher type unit root tests are in consonance with the outcomes of Liu et al. (2021).

In order to investigate the co-integration among the variables, given below Table 5a indicate Pedroni cointegration test.

Table 5 a, b, c demonstrates the cointegration test results: Pedroni and Kao (Pedroni 1999, 2004; Kao 1999), and Johansen Fisher cointegration tests (Maddala

Table 2 Descriptive summary

	$LECO_2$	LEGR	$LEGR^2$	LRENE	LNRR	LURG	LICT
Mean	3.027	4.927	34.580	35.093	6.073	2.980	9.459
Median	1.875	4.727	22.352	30.934	4.781	2.966	4.147
Std. Dev	3.091	3.214	38.963	28.706	6.219	1.221	11.908
Skewness	1.204	0.480	1.870	0.437	2.189	0.080	1.702
Kurtosis	3.710	2.883	6.879	1.889	9.872	2.707	5.075
Jarque–Bera	81.452***	12.115***	375.109***	25.828***	857.783***	12.443***	205.285***
Probability	0.000	0.002	0.000	0.000	0.000	0.002	0.000

Note *** indicates 1% significance level

Table 3 Cross-section dependence tests

Variables	Breusch-Pagan LM	Pesaran scaled LM	Bias-corrected scaled LM
$LECO_2$	778.160*** (0.000)	76.227*** (0.000)	76.061*** (0.000)
LEGR	129.445*** (0.000)	7.847*** (0.000)	7.680*** (0.000)
$LEGR^2$	101.175*** (0.000)	4.867*** (0.000)	4.700*** (0.000)
LRENE	664.111*** (0.000)	64.205*** (0.000)	64.039*** (0.000)
LNRR	276.266*** (0.000)	23.323*** (0.000)	23.156*** (0.000)
LURG	354.723*** (0.000)	31.593*** (0.000)	31.426*** (0.000)
LICT	655.228*** (0.000)	63.269*** (0.000)	63.102*** (0.000)
Pesaran Cross-section (CD)			
Variables: $LECO_2$, LEGR, $LEGR^2$, LRENE, LNRR, LURG and LICT			
		Statistic	Prob
Pesaran CD		0.0006	0.998

Note *** indicates *P*-value < 1%,. Probabilities are indicated by values in parentheses
Null Hypothesis: No indication of Cross-section Dependence

and Wu 1999). In accordance with the results of Pedroni cointegration, with-in dimension coefficients such as Panel statistics of v, rho, PP, and ADF are used while Panel (rho, PP, and ADF) statistics have significantly rejected the H_0 and have revealed the cointegration among variables. However, the weighted statistic of with-in dimensions such as panel rho and panel ADF statistic is significant and accepted the alternative hypothesis of indicating cointegration among variables. Further, the Pedroni cointegration test' between dimension statistics group rho, group PP and group ADF is used for cointegration existence purposes. Group PP and group ADF statistics of between dimensions have significantly accepted that variables have cointegration among them. After that, Kao cointegration is used to proceed with the findings of the Pedroni cointegration test. Its ADF t-statistic value significantly accepts Pedroni cointegration outcomes and indicates cointegration between variables of the model. Moreover, an unrestricted cointegration rank test named with Johansen Fisher cointegration test is practiced to indicate cointegration. This cointegration test consists of a hypothesized number of CE's starting from none to almost 6, having their trace and maximum eigen values with probability values. All the hypothesized numbers of CE's starting from none to almost 6 have significant trace and eigen values, indicating that the H_0 is rejected and cointegration exists among the model's variables. The results of Table 5 have assured the cointegration among variables which leads to long-run existence among variables, and these outcomes are in line with the findings of Chen et al. (2019), Liu et al. (2021), and Caglar et al. (2021).

After the endorsement to apply P-FMOLS and P-DOLS from unit root tests and long run presence from cointegration tests, Table 6 displays the outcomes of Panel FMOLS and DOLS. These findings have revealed the effect of EGR, ICT, NRR, RENE, and urbanization towards environmental deterioration and ES in developing East Asian and Pacific economies. The findings of Table 6 also ratify the presence

Table 4 Unit root tests (with intercept and trend)

Variables	Unit root tests	Intercept and trend	Intercept and trend	Conclusion
		At Level I(0)	At 1st Difference I(1)	
$LECO_2$	LL & C	0.675 (0.750)	−3.981*** (0.000)	I(1)
	IPS	1.784 (0.962)	−5.087*** (0.000)	I(1)
	ADF	13.754 (0.842)	67.756*** (0.000)	I(1)
	PP	16.522 (0.683)	408.432*** (0.000)	I(1)
LEGR	LL & C	0.504 (0.651)	−9.069*** (0.000)	I(1)
	IPS	1.443 (0.882)	−11.860*** (0.000)	I(1)
	ADF	9.236 (0.921)	144.101*** (0.000)	I(1)
	PP	11.653 (0.871)	796.465*** (0.000)	I(1)
$LEGR^2$	LL & C	0.610 (0.698)	−10.202*** (0.000)	I(1)
	IPS	1.072 (0.736)	−11.701*** (0.000)	I(1)
	ADF	6.611 (0.968)	142.787*** (0.000)	I(1)
	PP	13.738 (0.849)	861.353*** (0.000)	I(1)
LRENE	LL & C	0.951 (0.829)	−3.555*** (0.000)	I(1)
	IPS	0.884 (0.811)	−3.319*** (0.000)	I(1)
	ADF	14.725 (0.791)	45.158*** (0.001)	I(1)
	PP	13.811 (0.839)	88.771*** (0.000)	I(1)
LNRR	LL & C	1.108 (0.866)	−2.410*** (0.008)	I(1)
	IPS	0.691 (0.755)	−6.769*** (0.000)	I(1)
	ADF	15.480 (0.748)	80.969*** (0.000)	I(1)
	PP	17.041 (0.650)	158.714*** (0.000)	I(1)
LURG	LL & C	−1.137 (0.879)	−5.417*** (0.000)	I(1)
	IPS	−0.137 (0.411)	−5.572*** (0.000)	I(1)
	ADF	17.204 (0.671)	66.397*** (0.000)	I(1)
	PP	13.465 (0.856)	93.895*** (0.000)	I(1)
LICT	LL & C	−0.801 (0.211)	−1.303* (0.096)	I(1)
	IPS	1.179 (0.880)	−1.524* (0.063)	I(1)
	ADF	16.039 (0.714)	31.639** (0.047)	I(1)
	PP	5.686 (0.999)	53.502*** (0.000)	I(1)

Note *** denotes P-value < 1%, ** indicates P-value < 5%, and * specifies P-value < 10%. Probabilities are indicated by values in parentheses. I(1) concludes that variables are stationary at the first difference

of the EKC hypothesis in these developing nations. In the evidence of FMOLS, LEGR's significant value of 0.365 at a 1 percent significance level indicate that EGR positively contributes to carbon emissions and deteriorates the environment of concerned economies in the long run, and confirms the U-shape of EKC. However, the estimates of DOLS revealed that EGR is still deteriorating the environment. Still,

Table 5 Cointegration tests pedroni cointegration

H_0: No Cointegration				
Alternative hypothesis: common AR coefficients (within-dimension)				
Panel	Statistic	Probability	Weighted statistic	Probability
v-Statistic	–0.940	0.826	0.076	0.469
rho-Statistic	–3.710***	0.000	–3.489***	0.000
PP-Statistic	–1.666**	0.047	1.036	0.850
ADF-Statistic	–1.688**	0.045	–1.517*	0.067
Alternative hypothesis: individual AR coefficients. (between-dimension)				
	Statistic	Probability		
rho-statistic	4.531	1.000		
PP-statistic	–2.307**	0.010		
ADF-statistic	–2.267**	0.011		
On the other hand, Table b indicate Kao cointegration test b: Kao cointegration test				
H_0: No cointegration				
	t-statistic	Probability		
ADF	–1.910**	0.025		
Residual variance	0.138			
HAC variance	0.134			
Likewise, Table c indicate Johansen Fisher panel cointegration test c: Johansen Fisher panel cointegration test				
Unrestricted cointegration rank test (trace and maximum eigenvalue)				
Hypothesized number of CE's	Fisher Stat (trace test)	Probability	Fisher Stat (max-eigen test)	Probability
None	396.7***	0.000	229.5***	0.000
At most 1	244.4***	0.000	104.3***	0.000
At most 2	155.0***	0.000	65.17***	0.000
At most 3	102.1***	0.000	58.48***	0.000
At most 4	57.44***	0.000	39.27***	0.006
At most 5	35.92**	0.015	31.87**	0.044
At most 6	30.50*	0.062	30.50*	0.062

Note *** denotes P-value < 1%, ** indicates P-value < 5%, and * specifies P-value < 10%

its influence is less worsened in the long run than FMOLS, and EGR increases ECO_2 by about 0.234 percent in response to 10 percent growth in developing economies. Nevertheless, attaining the desired growth level leads to economic progress and preserving environmental sustainability. In FMOLS, EGR^2 mitigates $LECO_2$ about 0.023 percent in response to 5 percent surges and ascertain the inverted U shape of EKC in the long period. However, the inverted U shape of EKC is also validated in evidence of DOLS, EGR^2 value of -0.014 significantly influences ECO_2 at 10 percent significance level, while in consent of negative direction. In other words, the squared term of economic growth reduces ECO_2 by about 0.014 percent in the long run during 10 percent growths in developing economies lead to environmental improvement and determine the EKC hypothesis of inverted U shape. The findings are endorsed by the aforementioned studies of Al-Mulali et al. (2016), Danish et al. (2017), Dong et al. (2018), Danish et al. (2019), Avom et al. (2020), and Haini (2021).

Renewable energy consumption (RENE) coefficient values are –0.024 and –0.022 for FMOLS and DOLS, respectively, and are significant at a 1 percent significance level. This specifies that by one percent proliferation of consumption of RENE in the long run, $LECO_2$ secretions lessen about 0.024 and 0.022 percent in developing economies of East Asia and the Pacific. In the past few decades, the developing economies of this East Asia and Pacific region have shown immense interest in adopting the clean form of energy to reduce the influence of non-renewable energy and moderate the pressure of environmental deterioration. However, the findings of FMOLS and DOLS in this study reveal that renewable energy has expressively mitigated environmental stress and maintained environmental cleanliness in developing East Asia and Pacific countries. The findings are in consonance with the previous studies of Al-Mulali et al. (2016), Yao et al. (2019), Sinha and Shahbaz (2018), Chen et al. (2019), Altintas and Kassouri (2020), and Caglar et al. (2021). Furthermore, the sustainable consumption of NRR and their rents can contribute to economic progression and reduce environmental pressure (Fang et al. 2021). In contrast, the

Table 6 P-FMOLS and P-DOLS

P-FMOLS				
Dependent variable: $LECO_2$				
Variables	Coefficient	S.E	t-Statistic	Probability
LEGR	0.365***	0.122	2.971	0.003
$LEGR^2$	-0.023**	0.010	-2.272	0.023
LRENE	-0.024***	0.006	-3.983	0.000
LNRR	0.064**	0.025	2.522	0.012
LURG	0.182*	0.108	1.676	0.094
LICT	0.199***	0.014	13.501	0.000
Panel Dynamic Least Squares (P-DOLS)				
LEGR	0.234*	0.128	1.830	0.068
$LEGR^2$	-0.014*	0.010	-1.742	0.090
LRENE	-0.022***	0.006	-3.650	0.000
LNRR	0.061**	0.026	2.300	0.022
LURG	0.215*	0.112	1.908	0.057
LICT	0.207***	0.015	13.436	0.000

Note *** denotes *P*-value < 1%, ** indicates *P*-value < 5%, and * specifies *P*-value < 10%

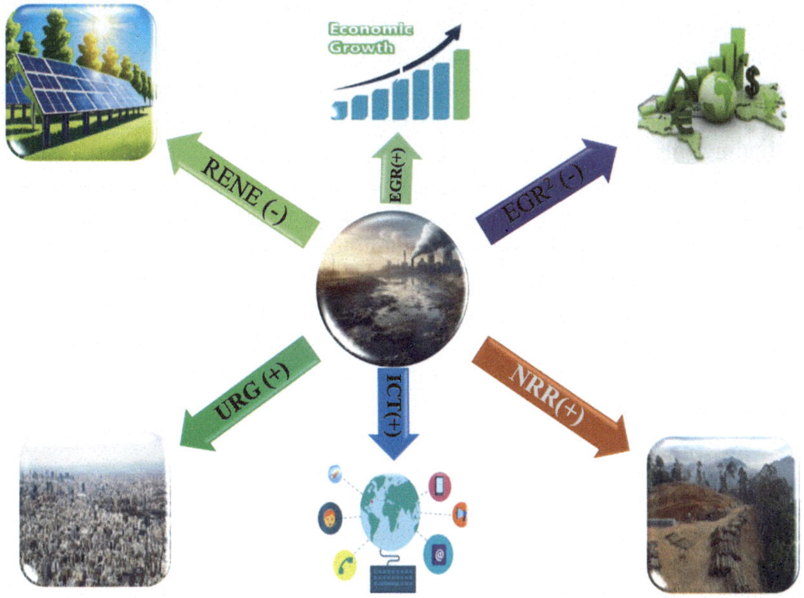

Fig. 1 Summary of long-run outcomes

findings of FMOLS and DOLS of this study make known that natural resource rents (LNRR) positively boost carbon dioxide emissions ($LECO_2$) about 0.064 and 0.061 percent in response to 5 percent significance level and worsens the environment of East Asia and Pacific economies in the long run. It is hard to find sustainability in the consumption of resources for developing countries, and inefficient use of natural resources leads to environmental deterioration. The findings are endorsed by Danish et al. (2019), Ahmed et al. (2020), and Fang et al. (2021) (Fig. 1).

Urban attractiveness no doubt participates in economic well-being also contributes to environmental sustainability. However, urbanization needs sustainability in its process to develop a better environment. Otherwise, it leads to severe emissions of greenhouse gases which resultantly deteriorate the environmental quality. Here in East Asia and Pacific developing economies, urbanization growth has worsened the quality of environment by increasing ECO_2 in the long-run, evident by the outcomes of FMOLS and DOLS. LURG coefficient values are 0.182 and 0.215 and significant at a 10 percent significance level, representing that the surged urbanization growth increases the $LECO_2$ in the long run while degrading the environment of developing economies. The reason is that the developing countries of East Asia and the Pacific are more concerned about urbanization from the last two decades to get urban attractiveness and stands with the countries having urban cities and are more globalized nations. Further, urbanization attracts tourism and proposer economic progress. However, the environmental pressure due to the urbanization process is unbearable and degrading the environmental efficiency in these countries. The findings are in accordance with the shreds of evidence of Ahmed et al. (2020), Asongu et al. (2020), Khan et al. (2021), Huo et al. (2021), and Liu et al. (2021). Further, information communication technology is also failed to mitigate the carbon secretions and put environmental pressure on developing economies. LICT values in FMOLS and DOLS are 0.199 and 0.207, respectively, significant at a 1 percent significance level. These findings illustrate that one percent progress in ICT increases carbon emissions by about 0.199 and 0.207 percent in the long run. It is possible that ICT is easily accessible and cheaper, which is why it tends to consume more and directly increases CO_2 emissions. However, the high consumption of ICT further processes the high energy consumption demand and indirectly influences CO_2 secretions and deteriorates the environmental quality. The results are also matched with the past evidence of Salahuddin et al. (2016), Danish et al. (2019), and Avom et al. (2020).

5 Conclusion

The emerging economies of East Asia and the Pacific have experienced astonishing economic growth, urbanization growth, and advancement in information communication technologies. Further, the rents from resources and renewable energy have met them with remarkable economic progression. However, these emerging economies have gone through massive and continuous environmental deficits, imposing distressing environmental problems. It is a fact that the sustainable urbanization process, EGR, renewable energy, and NRR leads to urban attractiveness, economic progression, and environmental sustainability. In contrast, instability leads to environmental deterioration pressure. However, the literature has been rarely looked over the relationship between these indicators for East Asia and the Pacific region and still has some shortcomings addressed in this research. The current study determines the influences of these indicators and determines which indicator leads to environmental sustainability and which opposes it and causes environmental deterioration. For the purpose of analysis, the data of selected developing East Asia and Pacific countries following their income levels have been collected from 1986 to 2016. To examine the unit root testing, LLC, IPS, and fisher type ADF and PP tests are employed, which have addressed the same order of integration at I(1) and leads to cointegration. The cointegration tests such as Pedroni and Kao and Johansen Fisher cointegration tests have confirmed the cointegration, and long run existence among variables and further proceed to Panel FMOLS and DOLS for long run estimation.

The estimates of Panel FMOLS and Panel DOLS for long run estimation reveal that EGR leads to environmental deterioration, while its squared term assistances to mitigate CO_2 emissions and proves the inverted U shape of EKC in developing East Asia and Pacific economies. In this regard, renewable energy has recorded its sustainable consumption, and its efficient use has mitigated CO_2 emissions and preserved environmental sustainability. In contrast, natural resource rents, urbanization growth, and information communication technologies are opposed to renewable energy and squared term of EGR and deteriorated the environment of East Asia and Pacific nations. According to the findings, it comes to the fact that information communication technologies have caused changes in consumer behavior. Its cheaper and easily accessible approach has gained massive consumer recognition and demands for energy consumption, leading to greater emissions and environmental deterioration.

5.1 Policy Implications

It is suggested that there is a need to update and upgrade the ICT infrastructure to maintain the environmental sustainability. There is a need for technological innovation, innovative instructional ICT approach, and advancement in ICT research and development to mitigate environmental pollution. Technological innovation, innovative instructional ICT approach, and ICT research and development will assist low-carbon machinery, which will help to reduce carbon releases. Further, a sustainable path towards ICT, urban attractiveness, and resource consumption will lead to environmental sustainability. Additionally, renewable energy policies such as low-cost renewables, availability of renewables at the household level, and electrification are required to implement to moderate non-renewable consumer behavior and greater emissions in East Asia and Pacific emerging economies. ICT enables energy efficiency in several key sectors. Smart grids, the Internet of Things, big data analytics, and artificial intelligence will enable monitoring, management, and optimization of energy use with better accuracy. Considering a fact smart grids would be able to facilitate adjustments in the distribution of electricity supply automatically in real-time, significantly reducing energy waste while also improving the ability of renewable sources of energy, such as solar and wind, to penetrate the grid. For instance, smart meters enable consumers to monitor their patterns of energy use in a way that better informs them about when and how much electricity to use. This reduces demand on the grid during peak times, which in turn reduces the amount of fossil fuels needed to produce energy. In the same vein, IoT-enabled devices in homes, offices, and industries can automatically adjust heating, cooling, and lighting systems toward efficient energy use with low emissions. The combining of ICT and renewable energy increases their efficiency. ICT tools, such as machine learning algorithms and AI, are important in the forecasting of weather patterns, which in turn increases the efficiency of wind and solar farms. Predictive analytics can forecast wind speeds and magnitudes of solar radiation; therefore, grid operators can manage energy storage and distribution effectively. This reduces dependence on emissions-reducing, fossil fuel-based backup systems. Similarly, ICT and renewable energy complement each other in facilitating green urbanization. It is also possible to cut down the carbon footprint in cities by a great margin using smart cities from ICT-enabled infrastructure, renewable-powered infrastructure, energy-efficient buildings, and sustainable transportation systems. Electrical vehicles replace combustion engines and run with renewable energy, supported by charging through ICT-enabled infrastructure, hence cutting down the CO2 emissions in urban areas. Similarly, ICT enables the monitoring of carbon emission levels in real time through satellite data, AI-based systems, and sensor networks. These allow both governments and businesses to comprehend their respective carbon footprints by monitoring activities and thereby making evidence-based decisions to reduce adverse environmental impacts. For example, in Brazil, through a satellite-based monitoring system, the rate of deforestation in the Amazon is tracked, an essential component in controlling carbon emissions related to land-use changes. Furthermore, ICT can enhance the effectiveness of operation and maintenance of renewable energy infrastructure. Drones, sensors, and remote monitoring systems can inspect for damage to wind turbines and solar panels to minimize time out of operation and ensure efficient continuous energy production. ICT supports the development of green technology sectors: renewable energy, electric vehicles, and energy storage. ICT solutions support data analytics and real-time monitoring needed to optimize operations of renewable energy infrastructure. In this way, it contributes to transitioning from the carbon-intensive production means of energy, like coal and gas, to sustainable sources of this vital resource. This can be extended further to circular economic models in which resources are reused, recycled, or repurposed to reduce demand for new raw materials and subsequently reduce environmental degradation. In agriculture, ICT contributes to enabling technology for precision farming. Equipped with sensors, drones, and AI-powered analytics, farmers can optimize water, fertilizers, and pesticides to obtain better yields while minimizing environmental harm. For example, fertilizers should be applied only in places where they are needed to reduce the rate of chemical runoff to nearby water bodies, thus protecting ecosystems.

5.2 Limitations and Future Direction of the Research

The study area of choosing East Asia and Pacific developing economies is the limitation of this research. Further, it directs to study in other regions of Asia, and there can be the possibility of comparison between Asian regions. However, this research is limited with the evidence of the Inverted U shape of the EKC hypothesis. Further for future research, it directs to N shape of EKC hypothesis for industrialized and technologically advanced nations of Asian regions. Moreover, this research is based on the latest data, which covers the time span from 1986 to 2019. However, the future direction of similar type research can cover during and after-effects of Covid-19, which will be interesting research.

References

Aghamolaei R, Fallahpour M (2023) Strategies towards reducing carbon emission in university campuses: a comprehensive review of both global and local scales. Journal of Building Engineering 107183

Ahmed Z, Asghar MM, Malik MN, Nawaz K (2020) Moving towards a sustainable environment: the dynamic linkage between natural resources, human capital, urbanization, economic growth, and ecological footprint in China. Resour Policy 67:101677

Ahmed Z, Nathaniel SP, Shahbaz M (2021) The criticality of information and communication technology and human capital in environmental sustainability: evidence from Latin American and Caribbean countries. J Clean Prod 286:125529

Alataş S (2021) The role of information and communication technologies for environmental sustainability: Evidence from a large panel data analysis. J Environ Manage 293:112889

Al-Mulali U, Ozturk I, Solarin SA (2016) Investigating the environmental Kuznets curve hypothesis in seven regions: The role of renewable energy. Ecol Ind 67:267–282

Altıntaş H, Kassouri Y (2020) Is the environmental Kuznets Curve in Europe related to the per-capita ecological footprint or CO2 emissions? Ecol Ind 113:106187

Asongu SA, Agboola MO, Alola AA, Bekun FV (2020) The criticality of growth, urbanization, electricity and fossil fuel consumption to environment sustainability in Africa. Sci Total Environ 712:136376

Asongu SA, Nwachukwu JC, Pyke C (2019) The comparative economics of ICT, environmental degradation and inclusive human development in Sub-Saharan Africa. Soc Indic Res 143(3):1271–1297

Atsu F, Adams S, Adjei J (2021) ICT, energy consumption, financial development, and environmental degradation in South Africa. Heliyon e07328

Avom D, Nkengfack H, Fotio HK, Totouom A (2020) ICT and environmental quality in Sub-Saharan Africa: effects and transmission channels. Technol Forecast Soc Chang 155:120028

Azam A, Rafiq M, Shafique M, Yuan J (2021) An empirical analysis of the non-linear effects of natural gas, nuclear energy, renewable energy and ICT-Trade in leading CO2 emitter countries: Policy towards CO2 mitigation and economic sustainability. J Environ Manage 286:112232

Bilan Y, Oliinyk O, Mishchuk H, Skare M (2023) Impact of information and communications technology on the development and use of knowledge. Technol Forecast Soc Chang 191:122519

Breusch TS, Pagan AR (1980) The Lagrange multiplier test and its applications to model specification in econometrics. Rev Econ Stud 47(1):239–253

Caglar AE, Mert M, Boluk G (2021) Testing the role of information and communication technologies and renewable energy consumption in ecological footprint quality: evidence from world top 10 pollutant footprint countries. J Clean Prod 298:126784

Charfeddine L, Kahia M (2019) Impact of renewable energy consumption and financial development on CO2 emissions and economic growth in the MENA region: a panel vector autoregressive (PVAR) analysis. Renewable Energy 139:198–213

Chen Y, Zhao J, Lai Z, Wang Z, Xia H (2019) Exploring the effects of economic growth, and renewable and non-renewable energy consumption on China's CO2 emissions: evidence from a regional panel analysis. Renewable Energy 140:341–353

Cheng C, Ren X, Wang Z, Yan C (2019) Heterogeneous impacts of renewable energy and environmental patents on CO2 emission-Evidence from the BRIICS. Sci Total Environ 668:1328–1338

Danish MSS, Senjyu T, Yaqobi MA, Nazari Z, Matayoshi H, Zaheb H (2018) The role of ICT in corruption elimination: a holistic approach. In: 2018 IEEE 9th annual information technology, electronics and mobile communication conference (IEMCON). IEEE, pp 859–864

Danish, Baloch MA, Mahmood N, Zhang JW (2019) Effect of natural resources, renewable energy and economic development on CO2 emissions in BRICS countries. Sci Total Environ 678:632–638

Danish, Zhang B, Wang B, Wang Z (2017) Role of renewable energy and non-renewable energy consumption on EKC: evidence from Pakistan. J Cleaner Product 156:855–864

Danish, Zhang J, Wang B, Latif Z (2019) Towards cross-regional sustainable development: The nexus between information and communication technology, energy consumption, and CO2 emissions. Sustain Develop 27(5):990–1000

Del Baldo M (2023) OECD guidelines for SMEs. Encyclopedia of sustainable management. Springer International Publishing, Cham, pp 1–5
Dileep GJRE (2020) A survey on smart grid technologies and applications. Renewable Energy 146:2589–2625
Dong K, Sun R, Jiang H, Zeng X (2018) CO2 emissions, economic growth, and the environmental Kuznets curve in China: What roles can nuclear energy and renewable energy play? J Clean Prod 196:51–63
Earthineni N, Rao VS (2023) Remote monitoring and control of battery management system using CAN communication and IoT device for cloud based analysis and management. In 2023 IEEE 7th conference on information and communication technology (CICT). IEEE, pp 1–4
Fang X, Shi X, Phillips TK, Du P, Gao W (2021) The coupling coordinated development of urban environment towards sustainable urbanization: an empirical study of Shandong Peninsula. China. Ecological Indicators 129:107864
Farrar NO, Ali MH, Dasgupta D (2023) Artificial intelligence and machine learning in grid connected wind turbine control systems: a comprehensive review. Energies 16(3):1530
Global e-Sustainability Initiative (2020) SMART 2020: enabling the low carbon economy in the information age
Grossman GM, Krueger AB (1995) Economic growth and the environment. Q J Econ 110(2):353–377
Haini H (2021) Examining the impact of ICT, human capital and carbon emissions: evidence from the ASEAN economies. International Economics 166:116–125
Haldar A, Sucharita S, Dash DP, Sethi N, Padhan PC (2023) The effects of ICT, electricity consumption, innovation and renewable power generation on economic growth: an income level analysis for the emerging economies. J Clean Prod 384:135607
Hanif I, Raza SMF, Gago-de-Santos P, Abbas Q (2019) Fossil fuels, foreign direct investment, and economic growth have triggered CO2 emissions in emerging Asian economies: some empirical evidence. Energy 171:493–501
Huo T, Cao R, Du H, Zhang J, Cai W, Liu B (2021) Nonlinear influence of urbanization on China's urban residential building carbon emissions: new evidence from panel threshold model. Sci Total Environ 772:145058
Ibekwe KI, Umoh AA, Nwokediegwu ZQS, Etukudoh EA, Ilojianya VI, Adefemi A (2024) Energy efficiency in industrial sectors: a review of technologies and policy measures. Engin Sci Technol J 5(1):169–184
Ikevuje AH, Kwakye JM, Ekechukwu DE, Benjamin O (2023) Energy justice: ensuring equitable access to clean energy in underprivileged communities
Im KS, Pesaran MH, Shin Y (2003) Testing for unit roots in heterogeneous panels. J Economet 115(1):53–74
Iram M, Zameer S, Asghar MM (2024) Financial development, ICT use, renewable energy consumption and foreign direct investment impacts on environmental degradation in OIC countries. Pakistan J Humanities Soc Sci 12(2):1303–1315
ITU, ICT Development Index (2017) The International Telecommunication Union (ITU) ICT Development Index 2017, IDI 2017 Rank. Available from https://www.itu.int/net4/ITU-D/idi/2017/index.html#idi2017byregion-tab
Kao C (1999) Spurious regression and residual-based tests for cointegration in panel data. J Economet 90(1):1–44
Kao C, Chiang M (2000a) On the inference of a cointegrating regression in panel data. Adv Econ 15(1):179–222
Kao C, Chiang MH (2000b) Testing for structural change of a cointegrated regression in panel data. Syracuse University, Manuscript
Khalid M (2024) Smart grids and renewable energy systems: perspectives and grid integration challenges. Energ Strat Rev 51:101299

Khan I, Hou F, Le HP, Ali SA (2021) Do natural resources, urbanization, and value-adding manufacturing affect environmental quality? Evidence from the top ten manufacturing countries. Resour Policy 72:102109
Kothari DP, Ranjan R, Singal KC (2021) Renewable energy sources and emerging technologies
Krishnan N, Kumar KR, Inda CS (2023) How solar radiation forecasting impacts the utilization of solar energy: a critical review. J Clean Prod 388:135860
Kuznets S (1955) Economic growth and income inequality. Am Econ Rev 45(1):1–28
Lahouel BB, Taleb L, Zaied YB, Managi S (2021) Does ICT change the relationship between total factor productivity and CO2 emissions? Evidence based on a nonlinear model. Energy Econ 101:105406
Lei D, Xu X, Zhang Y (2021) Analysis of the dynamic characteristics of the coupling relationship between urbanization and environment in Kunming city, southwest China. Cleaner Environ Syst 2:100018
Levin A, Lin CF, Chu CSJ (2002) Unit root tests in panel data: asymptotic and finite-sample properties. J Economet 108(1):1–24
Li J, Herdem MS, Nathwani J, Wen JZ (2023) Methods and applications for artificial intelligence, big data, internet of things, and blockchain in smart energy management. Energy and AI 11:100208
Liu X, Kong H, Zhang S (2021) Can urbanization, renewable energy, and economic growth make environment more eco-friendly in Northeast Asia? Renewable Energy 169:23–33
Maddala GS, Wu S (1999) A comparative study of unit root tests with panel data and a new simple test. Oxford Bull Econ Stat 61(S1):631–652
Mahmood H, Alkhateeb TTY, Furqan M (2020) Industrialization, urbanization and CO2 emissions in Saudi Arabia: asymmetry analysis. Energy Rep 6:1553–1560
N'dri LM, Islam M, Kakinaka M (2021) ICT and environmental sustainability: any differences in developing countries?. J Cleaner Product 297:126642
Panda DK, Das S (2021) Smart grid architecture model for control, optimization and data analytics of future power networks with more renewable energy. J Clean Prod 301:126877
Pata UK (2018) Renewable energy consumption, urbanization, financial development, income and CO2 emissions in Turkey: testing EKC hypothesis with structural breaks. J Clean Prod 187:770–779
Pedroni P (1999) Critical values for cointegration tests in heterogeneous panels with multiple regressors. Oxford Bull Econ Stat 61(S1):653–670
Pedroni P (2000) Fully modified OLS for heterogeneous cointegrated panels. Adv Econ 15:93–130
Pedroni P (2001) Fully modified OLS for heterogeneous cointegrated panels. In Nonstationary panels, panel cointegration, and dynamic panels. Emerald Group Publishing Limited
Pedroni, P. (2004). Panel cointegration: asymptotic and finite sample properties of pooled time series tests with an application to the PPP hypothesis. *Econometric theory*, 597–625.
Pesaran MH (2004) General diagnostic tests for cross-sectional dependence in panels. Empir Econ 1–38
Pesaran MH (2007) A simple panel unit root test in the presence of cross-section dependence. J Appl Economet 22(2):265–312
Rahman MM, Alam K (2021) Clean energy, population density, urbanization and environmental pollution nexus: evidence from Bangladesh. Renew Energy 172:1063–1072
Rehman A, Ma H, Ozturk I, Alvarado R, Oláh J, Liu R, Qiang W (2024) The enigma of environmental sustainability and carbonization: assessing the connection between coal and oil rents, natural resources, and environmental quality. Gondwana Res 128:1–13
Rehman SU, Gill AR, Ali M (2023) Information and communication technology, institutional quality, and environmental sustainability in ASEAN countries. Environ Sci Pollut Res 1–14
Salahuddin M, Alam K, Ozturk I (2016) The effects of Internet usage and economic growth on CO2 emissions in OECD countries: a panel investigation. Renew Sustain Energy Rev 62:1226–1235
Sayed ET, Olabi AG, Alami AH, Radwan A, Mdallal A, Rezk A, Abdelkareem MA (2023) Renewable energy and energy storage systems. Energies 16(3):1415

Sinha A, Shahbaz M (2018) Estimation of environmental Kuznets curve for CO2 emission: role of renewable energy generation in India. Renewable Energy 119:703–711

Ulucak R, Khan SUD (2020) Does information and communication technology affect CO2 mitigation under the pathway of sustainable development during the mode of globalization? Sustain Dev 28(4):857–867

UN (2019) Report of the secretary-general on the 2019 climate action summit and the way forward in 2020. Un.Org

Voronkova V, Nikitenko V, Oleksenko R, Andriukaitiene R, Kharchenko J, Kliuienko E (2023) Digital technology evolution of the industrial revolution from 4g to 5g in the context of the challenges of digital globalization. TEM Journal. 12(2):732–742

Wang B, Guo X (2024) Blockchain-enabled transformation: decentralized planning and secure peer-to-peer trading in local energy networks. Sustain Energy, Grids Netw 40:101556

Wang J, Jiang Q, Dong X, Dong K (2021) Decoupling and decomposition analysis of investments and CO2 emissions in information and communication technology sector. Appl Energy 302:117618

Wang Q, Hu S, Li R (2024) Could information and communication technology (ICT) reduce carbon emissions? The role of trade openness and financial development. Telecommun Policy 48(3):102699

World Bank (2020a) List of economies. https://databank.worldbank.org

World Bank (2020b) World development indicators database: 2020. https://databank.worldbank.org

World Bank (2021) World Development Indicators (WDI). https://databank.worldbank.org/source/world-developmentindicators#advancedDownloadOptions

World Bank (2023) World development indicators database: 2023. https://databank.worldbank.org

World Economic Forum (2020) Global information technology report 2020. Readiness index 2020: digital transformation at a glance. https://knoema.com/infographics/ljisicg/network-readiness-index-2020-digital-transformation-at-a-glance

Yao S, Zhang S, Zhang X (2019) Renewable energy, carbon emission and economic growth: a revised environmental Kuznets Curve perspective. J Clean Prod 235:1338–1352

Zhang C, Liu C (2015) The impact of ICT industry on CO2 emissions: a regional analysis in China. Renew Sustain Energy Rev 44:12–19

Zheng Z, Wu Z, Chen Y, Yang Z, Marinello F (2020) Exploration of eco-environment and urbanization changes in coastal zones: a case study in China over the past 20 years. Ecol Ind 119:106847

Environmental Sustainability: Nexus Between Green Conscientiousness, Green Motivation, Green Altruism, Green Attitudinal Purchase Intention, and Green Brand Evangelism

Adnan Ahmed Sheikh, Asif Hameed, Syed Abdul Rehman Khan, and Zeeshan Ahmad

Abstract Globally, the degradation of natural resources and its severe environmental effects is growing. The world is united to work for the environment's safety and natural resources. Consumers are more conscious of utilizing those products that are harmful to the environment, and organizations are taking the competitive edge of consumer consciousness by providing environment-friendly products. However, it is also essential for organizations to realize that a green and sustainable environment changes the consumption pattern of societies and introduces other factors that can lead to green purchase intention. Besides, to make a consumer green brand evangelist, it is crucial to understand the necessary factors for environmental protection. Therefore, to fill this literature gap, the study aims to examine the effects of green conscientiousness (GC), green motivation (GM), green altruism (GA), and green attitudinal purchase intention (GPI) on green brand evangelism (GBE). The study data of 276 green customers were gathered and analyzed using partial least square structural equation modeling (PLS-SEM). The theory of reasoned action and purposeful work behavior were applied to describe a clear analytical basis for the research model. The study findings reinforce new evidence that green conscientiousness directly affects green motivation and green attitudinal purchase intention. In the focused group, respondents were active green buyers with experience purchasing green products.

A. A. Sheikh (✉)
College of Business, University of Buraimi, Al Buraimi, Sultanate of Oman
e-mail: adnan.a@uob.edu.om

A. Hameed
Department of Environment Science and Engineering, Tianjin University, Tianjin, China
e-mail: asif@tju.edu.cn

S. A. R. Khan
School of Engineering Management, Xuzhou University of Technology, Xuzhou, China
e-mail: sarehman_cscp@yahoo.com

Z. Ahmad
Department of Business Administration, Air University, Islamabad, Pakistan
e-mail: Zeeshan.ahmad@aumc.edu.pk

S. A. R. Khan et al. (eds.), *Circular Economy and Technological Innovation*, Industrial Ecology, https://doi.org/10.1007/978-981-96-5650-9_10

Our analysis concludes that green motivation significantly mediates green conscientiousness and green attitudinal purchase intention. Besides, green motivation and brand evangelism are significantly mediated by green attitudinal purchase intention. Finally, green altruism significantly moderates the impact of green motivation on green attitudinal purchase intention. The developing country's government and management should invest in evangelists to disseminate the green note to delicate environmental sustainability. Future studies may investigate a composite model that assesses the impact of environmental awareness on brand evangelism, with green purchasing intentions considering a mediating variable.

Keywords Environmental sustainability · Green conscientiousness · Green motivation · Green attitudinal purchase intention · Green altruism · Green brand evangelism

1 Introduction

Environmental issues have drastically affected the business patterns of organizations and the associated consumers worldwide (Ambec and De Donder 2022; Lisniak 2024; Sreenivasan and Suresh 2023). Notably, natural resources are depleting continuously because of significant economic expansion, which is dragging on environmental issues (Hameed et al. 2021; Panda et al. 2020). Especially in promoting green consumer brands (Ambec and De Donder 2022; Hallez et al. 2023; Hong et al. 2024). Today, the world is not sustainable, not fair, and not resilient for the majority of human-being. The misuse of energy and resources leading to environmental problems has created alarming situations (Ali et al. 2021; Berman Caggiano et al. 2021; Hossain et al. 2022). The massive increase in consumption activities by the end-users, the natural resources are depleting, and the severe effect on the environment have raised concerns for humans and organizations (Haake and Seuring 2009; Jafari et al. 2022). Unfortunately, such disastrous consumption activities need abrupt remedies to control environmental and health-related issues. Therefore, to reduce the harmful effects on the environment, consumers must shift to environment-friendly products that are recyclable and healthy enough to protect human life and the surroundings precisely (Khan et al. 2023). Globally, the consumer concern about green products and the relevant information the organization has to protect the environment has emerged from a practical perspective. Consumers who are more conscious and conscientious in terms of personality traits will be more eco-friendly as they can choose between right and wrong (Chwialkowska et al. 2020; Majeed et al. 2022).

Moreover, the word conscious links with the personality trait of conscientiousness, which means to differentiate between right and wrong; therefore, customers who are more conscientious and motivated and are continuously involved in the buying process of sustainable products are considered eco-friendly consumers (Majeed et al. 2022). At the same time, conscientiousness is a core personality trait—one of the Big Five—characterized by a propensity for organizing, being responsible, goal-oriented, hard-working, and adhering to norms and regulations. Consumer decision-making about green products is considerably affected by their personality traits and green motivation to make a green attitudinal purchase decision and finally to perform as an evangelist of green products (Panda et al. 2020). To build motivation among customers and create altruistic love for green brands, marketers must depict the benefits of green products and their impact on individual life (Groening et al. 2018). Moreover, the organization's believability is another reason for building consumer attitudes toward green products, and customers play a better role as green brand evangelists. Green brand evangelist not only purchases a green product of the organization but also communicate and share a positive experience with society by creating green word of mouth. Such marketers can achieve an ethical profit for the organization (More 2023; Prakash and Pathak 2017).

The mechanism and logic behind green attitudinal purchase intention development were understood, limited studies have been identified in different contexts (Gadenne et al. 2011; Hong et al. 2024; Prakash and Pathak 2017; Waris and Hameed 2021). In scrutinizing the association between green purchase intention and the relevant consumer behavioral outcomes like green brand evangelism, the theory of reasoned action and purposeful work behavior are used to explain the phenomena. GC, also known as green consciousness, is a positive personality trait linked and examined with green attitudinal purchase intention. However, studies related to green attitudinal purchase intention with green behavior, for instance, green brand evangelism, are still under debate (Guiao and Lacap 2022; Panda et al. 2020). Further, the study on GPI about GC and GM lacks in literature. Specifically, the moderating role of GA is a unique combination of understanding and building consumer behavior towards eco-friendly products. Moreover, the theoretical lens to understand the consumer green consumption pattern is another gap that has been addressed in the current study.

Further, emerging countries that are developing in terms of eco-friendly products and trying to achieve sustainable goals need consideration to address the emerging issue in a purely research manner. Therefore, the current study will open avenues for sustainable development for developing countries by looking at the essential factors to establish an eco-friendly environment. In the past literature, green purchase intention was examined through eco-friendly consumer behavioral outcomes using the theory of planned behavior (TPB). Besides, assessing green purchase intention through environmental consciousness and green motivation in consumers as well as its influence on brand evangelism moderated by altruism, is rare.

The situation managed using specific coping strategies has emerged at different times; the rigorous step to overcoming the situation is to devise sustainable environmental strategies. Therefore, green production, consumption, and marketing will play a vital role (Asih et al. 2020; Hazaea et al. 2022; Paul et al. 2016). While to increase the acceptability of such products and the related benefits which remained unexplored, there is a dire need for promotional or motivational activities globally and specifically in developing countries where technologically innovated products have been found unrated (Ali et al. 2020; Hallez et al. 2023; Harjadi and Gunardi 2022; Prakash et al. 2019). However, past literature suggested that green electronics, particularly home appliances, have low acceptability by consumers due to a lack of knowledge, awareness, and resilience to technology (da Luz et al. 2020; Zhang and Liu 2022; Zhang and Luo 2023). The environment will only be protected, and fossil reserves can economize when the customers are well aware of energy-efficient products (Hossain et al. 2022). The Economic Information Center 2010 Census reports frequent increases in power use among urban and rural people over the previous few years. The yearly power consumption of rural and urban residents was 70.37 million kWh, which rose to 83.11 million kWh by 2024. It shows that household appliances account for the majority of energy usage (Ali et al. 2021; Pakistan Electricity Consumption 2024; Zhang and Liu 2022; Zhang and Luo 2023). Therefore, studying individual beliefs, social influence, and attitudes toward green home appliances is essential to understanding the green world. Sustainability protects the environment and human and ecological well-being and drives innovation (Ali et al. 2020; da Luz et al. 2020; Shah et al. 2023; Zhang et al. 2022).

Sustainable development believes that economic prosperity, human development, and nature protection are interrelated (Ali et al. 2023; Dalvi-Esfahani et al. 2020; Hong et al. 2024). Therefore, this dynamic era requires involvement and innovative technology for producing household equipment to establish close ties with customers (Siano et al. 2022; Steenkamp 2020; Swaminathan et al. 2020). Developing green electronic products and their consumption has become necessary, specifically in Pakistan (Ali et al. 2021; Hossain et al. 2022; Shah et al. 2023; Zhang et al. 2022). Both customers and organizations start thinking green and collectively feel affectionate for the clean climate (Ali et al. 2020; Berman Caggiano et al. 2021). Therefore, marketers must increase promotions, provide opportunities, and motivate customers to buy green electronic home appliances for a sustainable environment while running a profitable business (Horne et al. 2020; Sreenivasan and Suresh 2023; Terán-Yépez et al. 2020). Thus, it is necessary to understand which personality traits motivate and develop individuals' and groups' attitudes to the intention for buying green products and become green brand evangelists.

The overconsumption of energy resources causes the misuse of resources (Hummels and Argyrou 2021). It creates unnatural climate challenges without opting for the latest technologies like inverters and hybrids, which are directly related to consumers' purchasing patterns (Hossain et al. 2022; Zhang and Liu 2022; Zhang and Luo 2023). This competitive era has led many buyers to reconsider their consumption choices due to overuse and degradation of land resources, such as deforestation, fossil fuel, fossil gases, and natural resource scarcity (Ali et al. 2021; Hossain et al. 2022; Hummels and Argyrou 2021). Consequently, consumers are becoming green and conscientious about their usage because polluting nature can lead to a disaster of energy in general and health in specific (Shah et al. 2023; Zhang et al. 2022; Zhang and Liu 2022; Zhang and Luo 2023). Therefore, green motivation toward purchasing energy-efficient products can lead to a brand evangelist scenario where the customer can advocate and spread the importance of efficient technology after becoming an evangelist (Ali et al. 2020; Guiao and Lacap 2022).

Green conscientiousness personality rationale motivates consumers to acquire electronic products by realizing that these products save both energy and nature (Laurent et al. 2020; Panda et al. 2020). Green conscientiousness is a trait of being vigilant, careful, reliable, organized, goal-oriented, and preserving nature (Ababneh 2021; Duarte et al. 2024; Mahlamäki et al. 2019). The individuals are motivated by a significant love for nature. Green conscientiousness and nature love drive us to choose green appliances instead of conventional ones that save the environment due to energy-efficient performance (Ali et al. 2021; Berman Caggiano et al. 2021). Green motivation plays a positive role in behavior, leading to rearranging gratification and high regulation of desires and realizing that their purchasing decisions affect the environment (Ali et al. 2020, 2023).

Moreover, the motivated green consumer prefers environment-friendly measures (Li et al. 2020; Maitlo et al. 2022). The study examines green motivation and its influences on the green attitudinal purchase intention of prospects who are explicitly using green electronic home appliances. Such personalities with these traits have had a personality trait of green conscientiousness. Moreover, Wuertz (2015) recommended that green conscientiousness adopted by individuals or organizations will be a factor that plays an active role in a clean environment (Wuertz 2015). Next, some studies have found insignificant results with the mediating role of green motivation and green attitudinal purchase intention tested in China in similar sectors (Ali et al. 2020), Current research has examined how green motivation and green attitudinal purchase intention results in Pakistan, particularly the consumer attitude and behavior toward using green electronic home appliances.

Few researchers thought energy-efficient electronic items protect the environment. Green conscientiousness is a personality trait that influences organizations to produce home appliances that are energy efficient to make customers green brand evangelists (Berman Caggiano et al. 2021; Shah et al. 2023; Zhang et al. 2022). Therefore, there is a need to examine green motivation and green attitudinal purchase intention as mediation (Ali et al. 2020; Guiao and Lacap 2022). Further, testing a moderating effect of green altruism between these mediation variables makes this a novel study (Laurent et al. 2020). These motivations originate from an internal passion and lead to the intentional formation process for green electronic home appliances (Panda et al. 2020; Zhang et al. 2022). This study examines the effect of green conscientiousness on green brand evangelism, with a mediating role of green motivation and green attitudinal purchase intention (Fig. 1).

2 Theoretical Development: Theory of Reason Action and Purposeful Work Behavior

The studies have explored that attitude and norms develop an individual's intention to proceed with the behaviour (Asih et al. 2020; Prakash et al. 2019). The theory of reason action (TRA) states that subjective norms form attitudes towards behavioral intention. Today, collective motivation is required for individuals and businesses to collaborate and achieve sustainable development in all ways (Zhang and Liu 2022; Zhang and Luo 2023). For a sustainable business, the customer supports managerial

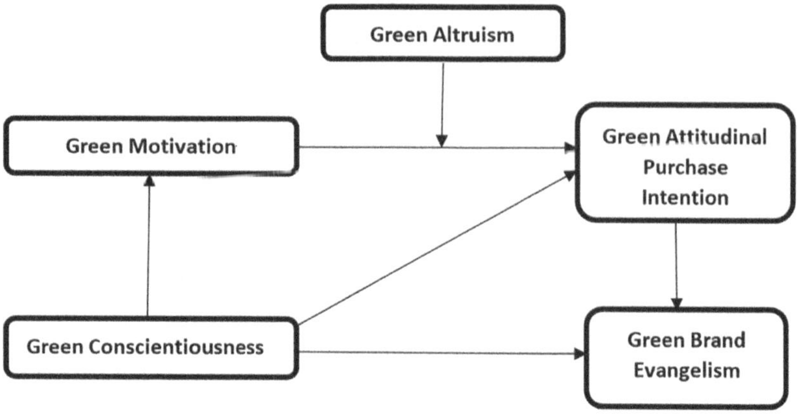

Fig. 1 Conceptual model

decisions and practices and spreads positive norms that help the business flourish (Ali et al. 2023; Asih et al. 2020). Achievements depend on individual motivation (intention) and ability (behavior) (Paul et al. 2016). The theory of reason action provides a sound theoretical model and has become the most commonly used model in rational choices (Asih et al. 2020). Ethical behavior in the theory of reason action (TRA) regarding the decision-making framework and association of individual belief and behavior. Previous literature shows that ecological problems can be get exaggerated by consumer purchase behavior to protect nature (Graça and Kharé 2023; Lopes et al. 2024). The theory of purposeful work behavior explains personality traits and motivates individuals to pursue the attitude. Purposefulness is a dynamic motivational process that endorses personality traits to pursue attitude (Dalvi-Esfahani et al. 2020).

In this model, human attitude requires significant attention to developing purchase intention and, ultimately, an individual's behavioral development. Specifically, attitude is the degree of likeness or unlikeness of an individual. Subjective norm is his belief or value perceived for the social environment (peers, friends, and family) (da Luz et al. 2020; Zhang and Luo 2023). In general, positive attitudes and favorable subjective norms correlate with a solid intention to perform the behavior. Conversely, intention can help predict the behavior's performance and stronger intention or solid willingness can lead to more chances of behavioral achievements. The consumer green attitudinal purchase decision comes under ethical behavior (Ambec and De Donder 2022; Majeed et al. 2022). In this research, consumers believe to be more conscious of climate and surroundings. This green attitude towards the environment becomes a part of the personality trait of an individual (Dalvi-Esfahani et al. 2020). To purchase a green electronic product (i.e., behavior) requires green motivation that directly links with purposeful work behavior and the theory of reason action to explain the study framework in examining the effect of green conscientiousness on green brand evangelism.

Green brand evangelism indicates a robust consumer-brand affiliation and is a form of persuasion (Hallez et al. 2023; Pornsrimate and Khamwon 2020). It is an act of promoting green electronic products that save energy and protect the environment. Environmental researchers investigated consumer sustainable and green behavior precursors from emerging and advanced economies and found that reliance, persuasion, and attitude towards purchasing a product have a vital role (Panda et al. 2020). A consumer having emotional solid commitment and behavior convinces others about the brand's benefits, purchasing favored brands, and acting as an unpaid spokesperson (Pornsrimate and Khamwon 2020; Steenkamp 2020). Motivation significantly influences product selection and adoption; people realize their role in protecting the environment (Ali et al. 2020, 2023; Dalvi-Esfahani et al. 2020). Consumers with the personality traits of green conscientiousness are more inclined to buy green products. Therefore, this communication attempts to influence others to purchase the eco-friendly brand and interact with consumers to make brand evangelism essential for company success.

3 Literature Review and Hypotheses Development

3.1 Green Conscientiousness and Green Brand Evangelism

Green brand evangelism is a type of persuasion that promotes green electronic products that save energy and protect the environment (Hazaea et al. 2022; Pornsrimate and Khamwon 2020; Steenkamp 2020). Past studies have elaborated on the relationship between brand evangelism and conscientiousness and the underlying importance (Hazaea et al. 2022; Panda et al. 2020). Past literature on brand evangelism shows an insignificant relationship with conscientiousness and further suggested checking the significance of this relationship in developing countries. Recent literature on green brand evangelism explained that the intention to establish green behavior is essential (Hazaea et al. 2022). A study conducted in China on green electronic product consumption found it insignificant (Ali et al. 2020). The study proposed to re-test the relationship in different regions of the world and establish the hypothesis below.

H_1: Green conscientiousness personality trait positively enhances the green brand evangelism behavior.

3.2 Green Conscientiousness and Green Motivation

Motivation is a drive, desire, or need that contributes to and explains behavioral changes. Motivated individuals strongly focus on conscientiousness and tend to be determined, systematic, purposeful, and inflexible regarding environmental protection and are willing to follow the consumption pattern that saves climate. Green conscientious individuals are motivated toward goal-oriented behavior. The well-documented correlation between conscientiousness and motivation performs a solid conceptual foundation. Some studies suggest a connection between green conscientiousness and green motivation (Laurent et al. 2020; Mahlamäki et al. 2019). Therefore, this study establishes the direct relation between green conscientiousness and green motivation by articulating the following hypothesis:

H_2: Green conscientiousness personality trait is positively related to green motivation.

3.3 Green Conscientiousness and Green Attitudinal Purchase Intention

Conscientious individuals tend to be organized, efficient, and motivated toward purchase intention, perform at a higher degree of adoption behavior, and take steps to improve efficiency. Therefore, they consider a particular product only after carefully evaluating its opportunities for further achievement (Mahlamäki et al. 2019). People with solid green conscientiousness are self-disciplined, and robust willing. However, innovative technology enhances efficiency and effectiveness in performing a specific action to increase trust and usage (Zhang and Liu 2022; Zhang and Luo 2023). Therefore, it establishes below hypothesis.

H_3: Green conscientiousness is positively related to green attitudinal purchase intention.

3.4 Green Motivation and Green Attitudinal Purchase Intention

Naturally, people are motivated by such pleasant and fascinating items. An encouraged consumer intends to buy green electronic products due to natural attachment and willingness to purchase intention. For instance, if their desire for green electronic home appliances succeeded due to discouraging factors like cost or marketing deception, consumers would be more motivated and inclined toward green attitudinal purchase intention (Shah et al. 2023; Zhang et al. 2022). A previous study suggested that customers with pleasure activities are constructed for the eco-friendly environment and got involved in purchasing green electronic home appliances (Li et al. 2020). Besides, a study found that green motivation plays a dominant role in developing consumers' attitudinal purchase intention to procure green electronic products (Ali et al. 2020). Therefore, a consumer with higher motivation pursues green attitudinal purchasing intentions and establish the following hypothesis.

H_4: Green motivation is positively related to green attitudinal purchase intention.

3.5 Green Attitudinal Purchase Intention and Green Brand Evangelism

A solid emotional attachment between consumer and brand leads to green brand evangelism, which builds bonding, not a brand. However, brands attempt to bias consumers through advertising and various promotional strategies. The consumer decides to wear the title of an evangelist (Guiao and Lacap 2022; Pornsrimate and Khamwon 2020). The consumer does not need to buy a particular brand to become brand evangelism which presents an insignificant relationship between consumer green attitudinal purchase-intention and green brand evangelism. The green brand evangelism and green attitudinal purchase intention relationship and found it significant positive (Harrigan et al. 2021). Further, a study recommended that green attitudinal purchase intention with green brand evangelism needs empirical investigation in various countries (Pornsrimate and Khamwon 2020). Therefore, the following hypothesis has been proposed;

H_5: Green attitudinal purchase intention is positively related to green brand evangelism.

3.6 Green Altruism as Moderation Between Green Motivation and Green Attitudinal Purchase Intention

The individual's willingness trait to share knowledge in virtual environments refers to green altruism (Ali et al. 2020; Hazaea et al. 2022; Prakash et al. 2019). It is an effective construct that stimulates individuals for energy-efficient consumption behaviors. In recent environmental research, green altruism is a robust and established personality trait (Ali et al. 2020; Panda et al. 2020; Tan et al. 2020) and is considered a construct that encourages individuals to choose a green electronic product. Green altruistic individuals realize that green attitudinal purchase decision plays a significant role in energy-saving and reducing waste to protect nature and the green environment for future generations (Hong et al. 2024). In past studies, green altruism positively correlates with green motivation and green attitudinal intention but is not tested as a moderator (Ali et al. 2020; Guiao and Lacap 2022). Past studies tested green altruism with green motivation, and the results found a significant relationship. Therefore, based on the recommendations, this variable has been considered a moderator between green motivation and green attitudinal purchase intention (Laurent et al. 2020).

Green altruism is the individual action on behalf of someone without expecting any benefit and is an effective predictor of nature care (Tan et al. 2020). Moreover, green, conscientious individuals benefit from their actions rather than their value. Previous research results show that green altruism significantly affects consumer purchase intention for green electronic items (Hong et al. 2024; Prakash et al. 2019)Future studies also recommend using green altruism to check the difference in results. So, the following hypothesis is established.

H_6: Green altruism positively moderates the relationship between green motivation and green attitudinal purchase intention.

3.7 Mediating Effects

Understanding green conscientiousness and green brand evangelism relationship through green attitudinal purchase intention needs further investigation (Duarte et al. 2024; Panda et al. 2020). Further, recommended in future studies for testing "How to encourage sustainability and the use of green and sustainable goods using motivation for green brand evangelists must be studied."

At the same time, the study aims to find the green motivation and green purchase intention, green conscientiousness, and brand evangelism relationship. Thus, establishing the link between conscientiousness and green motivation, the antecedent constructs, and their hypothesis.

H_7: Green motivation positively mediates between green conscientiousness and green attitudinal purchase intention.

H_8: Green attitudinal purchase intention has a mediating relationship with green motivation and green brand evangelism.

H_9: Green motivation and green attitudinal purchase intention both have a mediating relationship with green conscientiousness and green brand evangelism.

4 Research Methodology: Survey Method and Data Collection

The study has focused the user of green electronic home appliance. The target population was household consumers because the electronics industry in Pakistan is continuously working to produce energy-efficient products. However, marketers cannot convince the consumers or lack awareness about the benefits of such products ignored. To cater to the actual users of these electronic products, we adopted a convenient sampling technique. We circulated 285 self-administrated questionnaires at different electronic stores in three major cities (Lahore, Multan, and Faisalabad) in Punjab, Pakistan. The researcher has selected these cities because they have a good market where billions of rupees in business transactions are executed daily in link to electronic products. Secondly, most companies like Dawlance, Orient, Haier, PEL, Gree, Mitsubishi, Electrolux, and many other international brands have their head and sub-offices in these cities to facilitate the dealers and retailers. Thirdly, these companies are continuously producing energy-efficient products due to high competition. A price war is another challenge for customers to take price benefits

Table 1 Respondent's demographic profile

Demographic variables	Classification	Frequency	Percent
Gender	Male	171	74
	Female	60	26
Age	Below 25	24	10
	26–33	145	63
	34–41	45	20
	Above 41	16	7
Education	Graduate	65	28
	Post Graduate	42	18
	Doctor	23	10
	Others	101	44
Cities	Lahore	97	42
	Multan	85	37
	Faisalabad	49	21

and buy the product with easy access. Fourthly, customers and retailers from all over the province visit these cities for buying purposes.

Moreover, the response rate of this study was 97 percent (276), while 231 surveys were considered valid and usable for data analysis. Further, Seventy-four percent of male, and twenty-six percent female participants were responded. The maximum respondent's age was 26 to 33 years and belonged to Lahore, as shown in (Table 1). Frequency.

4.1 Measures

We adopted measures for green conscientiousness (GC) with five items from Ali et al. (2020), Vander Ark (1971), green motivation (GM) with four items from Mahadin et al. (2020), Mahadin and Akroush (2019), green altruism (GA) with three items from Andreu et al. (2015), and green brand evangelism (GBE) with four items from Panda et al. (2020), Riorini and Widayati (2016). However, the green attitudinal purchase intention (GPI) scale was adopted with five items (Panda et al. 2020). Using five-point Likert scale, 1 for strongly disagree to 5 for strongly agree for all without facing problems in measuring the reliability and validity of questions. Furthermore, socio-economic properties (gender, age, and education) of the respondents were adjusted for potential alternative effects (Wu 2024). To understand the information, a short description was described at the top of the questionnaire for awareness and promotion of green electronic home appliances before answering (Zhang et al. 2022).

5 Results

5.1 Measurement Model

The results of Cronbach's alpha (α) and composite reliability (CR) of all constructs were more outstanding than 0.70 during the measurement of model assessment. This is the minimum reliability requirement (Fornell and Larcker, 1981). The average variance extracted (AVE) value was more significant than 0.50 (Bagozzi and Yi 1988, 2012) and was validated by heterotrait-monotrait ratios (HTMT), with all ratios remaining below 0.95 (Edeh et al. 2023). Tables 2 and 3 validate the development of reliability and discriminatory validity.

The variance inflation factor (VIF) values confirmed no multicollinearity issues (Ali et al. 2020). All VIF values were below 3.3, which indicates no common method bias in the research (Rasoolimanesh et al. 2015). Further validation confirmed that all items in the study were reflective and conducted Harman's single-factor analysis using SPSS. Only 30.9 percent of the variance was elucidated, indicating no predominance by any single construct. Further, we applied Smart-PLS by testing all constructs against each other and found an inner VIF value below 3.3 of all tested constructs as recommended (Rasoolimanesh et al. 2015). The R-square value of 0.47 for green purchase intention indicates a satisfactory predictive capability for the research findings. Thus, the research fulfils all research analysis requirements.

5.2 Hypothesis Tests (Direct Relationships)

The hypotheses' direct, mediation, and moderation results (H1 to H9) are shown in Tables 4, 5, and 6. Each latent variable's direct influence on green brand evangelism represents the output generated by Smart PLS 3.2.9 (Rasoolimanesh 2022; Rasoolimanesh et al. 2015); p-value, t-value, coefficient value, and default errors are illustrated. The hypothesis decision was taken concerning any hypothesis level according to these threshold values. The Current research has developed t-values from bootstrapping guidelines (containing 5000 sampling iterations for 231 cases/observances). Furthermore, this research examines the impact of green altruism between green motivation and green attitudinal purchase intention as a moderator. The underlying objectives of this study are to explain the relationship in general and increase knowledge by considering these specific variables. The background of the research explains why the topic needs to be examined and established with relevant phenomena that emphasize its importance.

In direct analysis, green conscientiousness on green brand evangelism is sharply decreasing ($\beta = 0.060$, $t = 0.970$, $p = 0.166$) and turns out to be insignificant, so H1 is rejected, which means there must substantial need for a variable for connection. The effect of green conscientiousness increased on green motivation ($\beta = 0.474$, $t = 9.017$, $p < 0.01$) and green attitudinal purchase intention ($\beta = 0.136$, $t = 2.006$, p

Table 2 Reliability and validity of constructs

Construct items		Loading	VIF	A	CR	AVE
Green conscientiousness				0.842	0.888	0.614
1	I see myself as someone who can be somewhat careless for the environment	0.736	1.78			
2	I see myself as someone reliable for nature	0.799	2.07			
3	I see myself as someone who tends to be disorganized for the environment	0.788	1.74			
4	I see myself as someone who does things efficiently for the environment	0.776	2.01			
5	I see myself as someone who makes plans to protect the environment and follows through with them	0.816	2.24			
Green motivation				0.909	0.936	0.785
1	Green electronic (Hybrid or Inverter) products evaluate environmental performance	0.870	2.85			
2	I save both energy and money by using green electronic products	0.872	2.84			
3	Green electronic product performance includes environmental incidents, responsibilities, concerns, and policy	0.913	2.67			
4	I save energy by buying and using green electronic products	0.890	2.1			
Green attitudinal purchase intention				0.881	0.913	0.676
1	I plan to buy green electronic (Hybrid or Inverter) products due to their environmental consideration	0.813	2.36			

(continued)

Table 2 (continued)

Construct items		Loading	VIF	A	CR	AVE
2	I anticipate acquiring green electrical products due to their environmental efficacy in the future	0.818	2.42			
3	I am pleased to acquire green electrical products due to their eco-friendliness	0.796	2.12			
4	I am willing to purchase green electrical products due to their environmental efficacy	0.841	2.75			
5	I am prepared to pay a premium for environmentally sustainable electronic products	0.843	2.66			
Green altruism				0.878	0.925	0.804
1	I am motivated for saving the environment and money, also help society by green product purchasing	0.879	2.07			
2	I am fulfilling my duty for society and saving energy by green electronic (Hybrid or Inverter) products buying	0.895	2.69			
3	I contend that the world would improve if all capable individuals acquired environmentally friendly electronic products	0.915	2.79			
Green brand evangelism				0.859	0.904	0.703
1	I plan to buy eco-friendly electronic products (Hybrid or Inverter) due to environmental concern	0.883	2.7			

(continued)

Table 2 (continued)

Construct items		Loading	VIF	A	CR	AVE
2	I intend to acquire green electronic products in the future due to their environmental performance	0.874	2.72			
3	I am happy to buy green electronic products due to environmental efficacy	0.789	1.85			
4	I am motivated to purchase eco-friendly electrical products due to their sustainable performance	0.803	1.86			

Table 3 Discriminant validity (HTMT)

Constructs	GA	GBE	GC	GM	GPI
Green altruism					
Green brand evangelism	0.407				
Green conscientiousness	0.472	0.372			
Green motivation	0.483	0.639	0.539		
Green purchase intention	0.517	0.659	0.544	0.792	

Notes GC = Green Conscientiousness, GM = Green Motivation, GPI, Green Attitudinal Purchase Intention, GA = Green Altruism, GBE = Green Brand Evangelism

Table 4 Hypotheses assessment

Effect	Hypothesis	Path	β - value	t-value	p-value
Direct model analysis	H1	GC → GBE	0.060	0.970	0.166
	H2	GC → GM	0.474	9.017	0.000
	H3	GC → GPI	0.136	2.006	0.022
	H4	GM → GPI	0.593	9.978	0.000
	H5	GPI → GBE	0.550	9.513	0.000

NotesGC = Green Conscientiousness, GM = Green Motivation, GPI, Green Attitudinal Purchase Intention, GA = Green Altruism, GBE = Green Brand Evangelism

= 0.022) and turned to significant. Hence, H2 and H3 are supported. We contended that marketing and provocative activities tend to stimulate attention and interest in environmental initiatives. Green motivation significantly influences green attitudinal purchasing intention ($\beta = 0.593$, $t = 9.978$, $p < 0.01$), which in turn affects green brand evangelism ($\beta = 0.550$, $t = 9.513$, $p < 0.01$). So, we accept H4 and H5. The

Table 5 Results of hypothesis testing (Moderation effects)

Moderation analysis	Hypothesis	Beta	SD	T Stats	P-Value	Result	Decision
Moderation GA b/w GM*GPI - > Green Purchase Intention	H6	0.101	0.045	2.224	0.013	Moderation	*Strengthening the relationship b/w GM and GPI, due to positive beta-value*

Table 6 Results of hypothesis testing (Mediation effects)

Mediation analysis	Hypotheses	Beta	SD	T Stats	P-Value	5.00%	95.00%	Decision
Green Motivation - > Green attitudinal Purchase-Intention - > Green Brand Evangelism	H7	0.419	0.052	8.013	0.00	0.326	0.50	Mediation
Green Conscientiousness - > Green Motivation - > Green attitudinal Purchase-Intention - > Green Brand Evangelism	H8	0.200	0.039	5.139	0.00	0.136	0.26	Mediation
Green Conscientiousness - > Green Motivation - > Green Purchase Intention	H9	0.344	0.047	7.378	0.00	0.263	0.42	Mediation

direct effect of green altruism also increased on green attitudinal purchase intention ($\beta = 0.145$ $t = 2.438$, $p = 0.005$).

Introducing the mediator in model 2 effect's green conscientiousness ($\beta = 0.344$, $t = 7.378$, $p < 0.01$) on green attitudinal purchasing intention and green motivation ($\beta = 0.419$ $t = 8.013$, $p < 0.01$) on green brand evangelism, and green conscientiousness ($\beta = 0.200$, $t = 5139$, $p < 0.01$) on green brand evangelism sharply increased. So all mediators, H7, H8, and H9, proved significant and fully supported. Therefore we state that promotion and environmental cognition boost the individual toward green electronic home appliances. Green altruism's moderating effect has been found significant for green motivation and green attitudinal purchasing intention ($\beta = 0.101$, $t = 2.224$, $p = 0.013$). It clearly explains that moderator green altruism strengthens the green motivation and green attitudinal purchase intention relationship due to positive Beta. Thus H6 is supported (Fig. 2).

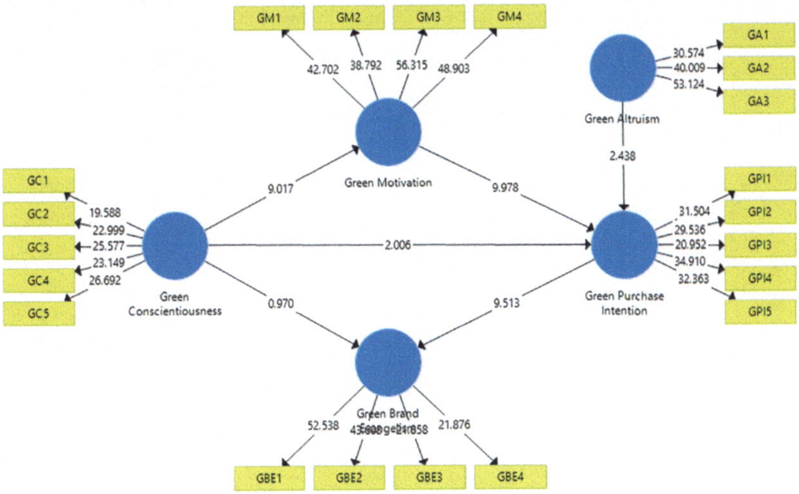

Fig. 2 Structural model assessment

5.3 Moderation Analysis

Green altruism positively moderates between green motivation and green attitudinal purchasing intention on green brand evangelism and strengthens their relationship. Figure 3 exhibits that higher individual green motivation encourages green attitudinal purchasing intention towards green brand evangelism. This derive that minor green motivation leads to green purchasing intentions decline.

5.4 Mediation Analysis

A mediator intervenes the effect between two constructs to explain the underlying mechanism (Edeh et al. 2023). This study incorporated green motivation and green attitudinal purchase intention to mediate between green conscientiousness and green brand evangelism. Table 6 shows that it fulfils the first condition of mediation analysis and relationships of dependent and independent variables are significant. The second condition found an insignificant direct effect of green conscientiousness on green brand evangelism. After introducing the mediators, we found direct effect of green conscientiousness on green brand evangelism prominently raised, which is 0.344, 0.419, and 0.200 beta coefficient values, respectively, that satisfying a third required condition of a mediation analysis (Edeh et al. 2023).

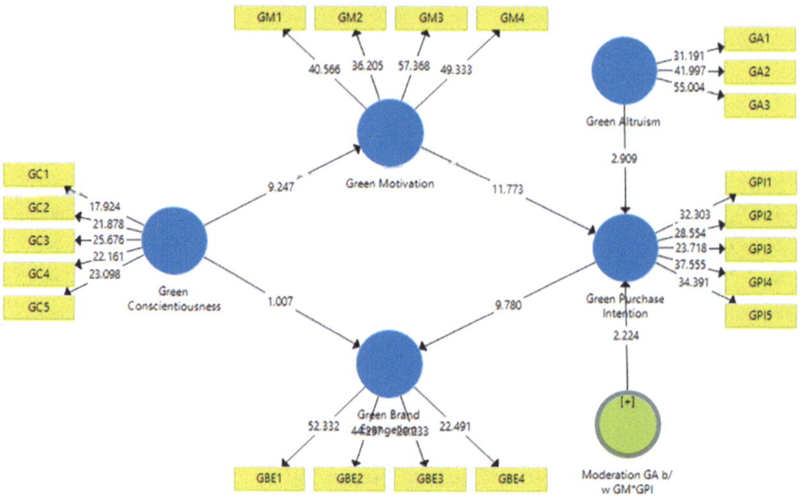

Fig. 3 Moderating effect between green motivation and green attitudinal purchase intention on green brand evangelism

6 Discussion

The research was conducted empirically to investigate the associations between green conscientiousness, green motivation, green attitudinal purchase intention, green altruism, and green brand evangelism, applying multiple regression analysis to test hypotheses. A direct correlation was analyzed, and the mediating effect of green motivation and green attitudinal purchase intention among independent and dependent variables. The green altruism's moderating effect in predicting motivation and purchase intention was also analyzed.

The study results show that the green conscientiousness and green brand evangelism relationship is insignificant and not supported ($\beta = 0.060$, $t = 0.970$, $p > 0.05$) as the p-value does not support hypothesis H1. Aydın (2017) explained that market mavenisim tendency is negatively related to conscientiousness (Aydın 2017). Due to the brand evangelism relationship, a potential association may exist between evangelism and conscientiousness. However, there is no substantial evidence in past studies that shows a significant relationship between green conscientiousness and green brand evangelism relationship. Consumers possessing conscientious personality traits may exhibit strong brand loyalty and perceive the dissemination of brand information as a social duty. Besides, consumers involved in buying energy-efficient products may lack to develop love or spread positive information about the brand among their network because sharing the usefulness of the product is the other thing and advocating the brand name is a different concept (Aydın 2017; Hong et al. 2024). Therefore, the relationship between green conscientiousness personality consumers and green brand evangelism has been insignificant in the current scenario. In line with the theory of reasoned action that people behave based on their pre-existing attitudes in current scenario. The consumer in Pakistan needs to be aware of the usage benefits of energy-efficient products. Afterwards, they might establish the specific behaviour of brand evangelists.

Further, H2 articulated that green conscientiousness has positive and significant influence on green motivation. Thus, results revealed a significant outcome of ($\beta = 0.474$, $t = 9.014$, $p < 0.005$). Moreover, studies have demonstrated that conscientious green consumers are self-motivated to protect the environment (Laurent et al. 2020). Conscientiousness is a personality trait characterized by diligence and carefulness. Therefore, it implies a wish to perform tasks well and honour duties to others seriously. Conscientious individuals are typically efficient and structured rather than relaxed. Therefore, they always feel motivated to do certain tasks directly or indirectly related to societal and environmental benefits.

Moreover, Hypotheses H3 proposed a positive relationship between green conscientiousness and green attitudinal purchase intention. The findings have shown positive and significant outcomes ($\beta = 0.136$, $t = 2.006$, $p = 0.022$). However, past literature has ignored testing this relationship specifically in the context of green electronic home appliance consumption. People with strong green conscientiousness stay firm on their rational opinions because they are self-disciplined and strongly willing. However, innovative technology enhances efficiency and effectiveness in performing a specific action to increase trust and usage. Past studies indicated that enriching green conscientiousness is more willing to green attitudinal purchase intention. Chains that the reaction theory explains that a person can develop certain actions based on subjective norms and attitudinal changes.

The green motivation and green attitudinal purchase intention direct relationship were positively significant, thus supporting hypothesized H4 ($\beta = 0.593$, $t = 9.978$, $p < 0.005$). In past research, green intrinsic motivation and green purchase intention were significant (Ali et al. 2020). It explains that customers with pleasure activities are constructed for the eco-friendly environment and get involved in purchasing green electronic home appliances (Zhang et al. 2022). Besides, a study found that green motivation plays a dominant role in developing consumers' attitudinal purchase intention to procure green electronic products (Ali et al. 2020). The corresponding theory of purposeful work behavior posits personality emerges from the interaction between the individual and their environment. Theories claim that conditioning predictable behavioural responses transpire through environmental interactions, which ultimately mould our personalities through intrinsic motivation and awareness.

The direct relation between attitudinal purchase intention and green brand evangelism was significant and supported H5 with ($\beta = 0.550$, $t = 9.513$, $p < 0.005$), concurred with previous studies, the results have found concurrent to past study (Panda et al. 2020). It implies that once a consumer has a solid emotional attachment to a particular brand, that eventually makes a consumer a brand evangelist. Therefore, green and energy-efficient products create a sense of attachment because of their attributes, usefulness, energy-efficient, innovative technology, cost-saving, and environment-friendly nature (Prakash et al. 2019; Zhang and Luo 2023). Such creation of attitudinal development towards the green product is related to consumer experience, motivation, and brand attributes that leads to creating evangelist behavior towards the brand, which is somehow uncontrollable by the consumer, and they become an evangelist (Aydın 2017).

According to the hypothesis, green altruism positively moderates green motivation and green attitudinal purchase intention relationship. However, the results revealed significant and positive moderating result ($\beta = 0.550$, $t = 9.513$, $p < 0.005$). This supported hypothesis 6. However, past studies have overlooked the importance of green altruism in environmental and consumer behavior research. The current study has found green altruism a significant predictor in moderating green motivation and green attitudinal purchase intention by strengthening the relationship. Green altruism is a well-established personality trait studied (Ali et al. 2020; Panda et al. 2020; Tan et al. 2020) and considered a construct that encourages individuals to choose a green electronic product. Green altruistic individuals realize that green attitudinal purchase decision plays a significant role in energy-saving and reducing waste to protect nature and the green environment for future generations (Ababneh 2021; Hazaea et al. 2022). Therefore, the study has found green altruism as a major contributor to establishing the green attitude purchase intention by multiplying with a green motivational personality perspective (Tan et al. 2020).

Further, as a single mediation, green attitudinal purchase intention between green motivation and green brand evangelism was significant and supported the hypotheses H7 with ($\beta = 0.419$, $t = 8.013$, $p < 0.005$). Moreover, the mediating relationship between the variables is significant and supported. Green motivation, green attitudinal purchase among green conscientiousness, and green brand evangelism, a serial mediation, have been significant. Supported hypothesis H8. Lastly, green motivation as mediating variable between green conscientiousness and green attitudinal purchase intention was significant and supported the hypothesis H9 with ($\beta = 0.344$, $t = 7.378$, $p < 0.005$). Based on the above discussion, the study has found that green motivation and green attitudinal purchase intention have mediated green conscientiousness and green brand evangelism relationship. Past studies remained scarce to explaining green motivation and green attitudinal purchase intention's mediating role with the relationship of green conscientious personalities in establishing the evangelist behavioral outcome. Therefore, when consumers establish a green motivation and subsequently develop a green attitudinal intention to buy an energy-efficient product, they become evangelists towards the particular brand (Panda et al. 2020).

7 Conclusion and Implications

This study concludes that novel variables, green conscientiousness, green altruism, and mediating role of green motivation, and green attitudinal purchase intention in explaining green brand evangelism have played a significant role. The current study's findings identify the most valid factors that affect green brand evangelism through green motivation and green attitudinal purchase intention. The green conscientiousness and green brand evangelism relationship is insignificant; there is a need to introduce the trait of green altruism as an independent variable and check that either direct relationship is significant in environmental protection.

Government policymakers, practitioners, and researchers insist that the manufacturers of electronic home appliances adopt green technology practices for the sustainability of the environment and to minimize the wastage of resources that cause environmental, air, and water pollution and scarcity of natural resources. The awareness, knowledge, and benefits of using green electronic home appliances must be for household consumers. Organizations need to adopt promoting techniques to motivate individuals to buy green electronic items to protect future generations' environment.

7.1 Theoretical Implications

The selection criteria of customers are focused intensely on the knowledge that they perceive. Generally, customers get additional knowledge and are more influenced by the endorsements of trusted individuals or sources. Promotion of goods, green altruism, and green brand evangelism play an essential role that significantly involves product co-creation. In this respect, the current study gives a substantial theory implication. Current literature offers no good discussion about consumers' knowledge regarding environmental sustainability in green altruism and green purchasing of green electronic home appliances. In the current study, a theoretical model where consumers' perception of environmental sustainability contributes to green altruism and green environmental conscientiousness explains how these most relevant buildings affect brand evangelists. Consequently, our theoretical model expands on the current TPB and TRA framework (Asih et al. 2020) and examines the framework for ethical decision-making.

The current study's findings include a theoretical framework that helps to explain factors affecting the mediation of green motivation and green attitudinal purchase intention between green conscientiousness and green brand evangelism toward the consumption of green electronic home appliances. The analysis results suggest the direct relationship of green conscientiousness and green brand evangelism is insignificant. In contrast, direct relationships of green conscientiousness with green motivation, green attitudinal purchase intention and green motivation with green attitudinal purchase intention and green attitudinal purchase intention with green brand evangelism are significant. That means green motivation and green attitudinal purchase intention mediate green conscientiousness and green brand evangelism the relationship. Firstly, green motivation mediates green conscientiousness and green attitudinal purchase intention. Secondly, green attitudinal purchase intention mediates green motivation and green brand evangelism. Thirdly, green attitudinal purchase intention mediates green conscientiousness and green brand evangelism. Moreover, green altruism's moderating effect also strengthened green conscientiousness and green brand evangelism relationship by mediating the green motivation and green attitudinal purchase intention.

The study's findings have emphasized the importance of green conscientiousness and green brand evangelism for the consumption of green electronic home appliances. These findings are helpful for academicians, scholars, and practitioners who failed to realize the importance of environmental sustainability. The research framework clarifies how consumers consider eco-friendly activities and are motivated to consume green products.

The existing framework extended the theoretical literature with the theory of reason action and purposeful work behavior, helping by introducing novel constructs of green conscientiousness, green altruism, and the mediation role of green motivation and green attitudinal purchase intention. This implies a connection between the most valid factors for examining a better understanding of how environmental factors affect brand evangelism.

7.2 Managerial Implication

The analysis of this research provides vital information for marketers to develop strategies for green brands, and optimize the impact of the examined variables. Sustainable green electronic product development and its consumption are becoming famous in Pakistan. People are becoming more inclined to use eco-friendly electronic home appliances and realize their role as citizens to protect the country's environment. Consumers and organizations start thinking green and collectively feel affectionate for the clean climate (Ali et al. 2020). Therefore, understanding consumer psychology regarding green electronic home appliances is crucial for marketers to increase green consumption due to the growing number of nature-protected electronic home appliance productions.

Due to the growing number of green manufacturers and enterprises and the advancement of household consumer understanding of green electronic home equipment, marketers must expand green consumption. In particular, this study shows that green consciousness and affective history of green altruism support consumers' green buying intention for home appliances in green electronics. Green motivation is crucial in this phase since it completely mediates the green consciousness and green purchase intention relationship, as well as the green purchasing and green brand evangelism relationship.

Companies must also follow approaches to draw customers' eco-friendly interests and feelings. Proper recycling reduces environmental pollution after a product's life has ended. However, it does not prevent the resource depletion and carbon emissions linked to the product's manufacturing in the first place. This analysis attempts to determine how committed manufacturers are to reducing their emissions of greenhouse gases, sustainably designing products with sustainable materials, and removing dangerous chemicals from their products.

Companies must adopt strategies to engage customers' environmental interests and sentiments. Effective recycling reduces environmental contamination following a product's life cycle. However, it does not prevent the resource depletion and carbon emissions associated with the product's initial manufacturing. This analysis attempts to determine the extent of manufacturers' commitment to reducing greenhouse gas emissions, sustainably designing products with green materials, and eliminating hazardous chemicals from their products.

Therefore, companies must take responsibility for the concentration implications of their acts and play their positions as responsible co-citizens to brand evangelism. Green home appliances have significant footprints due to different metals used in manufacturing to mitigate the effect of environmental sustainability. Before purchasing, consumers observe the energy efficiency of electronic items, which shows the quality of electronic consumption that impacts consumer green brand evangelism. So, sellers must adopt effective and encouraging techniques for individuals to purchase and consume home appliances. Therefore, this move toward green brand evangelism proposed green motivation for attaining the sustainability of the Environment (Asih et al. 2020; Paul et al. 2016).

8 Limitations and Future Research

The research focuses only on motivating consumer behavior by establishing their green attitudinal purchase intention. Secondly, considering the extensive surveys, the study has limited intention to purchase home appliances without taking into account actual consumer behavior. Third, cross-sectional research may inadequately notice the mediating effect of green motivation on green conscientiousness and green brand evangelism in terms of the green attitudinal purchase intention relationship. Therefore, experimental designs and longitudinal studies should emphasize. Fourthly, primarily samples consist of young individuals with relatively high cognitive abilities in Punjab, Pakistan, and may restrict the generalisation of these findings to other age demographics. Lastly, the moderating effect of green altruism on green motivation and green attitudinal purchase intent relationship is statistically significant at $P < 0.05$.

Furthermore, other personality traits from the Big 5 Personality dimensions may also be considered in future studies: agreeableness, introversion/extroversion, or neuroticism. Besides, in future studies, gender differences may share changed characteristics, opinions, and behaviors for adopting green electronic home appliances. Other perspectives of a gap for comparative analysis are also present, such as how marketing dissatisfaction could influence green purchase intent and how it could vary through cultures or markets to promote knowledge and understanding of this purchase process. The study mainly relates to the green perspective using the energy-efficient product from a consumer viewpoint. Therefore, future studies could include automotive industries specifically in understanding the hybrid and electric vehicles technologies towards low wastage of energy and their contribution towards the environment by saving fuel consumption and friendliness towards the atmosphere and bringing stability to the environment. Future studies could also include other variables like green environmental concerns, green consciousness, environmental performance, green brand practices, green brand attachment, green brand involvement, and green brand equity to deeply understand consumer behavior towards the environment in different contexts and industries. The studies could also make comparative studies between different demographics of the consumers to understand their nature of personalities and responses towards particular brands or industries.

References

Ababneh OMA (2021) How do green HRM practices affect employees' green behaviors? The role of employee engagement and personality attributes. J Environ Planning Manage 64(7):1204–1226. https://doi.org/10.1080/09640568.2020.1814708

Ali F, Ashfaq M, Begum S, Ali A (2020) How "Green" thinking and altruism translate into purchasing intentions for electronics products: The intrinsic-extrinsic motivation mechanism. Sustainable Production and Consumption 24:281–291. https://doi.org/10.1016/j.spc.2020.07.013

Ali MR, Shafiq M, Andejany M (2021) Determinants of consumers' intentions towards the purchase of energy efficient appliances in Pakistan: an extended model of the theory of planned behavior. Sustainability 13(2):565. https://doi.org/10.3390/su13020565

Ali M, Ullah S, Ahmad MS, Cheok MY, Alenezi H (2023) Assessing the impact of green consumption behavior and green purchase intention among millennials toward sustainable environment. Environ Sci Pollut Res 30(9):23335–23347. https://doi.org/10.1007/s11356-022-23811-1

Ambec S, De Donder P (2022) Environmental policy with green consumerism. J Environ Econ Manag 111:102584. https://doi.org/10.1016/j.jeem.2021.102584

Andreu L, Casado-Díaz AB, Mattila AS (2015) Effects of message appeal and service type in CSR communication strategies. J Bus Res 68(7):1488–1495. https://doi.org/10.1016/j.jbusres.2015.01.039

Asih D, Setini M, Soelton M, Muna N, Putra I, Darma D, Judiarni J (2020) Predicting green product consumption using theory of planned behavior and reasoned action. Manag Sci Lett 10(14):3367–3374. https://doi.org/10.5267/j.msl.2020.5.042

Aydın H (2017) Brand evangelism and big five personality traits. Glob J Business, Econom Manag 7(1):198–208

Bagozzi RP, Yi Y (1988) On the evaluation of structural equation models. J Acad Mark Sci 16:74–94. https://doi.org/10.1007/bf02723327

Bagozzi RP, Yi Y (2012) Specification, evaluation, and interpretation of structural equation models. J Acad Mark Sci 40:8–34. https://doi.org/10.1007/s11747-011-0278-x

Berman Caggiano H, Kumar P, Shwom R, Cuite C, Axsen J (2021) Explaining green technology purchases by US and Canadian households: the role of pro-environmental lifestyles, values, and environmental concern. Energ Effi 14(5):46. https://doi.org/10.1007/s12053-021-09959-8

Chwialkowska A, Bhatti WA, Glowik M (2020) The influence of cultural values on pro-environmental behavior. J Clean Prod 268:122305. https://doi.org/10.1016/j.jclepro.2020.122305

da Luz VV, Mantovani D, Nepomuceno MV (2020) Matching green messages with brand positioning to improve brand evaluation. J Bus Res 119:25–40. https://doi.org/10.1016/j.jbusres.2020.07.024

Dalvi-Esfahani M, Alaedini Z, Nilashi M, Samad S, Asadi S, Mohammadi M (2020) Students' green information technology behavior: beliefs and personality traits. J Clean Prod 257:120406. https://doi.org/10.1016/j.jclepro.2020.120406

Duarte N, Pereira C, Grzywińska-Rąpca M, Kulli A, Goci E (2024) Consumers' knowledge and decisions on circularity: Albanian, Polish, and Portuguese perspectives. Environ Develop Sustain 1–34. https://doi.org/10.1007/s10668-024-05077-4

Edeh E, Lo W-J, Khojasteh J (2023) Review of partial least squares structural equation modeling (PLS-SEM) using R: A Workbook: By Joseph F. Hair Jr., G. Tomas M. Hult, Christian M. Ringle, Marko Sarstedt, Nicholas P. Danks, Soumya Ray. Springer, Cham (2021). p 197. OpenAccess; 59.99, Hardcover Book. In: Taylor & Francis

Pakistan Electricity Consumption (2024) https://www.ceicdata.com/en/pakistan/electricity-generation-and-consumption/electricity-consumption-total

Fornell C, Larcker DF (1981) Evaluating structural equation models with unobservable variables and measurement error. J Mark Res 18(1):39–50. https://doi.org/10.1177/002224378101800104

Gadenne D, Sharma B, Kerr D, Smith T (2011) The influence of consumers' environmental beliefs and attitudes on energy saving behaviours. Energy Policy 39(12):7684–7694. https://doi.org/10.1016/j.enpol.2011.09.002

Graça SS, Kharé VP (2023) An investigation of the impact of sustainability drivers and transformative mediators on green buying behavior in the US and Brazil. Balt J Manag 18(4):428–449. https://doi.org/10.1108/BJM-10-2022-0377

Groening C, Sarkis J, Zhu Q (2018) Green marketing consumer-level theory review: a compendium of applied theories and further research directions. J Clean Prod 172:1848–1866. https://doi.org/10.1016/j.jclepro.2017.12.002

Guiao BGM, Lacap JPG (2022) Effects of environmental sustainability awareness and altruism on green purchase intention and brand evangelism. Asian J Business Res 12(3). https://doi.org/10.14707/ajbr.220134

Haake H, Seuring S (2009) Sustainable procurement of minor items–exploring limits to sustainability. Sustain Dev 17(5):284–294. https://doi.org/10.1002/sd.424

Hallez L, Vansteenbeeck H, Boen F, Smits T (2023) Persuasive packaging? The impact of packaging color and claims on young consumers' perceptions of product healthiness, sustainability and tastiness. Appetite 182:106433. https://doi.org/10.1016/j.appet.2022.106433

Hameed I, Hyder Z, Imran M, Shafiq K (2021) Greenwash and green purchase behavior: an environmentally sustainable perspective. Environ Develop Sustain 1–22. https://doi.org/10.1007/s10668-020-01202-1

Harjadi D, Gunardi A (2022) Factors affecting eco-friendly purchase intention: subjective norms and ecological consciousness as moderators. Cogent Business Manag 9(1):2148334. https://doi.org/10.1080/23311975.2022.2148334

Harrigan P, Roy SK, Chen T (2021) Do value cocreation and engagement drive brand evangelism? Mark Intell Plan 39(3):345–360. https://doi.org/10.1108/MIP-10-2019-0492

Hazaea SA, Al-Matari EM, Zedan K, Khatib SF, Zhu J, Al Amosh H (2022) Green purchasing: past, present and future. Sustainability 14(9):5008. https://doi.org/10.3390/su14095008

Hong Y, Al Mamun A, Masukujjaman M, Yang Q (2024) Significance of the environmental value-belief-norm model and its relationship to green consumption among Chinese youth. Asia Pac Manag Rev 29(1):127–140. https://doi.org/10.1016/j.apmrv.2023.10.002

Horne J, Recker M, Michelfelder I, Jay J, Kratzer J (2020) Exploring entrepreneurship related to the sustainable development goals-mapping new venture activities with semi-automated content analysis. J Clean Prod 242:118052. https://doi.org/10.1016/j.jclepro.2019.118052

Hossain I, Fekete-Farkas M, Nekmahmud M (2022) Purchase behavior of energy-efficient appliances contribute to sustainable energy consumption in developing country: moral norms extension of the theory of planned behavior. Energies 15(13):4600. https://doi.org/10.3390/en15134600

Hummels H, Argyrou A (2021) Planetary demands: redefining sustainable development and sustainable entrepreneurship. J Clean Prod 278:123804. https://doi.org/10.1016/j.jclepro.2020.123804

Jafari SQ, Shokouhyar S, Shokoohyar S (2022) Producer-consumer sustainability continuum: mutual understanding to implement extended producer responsibility. J Clean Prod 374:133880. https://doi.org/10.1016/j.jclepro.2022.133880

Khan S, Rashid A, Rasheed R, Amirah NA (2023) Designing a knowledge-based system (KBS) to study consumer purchase intention: the impact of digital influencers in Pakistan. Kybernetes 52(5):1720–1744. https://doi.org/10.1108/K-06-2021-0497

Laurent J, Chmiel N, Hansez I (2020) Personality and safety citizenship: the role of safety motivation and safety knowledge. Heliyon 6(1). https://doi.org/10.1016/j.jclepro.2020.123804

Li W, Bhutto TA, Xuhui W, Maitlo Q, Zafar AU, Bhutto NA (2020) Unlocking employees' green creativity: the effects of green transformational leadership, green intrinsic, and extrinsic motivation. J Clean Prod 255:120229. https://doi.org/10.1016/j.jclepro.2020.120229

Lisniak B (2024) Global environmental problems and their impact on international business. specialty 292 - international economic relations/research advisor M. D. Domashenko. Sumy : Sumy State University 2024. 69 p. https://essuir.sumdu.edu.ua/handle/123456789/96788

Lopes JM, Gomes S, Trancoso T (2024) Navigating the green maze: insights for businesses on consumer decision-making and the mediating role of their environmental concerns. Sustain Account, Manag Policy J. https://doi.org/10.1108/SAMPJ-07-2023-0492

Mahadin BK, Akroush MN (2019) A study of factors affecting word of mouth (WOM) towards Islamic banking (IB) in Jordan. Int J Emerg Mark 14(4):639–667. https://doi.org/10.1108/IJOEM-10-2017-0414

Mahadin B, Akroush MN, Bata H (2020) The effects of tourism websites' attributes on e-satisfaction and e-loyalty: a case of American travellers' to Jordan. Int J Web Based Communities 16(1):4–33. https://doi.org/10.1504/IJWBC.2020.105124

Mahlamäki T, Rintamäki T, Rajah E (2019) The role of personality and motivation on key account manager job performance. Ind Mark Manage 83:174–184. https://doi.org/10.1016/j.indmarman.2018.11.013

Maitlo Q, Wang X, Jingdong Y, Lashari IA, Faraz NA, Hajaro NH (2022) Exploring green creativity: the effects of green transformational leadership, green innovation climate, and green autonomy. Front Psychol 13:686373. https://doi.org/10.3389/fpsyg.2022.686373

Majeed A, Ahmed I, Rasheed A (2022) Investigating influencing factors on consumers' choice behavior and their environmental concerns while purchasing green products in Pakistan. J Environ Plann Manage 65(6):1110–1134. https://doi.org/10.1080/09640568.2021.1922995

More AB (2023) Implementing digital age experience marketing to make customer relations more sustainable. In: New horizons for industry 4.0 in modern business. Springer, pp 99–119. https://doi.org/10.1007/978-3-031-20443-2_5

Panda TK, Kumar A, Jakhar S, Luthra S, Garza-Reyes JA, Kazancoglu I, Nayak SS (2020) Social and environmental sustainability model on consumers' altruism, green purchase intention, green brand loyalty and evangelism. J Clean Prod 243:118575. https://doi.org/10.1016/j.jclepro.2019.118575

Paul J, Modi A, Patel J (2016) Predicting green product consumption using theory of planned behavior and reasoned action. J Retail Consum Serv 29:123–134. https://doi.org/10.1016/j.jretconser.2015.11.006

Pornsrimate K, Khamwon A (2020) Building brand evangelism through social media micro-influencers: a case study of cosmetic industry in Thailand. Int J Soc Sci Res 2(3):84–99. https://myjms.mohe.gov.my/index.php/ijssr/article/view/10804

Prakash G, Pathak P (2017) Intention to buy eco-friendly packaged products among young consumers of India: a study on developing nation. J Clean Prod 141:385–393. https://doi.org/10.1016/j.jclepro.2016.09.116

Prakash G, Choudhary S, Kumar A, Garza-Reyes JA, Khan SAR, Panda TK (2019) Do altruistic and egoistic values influence consumers' attitudes and purchase intentions towards eco-friendly packaged products? An empirical investigation. J Retail Consum Serv 50:163–169. https://doi.org/10.1016/j.jretconser.2019.05.011

Rasoolimanesh SM (2022) Discriminant validity assessment in PLS-SEM: a comprehensive composite-based approach. Data Anal Perspect J 3(2):1–8

Rasoolimanesh SM, Jaafar M, Kock N, Ramayah T (2015) A revised framework of social exchange theory to investigate the factors influencing residents' perceptions. Tourism Manag Perspect 16:335–345. https://doi.org/10.1016/j.tmp.2015.10.001

Riorini SV, Widayati CC (2016) Brand relationship and its effect towards brand evangelism to banking service. Int Res J Business Stud 8(1). https://doi.org/10.21632/irjbs.8.1.78.33-45

Shah R, Modi A, Muduli A, Patel JD (2023) Purchase intention for energy-efficient equipment appliances: extending TPB with eco-labels, green trust, and environmental concern. Energ Effi 16(4):31. https://doi.org/10.1007/s12053-023-10111-x

Siano A, Vollero A, Bertolini A (2022) From brand control to brand co-creation: an integrated framework of brand paradigms and emerging brand perspectives. J Bus Res 152:372–386. https://doi.org/10.1016/j.jbusres.2022.08.001

Sreenivasan A, Suresh M (2023) Exploring the contribution of sustainable entrepreneurship towards sustainable development goals: a bibliometric analysis. Green Technol Sustain 100038. https://doi.org/10.1016/j.grets.2023.100038

Steenkamp J-BE (2020) Global brand building and management in the digital age. J Int Mark 28(1):13–27. https://doi.org/10.1177/1069031X19894946

Swaminathan V, Sorescu A, Steenkamp J-BE, O'Guinn TCG, Schmitt B (2020) Branding in a hyperconnected world: refocusing theories and rethinking boundaries. J Mark 84(2):24–46. https://doi.org/10.1177/0022242919899905

Tan LL, Abd Aziz N, Ngah AH (2020) Mediating effect of reasons on the relationship between altruism and green hotel patronage intention. J Market Anal 8:18–30. https://doi.org/10.1057/s41270-020-00067-7

Terán-Yépez E, Marín-Carrillo GM, del Pilar Casado-Belmonte M, de las Mercedes Capobianco-Uriarte M (2020) Sustainable entrepreneurship: review of its evolution and new trends. J Cleaner Product 252:119742. https://doi.org/10.1016/j.jclepro.2019.119742

Vander Ark SD (1971) Handbook of personality theory and research. J Music Therapy 8(2): 75–76 https://doi.org/10.1093/jmt/8.2.75-a

Waris I, Hameed I (2021) An empirical study of consumers intention to purchase energy efficient appliances. Soc Responsib J 17(4):489–507. https://doi.org/10.1108/SRJ-11-2019-0378

Wu H (2024) Material flows with nexus of regional socioeconomic system. Springer. https://doi.org/10.1007/978-3-031-54299-2

Wuertz T (2015) Personality traits associated with environmental concern Walden University]. https://www.proquest.com/openview/f425c164f6b1921a0de75c9ef707de98/1?pq-origsite=gscholar&cbl=18750

Zhang W, Luo B (2023) Predicting consumer intention toward eco-friendly smart home services: extending the theory of planned behavior. Econ Chang Restruct 56(5):3335–3352. https://doi.org/10.1007/s10644-022-09477-2

Zhang J, Cherian J, Abbas Sandhu Y, Abbas J, Cismas LM, Negrut CV, Negrut L (2022) Presumption of green electronic appliances purchase intention: the mediating role of personal moral norms. Sustainability 14(8):4572. https://doi.org/10.3390/su14084572

Zhang W, Liu L (2022) How consumers' adopting intentions towards eco-friendly smart home services are shaped? An extended technology acceptance model. Ann Region Sci 1–24. https://doi.org/10.1007/s00168-021-01082-x

Innovations Driving Green Transformation

Revolutionizing Agriculture: Harnessing High-Performance Computing and Artificial Intelligence for Innovative Farming Practices

Shad Ahmad Khan, Bhanupriya Khatri, Henry Jonathan, Arshi Naim, and Shaina Arora

Abstract This chapter discusses the need for the agriculture sector to enhance the sustainability and production due to the rising population on the planet and the climate change. This chapter highlights the transformative potential of incorporating Artificial Intelligence (AI) and High-Performance Computing (HPC) technologies into conventional farming practices. This study is based on review of literature and case studies. The study explores that way data-driven approach optimizes resource use, reduces environmental impacts, and improves decision-making through advanced algorithms, with applications including disease detection, yield prediction, and crop monitoring. It also underscores the ways the technology like IoT devices and smart sensors in the field enables ongoing data collection, generation of a feedback loop that enhances agricultural strategies. The socioeconomic aspects of using AI and HPC in agriculture is also discussed that covers the possibilities for improved food security, job creation, and rural development. The results provided here highlight how this integration has the potential to propel a sustainable agricultural future, guaranteeing the sector's adaptation and resilience in the face of ever-changing global problems.

Keywords Agriculture · Agri-business · High performance computing · Artificial intelligence · Farming · Rural development

---

S. A. Khan (✉)
College of Business, University of Buraimi, Al Buraimi, Oman
e-mail: khan.shadahmad@gmail.com

B. Khatri
University School of Business, Chandigarh University, Mohali, India

H. Jonathan
Modern College of Business and Science, Muscat, Oman

A. Naim
Business Management, King Khalid University, Abha, Kingdom of Saudi Arabia

S. Arora
University Institute of Tourism and Hospitality Management, Chandigarh University, Mohali, India
e-mail: shyna150796@gmail.com

S. A. R. Khan et al. (eds.), *Circular Economy and Technological Innovation*, Industrial Ecology, https://doi.org/10.1007/978-981-96-5650-9_11

1 Introduction

Increased productivity in the agriculture sector is critical to the prosperity of any nation (Jain et al. 2021). The increasing global population and the associated demands on food production have placed unprecedented pressure on the agricultural sector to adopt more sustainable practices (Khan et al. 2024). Climate change exacerbates these challenges, necessitating a shift towards innovative solutions that can enhance productivity while minimizing environmental impact. This chapter investigates the transformative potential of integrating Artificial Intelligence (AI) and High-Performance Computing (HPC) into conventional farming methodologies. By leveraging advanced computational capabilities and sophisticated algorithms, this integration aims to optimize resource utilization, reduce ecological footprints, and revolutionize agricultural decision-making processes.

The adoption of a data-driven approach, facilitated by AI and HPC, allows for real-time data analysis, predictive modeling, and precision farming techniques (Naim et al. 2024a, b). These technologies empower farmers to make informed decisions that enhance crop yields, minimize waste, and optimize resource allocation. Specific applications such as disease detection, yield prediction, and crop monitoring are explored within this study, illustrating how AI and HPC can significantly improve agricultural outcomes. Furthermore, the implementation of Internet of Things (IoT) devices and smart sensors enables continuous data collection in the field, establishing a feedback loop that enhances agricultural strategies.

This research also addresses the socioeconomic implications of utilizing AI and HPC in agriculture, focusing on their potential to bolster food security, create job opportunities, and promote rural development (Gangwar and Khan 2022). As the agricultural industry stands on the brink of a technological revolution, this study contributes to the ongoing discourse regarding the benefits and challenges associated with the convergence of HPC and AI in agriculture. The findings presented herein underscore the potential of these technologies to drive sustainable agricultural practices, ensuring that the sector can adapt and thrive amidst evolving global challenges.

2 Review of Literature

The country development is mostly reliant on the expansion of the agricultural sectors (Paymode et al. 2021). Food production and its position as the backbone of the economics of many emerging nations make agriculture an important part of society (Rathi and Gomathy 2023). Technologies can be used to increase agriculture's intelligence (Revathi et al. 2022). Precision agriculture is a data-driven farming technique that optimizes farming operations by utilizing information from both within and between fields (Tan et al. 2016). To fully reap the benefits of agriculture 4.0, it is imperative to identify and address its associated issues and obstacles (Sun et al. 2018).

As technology permeates contemporary life more and more, digital computing and data-driven technologies are beginning to be adopted by agriculture. The advent of "smart" farming has brought about a number of improvements in the industry, such as self-governing machinery and the gathering of data on plants, cattle, and climate (Tomar and Kaur 2021). A variety of technologies have been implemented into modern agriculture to meet the food demands, both in terms of quantity and quality. This portfolio of technologies has helped farmers in this era of technology-driven farming solve many of the difficulties related to the farming operations by facilitating accurate and quick decision making based on facts that are observed and then consolidated (Thilakarathne et al. 2022).

The decision support system must incorporate AI, machine learning, the cloud, sensors, and other automated devices in order to deliver accurate information quickly (Senapaty et al. 2023). Important information and communication technologies are combined with sensor technologies in smart agriculture to deliver efficient and productive agricultural services (Shaikh et al. 2022). Using an intelligent cloud-based system, AI and the IoT offer a comprehensive foundation for remote farm monitoring (Sharma et al. 2023; Khan et al. 2023a, b; Magd et al. 2023a, b). Over the past century, new farming methods have been developed, which has enabled agriculture to keep up with the rising demand for food and other agricultural goods (Sishodia et al. 2020; Khan et al. 2022a, b).

Ensuring food security is widely acknowledged to depend heavily on the agricultural sector. The need for agri-food, however, is growing along with the global population, which means that conventional agricultural methods must give way to smart agriculture techniques, or agriculture 4.0 (Singh et al. 2022; Bui et al. 2024). By monitoring at three levels: administrative, technical, and financial, integrated software solutions and ERP systems assist farmers in the farming and cattle industries in optimizing farm performance and more effectively organizing production (Trichkova-Kashamova and Paunova-Hubenova 2021). The application of information and communication technologies in the cyber-physical farm management cycle is emphasized by the trend known as "smart farming." It is anticipated that emerging technologies like cloud computing and the IoT will take advantage of this advancement and increase the use of robots and AI in farming (Wolfert et al. 2017). The IoT's application sceneries, which are based on these technologies, are constantly expanding across a wide range of fields due to the quick development of big data, sensor, and communication technologies (Yang et al. 2018).

Smart agriculture has undergone a transformation thanks to the IoT, which has increased productivity, reduced production costs, and optimized resource use (Tripathy et al. 2022a, b). 'Smart farming' is a new concept that uses advanced information technologies to boost agricultural productivity and effectiveness. With the latest advancements in automation, AI, and networking, farmers can now monitor every stage of the process more effectively and apply precise treatments that robots have chosen with superhuman precision (Tripathy et al. 2022a, b). It integrates the information and communication technology (ICT) with agricultural production systems' machinery, equipment, and sensors. It is anticipated that new technologies like cloud computing and the IoT will accelerate this trend and increase the number of robots and AI used in farming (Pivoto et al. 2018). The old farming methods will soon be replaced by precision agriculture and smart farming. These technologies can maximize crop yield, optimize input use, and preserve environmental resources all at the same time (Pranuthi and Srikanth 2023). The focus must be on quantitative methods supported by technology in order to maximize yield and value addition (Preethi and Reddy 2022). Taking advantage of the developments can transform agriculture by enabling quicker decision-making, lower costs, and higher yields (Lachgar et al. 2023). The latest technological advancements, such as IoT-enabled sensors, drones, and autonomous robots, have applications in agriculture and work in tandem with AI to create smart agriculture (Sankaranarayanan 2021).

The need for greater agricultural productivity is only growing as the population grows. Only with advancing technology will this growing demand be met. Because the IoT allows us complete control over data with little to no human intervention, it is significantly improving our quality of life (Joshi et al. 2017). The "Internet of Plants" is anticipated to support agriculture's bottom-up progress, spearheaded by astute farmers equipped with IoP capabilities (Kitano et al. 2022). Utilising the IoT, smart agriculture is an Industry 4.0 application that is utilised in both urban and rural settings (Mahajan et al. 2022). It is imperative that agriculture adopt new technology and methods in line with the global trend towards technological advancement (Moses et al. 2023). As technology advances, most industries are becoming smarter (Obien et al. 2022).

Farmers are turning to new technology to maintain or expand the quantity and quality of agricultural goods as a result of the population growth and reduction in the amount of land accessible for agriculture (Öztürk et al. 2021). The fourth agricultural revolution, known as "agriculture 4.0," seeks to use digital technologies to increase farming's productivity, predictability, and level of planning (Malik et al. 2023). Smart farming, or precision agriculture, is one of the keystones of contemporary society's efforts to fulfil the Sustainable Development Goals (Massaoudi et al. 2023). Precision agriculture decision-making has been aided by industrial technologies like AI and the IoT applied to agricultural productivity (Molin et al., 2021). One of the biggest challenges facing scientists and academics is how sustainable agriculture will adapt to the continuous changes in the environment and societal structure (Muniasamy 2020). Researchers in smart agriculture offer a wealth of resources and opportunities to enhance the agricultural ecosystem's sustainability and production (Nicolas et al. 2022). Large-scale data collection, storage, and analysis from a variety of agricultural sources—such as weather stations, soil sensors, satellite imaging, crop yield records, pest and disease reports, and other sources—is made possible in large part by big data (Nurcahyo et al. 2023).

Using modern smart technologies, the fourth industrial revolution, or Industry 4.0, has drastically changed traditional manufacturing and industrial practices. In a similar vein, the agriculture industry has changed to become more accurate, data-driven, and intelligent in order to meet upcoming problems (Singh 2022). Modern computer techniques, such as cloud computing, AI, and the IoT, are utilized in smart agriculture. The main goal is to support the farming process (Vrbančič et al. 2022). Wide-ranging consequences have resulted from the introduction of IoT devices in agriculture (Mustafa and Kutucu 2022). Industry 4.0 has completely changed how all industry domains, including agricultural systems, produce goods. The IoT, AI, big data, and automated digital processes are just a few of the sophisticated digital technologies being established by the Industry 4.0 trend, which is a revolutionary force (Naqvi et al. 2020; Khan et al. 2023a, b; Magd et al. 2022, 2023a, b). The d2024; Khan et al. 2022a, b; Khan et al. 2020). With the introduction of technology, this decade has seen a transition from traditional methods to the most cutting-edge ones. Both the quantity and quality of the agriculture industry have changed as a result of the IoT (Kour and Arora 2020; Khan et al. 2024; Khan et al. 2023a, b; Naim et al. 2024a, b). These technologies have profoundly transforming effects on people's lives because they help to demystify smart healthcare, plant pathology, and the planning, design, and development of smart cities and villages (Kumar et al. 2023; Magd et al. 2023a, b).

The fourth agricultural revolution, known as "Agriculture 4.0," makes use of digital technologies to transform the agricultural industry into one that is more environmentally conscious, intelligent, and productive (Bui et al. 2024). New agricultural technology have been developed to improve sustainability and find more efficient farming practises (Javaid et al. 2022; Khan et al. 2022a, b). In order to improve monitoring, decision support systems are being built using wireless sensor networks. Among the most fascinating industries with a growing demand for decision support systems is agriculture. Farmers lose money and effort as a result of ineffective and wasteful agricultural monitoring techniques (Jiber et al. 2011). It is imperative to irrigate more effectively in order to maximise water consumption when water supplies become scarce due to climate change. It is inevitable for farmers to adopt a decision-support system in this situation (Karim and Karim 2017). Precision farming has given rise to a new way of thinking about agriculture that incorporates state-of-the-art technical advancements. The biggest problem facing modern growers is identifying fruit illnesses early on. Farmers may see a decline in revenue if diseases are not detected in a timely manner (Kabilesh et al. 2023).

In contemporary agriculture, "Agriculture 4.0" is an unavoidable and irreversible development (Albiero et al. 2020). Industry 4.0 technology integration is required to improve aquaponics system production capacities and maximize crop yield on a commercial basis (Abbasi et al. 2022). Innovative horticulture uses a variety of technologies, tools, traditions, and computerized ideal models to enhance farming cycles. Blockchain, big data, AI, cloud computing, and edge processing provide the means and means to capture, store, and analyze the vast amounts of data generated by many sources(Ahamed and Vignesh 2022; Verma et al. 2024).

AI is a rapidly evolving science that is influencing every aspect of our life, from smart farming to autonomous cars, facial recognition, and online shopping recommendation systems (Guerrouj et al. 2020). ICT employed in machinery, equipment, and sensors in network-based high-tech farm supervision cycles is the focus of the emerging field of "smart farming" (Dhanaraju et al. 2022). The benefits of soil and soil fertility will be strengthened with the automation of farming operations.

Thus, a current data-centric era of agricultural exploration is made possible by the advancements in practical application and solutions (Donde et al. 2021).

The technologies support farmers at every step of the crop cycle, from planting to harvesting, packing to shipping. AI enables farmers to make equitable use of their farmland and to use their resources more profitably. With the aid of sensors, IoT offers a solution (Gupta et al. 2022). From farmers to business owners, a wide range of people use smart devices. These technologies are employed in many different contexts, ranging from monitoring the condition of crops and soil moisture content in real time to sending drones to help with pesticide spraying (Gupta et al. 2020). Along with improving plans and facilities, modern agriculture technology has been crucial to the progress (Habib et al. 2022).

Agriculture may now transition from an input-intensive to a knowledge-intensive one thanks to digitalization. Numerous digital technologies are available for intelligent and accurate animal production. Which digital technologies, though, are currently applicable to the management and running of cattle farms remains to be seen (Haldar et al. 2022). With the world's population growing, ensuring food security has become crucial. Particular difficulties for the agriculture industry include an ageing farmer population and a shrinking labour force. The acknowledgment of smart farms as a viable solution has resulted from these difficulties (Han et al. 2023).

A multitude of issues related to agriculture are persistently impacting the activities taking place around the nation. The eradication of such problems may be achieved by fusing ongoing agricultural practices with technological breakthroughs (Edwin et al. 2022) Most notably, crop monitoring has changed from being a qualitative and experience-based effort to a quantitative and data-driven endeavor with the advent of IoT into crop, soil, and microclimate sensing (Chamara et al. 2022). In the realm of the IoT, one of the most exciting possible applications is smart agriculture. The existing intensive production style of farming is surpassed by more precise and controlled farming thanks to big data analysis and sensor and networking technology (Bruno et al. 2021). Through the incorporation of modern technologies, Industry 4.0 transforms farming operations in a revolutionary way. It is possible that these emerging technologies will make data-driven smart farming feasible (Garg and Alam 2023).

Under the auspices of Industry 4.0, a novel approach known as "Smart Farming" is being implemented as an endeavor to create sustainable and effective standards in the agriculture sector (Haq et al. 2022). Agriculture is undergoing above-average rate and intensity change as a result of the digital revolution of the economy and society. It is true that agriculture has been able to provide food security by achieving significant yield gains in recent decades, in part due to high levels of mechanization (Härtel 2022).

Professionals in the sector and communities affected by the technologies are worried about AI ethics, responsibility, trust, and transparency as a result of the technology's ongoing development in agriculture (Hingle and Johri 2023). Future generations will depend on the intelligent modelling, analysis, and management of agricultural and forest ecosystems as well as the usage and preservation of soils, all of which are presently critical to the survival of our planet (Holzinger et al. 2022).

Low-power, inexpensive sensors and airborne devices and share data/images for crop monitoring and control can be very helpful to improve agriculture in rural regions (Chakraborty et al. 2022). Data-driven and automated agriculture has emerged in recent years, mostly due to technological advancements in fields like AI and the IoT (Dakhole and Jeno Lovesum 2021). It is well known that technical advancements can help humans escape these situations, resolving the linkages between the food, water, energy, and climate nexus and facilitating the transition of agriculture from traditional to digital methods (Dayioğlu and Türker 2021).

The IoT technology is rapidly transforming labor-intensive traditional agriculture into data-driven smart farming. It does this by offering theoretical and technological support to address the problems of food shortages brought on by rapid population growth and the challenges of sustainable development brought on by the depletion of natural resources as a result of climate change (Huo et al. 2024).

Since its introduction to the agricultural industry, the IoT has had a significant impact (Idoje et al. 2021). In agriculture, which is mostly dependent on customized solutions, the introduction of AI undoubtedly generated a lot of buzz and led to overly optimistic plug-and-play solutions. When a disruptive breakthrough is marketed as sustainable, there is a significant risk of failure (Jacobs et al. 2022). Temperature, humidity, and soil moisture are the three input factors of a plant that are managed and monitored through the use of mobile applications and the IoT (Ahmad et al. 2021). All agri-food industry sectors now have to meet a wider range of requirements due to the highly competitive and globalized global market (Alonso et al. 2020).

Over many thousands of years, agriculture has been a significant source of food for humans, and with it, the development of suitable agricultural techniques for various crop types. New, cutting-edge IoT solutions could monitor the agricultural environment and guarantee high-quality products (Alreshidi 2019). Modern technical developments in computer vision, cloud computing, AI, and the IoT have made it possible to replace conventional agricultural methods with smart ones (Alrowais et al. 2022). These days, the IoT and cloud computing paradigms are driving an increasing amount of enhanced agricultural production at reduced costs. Its goal is to use less energy, less resources, and less human labor (Baghrous et al. 2020).

Since agriculture has long been ingrained in Indian culture, it is the most significant and productive industry in the nation. The smart irrigation system is one of the sophisticated methods that have been created over time to maximize farming practices (Bobade et al. 2023). The Food and Agriculture Organization of India (FAO) states that plants that are used in agriculture have the potential to prevent a 20–40% loss in global output. AI and current technologies were used to build smart farming for farmers, which aims to prevent these overpowering insect plants and boost agricultural productivity (Deepika and Arthi 2022). With the help of distributed computing, AI, and the IoT, farming has improved today. In fact, evaluating the soil characteristic makes the development of yields possible even in areas where water is scarce (Dewari et al. 2023).

3 Methodology

Using the system review and case exploration in qualitative study, the major goal of this study is to comprehend and analyze the differences of the selected field, which is HPC and AI in connection to know the innovative farming techniques in agriculture. The goal to understand and awareness of hypothetical concepts acquiring available knowledge is adequate justification for the decision to adopt a qualitative approach.

3.1 Case Selection

As the study is totally based upon the literature review and case approach and the data collection is through the specific articles, research papers, book chapters and official websites. To know about the reason to choice of case approach, below is the reason and justification to the study—The study utilized the publications available on google scholar, considering the smaller number of studies conducted in this field. Thus, to achieve the relevance of the study sources to the current context of the study, the keywords utilized were "Agriculture"; "High Performance Computing"; "Innovative Agriculture"; and "Innovative Agriculture". To time frame chosen for the selection of the literature was from the year 2015 to 2024. The study considered the studies published in journals, edited books, and conference proceedings published in English language. The case study adopted for this study were selected based on the pretext of their relevance to the main theme of this study available on the open sources.

The agricultural industry is anticipated to experience unusual involvements with population growth, resource shortage and climate transformation. To see the rising dietary demands of these interactions, the use of cutting-edge technologies is serious. HPC is a technology that practices existing computing resources to process and analyze large dimensions of data at very high speeds. Agricultural modeling, data analysis, and imitations can be better if HPC provides useful information for decision-making.

4 Case Analysis

4.1 Case 1

Now let's discover the applications of HPC in agriculture: (Developing Integrated Climate-Smart Precision Crop Management Systems—UNIV OF MINNESOTA, n.d.)

A. Climate modeling and prediction for precision agriculture:

Climate modeling practices complex algorithms and simulations to forecast and study weather patterns and climate conditions. This data is perilous for precision agriculturalists to make informed crop management decisions. Farmers can use HPC to develop large amounts of environmental data in real time and soon gain exact atmospheric material. Using this data will help advance planting and collection plans, expand resource use, and moderate the effects of thrilling weather events.

B. Optimizing plant breeding through genomic analysis:

Probing a crop's genetic makeup over genomic analysis authorizations for rapid identification of wanted qualities and development of breeding. Thoughtful agricultural genetics is grave to evolve crop varieties with better yields, disease confrontation and stress tolerance. HPC can analyze a wide assortment of genomic statistics speedily, making it easier for investigators to notice genetic markers associated with desired traits. This speeds up the breeding course and leads to further enhancements in plant flexibility and productivity, as it is easier to pick plants with precise characteristics.

C. Simulation of environmental factors in sustainable agriculture:

Sustainable action in agriculture requires a complete understanding of the links amongst agricultural activities and other natural factors such as soil composition, water accessibility and land use. Circulation representations can be used to predict how certain developments affect the atmosphere. HPC enables the expansion of multiple simulation models that deliberate multiple conserved variables instantaneously. By simulating the long-term effects of different farming techniques, these models enable agriculturalists to choose methods that reduce conservational impact, improve soil health, and certify the long-term achievement of their operations.

4.2 Case 2

Supercomputing for Climate Modeling in Agriculture (Case Study: European Centre for Medium-Range Weather Forecasts) (ECMWF 2023).

To support agriculture, the European Center for Medium-Range Weather Forecasts (ECMWF) has been at the forefront of applying supercomputing to advance climate modelling. Headquartered in Reading, UK, ECMWF operates one of the world's most important supercomputers and provides high-resolution climate models and predictions.

The main goal is to improve the accuracy and precision of weather forecasts so farmers can make more informed decisions about crop management, irrigation and pest control. ECMWF uses sophisticated numerical weather prediction models running on high-performance supercomputers to simulate complex atmospheric processes. These models combine large amounts of observational data to produce medium-term estimates. Highly accurate weather forecasts help farmers and other agricultural stakeholders plan planting, optimize irrigation and minimize the negative impact of severe weather on crops.

4.3 Case 3

Genomic Research and Crop Breeding Optimization (Case Study: International Maize and Wheat Improvement Center—CIMMYT) (CIMMYT 2023).

The International Maize and Wheat Improvement Center (CIMMYT), a Mexican institution, is accelerating genomic research and improving plant breeding for major crops such as corn and wheat through the use of HPC. CIMMYT uses HPC to evaluate massive genomic data sets, identify important genetic markers, and accelerate the breeding process to produce high-yielding and climate-resilient agricultural varieties. CIMMYT researchers leverage HPC capabilities and advanced bioinformatics techniques to study the genetic characteristics of different crop species.

This enables the identification of genes associated with desired traits such as drought tolerance, disease resistance and higher nutrient content. The use of HPC in genomic research has accelerated the development of new crop varieties.

5 Managerial Implications

Managers must set aside funds for the purchase and upkeep of AI and sophisticated computer systems. Although there can be a large initial cost, there might be long-term efficiency improvements from this. Farmers need to be trained in the use and operation of AI and HPC technologies. The key to a successful implementation is equipping the workforce with the digital skills they need. Agricultural methods differ depending on the crop and the locality. Farmers ought to look for adaptable solutions that offer flexibility in implementation and may be tailored to certain farm situations and production requirements. Managerial control is necessary when implementing AI for real-time crop status, weather, and equipment performance monitoring. To get the most out of the technology, control mechanisms must be established that work. Managers must communicate the benefits of combining AI and HPC in agriculture to a range of stakeholders, such as investors, producers, and governmental organizations. This entails stressing the advantages of sustainability, resource efficiency, and productivity increases.

6 Conclusion

In conclusion, a turning point in the history of the farming sector has been reached with the revolutionization of agriculture through the integration of AI and HPC. The combination of these technologies presents hitherto unseen chances to improve farming practices' overall efficiency, sustainability, and production. Farm managers and other stakeholders need to be aware of the revolutionary consequences of using HPC and AI, and they need to actively participate in strategic planning and adaptation. The advantages are numerous and include data-driven decision-making, precision farming, and real-time monitoring. However, careful consideration of a number of aspects is necessary in order to fully realize these benefits. The determination of business executives, legislators, and technological innovators to work together and clear the path for a more intelligent, sustainable agricultural landscape is what will determine whether or not the revolution in agriculture is successful.

6.1 Current Study Limitations and Future Avenue

While every attempt has been made to make this study as reliable as possible, like every study this study also suffers a few limitations. As open source i.e., google scholar was used, there can be issues of the reliability of the literature utilized. Google scholar, unlike the other databases like Scopus comes with limited filtering options, the literature inclusion and exclusion criteria rely more on the wisdom and judgment of the researchers. Future studies can be based on systematic literature review where the literature is extracted from more reliable sources (Scopus, Web of Science etc.). As HPC is still a growing field and the way technology is changing, more such kinds of studies are recommended in quick succession to maintain the relevancy for the future contemporary world. Being a study based on technology; the researchers feel that an empirical investigation can bring more contemporary issues to the surface leading to better understanding of the phenomenon. Thus, the future studies can adopt a method that can be based on robust systematic literature review and empirical investigations.

References

Abbasi R, Martinez P, Ahmad R (2022) An ontology model to represent aquaponics 4.0 system's knowledge. Inf Process Agric 9(4):514–532. https://doi.org/10.1016/j.inpa.2021.12.001

Ahamed NN, Vignesh R (2022) Smart agriculture and food industry with blockchain and artificial intelligence. J Comput Sci 18(1):1–17. https://doi.org/10.3844/JCSSP.2022.1.17

Ahmad I, Shariffudin SE, Ramli A, Maharum SMM, Mansor Z, Kadir KA (2021, August). Intelligent plant monitoring system via IoT and fuzzy system. In 2021 IEEE 7th International Conference on Smart Instrumentation, Measurement and Applications (ICSIMA), IEEE, pp 123–127

Albiero D, Paulo RLD, Félix JC, Santos JDSG, Melo RP (2020) Agriculture 4.0: a terminological introduction. Rev Ciênc Agron 51(spe), e20207737

Alonso RS, Sittón-Candanedo I, García Ó, Prieto J, Rodríguez-González S (2020) An intelligent Edge-IoT platform for monitoring livestock and crops in a dairy farming scenario. Ad Hoc Netw 98:102047

Alreshidi E (2019) Smart sustainable agriculture (SSA) solution underpinned by internet of things (IoT) and artificial intelligence (AI). arXiv preprint arXiv:1906.03106

Alrowais F, Asiri MM, Alabdan R, Marzouk R, Hilal AM, Gupta D (2022) Hybrid leader based optimization with deep learning driven weed detection on internet of things enabled smart agriculture environment. Comput Electr Eng 104:108411

Baghrous M, Ezzouhairi A, Benamar N (2020) Smart farming system based on fog computing and lora technology. In Embedded systems and artificial intelligence: Proceedings of ESAI 2019, Fez, Morocco. Springer Singapore, pp 217–225

Bobade G, Dhule C, Khadilkar R, Agrawal R, Morris NC (2023, July) Design of smart irrigation system based on MLA. In 2023 IEEE World Conference on Applied Intelligence and Computing (AIC), IEEE, pp 174–179

Bruno C, Licciardello A, Nastasi GAM et al (2021, April) Embedded artificial intelligence approach for gas recognition in smart agriculture applications using low cost mox gas sensors. In 2021 smart systems integration (SSI), IEEE, pp 1–5

Bui HT, Aboutorab H, Mahboubi A et al (2024) Agriculture 4.0 and beyond: evaluating cyber threat intelligence sources and techniques in smart farming ecosystems. Comput Secur 103754

Chakraborty S, Choudhury N, Kalita I (2022) AI-based smart agriculture monitoring using ground-based and remotely sensed images. In: The New Advanced Society: Artificial Intelligence and Industrial Internet of Things Paradigm, pp 191–221

Chamara N, Islam MD, Bai GF, Shi Y, Ge Y (2022) Ag-IoT for crop and environment monitoring: Past, present, and future. Agric Syst 203:103497

Dakhole DK, Jeno Lovesum SP (2021) Study of new trends in precision agriculture. In: Computer networks and inventive communication technologies: proceedings of third ICCNCT 2020. Springer Singapore, pp 167–177

Dayıoğlu MA, Turker U (2021) Digital transformation for sustainable future-agriculture 4.0: a review. Journal of Agricultural Sciences 27(4):373–399

Deepika P, Arthi BJMS (2022) Prediction of plant pest detection using improved mask FRCNN in cloud environment. Measur Sens 24:100549

Developing Integrated Climate-Smart Precision Crop Management Systems—Univ Of Minnesota. (n.d.). https://portal.nifa.usda.gov/web/crisprojectpages/1031103-developing-integrated-climate-smart-precision-crop-management-systems.html

Dewari S, Gupta M, Kumar R, Obaid AJ, AL-Hameed MR (2023) A review analysis on measuring the soil characteristic in agriculture using artificial intelligence and IOT. In Micro-electronics and telecommunication engineering: proceedings of 6th ICMETE 2022, Springer Nature Singapore, Singapore, pp 325–334

Dhanaraju M, Chenniappan P, Ramalingam K, Pazhanivelan S, Kaliaperumal R (2022) Smart farming: Internet of Things (IoT)-based sustainable agriculture. Agriculture 12(10):1745

Donde R, Gouda G, Sabarinathan S et al (2021) Artificial intelligence and machine learning in rice research. Appl Bioinf Rice Res 239–275

ECMWF (2023, November 13). ECMWF. https://www.ecmwf.int/

Edwin B, Veemaraj E, Parthiban P, Devarajan JP, Mariadhas V, Arumuganainar A, Reddy M (2022) Smart agriculture monitoring system for outdoor and hydroponic environments. Indonesian J Electr Eng Comput Sci 25(3):1679–1687

Gangwar VP, Khan SA (2022) Analyzing the role of micro-entrepreneurship and self-help groups (SHGs) in women empowerment and development: a bottom-of-pyramid perspective. In: Arafat M, Saleem I, Ali J, Khan A, Balhareth H (eds) Driving factors for venture creation and success in agricultural entrepreneurship. IGI Global, pp 213–226. https://doi.org/10.4018/978-1-6684-2349-3.ch011

Garg D, Alam M (2023) Smart agriculture: a literature review. J Manage Analyt 10(2):359–415
Guerrouj FZ, Latif R, Saddik A (2020, November) Evaluation of NDVI and NDWI parameters in CPU-GPU heterogeneous platforms based CUDA. In 2020 5th international conference on cloud computing and artificial intelligence: technologies and applications (CloudTech). IEEE, pp 1–6.
Gupta M, Abdelsalam M, Khorsandroo S, Mittal S (2020) Security and privacy in smart farming: challenges and opportunities. IEEE Access 8:34564–34584
Gupta P, Jhajharia K, Mathur P (2022) Intelligent computing for precision agriculture. In Handbook of intelligent computing and optimization for sustainable development, pp 677–692
Habib S, Alyahya S, Islam M, Alnajim AM, Alabdulatif A, Alabdulatif A (2022) Design and implementation: an IoT-framework-based automated wastewater irrigation system. Electronics 12(1):28
Haldar A, Mandal SN, Deb S, Roy R, Laishram M (2022) Application of information and electronic technology for best practice management in livestock production system. Agriculture, livestock production and aquaculture: advances for smallholder farming systems, vol 2. Springer International Publishing, Cham, pp 173–218
Han SH, Mutahira H, Jang HS (2023) Prediction of sensor data in a greenhouse for cultivation of paprika plants using a stacking ensemble for smart farms. Appl Sci 13(18):10464
Haq ZA, Jaffery ZA, Mehfuz S (2022, January) A novel framework for smart agriculture using internet of things and enabling technologies. In 2022 international conference for advancement in technology (ICONAT), IEEE, pp 1–6
Härtel I (2022) Agricultural Law 4.0: digital revolution in agriculture. In Handbook Industry 4.0: law, technology, society. Springer Berlin Heidelberg, Berlin, Heidelberg, pp 331–350
Hingle A, Johri A (2023, June) Recognizing principles of AI ethics through a role-play case study on agriculture. In: ASEE conferences
Holzinger A, Saranti A, Angerschmid A, Retzlaff CO, Gronauer A, Pejakovic V, Stampfer K (2022) Digital transformation in smart farm and forest operations needs human-centered AI: challenges and future directions. Sensors 22(8):3043
Home. (2023, November 30). CIMMYT. https://www.cimmyt.org/
Huo D, Malik AW, Ravana SD, Rahman AU, Ahmedy I (2024) Mapping smart farming: addressing agricultural challenges in data-driven era. Renew Sustain Energy Rev 189:113858
Idoje G, Dagiuklas T, Iqbal M (2021) Survey for smart farming technologies: challenges and issues. Comput Electr Eng 92:107104
Jacobs M, Remus A, Gaillard C et al (2022) ASAS-NANP symposium: mathematical modeling in animal nutrition: limitations and potential next steps for modeling and modelers in the animal sciences. J Anim Sci 100(6):skac132
Jain N, Awasthi Y, Jain RK (2021, February) Ubiquitous sensor based intelligent system for net houses. In: 2021 international conference on computing, communication, and intelligent systems (ICCCIS), IEEE, pp 219–225
Javaid M, Haleem A, Singh RP, Suman R (2022) Enhancing smart farming through the applications of Agriculture 4.0 technologies. International Journal of Intelligent Networks 3:150–164
Jiber Y, Harroud H, Karmouch A (2011, July) Precision agriculture monitoring framework based on WSN. In 2011 7th international wireless communications and mobile computing conference, IEEE, pp 2015–2020
Joshi J, Polepally S, Kumar P et al (2017, January) Machine learning based cloud integrated farming. In: Proceedings of the 2017 international conference on machine learning and soft computing, pp 1–6
Kabilesh SK, Mohanapriya D, Suseendhar P, Indra J, Gunasekar T, Senthilvel N (2023) Research on artificial intelligence based fruit disease identification system (AI-FDIS) with the internet of things (IoT). Journal of Intelligent & Fuzzy Systems 44(4):6593–6608
Karim F, Karim F (2017) Monitoring system using web of things in precision agriculture. Proc Comput Sci 110:402–409

Khan SA, Epoc F, Al Shamsi IR, Al Naimi MS (2023a, December) Perspectives on utilizing green practices and digital technologies for vertical farming in Oman. In: Proceedings of international conference on recent advancements in artificial intelligence. Springer Nature Singapore, Singapore, pp 317–328. https://doi.org/10.1007/978-981-97-1111-6_26

Khan SA, Magd H, Al Shamsi IR, Masoom K (2022a) Social entrepreneurship through innovations in agriculture. In Magd H, Singh D, Syed R, Spicer D (eds) International perspectives on value creation and sustainability through social entrepreneurship, IGI Global, pp 209–222. https://doi.org/10.4018/978-1-6684-4666-9.ch010

Khan SA, Magd H, Khatri B, Arora S, Sharma N (2023b) Critical success factors of internet of things and digital marketing. In Naim A, Devi V (eds) Global applications of the internet of things in digital marketing. IGI Global, pp 233–253. https://doi.org/10.4018/978-1-6684-8166-0.ch012

Khan SA, Devi TP, Sharma PP (2020) Vertical farming: Why it matters for Bhutan. Stud Indian Place Names 40(01):1323–1329

Khan SA, Epoc F, Al Shamsi IR, Shamim A (2022b) How far modern vertical farming is appropriate for developing countries like Oman? A review based analysis. Delhi Bus. Rev. 23(2):9–15 https://doi.org/10.51768/dbr.v23i2.232202202

Khan SA, Epoc FJ, Al Shamsi IR, Al Naimi MS (2024) Exploring critical success factors for vertical farming in developing countries. In: Kumar N (eds) Hydroponics. Encyclopedia of sustainability science and technology series. Springer, New York, NY. https://doi.org/10.1007/978-1-0716-3993-1_12

Kitano M, Nomura K, Yamazaki T, Iwao T, Saitou M, Mori M, Okabayashi T (2022) Internet of Plants (IoP) empowers bottom-up innovations in greenhouse horticulture. Environ Control Biol 60(1):3–12

Kour VP, Arora S (2020) Recent developments of the internet of things in agriculture: a survey. IEEE Access 8:129924–129957

Kumar A, Bhushan M, Galindo JA, Garg L, Hu YC (eds) (2023) Machine intelligence, big data analytics, and IoT in image processing: practical applications. John Wiley & Sons.

Lachgar M, Hrimech H, Kartit A (2023) Unmanned aerial vehicle-based applications in smart farming: a systematic review. Int J Adv Comput Sci Appl 14(6):1150–1165

Magd H, Ansari MSA, Khan SA (2023a) Need for explainable artificial intelligence ethnic decision making in society 5.0. In Al-Turjman F, Nayyar A, Naved M, Singh AK, Bilal M (eds) XAI based intelligent systems for society 5.0, Elsevier, pp 103–127. https://doi.org/10.1016/B978-0-323-95315-3.00010-3

Magd H, Jonathan H, Khan SA, El Geddawy M (2022) Artificial intelligence—the driving force of Industry 4.0. A roadmap for enabling Industry 4.0 by artificial intelligence. Wiley, pp 1–15. https://doi.org/10.1002/9781119905141.ch1

Magd, H., Khan, S. A., Khatri, B., Sharma, N., & Arora, S. (2023). Understanding the Relationship Between IoT and Digital Marketing: A Bibliometric Analysis. In A. Naim & V. Devi (Eds.), Global Applications of the Internet of Things in Digital Marketing (pp. 123–140). IGI Global. https://doi.org/10.4018/978-1-6684-8166-0.ch007

Mahajan HB, Junnarkar AA, Tiwari M, Tiwari T, Upadhyaya M (2022) LCIPA: lightweight clustering protocol for industry 4.0 enabled precision agriculture. Microprocess Microsyst 94:104633

Malik M, Gahlawat VK, Mor R, Rahul K, Singh BP, Agnihotri S (2023) Industry 4.0 technologies in postharvest operations: current trends and implications In: Postharvest management of fresh produce. Academic Press, pp 347–368

Massaoudi A, Berguiga A, Harchay A, Ben Ayed M, Belmabrouk H (2023) Spectral and energy efficiency trade-off in UAV-based olive irrigation systems. Appl Sci 13(19):10739

Molin JP, Bazame HC, Maldaner L, Corredo LDP, Martello M (2021) Agricultura de precisão e as contribuições digitais para a gestão localizada das lavouras. Rev Cienc Agron 51:e20207720

Moses D, Kumar TP, Varalakshmi S, Pamulaparty L (2023) A cyber physical system enabled intelligent farming system with artificial intelligence, machine learning and cloud computing

Muniasamy A (2020) Applications of data mining techniques in smart farming for sustainable agriculture. In: Modern Techniques for Agricultural Disease Management and Crop Yield Prediction. IGI Global pp 142–178

Mustafa MS, Kutucu H (2022, October) Intelligent irrigation system-automation using IoT technology: a review. In: 2022 international symposium on multidisciplinary studies and innovative technologies (ISMSIT). IEEE, pp 687–692

Naim A, Khan SA, Mohammed AB, Malik PK (2024) Applications of high performance computing and AI in green digital marketing. In Naim A (ed) AI applications for business, medical, and agricultural sustainability, IGI Global, pp 47–67. https://doi.org/10.4018/979-8-3693-5266-3.ch003

Naim A, Mohammed AB, Fatima N, Khan SA, Alnfiai MM, Malik PK (2024) Applications of artificial intelligence in environmental resource business management and sustainability. In: Naim A (ed) AI applications for business, medical, and agricultural sustainability. IGI Global, pp 1–22. https://doi.org/10.4018/979-8-3693-5266-3.ch001

Naqvi RZ, Farooq M, Naqvi SAA, Siddiqui HA, Amin I, Asif M, Mansoor S (2020) Big data analytics and advanced technologies for sustainable agriculture. Handbook of Smart Materials, Technologies, and Devices: Applications of Industry 4:1–27

Nicolas C, Naila B, Amar RC (2022, July) Tinyml smart sensor for energy saving in internet of things precision agriculture platform. In: 2022 thirteenth international conference on ubiquitous and future networks (ICUFN). IEEE, pp 256–259

Nurcahyo A, Soeparno H, Gaol FL, Arifin Y (2023, September) Developing smart precision farming using big data and cloud-based intelligent decision support system. In 2023 10th international conference on ICT for smart society (ICISS). IEEE, pp 1–6

Obien JB et al (2022) AEaaS: artificial intelligence edge-of-things as a service for intelligent remote farm security and intrusion detection pre-alarm system. In 2022 IEEE 14th international conference on humanoid, nanotechnology, information technology, communication and control, environment, and management, HNICEM 2022. Institute of Electrical and Electronics Engineers Inc. https://doi.org/10.1109/HNICEM57413.2022.10109572

Öztürk M, Alonso RS, García Ó, Sittón-Candanedo I, Prieto J (2021) Livestock welfare by means of an edge computing and IoT platform. In Ambient intelligence–software and applications: 11th international symposium on ambient intelligence. Springer International Publishing, pp 156–165

Paymode AS, Magar SP, Malode VB (2021, March) Tomato leaf disease detection and classification using convolution neural network. In 2021 international conference on emerging smart computing and informatics (ESCI). IEEE, pp 564–570

Pivoto D, Waquil PD, Talamini E, Finocchio CPS, Dalla Corte VF, de Vargas Mores G (2018) Scientific development of smart farming technologies and their application in Brazil. Inf Process Agric 5(1):21–32

Pranuthi G, Srikanth R (2023) Globally scalable and locally adaptable solutions for agriculture. In Digital ecosystem for innovation in agriculture. Springer Nature Singapore, Singapore, pp 89–108

Preethi A, Reddy PK (2022, August) Survey on smart agriculture a roadmap for India: role of IoT, AI. In 2022 3rd international conference on electronics and sustainable communication systems (ICESC). IEEE, pp 434–439

Rathi M, Gomathy C (2023, September) Revolutionizing agriculture with IoT—a review. In 2023 4th international conference on smart electronics and communication (ICOSEC). IEEE, pp 370–381

Revathi K, Tamilselvi T, Arunkumar R, Samydurai A (2022) A smart drone for ensuring precision agriculture with artificial neural network. Indian J Comput Sci Eng 13(3):897–906

Sankaranarayanan S (2021) Applications of artificial intelligence for smart agriculture. In AI-based services for smart cities and urban infrastructure. IGI Global, pp 277–288

Senapaty MK, Ray A, Padhy N (2023) IoT-enabled soil nutrient analysis and crop recommendation model for precision agriculture. Computers 12(3):61

Shaikh FK, Karim S, Zeadally S, Nebhen J (2022) Recent trends in internet-of-things-enabled sensor technologies for smart agriculture. IEEE Internet Things J 9(23):23583–23598

Sharma AK, Chanderwal N, Khan R (eds) (2023) Convergence of cloud computing, AI, and agricultural science. IGI Global

Singh AK (2022) Smart farming: applications of IoT in agriculture. In Handbook of smart materials, technologies, and devices: applications of Industry 4.0. Springer International Publishing, Cham, pp 1655–1687

Singh G, Kalra N, Yadav N, Sharma A, Saini M (2022) Smart agriculture: a review. Siberian Journal of Life Sciences and Agriculture 14(6):423–454

Sishodia RP, Ray RL, Singh SK (2020) Applications of remote sensing in precision agriculture: a review. Remote Sens 12(19):3136

Sun ZG, Wang YS, Zhang L, Guo W (2018) Design and realization of intelligent service system for monitoring and warning of meteorological disasters in facility agriculture in North China. Trans Chin Soc Agric Eng (Trans CSAE) 34(23):149–156

Tan L, Hou H, Zhang Q (2016, July) An extensible software platform for cloud-based decision support and automation in precision agriculture. In: 2016 IEEE 17th international conference on information reuse and integration (IRI). IEEE, pp 218–225

Thilakarathne NN, Bakar MSA, Abas PE, Yassin H (2022) A cloud enabled crop recommendation platform for machine learning-driven precision farming. Sensors 22(16):6299

Tomar, P, Kaur G (eds) (2021) Artificial intelligence and IoT-based technologies for sustainable farming and smart agriculture. IGI Global.

Trichkova-Kashamova E, Paunova-Hubenova E (2021, September) Integrated software solutions in animal husbandry. In 2021 international conference automatics and informatics (ICAI), pp 248–251. IEEE

Tripathy N, Tripathy SS, Rath M, Swain J (2022a, December). An IoT assisted fog enabled framework for smart green house. In 2022 5th international conference on computational intelligence and networks (CINE), pp 1–6. IEEE

Tripathy SS, Tripathy N, Rath M, Pati A, Panigrahi A, Dash M (2022b, November) Smart farming based on deep learning approaches. In 2022 2nd Odisha international conference on electrical power engineering, communication and computing technology (ODICON). IEEE, pp 1–5

Verma D, Kansra P, Khan SA (2024) Apparent advantages and negative facet of block chain in banking sector: an innovative theoretical perspective. In: Irfan M, Muhammad K, Naifar N, Khan MA (eds), Applications of block chain technology and artificial intelligence: lead-ins in banking, finance, and capital market. Springer International Publishing, Cham, pp 19–27. https://doi.org/10.1007/978-3-031-47324-1_2

Vrbančič G, Podgorelec V, Salcedo-Sanz S, Fister I (2022, November). Profiling the Arion rufus snails with computer vision. In 2022 IEEE 22nd international symposium on computational intelligence and informatics and 8th ieee international conference on recent achievements in mechatronics, automation, computer science and robotics (CINTI-MACRo). IEEE, pp 000369–000374

Wolfert S, Ge L, Verdouw C, Bogaardt MJ (2017) Big data in smart farming—a review. Agric Syst 153:69–80

Yang J, Liu M, Lu J, Miao Y, Hossain MA, Alhamid MF (2018) Botanical internet of things: toward smart indoor farming by connecting people, plant, data and clouds. Mobile Netw Appl 23:188–202

Online to Offline Recycling—An Analysis of Recycling Waste in an Internet-Integrated World

Adeel Shah, Muhammad Arif, and Saheer Ali

Abstract As the escalated destructive impacts of climate change become more and more apparent year after year, people are comprehending the significance of preserving their planet more than ever before. Businesses and manufacturers are moving towards sustainable practices and playing their part in preserving the environment. An important part of sustainability is waste recycling. Treatment of industrial and domestic waste is a major challenge for businesses and authorities. Due to the major need for recycling, this research is based on online to offline recycling (O2O). The impact of online to offline recycling is studied on the customer's perception and their choice to pick the Internet as a medium to recycle their electronic waste. This choice is termed customer choice (CC), and its influence is studied on constructs such as Better Inspection Facilities (BIF), Fast Pick Services (FPS), Fast Money Transfer (FMT) and Fast Product Return Services (FPRS) and relations between the constructs. The data for the research was collected from two hundred and twenty-one organizations in the Malaysian manufacturing sector. Regression analysis was used for statistical inference through the Smart PLS. Substantial results are found between BIF and FPS and between BIF and FMT. The study's results also confirmed that a weak significant value was found between CC and FPRS.

Keywords Online to offline recycling · Customer choice · Better inspection facilities · Fast pick-up service · Fast money transfer · Fast product return service · Electronic waste · Internet recycling · Online recycling · Online recycler

---

A. Shah (✉)
Department of Supply Chain Management, Institute of Business Management, Karachi, Pakistan
e-mail: adeel.shah@iobm.edu.pk

M. Arif
Institute of Business Management, Karachi, Pakistan
e-mail: muhammad.arif@iobm.edu.pk

S. Ali
Faculty of Economics and Management, Universiti Kebangsaan Malaysia, Selangor, Malaysia
e-mail: p114938@siswa.ukm.edu.my

S. A. R. Khan et al. (eds.), *Circular Economy and Technological Innovation*, Industrial Ecology, https://doi.org/10.1007/978-981-96-5650-9_12

Chapter Objectives
Below are the intended objectives of this chapter.

- To present a brief overview of electronic waste (E-Waste) generated around the world and Malaysia.
- Reiterate the importance of recycling E-Waste.
- Determine the factors that drive people to recycle their items through online networks.
- Present an applicable and inclusive model of the flow of material and money for recycling via online channels.

Learning Outcomes of the Chapter
The learning outcomes of the chapter are presented below. After reading this chapter, the readers will:

- Understand the magnitude of E-waste which is generated in the world and its adverse effects
- Have an understanding of the process of recycling E-waste, which is a need in the present internet-integrated world.
- Develop an idea that the internet can bridge the gap between producers of E-waste who are willing to recycle their items via recycling facilities in exchange for monetary benefits

1 Introduction

Humans, in any era, have heavily relied on tools and apparatus in their daily walk of life. The twenty-first century is no different. The current century is heavily reliant on electronic appliances and products. On observing our daily routine, it becomes evident that life without such devices is unimaginable. This avid usage of electronic devices by billions of humans globally leads to very significant management and environmental concerns, such as how to deal with used devices and products at the end of their product life cycle. The benefits of recycling discarded mobile phones for the benefit of the economy and the environment have attracted much public interest (Liu et al. 2023). According to Victoria Gill (2022), five billion cellular phones will end up in landfills in the year 20, and the forecasted waste will be higher in the year 2024.

Electronic recycling is a heterogeneous combination of a few unsafe and harmful synthetics, which includes materials like ceramics, polymers, metals and glass. It is essential to accumulate and eliminate such materials appropriately to guarantee the reuse of resources and safeguard the environment. Some prominent manufacturers of electric and technology-related products, such as Huawei (2024) and Apple (2022), are refurbishing items using recycled parts. With their refurbished items and recycled parts, these manufacturers succeeded in attaining the same degree of functionality and craftsmanship that they accomplished with their newly developed goods with virgin raw materials. The recycling of discarded mobile phones must be improved, customer involvement in recycling campaigns should be encouraged, and these devices must be made easier to recycle and reuse (Ramakrishna and Srivastava 2024). Online recycling, which merges the Internet with the old electronic items recycling industry, is quickly gaining momentum in this respect. As the internet economy evolved, various online recycling platforms (ORPs) emerged as significant players in the recycling business. These platforms, such as the European Recycling Platform, Eco ATM and Aihuishou in China, have grown in prominence and prominent position (Islam et al. 2020; Liu et al. 2022a).

Malaysia is a viable country for the O2O recycling business. Malaysians generate a considerable tonnage of electronic waste, which needs to be managed every year in a way that is similar to that of developed nations in the world. Globally, there was an increase in e-waste production by 60% from the years 2010 to 2019; the total global e-waste will surpass 74 million tons by the year 2030 and as for Malaysia, the estimated e-waste production in the year 2021 was 2,459 tons, and Malaysians will produce 24.5 million items as e-waste by the year 2025 (Azman et al. 2024). In contrast, the recycling rate for such waste is merely 25% in Malaysia (Akhtar 2024). The reason for such an increase in electronic items being discarded as waste is that Malaysia is a progressing economy where citizens and their lifestyles are on an upward elevated trend. This positive growth allows for more purchases and rapid consumption of the latest electronic gadgets. Moreover, several businesses offer the latest electronic devices, especially recent laptop computers and cellphones, at quite a significant discounted rate for students in Malaysia.

Online recycling and ORPs occupy only a marginal share despite their swift growth in the recycling market, mainly due to a lack of rules and regulations. Another possible reason for marginal market share is that it is comparatively more difficult for recycling firms to establish a reverse supply chain along with customer loyalty than for a manufacturer in a traditional downstream flow of materials. As in a supply chain structure of the forward or downstream flow of products, customers build their loyalty based on the manufacturer's product differentiation, product features, price or quality. However, the work of Adesoga et al. (2024) on reverse supply chain highlighted that businesses focusing on the reverse supply chain could also foster strong brand loyalty by accepting, promoting and implementing technological innovations, adjusting to regulations and fostering a research-based culture.

In the case of internet recycling, there are no major market regulations or pricing established by demand and supply parameters, and there will always be contention between the parties on selling and buying prices until the market evolves to follow a framework accepted by all. Even though the "Internet + recycling" ventures have gained some momentum, they have encountered a variety of problems during the span of their evolution. For instance, some people disagree about the cost of recyclable materials and are concerned about information security. The biggest issue with recycling is that the residents of the locality or region do not completely comprehend Internet recycling, which results in limited participation and a lack of passion (Liu et al. 2022c).

One of the most significant ethical challenges of the digital era is data privacy. This problem stemmed from the time when electronic devices such as personal computers or cell phones started to become popular for domestic use. This issue of data privacy still exists for computers (Corcoran et al. 2024). Due to this, online or internet recycling is behind in gaining more prominence than traditional recycling.

As a result, the variables influencing a consumer's intention to recycle via the Internet are classified as general attitude, subjective norms, and perceived behavioral control. Other than these, there are several personal and social influencers crafting a person's intention and final behavioral outcome to recycle via an ORP, such as a person's perception and trust in their ability to use the Internet for recycling. Emotional factors also play a role in determining how a person feels about recycling, and the moral ideals and social pressure governed by subjective norms and all these personal and social influencers impact a consumer's decision to have their electronic items recycled via an ORP (Bhutto et al. 2023). ORPs should also take into consideration the benefits they already possess, which include imparting information about recycling to reduce the cost incurred for information exchange between parties.

Previously, only a few studies discussed consumer recycling, which was categorized as either online or offline recycling (Cho et al. 2024). However, online-to-offline recycling between consumers and internet recyclers requires further investigation to determine if the two mechanisms are interconnected using Internet recycling platforms. This has several advantages over conventional ways of recycling. Primarily because it substantially reduces the knowledge gap between buyers and sellers, encouraging better information sharing. Secondly, people may schedule door-to-door recycling using online recycling platforms, which will expedite and simplify the procedure. Finally, internet recycling processes have become more standardized, trained recyclers provide consumers with professional services and the online platform tracks recycled materials to make sure they enter authorized routes for disposal. Based on the available gap in the literature, an empirical study must be conducted to understand the customer behavioral intention for using online-to-offline systems in recycling and reverse logistics.

The study is organized as follows: Sect. 2 encompasses a synopsis of the relevant literature, an explanation of the variables adopted, their theoretical implications and the development of hypothesis statements. Section 3 entails the methodology of the study. Section 4 presents statistical inferences about data collection, data processing and results obtained. Section 5 summarizes the findings and suggests avenues for further studies on the subject.

2 Literature Review for Online Recycling, Its Theoretical Implications, Global Outlook and Hypothesis Development

The worldwide approach to climate change is astoundingly crucial today. To combat global warming and achieve sustainable development, many countries and businesses have considered carbon neutrality, which is balancing the quantity of carbon dioxide emissions with carbon dioxide being reduced or compensated by sustainable practices, as their objective in the coming year. China, being a major economy that consumes and manufactures electronic items, has declared an official commitment to carbon neutrality, waste reduction, and the consumption of virgin raw materials through national laws (Wang et al. 2022). The Chinese government's agreements and strategy proclamations to combat global warming and to decrease emissions of greenhouse gases such as carbon dioxide (Liu et al. 2022d) Demonstrate and set an astounding standard in the world for other countries to follow for environmental concerns. Among many methods to curb carbon emissions and attain carbon neutrality in the world on domestic and commercial levels, one way is to recycle the waste generated most appropriately and swiftly. As explained by Shah (2024), recycling propagates sustainability in the following ways as described in Table 1:

2.1 Segregation of Recyclable Items

Recycling helps to reduce carbon emissions, making it a crucial step towards attaining carbon neutrality. According to Paper Excellence (2024) recycled paper can save energy use by 60–70% and, similarly, Air pollution by the same percentage. Recycling copper has the potential to cut energy consumption by 85% (Copper Sustainability Partnership 2024) and reduce carbon emissions of greenhouse gases by 4.1 tCO_2e (Carbon et al.) per ton of ingested copper. Outdated online market platforms such as eBay.com, taobao.com, and others exchanged huge amounts of utilized and out-of-date parts, and their purchasers were available all around the world. Returned materials can be classified as:

(I) End of Life (EOL)
(II) Finish of Purpose
(III) Reusable returns

End-of-life return (EOL) is hardware or items that have been utilized for a determined time and arrangement and now usually are at the end of their reported life or those items for which the need to substitute them with a new, most recent variant has arrived. End-of-purpose returns are those items that organizations obtain on rent or lease rather than purchasing them and then return those items or machinery later after their determined period, such as in the construction industry. Reusable things are reusable pieces from rejected or thrown-away items or hardware. Recovery of

Table 1 Key areas of application for recycling

Key points	Conceptual understanding	Importance	Practical applications
Conserving Resources	Protecting natural resources such as freshwater, oil and forestation. Manufacturing consumes resources such as oil, gas and coal, which are causes of greenhouse gases (Lu and Wang 2023)	Recycling decreases the need for material used in production, reducing the use of resources	Recycling a ton of paper would protect 17 trees, 7,000 gallons of water, and 3.3 cubic yards of landfill space
Saving Energy	Reducing energy consumption. Re-inducting material from discarded waste, especially the recovered items (circuits and wires) from electric waste (E-waste), will allow manufacturers to produce less and use less energy. The manufacturing sector consumes almost 30% of the total energy produced in the world (Farghali et al. 2023)	Less energy is used, as items recovered from recycling could be inducted in one of the later stages of manufacturing	Recycling aluminum cans saves up to 95% of energy compared to the amount of energy used to produce the cans from scratch
Reducing Waste	Reduction in discarded material. Reduction takes place by using the material for longer periods, reusing it or making the discarded material usable again. Presently developed regions of the world, such as European nations, have enacted strict laws for waste disposal and preventing waste generation by focusing on repairable items and reducing food waste. Collectively, the EU recycles 49% of municipal waste at present (European Environment Agency 2024)	Recycling saves a significant amount of waste from being thrown into landfills. Landfills deteriorate the soil quality	Recycling plastic bottles would save a considerable area of land from being used for landfill
Saving Costs	Any activity that contributes to the reduction of expenses and costs and helps bring financial benefit	A new sector would be established, offering entrepreneurial opportunities to earn by helping the environment	The United States is prominent in this regard. The country has 681,000 jobs, and USD 37.8 billion is paid in compensation

such parts begins right from when the hardware or machinery is rejected. The requirements of recyclers in this type of material recovery are often unique. For example, people who are looking to recover metallic pieces are not worried about electrical things. Those keen on recovering electrical parts do not consider metallic pieces.

A lot of developing countries are secondary markets for electronic and metallic equipment from the developed world. Used electronic devices and metallic equipment are imported as scrap to save the expense of imports. At the point when assortment is made in a market, the purchaser spreads everything over the ground and then the material is picked, selected and sold. In such purchases, sellers generally do not offer any return policy in case anything sold does not work.

2.2 *Global Outlook—Recycling Initiatives Around the World*

Several developed nations have devised comparatively extensive recycling systems through legislation for recyclable domestic materials, and their pertinent policies and procedures reflect cutting-edge resource management concepts. The United States has established a model that combines backing from public policy with engaged citizenry in the growth of the recycling sector. The Resource Conservation and Recovery Act was passed in the United States in 1976, and more than half of its states now have recycling regulations in effect (Liu et al. 2022b). Germany is a forerunner in the development of a circular economy, which is a notion based on reusing, refurbishing and producing products with material that can later be recycled after its useful life (Khan et al. 2022), with a rather comprehensive legal framework comprising of laws, norms, and suggestions. Non-governmental organizations, such as the Duales System Deutschland, have developed recycling systems to promote resource recycling programs and establish compliance with that comprehensive legal framework (Kitagawa 2021). The garbage sorting and recycling processes in Japan are highly structured and controlled. They are governed by a legislative framework that binds the responsibilities and obligations of the municipalities, corporations, and individuals engaged in the recycling chain. The country has reduced landfills with a high level of public participation in recycling operations (Acatech 2021) for such landfills, apart from a major portion of electronic items, textiles also contribute due to their increased and rapid purchasing in last few years (Costin-Weiterschan and Matiou 2017). Recycling reusable products is a vital step in the approach to achieving carbon neutrality, which has surfaced as a renowned sustainability plan. A new Internet based recycling model has potential to raise the recycling rate for end of life batteries in China (Qiao et al. 2021).

2.3 *Implication of Stakeholder Theory to an Online Recycling Business*

Stakeholder theory is a framework used to analyze and manage the relationships between a company and its stakeholders (Awa et al. 2024). A stakeholder is any individual or group that can be affected by or can affect the company's decisions and actions. In the case of an online internet recycler, stakeholders may include customers, employees, investors, suppliers, regulators, and the wider community. Stakeholder theory could be leveraged to describe an online internet recycler in the manners listed below:

Community: The local community is affected by an online internet recycler. Local community members and responsible citizens could organize and collaboratively gather waste material and volunteer to deliver the material for recycling directly to the internet recycler's facility as a part of keeping their neighborhood sustainable. The businesses should make a conscious decision to forge advantageous relationships with neighboring communal organizations and take part in efforts that enhance the local community, economic benefits, and ecosystem.

Suppliers: An online internet recycler could collaborate with an array of suppliers, notably IT firms, transportation businesses, and waste management organizations. Internet recyclers or ORPs should maintain positive relationships with such suppliers and make sure they adhere to ethical and ecological requirements (Feng et al. 2024), especially when disposing of their waste material.

Customers: The most essential stakeholders for any business, particularly for an online internet service-based recycler, are the customers. Internet recyclers should place their clients' wants and desires foremost by imparting consistent excellent customer service and comparably low prices. Likewise, ORPs should take precautions to safeguard client privacy and ensure that any personally identifiable information is safeguarded discreetly.

Investors: Investors contribute the capital that enables an online internet recycler to remain and expand their operations. Investors should get reliable and up-to-date monetary data from the firm in a transparent manner. To safeguard the longer-term objectives of its investors, an online recycling business should also make sure that it is doing its business in a way that is ethical and environmentally friendly.

Employees: An online internet recycler's workforce is essential to its ongoing success. The organization ought to provide a healthy and secure working atmosphere for every staff member. Additionally, organizations presently have started to inculcate a reward system based on sustainable actions of their employees, which has shown to add positive impact on organization's long term sustainable performance (Das and Dash 2024). A motivated employee is an asset in a service-based business such as for internet recycling, where employees visit residences, provide information about recycling processes and collect materials from users.

Regulators: An online internet recycler must abide by several legal obligations, including laws governing data privacy and the environment. A list of products composed by authorities, such as in Europe, in which electronic and electrical items are labelled and categorized to become E-Waste by the end of their useful life is one important point of information provided by regulators to online recyclers, this directive is termed as WEEE (Waste Electrical and Electronic Equipment), which is considered quite a valuable regulatory contribution in many countries for manufacturers and recyclers (Liu et al. 2023).

One way internet recyclers can do this is to motivate and promote recycling as the need of the hour and concern that impacts everyone alike regardless of identity, geography and social status.

2.4 Implication of Resource-Based Theory for an Online Internet Recycler

Recycling pertains to acts of preserving the environment, theoretically in strategic management, a popular theoretical notion termed a resource-based theory emphasizes on internal assets and competencies of a corporation as sources of long-term competitive advantage. Proposed in 1991, resource based theory focuses on organizational resources which are precious, not readily available to others, those which can be copied and resources which can not be easily replaced (Chatterjee et al. 2023) and iterates that organizations must look inward and exploit such valuable resources to gain edge over others in the industry. Nwikinaka and Poi (2024).published a study on implementation of recycling logistics and integrated their work with resource-based view (RBV) while presenting that managing logistics of recyclable waste such as liquid drinks bottle from consumers; manufacturers can uplift their marketing image and performance significantly. The study was conducted in Nigeria with Nigerian breweries.

Below are a few instances when resource-based theory is used to describe an online internet recycler. The resource-based theory can be elaborated in various aspects, which are as follows:

Technological Proficiency: An internet recycler who operates online could possess special technological proficiency in recycling and dispose of electronic waste such as electronic hardware and devices and the worth of material which is contained in such devices. This knowledge may be a priceless asset that helps the business stand out from rivals and offer consumers high-quality services.

Client Information: An online internet recycler may have access to immense amounts of client information, including preferences, buying patterns, and demographics. This increase in depth and volume of information about customers in the present times can provide a recycling business with number of options to establish recycling channels for collecting items from residential areas in contrast to traditional approaches where recycling was dependent on individual initiatives or actions (Wang et al. 2023).

Reputation for sustainability and environmental responsibility: An online recycler may have a positive brand reputation in several areas, such as in the recycling of cell phones. A useful asset that draws clients and sets the company apart from rivals might be its reputation (Liu et al. 2022e).

Network of alliances: An online internet recycler could establish alliances with other businesses, such as waste management companies and neighborhood associations. The company may be able to make use of the knowledge and resources obtained from collaboration with other companies through this network of partnerships, adding value for consumers (Liu et al. 2022b).

According to resource-based theory, an online internet recycler's capacity to generate value and establish a long-term competitive advantage is reliant on its knowledge-based assets and skills. They could distinguish the business from rivals, offer clients high-quality services and succeed over the long run by properly using these resources.

2.5 Hypothesis Development

This section elaborates on the hypothesis development, highlighting the works from the literature and framing the hypothesis statements.

2.5.1 Consumer Behavior Towards Internet Recyclers for Better Inspection Facility

The literature suggests that convenience, trust, and environmental consciousness are variables that affect how consumers behave when interacting with online recyclers (Zhong et al. 2022). For a better understanding, consider the following aspects below, which affect how consumers behave towards online recyclers:

Convenience: Online recyclers save consumers time, effort and money. Customers don't have to move their electronic garbage to recycling centers. Online recyclers provide the convenience of doorstep pick-up. Customers save time and effort by doing this, and as a result, they could be more likely to utilize online recyclers.

Trust: Consumer behavior towards online recyclers is significantly influenced by trust. They must feel confident in the safe and secure handling of their used electronic items. Consumers are more likely to trust online recyclers who have received regulatory approval or a strong reputation in the sector (Islam et al. 2021a, b).

Environmental Concerns: As consumers become more conscious about the effects of electronic waste on the environment, they search for ethical ways to dispose of it, ways that do not negatively impact the environment. Internet recyclers would provide customers with environmentally friendly means of getting rid of their electronic garbage. In this way, customers would be satisfied that their discarded electronic items are disposed of in an ecologically friendly manner via a certain online recycler (Issah et al. 2021).

Companies must educate customers on the positive aspects of utilizing such services if they are to persuade them to utilize online recyclers. An aspect of education would be to highlight the benefit of online recycling's properly organized and managed inspection facilities. Advertising campaigns or informational content on the business website can do this. Internet recyclers can attract more customers to utilize their services by addressing consumers' concerns about convenience, trust, and environmental responsibility. This will result in improved inspection facilities (Zhang et al. 2023).

H1: Better Inspection Facilities Significantly Impact Consumer's Choice for Internet Recyclers

2.5.2 Consumer Behavior Towards Internet Recyclers for Fast Pick-Up Service

The area of material recycling has been extensively introduced with technologies such as the Internet and the Internet of Things. To increase the capacity and effectiveness of recycling materials, several businesses have started to concentrate on developing Internet recycling (Liu et al. 2022c). Businesses often act as the intermediary buyers and collectors of recyclable items submitted by consumers to recycle appropriately. Among them, Aihuishou is the most prominent one. It operates in more than 700 stores in China. Shoppers can submit recycling orders through the Aihuishou webpage. It enables the customers to have their items, such as an out-of-date cell phone, assessed and picked up from their location. Customers can also visit a drop box at a retail outlet or network to have their telephones assessed and get a prompt prize. Based on a study of NBD (Public Business Day to Day) in 2020, Aihuishou processed more than 20 million arrangements of outdated cell phones in the year 2019 (Zhang et al. 2021).

Implementation of Internet recycling platforms has several benefits over conventional recycling. First, information transparency should be achieved to reduce knowledge asymmetry between buyers and sellers. Furthermore, consumers will choose speedier and more practical door-to-door pick-ups and item assessments, as such described in Table 2 below as variables of Fast Pickup Facility. Internet recycling is also more lucrative since employees undergo training to provide professional services to individuals, businesses and communities. An online recycling platform keeps records of documents about the inspection and movement of material received. Ensuring that the material travels via authorized routes for appropriate disposal (Liu et al. 2022c).

H2: Fast Pick-up Service Significantly Impacts Consumer's Choice for Internet Recyclers

2.5.3 Consumer Behavior Towards Internet Recyclers for Fast Product Return Service

This variable is dedicated to EOL items. Customer engagement is essential for the successful execution of the recovery process for EOL products via Reverse Supply Chain Management (RSCM). In response to concerns about resource depletion and environmental damage, businesses are required to collect EOL products for reuse, recycling, and refurbishment. Customers' active participation plays an essential role in demonstrating the success rate of RSCM. Customer's keen interest in engagement has a direct impact on the effectiveness of collecting EOL artifacts. Companies must encourage consumer interaction through outreach efforts, education programs and accessible return routes to achieve positive outcomes (Ao et al. 2023). The viability of such reverse supply chain channels heavily depends on collectors' efforts, including their expenditures on advertising and promotional services that encourage customers to return their used items for recycling. Online recycling service providers allow for collection efforts to serve a variety of objectives, including strengthening user experiences and service quality. For instance, Aihuishou opened more than 300 locations in 35 cities by the year 2018 to enable face-to-face contact and transactions (Jian et al. 2019). This variable for rapid or fast product return service differentiates from the variable of fast pick-up service discussed above, as in the former, online recyclers would initiate contact by establishing reverse supply chain channels to obtain EOL material only. So, there is an imparting of knowledge about certain items' lifetimes (such as a chainsaw, which has a useful life of 10 years). In the latter variable for fast pick-up services, we initiate processes, and contacts are established when a customer places an order. This order can be for any item which is being discarded for any reason.

H3 Fast Product Return Service Significantly Impacts Consumer's Choice for Internet Recyclers

2.5.4 Consumer Behavior Towards Internet Recyclers for Fast Money Transfer

The study we conducted additionally delves into the impact of monetary rewards on consumer's perceptions of recycling. When it comes to online recycling, the researchers came across individuals with comparatively lower incomes than other participants who were more concerned about higher lucrative returns. This is extremely important as online recycling provides significantly more economic benefits than normative recycling techniques. This promise of lucrative and faster monetary returns, as such described as Fast Money Transfer variable in the Table 2 below, has also led numerous online recycling platforms to risk going bankrupt and running into other operational issues. Even so, since businesses and governments globally are assertively promoting the Internet recycling model, it is necessary to investigate the current situation and the variables affecting people's participation in online recycling (Liu et al. 2022d). Internet recycling platforms should reap the rewards of their inherent benefits, which include offering reasonable collection pricing that satisfies customers' expectations. Presently, in China, most internet recycling businesses are privately owned, have quick start-up times and have modest initial revenues. These businesses frequently struggle with issues like high operating costs, dismal profit margins and a lack of effective profit models; as a result, their growth is dependent on government policy and financial support (Gibson 2023).

H4 Fast Money Transfer Significantly Impacts Consumer's Choice for Internet Recyclers

Table 2 Theoretical model construct with definitions

Construct	Definition	Citation
Customer Choice	This measure represents decision-making and activities based on intellect and information at a separate or individual level of the customer. Which is a necessary part of human life	(Cho et al. 2024; Odhiambo and Murori (2024)
Internet Recycler	A term to denote people/customers who may schedule collection using a range of online platforms and those who collect waste would then pick up the waste locally for recycling	(Kang et al. 2020; Wirani et al. 2024)
Inspection Facility	A zone or area where waste materials are inspected and sorted according to their condition, hazard, quality and size classifications to determine various grades	(Gundupalli et al. 2017; Silva et al. 2023)
Fast Pick-up Facility	Reduced time between waste generation and its removal by using a waste collection service or system that prioritizes prompt and effective pick-up of waste products and mitigating the adverse consequences of delayed pick-up	(Wen et al. 2018; Wu et al. 2024)
Fast product return service	To effectively collect end-of-life products as submitted by customers at a collection point for reuse, recycling, or refurbishment, thus minimizing the negative effects on the environment, maximizing resource efficiency, and streamlining the reverse logistics	(Islam and Huda 2018; Mishra et al. 2023)
Fast Money Transfer	Quick and effective money transactions related to the purchasing and selling of recyclable materials	(Khan and Ahmad 2022; Wu et al. 2024)

2.6 *Construct and Definitions*

2.7 *Proposed Framework*

The strategy hinges on an online recycling platform where consumers may sell their used or surplus products to internet recyclers. After receiving these products, these online recycling platforms companies examine and categorize them before dropping them to manufacturers for refurbishment or recycling. The internet recycler receives the products and undertakes testing, inspection, and rectification of any misclassified items throughout this period. If the items comply with the prerequisites, they will be awarded the "Success" label. If the items do not fulfill the prerequisites, they are labeled "Failure" and returned to the customers.

The flow of material (green dotted lines) suggests that the material is transported from a customer to the internet recycler's logistical team. Then, it is received at the facility for further processing. Further processing includes correction of orders and inspection of material. Inspection of material is where the cleansing of the material takes place to extract the most useable parts or decide if the entire item received can

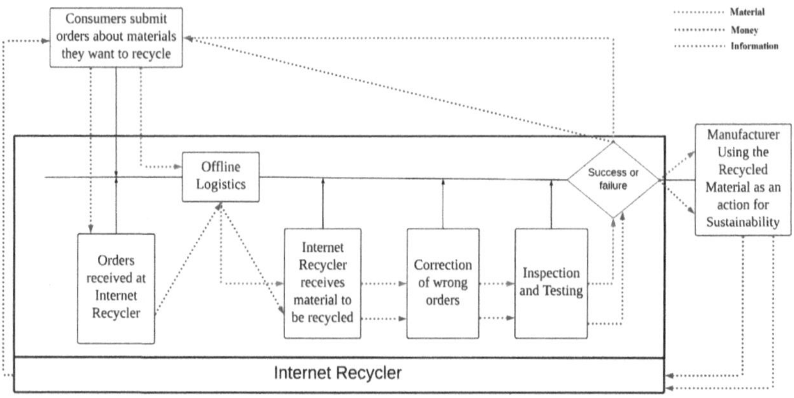

Fig. 1 Timeline and Process Flow of O2O (Online-to-Offline) recycling between consumers, internet recyclers and then manufacturers. Consistent black-colored lines define boundaries and timelines for each process. Green dotted lines represent the flow of material. Red dotted lines represent the flow of money or funds, and blue dotted lines represent the flow of information

be reused. Upon success of inspection, the material is then transported to manufacturers. Since several manufacturers have implemented notions of circular economy, it becomes necessary for them to induct recycled material for better sustainability and environmental performance.

In the process below (Fig. 1), the role of information flow (blue dotted lines) is crucial. The most important promise of any O2O recycler should be the protection of customers' information. This is possible by restricting access to information at each level of the business. Limited information should be imparted within the company, only on a need basis, and it must be retracted once any function (such as transportation from customer to facility) is completed. Information after receiving the material travels in the same direction as the material. If the inspection is passed, then information needs to be shared with the customer and with the manufacturer down the line.

The flow of money or funds (denoted by red dotted lines) is first from the cleansed and recycled material purchased by manufacturers and sold by the O2O recycler. These funds act as the business's input. Then, the monetary rewards paid by the business to customers in exchange for giving their items to for recycling. Such rewards will be imparted after a thorough evaluation of the item on-site (customer's location) by O2O professionals or at the facility.

Theoretically, we investigate variables that this study has inculcated to examine consumers' decisions about selecting online recyclers for recycling their items by placing online orders. The figure below summarizes the impact each variable has on the final consumer selection for recycling of materials.

3 Methodology

Research is a purposeful and coordinated course of focus that includes getting, dissecting, and deciphering information to find an answer to a particular issue, tackle a challenge, or get a more significant understanding of a subject.

This research investigated the relationship between customers' perceptions of online and offline recycling via internet recyclers. To do this, a questionnaire was drafted and distributed to 330 businesses in Malaysia's manufacturing industry. The relationship between the constructs, depending on the relevant criteria, was subsequently assessed using regression analysis of the acquired data. Likewise, the model's components and constructs have been proven using statistical tests of convergent and discriminant validity (Liu et al. 2022d).

Partial least square structural equation modeling (PLS-SEM) was used to investigate the relationship between the constructs in this study. To evaluate the connections between the model's pathways, this method increases the indicators of independent variables and generates moderating variables (Raykov 2001). Linking variables to their factors, increasing the robustness of estimators, maximizing the interpretation of interaction effects and controlling for measurement error are all made simpler by utilizing PLS-SEM (DeVito and Drysdale 2022).

To obtain data, 330 questionnaires were emailed to various manufacturing businesses in Malaysia. 221 responses were received in total. 10 questionnaires were found to be inaccurate or missing data. The remaining information from the remaining 211 surveys was used for statistical inference, resulting in a response rate for the research of around 67%. The demographics of the respondents are shown in Table 3, which shows that the data is adequately generalized. The participants are from diverse expertise and hold positions across multiple organizational levels, from directors to line managers in Malaysia's manufacturing sector.

4 Results and Discussion

The structural representation of the research model is presented below while working on PLS-SEM (Fig. 2).

4.1 Model Measurement

The measurement model verifies and validates latent constructs' reliability and dimensionality (Hair et al. 2020). Table 4 shows loading factor values for all the indicators, which are significantly higher than 0.60. Furthermore, the values of the constructs derived through Cronbach's Alpha and Composite Reliability (CR) are more significant, at more than 0.7, confirming the constructs' reliability. Likewise, the

Table 3 Demographic characteristics of respondents

Characteristics	N	%
Job title		
Vice President	4	1.9
Operation manager	73	34.6
General manager	17	8.1
Logistics manager	29	13.7
Procurement manager	43	20.4
Information system manager	45	21.3
Job Experience		
Less than 5	21	10.0
5 to 10	62	29.4
10 to 15	69	32.7
15 to 20	33	15.6
20 to 25	20	9.5
Over 25 years	6	2.8
Firms age		
Less than 5 years	27	12.8
5 to 10	72	34.1
10 to 15	66	31.3
15 to 20	35	16.6
Over 20 years	11	5.2

values of all the Average Variance Extracted (AVE) constructs are statistically significant and greater than 0.5 (dos Santos and Cirillo 2023). The high values of Cronbach's Alpha and Composite Reliability indicate the constructs' internal consistency and reliability. The Average Variance Extracted values suggest that the constructs account for more than half of the variance in their indicators, ensuring convergent validity.

Table 5 shows the latent variables' relationships with the square roots of the AVE values. These values are higher than the correlation mentioned in the model's other constructs, confirming the constructs' discriminant validity and reliability.

4.2 The Structural Model

The structural equation model (SEM) depicted in the provided diagram assesses the relationships between several constructs related to a Customer's Choice (CC). Table 6 shows the hypothesis testing result, which shows that improvements in the construct for Customs Choice and (CC) are likely to be impacted by Better Inspection Facility (BIF), Fast Pick-up Service (FPS), and Fast Money Transfer (FMT) services but might not significantly impact Fast Product Return Service (FPR).

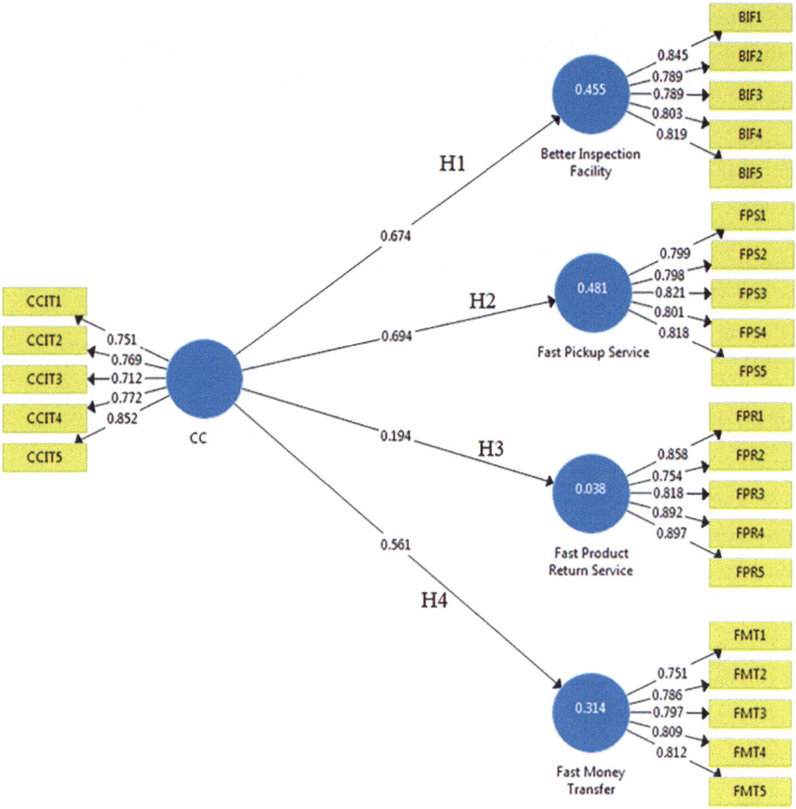

Fig. 2 Structural representation of the model

Table 4 Instrument reliability and validity

Constructs	Items	Factor loading ranges	Cronbach's Alpha	Composite Reliability (CR)	Average Variance Extracted (AVE)
BIF	5	0.789–0.845	0.868	0.905	0.655
C	5	0.712–0.852	0.831	0.881	0.597
FMT	5	0.751–0.812	0.851	0.893	0.626
FPS	5	0.799–0.818	0.867	0.904	0.653
FPR	5	0.754–0.897	0.918	0.926	0.715

The results indicate that the influence of better inspection facilities can contribute to the customer's choice to adopt the Internet as a medium for their recycling, which can lead to improved sustainable practice and the manufacturers using that recycled material from O2O recycler improves the environmental performance of the manufacturer and promotes carbon neutrality.

Table 5 Discriminant validity analysis

Construct	Better Inspection Facility	CC	Fast Money Transfer	Fast Pick-up Service	Fast Product Return Service
Better Inspection Facility (BIF)	0.809				
Customer Choice (CC)	0.674	0.773			
Fast Money Transfer (FMT)	0.472	0.561	0.791		
Fast Pick-up Service (FPS)	0.568	0.694	0.488	0.808	
Fast Product Return Service (FPRS)	0.261	0.194	0.319	0.202	0.846

Table 6 Hypotheses summary

Hypotheses	Path Coefficient	R-squared Value	Support
H1: CC is positively influenced by BIF	0.674	0.455	Supported
H2: CC is positively influenced by FPS	0.694	0.481	Supported
H3: CC is positively influenced by FPR	0.194	0.038	Not Supported
H4: CC is positively influenced by FMT	0.561	0.314	Supported

Furthermore, the results also indicate that the influence of fast pick-up services also impacts customer's choice for online recycling. As stated by (Liu et al. 2022c) Internet recycling can successfully lessen the knowledge asymmetry between buyers and sellers to achieve information transparency. Second, residents can decide on speedier and more practical door-to-door recycling through online recycling platforms.

This is extremely important for many individuals because online recycling provides significantly more economic benefits than normative recycling techniques. Prospects of more lucrative monetary rewards or earnings, residents with lower earnings would be more inclined to participate in online recycling (Wang et al. 2019). According to the authors and based on the current findings, fast money transfers are very important from the individual perspective; if they do not provide the right number of returns, people will not use this service.

The weak relationship between fast product return services in this research means that it does not significantly impact the customers' choice for O2O recycling. However, many different researchers have identified it as a major issue and stated that the viability of the reverse channel greatly depends on collectors' efforts to collect, including their investment in advertising and promotional services, which motivate customers to return their used items (Jian et al. 2019).

5 Conclusion and Recommendations

The current literature examines the role of online-to-offline recycling between consumers and internet recyclers in the Malaysian manufacturing sector. The data were collected from line managers, high-level executives, and directors working in the Malaysian manufacturing industry. The results indicate that adopting online-to-offline recycling will further strengthen the recycling process and improve overall sustainable supply chain practices. The results indicate that CC is strongly influenced by Better Inspection Facility, Fast Pick-up Service, and Fast Money Transfer but has a minimal impact on Fast Product Return Service.

Recommendations

The reusing of discarded hardware is a significant element of a circular economy. An Australian review detailed loads of light and weighty uncommon earth metals in family electronic gadgets, for example, cell phones and personal computers (PCs), to be 105,199 kg and roughly 35,412 kg, individually. In China, these figures are recommended to be much higher. Notwithstanding, the internet recycling model is in its novelty, and participation by consumers is not very high at present.

Based on the research, the following recommendations are advised for the manufacturing sectors of Malaysia which are as follows:

1. The application of online to offline recycling to induct useful recycled material into production (as in a circular economy model) will play a pivotal part in reducing manufacturing costs, provided that a good and consistent volume of useful material is received, retrieved and then sold by online recyclers to manufacturers.
2. This O2O model will assist in elevating a manufacturer's environmental performance. Especially for manufacturers operating in regions with strongly imposed environmental taxes, such as Europe, this elevation in environmental performance will result in cutting taxation expenses. European corporations paid a hefty EUR 164.9 billion in environmental taxation in the year 2022 (European Union 2024)
3. Manufacturers can adopt the proper Internet recycling model method if they have a better inspection facility through which they can inspect and separate the waste and recycling materials. Focusing on items that would help them extract the material of their need.
4. For personal devices such as cell phones, data security is the greatest limitation to their recycling. Authorities would need to enforce regulations and procedures upon internet recyclers to have the data removed safely before inducting the item. This removal of data could act as an additional service, being provided at the customer's doorstep. Such services would help reinforce customers' confidence in internet recycling and cultivate a mutually beneficial situation in which customers' data is being removed safely (Liu et al. 2023).

Appendix

Questionnaire

The following questions were included in the questionnaire. Respondents' responses were recorded on a 5-point Likert Scale, with points '1' being Strongly Disagree 'and 5' being Strongly Agree against the set of statements below. This survey questionnaire aimed to understand the factors that influence customers' choice of online recycling. The questionnaire was divided into 5 sections. Out of these sections, the first one was about the respondent's demographic information. The questionnaire also included a note for respondents in the beginning, stating that the information provided by any respondent shall be kept confidential and will only be used for research purposes.

Better Inspection Facilities (Chen and Chen 2024; Price and Pitt 2012)

1. The quality of service provided by local recycling facilities impacts my decision to recycle.
2. Online recyclers save time by offering their services for pickup from my place of choice.
3. Online recyclers offer more convenience by offering their services for pickup from my doorstep.
4. I would find my local recycler to be trustworthy if the recycler has regulatory approval from local authorities.
5. You recycle more if I am sure that your discarded items collected by the recycler will be given the best inspection and treatment for recycling.

Fast Pickup Services (Nguyen and Qi 2019)

1. Quick and fast pickups impact my choice of recycling.
2. I find quick and fast pickup services from my doorstep to be useful for recycling.
3. I find on-spot checking and assessment of discarded material by recycling professionals to be very useful.
4. I have found online recyclers to be faster than traditional recyclers offering the same pickup service
5. I have found the entire process, from pickup to recycling of material at a local facility, to be transparent

Fast Product Return Service (Philippsen 2015; Price and Pitt 2012)

1. I always recycle items that are at the end of their useful life.
2. I believe that online recycling for items that are at the end of their useful life is better than traditional recyclers
3. I have found online recyclers to be more interactive due to the flow of information and communication
4. I have come to know much about a product's useful life from online recyclers
5. I find interaction and engagement by exchange of information and knowledge with recyclers to be useful

Fast Money Transfer (Noor et al. 2023)

1. I have found it very useful to quickly transfer funds in my account from my recycled item.
2. I believe that the amount I received fairly represents the value of the material I recycled
3. The fast transfer of money from recycling motivates me to recycle more.
4. I believe the money received from online recycling is more than that would be received from traditional recyclers for the same item.
5. Fast and fair money transfer enables me to recycle more items in the future.

'To Give a Second Life to All Idle Goods'—Success Case of Aihuishou

One of the most prominent brands in implementing circular economy practices within one of the biggest economies of the world is ATRenew (All Things Renew) or AiHuiShou. The business model for AiHuiShou is based upon collecting items that seem 'used' or 'wasted' (EOL items) by consumers. Collect them, inspect the items, sort them and then recycle their parts or refurbish the whole item. The items then are sold by AiHuiShou as second-hand but fairly useable 'green' or 'sustainable' products. This business model markets **AiHuiShou** as a business that is re-inducting used items into the economic system rather than the items ending in a landfill somewhere.

Established in China in 2011 and then turned ATRenew after 9 years in 2020, AiHuiShou works on multiple channels to collect items from consumers. Their engagement with customers has enabled them to establish themselves as a prominent name worldwide in the recycling industry.

Their technological innovations include using high-end cameras and imagery for cellphone inspection, which consumers are returning. AiHuiShou uses X-rays to examine the inside of an item, such as circuits in an electronic item. Lastly, a hardware-testing module allows AiHuiShou to carry out testing in an automated way.

The trend based on the above information depicts that it is high time presently to capitalize upon all the electronic waste which is being generated in any business model similar to AiHuiShou. Firstly consumers are getting more and more cognizant recycling of their Waste Electrical and Electronic Equipment (WEEE) category items and secondly, the governing authorities all over the world especially in the Europe, are encouraging recycling businesses pertaining. It helps governments fulfill their aims for the United Nations Sustainable Development Goals (UNSDG). For UNSD goal number 12 of 'Ensure Sustainable Consumption and Production Patterns' in particular. Furthermore, it can also be observed in the case of AiHuiShou that since Omnichannel distribution and sales are being adopted by manufacturers all over the world, a need is there to design omnichannel reverse supply chains for recycling items also as did by AiHuiShou.

In 2021, AiHuiShou's revenue jumped 56% owing to the rise in electronic recycling. With its mission statement 'To give a second life to all idle goods', the company currently employs 2,438 people, is valued at USD 356 million and had a 31% revenue growth in 2023 from 2022.

References

Acatech (2021) Germany—circular economy roadmap. December, 104. http://ec.europa.eu/smart-regulation/impact/planned_ia/docs/2015_env_065_env+_032_circular_economy_en.pdf

Adesoga TO, Olaiya OP, Onuma EP, Ajayi OO, Olagunju OD (2024) Review of reverse logistics practices and their impact on supply chain sustainability. https://doi.org/10.30574/ijsra.2024.12.2.1216

Akhtar R (2024, March 4) Managing e-waste is key to our sustainability. The Edge Malaysia; The Edge Communications. https://theedgemalaysia.com/node/703393

Apple expands the use of recycled materials across its products—Apple (2022) Retrieved August 23, 2023, from https://www.apple.com/newsroom/2022/04/apple-expands-the-use-of-recycled-materials-across-its-products/

Azman NANN, Salleh SM, Hanafi WNW, Ya'acob NS, Alrazi B, Yusoff H (2024) An exploratory study on e-waste reporting: a review of annual reports from Malaysian public listed companies. Eur J Sust Dev 13(3):504–504. https://doi.org/10.14207/ejsd.2024.v13n3p504

Awa HO, Etim W, Ogbonda E (2024) Stakeholders, stakeholder theory and corporate social responsibility (CSR). Int J Corp Soc Responsib 9(1):11. https://doi.org/10.1186/s40991-024-00094-y

Bhutto MY, Rūtelionė A, Šeinauskienė B, Ertz M (2023) Exploring factors of e-waste recycling intention: the case of generation Y. PLoS ONE 18(10):e0287435

Chatterjee S, Chaudhuri R, Vrontis D, Thrassou A (2023) Revisiting the resource-based view (RBV) theory: from cross-functional capabilities perspective in post COVID-19 period. J Strateg Mark 1–16. https://doi.org/10.1080/0965254X.2023.2182447

Chen S, Chen Z (2024) Influencing factors of consumers' participation in express packaging recycling: a questionnaire survey on the current situation of five provinces in China. J Mater Cycles Waste Manage 26(2):986–1000. https://doi.org/10.1007/s10163-023-01875-6

Cho S, Ferguson M, Pekgun P, Im J (2024) Robust demand estimation with customer choice-based models for sales transaction data. Prod Oper Manage

Corcoran E, Clement A, Gabrielli J (2024) A measurement model of online privacy cognitions in a sample of US adolescents. Behav Inf Technol 43(16):4150–4171. https://doi.org/10.1080/0144929X.2024.2305286

Costin-Weiterschan S, Matiou C (2017) Value stream in the reverse supply chain: case study of the second-hand concept of a swedish multi-brand fashion retailer. https://www.diva-portal.org/smash/get/diva2:1142145/FULLTEXT01.pdf

Das S, Dash M (2024) Green compensation and reward system: a novel approach towards the growth and sustainability of organization. J Adv Zool 45(2):1213–1219. https://doi.org/10.53555/jaz.v45i2.4100

DeVito NJ, Drysdale H (2022) Issues with reporting and interpretation of Khan et al. 2021. BMC Infect Dis 22(1). https://doi.org/10.1186/S12879-022-07551-8

dos Santos P M, Cirillo M Â (2023). Construction of the average variance extracted index for construct validation in structural equation models with adaptive regressions. Commun Statistics-Simulation Comput 52(4):1639–1650. https://doi.org/10.1080/03610918.2021.1888122

European Environment Agency. (2024, August 24). Waste and recycling. Retrieved October 11, 2024, from www.eea.europa.eu; https://www.eea.europa.eu/en/topics/in-depth/waste-and-recycling#:~:text=The%20EU's%20recycling%20rate%20of,of%20municipal%20waste%20is%20landfilled

European Union (2024, July 16) Environmental tax statistics. Ec.europa.eu. https://ec.europa.eu/eurostat/statistics-explained/index.php?title=Environmental_tax_statistics#Environmental_taxes_in_the_EU
Feng Z, Luo N, Wu S, Yan ZJ (2024) Navigating the recycling intention of electronics manufacturers in collaborating with a third-party collector: a Stackelberg game analysis. J Clean Prod 457:142460. https://doi.org/10.1016/j.jclepro.2024.142460
Farghali M, Osman AI, Mohamed IM, Chen Z, Chen L, Ihara I, Yap P, Rooney DW (2023) Strategies to save energy in the context of the energy crisis: a review. Environ Chem Lett 21(4):2003–2039. https://doi.org/10.1007/s10311-023-01591-5
Gibson T (2023) Closing the loop. Mech Eng 145(3):42–47. https://doi.org/10.1115/1.2023-May3
Gundupalli SP, Hait S, Thakur A (2017) Multi-material classification of dry recyclables from municipal solid waste based on thermal imaging. Waste Manag 70:13–21. https://doi.org/10.1016/j.wasman.2017.09.019
Hair JF, Black WC, Babin BJ, Anderson RE (2020) Multivariate data analysis (8th ed.). Cengage Learning
Huawei (2024) Huawei consumer business sustainability progress report (2023–2024). In: https://www-file.huawei.com/ (p 52). Shenzhen, China: Huawei Device Corporation. Retrieved from Huawei Device Corporation website: https://www-file.huawei.com/-/media/corp2020/pdf/sustainability/others/huawei-consumer-business-sustainability-progress-report-2023-2024-en.pdf
Islam MT, Huda N (2018) Reverse logistics and closed-loop supply chain of Waste Electrical and Electronic Equipment (WEEE)/E-waste: a comprehensive literature review. Resour Conserv Recycl 137:48–75. https://doi.org/10.1016/j.resconrec.2018.05.026
Islam MT, Dias P, Huda N (2021a) Young consumers' e-waste awareness, consumption, disposal, and recycling behavior: a case study of university students in Sydney, Australia. J Clean Prod 282. https://doi.org/10.1016/J.JCLEPRO.2020.124490
Islam MT, Huda N, Baumber A, Shumon R, Zaman A, Ali F, Sahajwalla V (2021b) A global review of consumer behavior towards e-waste and implications for the circular economy. J Clean Prod 316:128297
Islam T, Dias P, Huda N (2020) Young consumers' e-waste awareness, consumption, disposal, and recycling behavior: a case study of university students in Sydney, Australia. J Clean Prod 124490. https://doi.org/10.1016/j.jclepro.2020.124490
Issah I, Arko-Mensah J, Agyekum TP, Dwomoh,D, Fobil JN (2021). Electronic waste exposure and DNA damage: a systematic review and meta-analysis. Rev Environ Health 38(1):15–31. https://doi.org/10.1515/reveh-2021-0074
Jian H, Xu M, Zhou L (2019) Collaborative collection effort strategies based on the "Internet + recycling" business model. J Clean Prod 241:118120. https://doi.org/10.1016/j.jclepro.2019.118120
Khan AUR, Ahmad RW (2022) A blockchain-based IoT-enabled E-waste tracking and tracing system for smart cities. IEEE Access, 10:86256–86269. https://doi.org/10.1109/ACCESS.2022.3198973
Kang KD, Kang H, Ilankoon IMSK, Chong CY (2020) Electronic waste collection systems using Internet of Things (IoT): household electronic waste management in Malaysia. J Clean Prod 252: 119801. https://doi.org/10.1016/j.jclepro.2019.119801
Khan SAR, Shah A, Zhang Y (2022, January) The impact of IR 4.0 on circular economy and operational performance to spur financial performance: a game changer strategy. In: 4th international seminar on education research and social science (ISERSS 2021). Atlantis Press, pp 83–88
Kitagawa S (2021) German packaging waste policy: its development and significance. In: Origins and evolution of environmental policies (pp 149–170). Edward Elgar Publishing. https://doi.org/10.4337/9781800378827.00015
Liu K, Tan Q, Yu J, Wang, M (2023) A global perspective on e-waste recycling. Circ Econ 2(1), 100028. https://doi.org/10.1016/j.cec.2023.100028

Liu T, Zhang Q, Zheng Z, Wu S, Weng Z (2022a). Stakeholder analysis of the waste electrical and electronic equipment internet recycling industry. Int J Environ Res Pub Health 19(16). https://doi.org/10.3390/ijerph191610003

Liu T, Zhang Q, Zheng Z, Wu S, Weng Z (2022b) Stakeholder analysis of the waste electrical and electronic equipment internet recycling industry. Int J Environ Res Pub Health 19(16). https://doi.org/10.3390/IJERPH191610003

Liu T, Zheng Z, Wen Z, Wu S, Liu Y, Cao J, Weng Z (2022c) Factors influencing residents' behavior in internet recycling: from the perspective of the adoption of new technology. Int J Environ Res Pub Health 19(10). https://doi.org/10.3390/ijerph19106166

Liu T, Zheng Z, Wen Z, Wu S, Liu Y, Cao J, Weng Z (2022d) Factors influencing residents' behavior in internet recycling: from the perspective of the adoption of new technology. Int J Environ Res Pub Health 19(10). https://doi.org/10.3390/IJERPH19106166

Liu T, Zheng Z, Wen Z, Wu S, Liu Y, Cao J, Weng Z (2022e) Factors influencing residents' behavior in internet recycling: from the perspective of the adoption of new technology. Int J Environ Res Pub Health 19(10):6166. https://doi.org/10.3390/IJERPH19106166

Lu C, Wang K (2023) Natural resource conservation outpaces and climate change: Roles of reforestation, mineral extraction, and natural resources depletion. Resour Policy 86:104159. https://doi.org/10.1016/j.resourpol.2023.104159

Mishra S, Ghosh S, van Hullebusch ED, Singh S, Das AP (2023) A critical review on the recovery of base and critical elements from electronic waste-contaminated streams using microbial biotechnology. Appl Biochem Biotechnol 195(12):7859–7888. https://doi.org/10.1007/s12010-023-04440-x

Nguyen Q, Qi H (2019) Design of questionnaire for the study of consumers' awareness and behavior towards electronic waste (E-waste) collection and recycling. In Proceedings of the 2019 ASEE North Central Section Conference Copyright. https://asee-ncs.org/proceedings/2019/1/84.pdf

Noor NHM, Soleman NAF, Azuan ASK (2023) To recycle or not to recycle? Factors affecting Malaysian residents' intention for recycling e-waste. Malaysian J Soc Sci Human (MJSSH) 8(2):e002102–e002102 https://doi.org/10.47405/mjssh.v8i1.2102

Nwikinaka LB, Poi EL (2024) Recycle logistics practices and marketing performance of registered breweries in Nigeria. BW Acad J https://www.bwjournal.org/index.php/bsjournal/article/view/2274

Odhiambo JD, Murori CK (2024) Utility function's influence on insurance policy customer choices. East Afr Financ J 3(2):215–222. https://doi.org/10.59413/eafj/v3.i2.6

Philippsen Y (2015) Factors influencing students' intention to recycle (Master's thesis, University of Twente). https://purl.utwente.nl/essays/66693

Price S, Pitt M (2012) The influence of facilities and environmental values on recycling in an office environment. Indoor Built Environ 21(5):622–632. https://doi.org/10.1177/1420326X11427340

Qiao D, Wang G, Gao T, Wen B, Dai T (2021). Potential impact of the end-of-life batteries recycling of electric vehicles on lithium demand in China: 2010–2050. Sci Total Environ 764:142835. https://doi.org/10.1016/j.scitotenv.2020.142835

Ramakrishna Y, Srivastava B (2024) Strategies for environmentally responsible supply chain and production management. IGI Global

Raykov T (2001) Estimation of congeneric scale reliability using covariance structure analysis with nonlinear constraints. Br J Math Stat Psychol 54(2):315–323. https://doi.org/10.1348/000711001159582

Shah A (2024) Industrial ecology: a fusion of material and energy in green supply chain context. Springer Nature

Silva M, Lagarto J, Sousa J, Mil-Homens F, Viveiros C, Barata F (2023) Impact of the new electricity remuneration scheme on the waste-to-energy recovery activity in portugal. Energies 16(18): 6624. https://doi.org/10.3390/en16186624

Wang B, Yu J, Wu R (2022) Achieving carbon neutrality in China: Legal and policy perspectives. Front Environ Sci 10:1043404. https://doi.org/10.3389/fenvs.2022.1043404

Wang B, Ren C, Dong X, Zhang B, Wang Z (2019) Determinants shaping willingness towards online recycling behaviour: an empirical study of household e-waste recycling in China. Resour Conserv Recycl 143(July 2018):218–225. https://doi.org/10.1016/j.resconrec.2019.01.005

Wang Y, Jiang Q, Guan X, Guan X (2023) Recycling channel design and coordination in a reverse supply chain with customer green preference. Transp Res E Log Transp Rev 179:103329. https://doi.org/10.1016/j.tre.2023.103329

Wen Z, Hu S, De Clercq D, Beck MB, Zhang H, Zhang H, Fei F, Liu, J (2018) Design, implementation, and evaluation of an Internet of Things (IoT) network system for restaurant food waste management. Waste manag 73:26–38. https://doi.org/10.1016/j.wasman.2017.11.054

Wirani Y, Eitiveni I, Sucahyo YG (2024) Framework of smart and integrated household waste management system: a systematic literature review using PRISMA. Sustainability 16(12):4898. https://doi.org/10.3390/su16124898

Wu W, Zhang M, Jin D, Ma P, Wu W, Zhang X (2024) Decision-making analysis of electric vehicle battery recycling under different recycling models and deposit-refund scheme. Comput Ind Eng 191:110109. https://doi.org/10.1016/j.cie.2024.110109

Zhang C, Hu M, Van der Meide M, Di Maio F, Yang X, Gao X, Li K, Zhao H, Li C (2023) Life cycle assessment of material footprint in recycling: a case of concrete recycling. Waste Manag 155:311–319. https://doi.org/10.1016/j.wasman.2022.10.035

Zhang L, Ran W, Jiang S, Wu H, Yuan Z (2021) Understanding consumers' behavior intention of recycling mobile phone through formal channels in China: the effect of privacy concern. Resour Environ Sustain 5:100027. https://doi.org/10.1016/j.resenv.2021.100027

Zhong H, Zhou S, Zhao Z, Zhang H, Nie J, Simayi P (2022) An empirical study on the types of consumers and their preferences for E-waste recycling with a points system. Clean Responsib Consum 7:100087. https://doi.org/10.1016/j.clrc.2022.100087

Building Capacity for Circular Economy Transitions: Exploring Knowledge of 3D Printing in Nigerian Universities

Silifat Abimbola Okoya, Oluwaseun Kolade, Olubunmi Ajala, and Muyiwa Oyinlola

Abstract The circular plastic economy offers a promising pathway toward sustainable resource management, but its adoption in developing contexts, particularly in Nigeria, remains underexplored. This chapter examines the capacity of Nigerian universities to drive the transition to a circular plastic economy through the integration of 3D printing technologies. By investigating the relationship between students' knowledge of the plastic waste problem, their understanding of 3D printing and sub-technologies such as Filtech, and their engagement in plastic waste management actions, the chapter provides critical insights into this emerging field. Using Structural Equation Modelling (SEM) to analyse data collected from 151 university students, the findings highlight the statistically significant role of knowledge in influencing plastic waste management actions. However, the results reveal that 3D printing technologies and their sub-technologies have not yet significantly impacted plastic waste management, suggesting systemic gaps in infrastructure, policy, and institutional capacity. The chapter underscores the importance of universities as hubs of innovation, advocating for targeted investments in infrastructure, curricula, and policies to enhance capacity in 3D printing technologies. These measures are critical for fostering sustainable innovation and entrepreneurship, particularly in resource-constrained settings. The chapter concludes with recommendations for multi-sectoral partnerships and international support to bridge identified gaps and position Nigerian universities as leaders in sustainability and the circular plastic economy.

S. A. Okoya · M. Oyinlola
Institute of Sustainable Futures, De Montfort University, Leicester, UK

O. Kolade (✉)
Sheffield Business School, Sheffield Hallam University, Leicester, UK
e-mail: s.kolade@shu.ac.uk

O. Ajala
School of Economics, Finance and Accounting, Coventry University, Coventry, UK

S. A. R. Khan et al. (eds.), *Circular Economy and Technological Innovation*, Industrial Ecology, https://doi.org/10.1007/978-981-96-5650-9_13

1 Introduction

As the global conversation on environmental sustainability gathers pace, the cricular economy emerged as an important operational frontier for scholars and practitioners interested in driving forward the sustainability agenda (Agyemang et al. 2019). This increasing interest is noticeable in both the public sector and the business world, as the shortcomings of the traditional linear economy become increasingly evident (Skýpalová 2024). It has been progressively applied in an effort to curb unsustainable utilisation of resources and production (Kirchherr et al. 2017). The circular economy is underpinned by three core principles, otherwise known as the 3Rs: reduce, reuse and recycle (Manickam and Duraisamy 2019). In its expanded form, it incorporates the 9Rs: include refuse, rethink, reduce, reuse, repair, refurbish, remanufacture, repurpose, recycle and recover (Potting et al. 2017). The strategy is a paradigm shift from the linear economy model of manufacturing using virgin materials (Korhonen et al. 2018) using a "take, make, dispose" approach (Alamelu et al. 2024). Therefore, the concept of a circular economy is increasingly attracting global attention from a range of stakeholders, especially businesses and governments (Korhonen et al. 2018). It focuses on closing material loops and prolonging the life of resources, standing in stark opposition to the conventional 'take-make-dispose' approach (Antikainen et al. 2018). This transition necessitates collaboration among companies, consumers and policymakers to develop innovative business models, stimulate demand for sustainable products, and establish effective governance structures.

Alternatively, some scholars claim the circular economy concept is vague with varied definitions (Kirchherr et al. 2017), criticised as a "melting pot of concepts" lacking harmony among scholars and societal stakeholders (Reike 2024). While it has gained international support from multilateral agencies like the EU and has gained traction with academia, industry and policymakers, some continue to view the concept as ambiguous and superficial with uncertain contributions to sustainability (Corvellec et al. 2022; Geissdoerfer et al. 2017; Korhonen et al. 2018).

Nonetheless, there have been calls from industry for guidance as the circular economy demonstrates the sustainable synthesis of economic actions and environmental wellbeing (Murray et al. 2017). This is a positive signal as organisations must consider the circular economy strategies and reassess wasteful manufacturing practices to tackle the emerging waste management crisis. As according to Geng et al., "*it takes a tonne of metal, silicon and plastic to produce a laptop computer weighing a few kilograms*" (Geng et al. 2019). However, the transition to a circular economy needs planning and policies (Morseletto 2020).

Today, studies show that due to Big Data and the Internet of Things (Alcayaga and Hansen 2024; Pagoropoulos et al. 2017), technologies are critical enablers for the establishment of servitised business models such as the circular economy in enterprises (Bressanelli et al. 2018). Therefore, digital technologies are seen as a viable solution for the adoption of the circular economy (Uçar et al. 2020). Nonetheless, some critics have mentioned that this approach is not always sustainable (Bressanelli et al. 2024) and it is difficult to establish a complete perspective on the implementation of digital technologies on the circular economy transition as further discussions on operationalisation are still required (Cagno et al. 2021).

Despite the criticisms, considerable empirical evidence and scholarly observations (Berg et al. 2018; Gall et al. 2020; Galvão et al. 2018; Murray et al. 2017) have indicated that digital technologies including mobile applications, geographical information system (GIS) and 3D printing, can play a key role in driving the circular economy. Creative applications of digital innovations can play a keyrole in disrupting societal lock-in to linear habits of production and production (Hariyani et al. 2024). It has the potential to bridge the circularity divide (Barrie et al. 2022; Berg et al. 2018; Gall et al. 2020; Galvão et al. 2018; Murray et al. 2017) and positively impact the landscape (Kolade et al. 2022a), as exemplified by recent empirical evidence on the potentials and promise of digitally-enabled circular plastic economy in Africa (Kolade et al. 2022b; Oyinlola et al. 2022).

3D printing, also known as additive manufacturing, has been identified as a disruptive technology that would transform the manufacturing sector and have a significant impact on other fields such as aerospace, defence, art and design. Over the years, its popularity and adoption has grown due to its features (Pîrjan and Petroşanu 2013). Its speed, cost effectiveness and ability to build prototypes from three-dimensional computer-aided designs (CAD) (Noorani 2017) has also enhanced its growing popularity. The technology has allowed businesses to adopt the circular economy principles through re-design and re-manufacturing of new products that promote a shared economy (Nikolaou and Tsagarakis 2021), especially in developing economies (Kolade et al. 2022a; Oyinlola et al. 2022).

The 3D printing technology has varied functionalities in the manufacturing sector such as mass customisation of products, on demand component production and ability to produce physical component which can be utilized to make alterations (Madhav et al. 2016). Its rapid growth is spreading to various disciplines such as mechanical, medical, civil, electrical, amongst others (Mahapatra et al. 2024). In the medical field, it directly impacts tissue engineering, dental (Dawood et al. 2015), drug delivery, crisis delivery (Manero et al. 2020), nutrition (Severini and Derossi 2016), prosthetics, and implants as it has the ability to create precision and difficult components (Barua et al. 2021).

The 3D printing technology operates by transforming waste material, specifically plastics, to feedstock (filaments) for production (Garmulewicz et al. 2016; Pavlo et al. 2018; Sanchez et al. 2017). It aims to utilise available resources at maximum capacity to derive the best value during their useful life (Grdic et al. 2020), thereby achieving circular value chains (Oyinlola et al. 2022). This strategy is promoted by various multilateral organisations as an important frontier to drive sustainable development (Ramalingam et al. 2016). It is viewed as an approach that would empower developing countries to leapfrog from traditional manufacturing to sustainable alternatives (Kolade et al. 2022a; Swiss 2018), as they would be able to reuse materials, such as plastics, in remote areas and gain economic value by up to 20 times (Oyinlola et al. 2023). This approach also has the potential of incentivizing sustainable plastic protocols in communities (Adefila et al. 2020).

While it offers promising opportunities, it is important to consider that the 3D printing technology is still at an early stage of development. Therefore, capacity needs to be built to accelerate its adoption and optimise it benefits. This would need to be supported by adequate infrastructure (Oyinlola et al. 2022) and appropriate policy landscape (Schröder et al. 2023). In addition, the technology is suited to customisation at a small-scale such as replacement parts and high value items and not large-scale production (Kolade et al. 2022a). It replaces the economy of scale, associated with traditional manufacturing, with the economy of one. It also works on much simplified logistics, with no requirements for centralised high-volume production and large inventory stocking.

3D printing technology application has the capacity to improve day-to-day life while evolving our economic and social standing (Chatzoglou and Michailidou 2019). Nonetheless, there has to be the readiness to use the technology regardless of experience to make a real impact. A study found that there is an absence of correlation between experience and behavioural intention to use 3D printers which indicates that people can introduce 3D printer technology notwithstanding the experience of the possible user (Chatzoglou and Michailidou 2019). Another study on the manufacturing industry suggested some success factors small and medium enterprises (SME's) could consider for the adoption of 3D printing technology, which includes:

- Identification of the main factors for its implementation provides valuable contributions to manufacturers and their decision-making process.
- Cost and environment should be taken into consideration for evaluating the feasibility of its adoption.
- Different parties have different concerns which should all be considered.

(Yeh and Chen 2018)

Scholars have also highlighted the need to build capacity and develop technical skills that will accelerate uptake of digital technologies among SMEs for local manufacturing of products using 3D printing (Balogun et al. 2018; Rogge et al. 2017; Sæterbø and Solvang 2023). It is also important that in a local context such as sub-Saharan Africa, 3D printers and extruders are sustainably manufactured as it requires being robust, reliable and durable to avert the need for frequent repairs (Minetola and Galati 2018). This is vital as the population consists of mainly low-income communities with a dearth of highly skilled labour.

The main goals of universities have been widely accepted as the production, dissemination and- more recently application- of knowledge which are viewed as the linchpin of the new knowledge economy. 3D printing technology is knowledge intensive, and offers a potentially transformative promise in the economy of knowledge (Birtchnell et al. 2017; Olatunji et al. 2023). The responsibility is now for the schools to react swifty by building capacity through the design of plans (labs, teachers and curricula) that would prepare students for the modern reality (Huleihil 2017). This is critical as the evolution of 3D printing technology creates an opportunity for contemporary teaching practices in different educational environments and subjects (Ford and Minshall 2019).

Accordingly, the required actions of universities are clear as it includes building knowledge by conducting fundamental and applied research, generating essential innovations, training, and harnessing human capital development of researchers, scientists and engineers. Universities are therefore critical actors in the societal ecosystem with the primary function of bridging the divide between industry and innovative systems such as 3D printing technology (Oyelaran-Oyeyinka and Adebowale 2017). This can also be achieved through the application of the triple helix model of university-industry-government in promoting a sustainable manufacturing future for SMEs (Kolade et al. 2022a). The universities can achieve this by driving environmental policy formulation that support decentralized recycling, upcycling, reuse and distributed manufacturing (Sanchez et al. 2020).

Although available literature has established that 3D printing technology is positively disruptive and critical for the facilitation of the circular economy, there are still limited studies on the roles required by universities to drive positive actions. In particular, its impact on waste management, especially the menace of plastic waste. This paper looked at variables such as knowledge and building capacity in Nigerian universities and their relationship to foster positive circular plastic economy actions in the society.

2 Africa: The New Frontier of 3D Printing for Circular Economy?

Africa holds immense potential to lead in sustainable 3D printing applications, but its adoption of the technology remains uneven, with South Africa standing as a notable outlier. While 3D printing has seen significant growth in regions such as Asia, Middle East and North Africa, Africa still lags behind (Alzhrani et al. 2024). However, the continent offers immense opportunities for technological leapfrogging, where strategic investments in additive manufacturing could address pressing challenges in manufacturing, waste management, and sustainability. For instance, Pilogallo (2018) estimated a 23% growth in 3D printing purchases through 2017, highlighting the sector's latent potential.

South Africa has the most advanced 3D printing ecosystem on the continent, with significant investments and dynamic partnerships between government, academia, and industry. Initiatives such as Aeroswift, a homegrown additive manufacturing platform supported by the South African Council for Scientific and Industrial Research and private aerospace firms like Aerosud, underscore the country's success, (Desiderio 2018). Between 2012 and 2015, the number of 3D printers grew by over 400%, with investments exceeding $30 million (de Beer et al. 2016). The Rapid Product Development Association of South Africa (RAPDASA) has also been instrumental in promoting technology diffusion, fostering a robust innovation ecosystem (Cruywagen 2017). South Africa's coordinated efforts among government, academia, and private enterprises illustrate the transformative potential of additive manufacturing when supported by strategic collaboration.

In other parts of Africa, the 3D printing landscape is less developed but demonstrates significant ingenuity. For instance, Elephab, a Nigerian start-up supported by GE Lagos Garage, aims to address Nigeria's chronic energy challenges by producing replacement parts with lower power requirements than traditional manufacturing (Desiderio 2018; Scott 2017). In Togo, Woelabs exemplifies innovative approaches by using electronic waste to produce Africa's first homegrown 3D printers. This initiative addresses the continent's e-waste problem while fostering sustainable local manufacturing. Woelabs has further expanded to develop 3D printing materials from recycled plastics, promoting circular economy principles (Besliu 2018; Matthews 2016).

Rwanda's Great Lakes Energy leverages 3D printing to create packaging for solar products, showcasing the synergy between renewable energy and additive manufacturing (Davis College Akilah 2016). In Uganda, the Comprehensive Rehabilitation Services Hospital has partnered with Canadian organisations to produce prosthetic limbs for amputees using 3D printing, meeting critical healthcare needs in a resource-constrained environment (Baike 2016; Simon 2020). These initiatives underline the potential of 3D printing to address diverse societal challenges, from healthcare to renewable energy, while promoting sustainable practices.

Despite these promising cases, significant barriers hinder the widespread adoption of 3D printing across Africa such as limited infrastructure, high costs and the need for specialised training (Olatunji et al. 2023). Unlike South Africa, where the government plays an active role, the growth of additive manufacturing in most African countries relies predominantly on private sector initiatives. This lack of coordinated support from universities, governments, and research institutions limits the scalability and integration of 3D printing technologies into national development strategies. For example, while South Africa benefits from government-funded R&D grants and policy direction, countries like Nigeria and Rwanda lack such institutional frameworks to drive the sector forward.

Universities, in particular, are underutilised in fostering 3D printing innovations. In most African countries, higher education institutions have not fully integrated additive manufacturing into their curricula or research agendas, thereby missing an opportunity to develop skilled professionals and advance localised solutions. The absence of university-led initiatives contrasts sharply with South Africa's model, where academic institutions have been central to the development and diffusion of additive manufacturing technologies.

To address these challenges, African policymakers must prioritise the establishment of supportive ecosystems that promote 3D printing (Fahfouhi et al. 2024). Governments should provide funding for R&D, create incentives for businesses adopting sustainable practices, and establish recycling hubs to convert waste into 3D printing feedstock. Universities must integrate additive manufacturing into their teaching and research activities, fostering partnerships with industry to bridge the gap between academic knowledge and practical application. Triple Helix partnerships, which bring together government, academia, and industry, could provide a framework for scaling 3D printing technologies across the continent.

The role of 3D printing in promoting the circular economy is particularly significant. By enabling the reuse of materials and reducing reliance on virgin resources, 3D printing supports closed-loop manufacturing systems that align with sustainability principles. For instance, initiatives such as Woelabs' use of e-waste and recycled plastics demonstrate how additive manufacturing can address environmental challenges while creating economic opportunities (Besliu 2018). However, scaling such efforts requires targeted interventions to address systemic barriers, such as fragmented supply chains, inadequate infrastructure, and limited awareness of 3D printing technologies.

Africa's ability to harness 3D printing for sustainable development hinges on building inclusive, innovative ecosystems. Drawing on successful examples like Aeroswift in South Africa, Woelabs in Togo, and Elephab in Nigeria, the continent has the potential to lead in sustainable additive manufacturing. By addressing gaps in infrastructure, policy, and education, African countries can position themselves as global leaders in leveraging 3D printing to meet critical societal and environmental challenges. This would not only accelerate the transition to a circular economy but also promote economic empowerment and resilience across the continent.

3 Methodology

The study collected quantitative data which was then analysed and modelled. The data was analyses based on the following hypothesis:

H_1 Knowledge of plastic waste problem has a positive relationship with plastic waste management action.

H_2 Understanding of 3D printing technology has a positive relationship with plastic waste management action.

H_3 Understanding of 3D printing sub-technology has a positive relationship with plastic waste management action.

3.1 Data Collection

With the use of a Likert scale, the questionnaire was created to capture respondents' perceptions on the circular plastic economy (Bell and Waters 2018). The quantitative data was gathered through an electronic questionnaire for students. Participants were randomly selected via invitation from professors, university departments, social media profiles and several WhatsApp university groups. To ensure a balanced pool of respondents, in terms of gender, study level and course of study, interested participants were asked for basic demographic information, contact information and

Table 1 Profile of questionnaire respondents

Variable		Frequency	Percent
Gender	Male	103	31.8
	Female	48	68.2
	Total	151	100
Age	18–24	71	47
	25–34	56	37.1
	35–44	17	11.3
	45–54	7	4.6
	Total	151	100
University	Ahmadu Bello University	56	37.1
	University of Nigeria	23	15.2
	University of Lagos	40	26.5
	Obafemi Awolowo University	29	19.2
	Other	3	2.0
	Total	151	100
Current Level of Study	Post PhD	5	3.3
	PhD	17	11.3
	Masters	44	29.1
	Undergraduate	82	54.3
	Others	3	2.0
	Total	151	100

their area of study or specialisation. The questionnaire obtained responses from 151 respondents (Okoya et al. 2024; Oyinlola et al. 2024). Table 1 below summarises the respondents' profiles:

3.2 Model Specification

A model was built to investigate the relationship between student's 3D printing technology capabilities and their plastic waste management action. With emphasis on micro capability around 3D printing, an assessment was conducted to establish the relationship between understanding of 3D printing and understanding of another sub technology of 3D printing (FILTECH) with plastic management action. To avoid the error of over-simplification of the relationship, a control for student's knowledge of the plastic waste problem was incorporated in the model. To assess the sensitivity of the result, the model was extended to create control for other very common capacities i.e., mobile application awareness and web application awareness.

Table 2 Summary statistics of variables

Variables	Mean	Std. dev	Min	Max
KNOW1	2.9073	0.9754	1	5
KNOW2	3.0596	1.0213	1	5
KNOW3	2.6887	1.3913	1	4
ACTN	1.5563	0.4985	1	2
UND3D	3.3576	1.2347	1	5
UNDS3	1.2450	0.4315	1	2
MOAPP	1.9536	0.2110	1	2
WEAPP	1.9205	0.2714	1	2

In both models, the outcome was evaluated using a binary variable that indicated whether a student had taken any action to manage plastic waste in their environment. Each model included four endogenous variables, with the outcome variable (ACTN) being one of them. The other three endogenous variables, KNOW1, KNOW2, and KNOW3, were used to measure the latent variable "Knowledge." Respondents' answers to questions about their knowledge of the circular plastic economy, their awareness of the connection between plastic pollution and climate change and their concerns regarding the environmental effects of plastic waste were analysed. The distinction between Model 1 and Model 2 was based on the number of exogenous variables included. Model 1 accounted for students' understanding of 3D printing technology and their familiarity with Filtech, a technology that converts plastic waste into filaments for 3D printing. In contrast, Model 2 introduced additional exogenous variables related to common resources in the country, specifically by assessing respondents' awareness of mobile and web applications designed to address these issues.

Table 2 presents the summary statistics of variables used in the study. Variables with maximum values of 2 are binary while others were measured in 5 Linkert scales, except for KNOW3 which was collapsed to 4 because of an insignificant number of respondents in one of the categories.

Table 3 maps the link between the variables and their corresponding survey questions. It presents all variables for model 1 and model 2.

4 Data Analysis and Results

To analyse the data, the study employed Structural Equation Modelling (SEM). The model choice was determined by the view that SEM is a powerful and robust statistical method used in many fields and its suitability for understanding relationships between variables such as the model developed (Hair et al. 2012). As the study was interested in investigating the relationship between knowledge, capacity and plastic

Table 3 Model variables and their corresponding measures

Variable	Names	Survey question
Dependent Variable	ACTN	Taken action to manage plastic waste
Knowledge	KNOW1	Knowledge of circular plastic economy
	KNOW2	Awareness of climate change
	KNOW3	Plastic challenge concern
3D Printing Technology	UND3D	Understanding of 3D printing
3D Printing sub-Technology	UNDS3	Understanding of FIltech
Mobile Application	MOAPP	Awareness of mobile application
Web Application	WEAPP	Awareness of web application

waste management action, it opted for the covariance-based SEM (CB-SEM) instead of the partial least squares SEM (PLS-SEM). This choice hinged on the fact that the study was interested in exploring likely factors that influence actions of students to manage plastic waste rather than attempting to predict the factors.

Measurement and Structural Models: Prior to discussing the estimation results, the study undertook analysis of goodness of fit of the models. Due to high similarity in results, it discussed the measurement model and the structural model evaluation in the same segment. Table 4 presents the table of relevant indices for judging the models. It evaluated their reliability by comparing the fit indices with some established benchmarks (Kolade et al. 2022a; Weston and Gore 2006). The chi^2 likelihood ratio divided by the degree of freedom (CMIN/DF) for both models were approximately 1 in which they were less than the theoretical cut-off (expected to be less than 3). Likewise, the Comparative Fit Index (CFI) was close to 1 in both models and the Root Mean Square Error of Approximation (RMSEA) was close to 0 for both models. The results holds for both measurement and structural parts of the developed models. Therefore, the study concluded that the model's goodness of fit was good.

Table 4 Check of estimation goodness of fit

Fit indices	Measurement model	Structural model	Model criteria
Model 1			
CMIN/DF	<1	<1	<3
CFI	~1	~1	>0.90
RMSEA	~0	~0	<0.08
Model 2			
CMIN/DF	<1	1.15	<3
CFI	~1	~1	>0.90
RMSEA	~0	0.03	<0.08

4.1 Results

The results of the models were presented in the figures and tables respectively. Figures 1 and 2 highlighted the path estimation results which reflect same results as shown in the Tables 5 and 6. Model 2 was used as a sensitivity test and conclusions from the 2 models regarding the parameters of interest were the same, the interpretation of results and hypotheses discussion used model 1. Knowledge was found to be positively associated with plastic waste management action and it is statistically significant at 5%. While the results for the two components of 3D printing that were investigated (understanding of 3D printing and understanding of a sub-technology that can power 3D printing—Filtech), showed a positive relationship with plastic waste management action, they were both statistically insignificant in affecting plastic waste management action of respondents in the Nigerian universities surveyed.

The extension of the model to consider other common capabilities such as mobile application and web application (model 2) to further test the robustness of the conclusion returned same conclusion for knowledge and the two components of 3D printing. Interestingly, the study found web application statistically significant in the second model (discussion of which was outside the scope of the study).

Table 7 presents the mapping of the results to the hypotheses. It rejected the implicit null hypothesis for the hypothesis 1 and concluded that knowledge of plastic waste problem has a positive and significant relationship with plastic waste management action of respondents in Nigerian universities. For hypotheses 2 and 3, it failed to reject their implicit null hypotheses and concluded that the understanding of 3D printing and understanding of 3D printing sub technology has a positive relationship with plastic waste management action, but they do not have significant impacts on the plastic waste management actions of respondents in Nigerian universities.

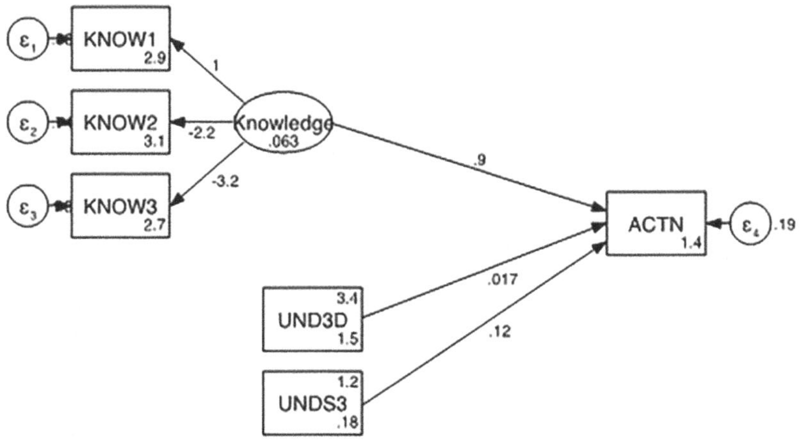

Fig. 1 Model 1 path diagram results

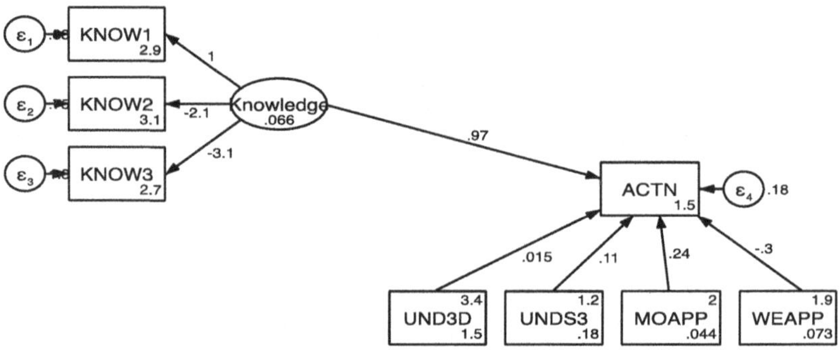

Fig. 2 Model 2 path diagram results

Table 5 Model 1 results

Variables	ACTN	KNOW1	KNOW2	KNOW3	/
var(e.KNOW1)					0.882***
					(0.108)
var(e.KNOW2)					0.736***
					(0.135)
var(e.KNOW3)					1.293***
					(0.262)
var(e.ACTN)					0.191***
					(0.0290)
var(Knowledge)					0.0633
					(0.0548)
UND3D	0.0168				
	(0.0332)				
UNDS3	0.120				
	(0.0958)				
Knowledge	0.900**	1	–2.718**	–3.156*	
	(0.436)	(0)	(1.024)	(1.627)	
Constant	1.350***	2.907***	3.060***	2.689***	
	(0.194)	(0.0791)	(0.0828)	(0.113)	
Observations	151	151	151	151	151

Standard errors in parentheses
***$p < 0.01$, **$p < 0.05$, *$p < 0.1$

Table 6 Model 2 results

Variables	ACTN	KNOW1	KNOW2	KNOW3	/
UND3D	0.0150				
	(0.0327)				
UNDS3	0.106				
	(0.0946)				
MOAPP	0.239				
	(0.191)				
WEPP	–0.298**				
	(0.146)				
Knowledge	0.970**	1	–2.096**	–3.129**	
	(0.445)	(0)	(0.961)	(1.552)	
var(e.KNOW1)					0.879***
					(0.108)
var(e.KNOW2)					0.747***
					(0.128)
var(e.KNOW3)					1.279***
					(0.252)
var(e.ACTN)					0.179**
					(0.0295)
var(Knowledge)					0.0657
					(0.0551)
Constant	1.480***	2.907***	3.060***	2.689***	
	(0.442)	(0.0791)	(0.0828)	(0.113)	
Observations	151	151	151	151	151

Standard errors in parentheses
***$p < 0.01$, **$p < 0.05$, *$p < 0.1$

Table 7 Hypotheses testing, results and conclusion

Hypothesis	Coeefficient	P-value	Conclusion
H_1	0.9355	0.0370	Positive and significant at 5%
H_2	0.1272	0.8910	Positive but statistically insignificant
H_3	0.0034	0.9190	Positive but statistically insignificant

5 Discussion

The findings highlight that knowledge plays a statistically significant role in advancing plastic waste management actions within a circular economy framework. This aligns with the university's mission to transfer and disseminate knowledge, positioning it as a key driver of innovation in sustainability. For example, Kolade et al. (2022a, b) discuss the potential of university-industry-government collaborations in leveraging 3D printing technologies to address pressing sustainability issues. By equipping students with contemporary tools like 3D printing, universities can foster entrepreneurial thinking and sustainable innovation, thereby contributing positively to Nigeria's environmental challenges (Kolade et al. 2022a).

However, this role necessitates significant investment in infrastructure, resources, and policy support, which remain underdeveloped in many Nigerian universities. Without targeted governmental and international backing, these institutions may struggle to meet the technological and pedagogical demands required to catalyze a sustainable circular economy.

Despite its promising potential, the study found that 3D printing technologies and sub-technologies like Filtech were statistically insignificant in influencing plastic waste management actions among Nigerian universities. This finding contrasts with global success stories in additive manufacturing, where 3D printing has been pivotal in achieving sustainable manufacturing practices. Kolade et al. (2022a, b) argue that such technologies are uniquely suited to disrupting traditional supply chains, enabling localised production with minimal waste (Kolade et al. 2022a). The lack of impact in Nigeria suggests a technology gap, which universities must urgently address through targeted capacity-building initiatives.

The low adoption rates of 3D printing in Nigerian universities also reveal systemic barriers, including inadequate infrastructure, limited access to funding, and insufficient awareness among stakeholders. As Oyinlola et al. (2022) note, transitioning to a circular plastic economy requires an ecosystem that supports technological integration and policy innovation. For Nigeria, this underscores the need for multi-sectoral partnerships to address structural deficiencies in higher education and foster a culture of innovation (Oyinlola et al. 2022).

In contrast to the limited impact of 3D printing technologies, the study found a positive relationship between web applications and plastic waste management actions. This finding highlights the practical utility of digital innovations, which are more accessible and scalable in resource-constrained environments. Oyinlola et al. (2022) discuss similar innovations in Africa, where web-based platforms have been employed to incentivise waste collection and recycling. These solutions demonstrate that even in the absence of advanced technologies like 3D printing, digital tools can drive meaningful progress toward sustainability (Oyinlola et al. 2022).

For Nigerian universities, web applications represent a low-cost, high-impact opportunity to engage students and staff in sustainability initiatives. By integrating these tools into curricula and campus operations, universities can build a foundation for broader technological adoption and environmental stewardship.

The findings expose critical gaps in the capacity of Nigerian universities to act as hubs of innovation for the circular economy. While their role as knowledge institutions is well-established, their ability to translate this knowledge into practical action remains limited. The low traction of 3D printing technologies highlights the disconnect between global advancements and local realities, suggesting a need for tailored strategies that account for Nigeria's unique challenges.

Moreover, the study underscores the importance of aligning academic curricula with industry needs. Kolade et al. (2022a, b) advocate for a Triple Helix model, where universities, industry, and government collaborate to drive technological leapfrogging (Kolade et al. 2022a). For Nigerian universities, adopting such a model could facilitate the integration of disruptive technologies like 3D printing into teaching and research, fostering a new generation of sustainability-oriented entrepreneurs.

6 Conclusion and Recommendations

The study offers valuable insights into the challenges and opportunities facing Nigerian universities in their quest to contribute to the circular plastic economy. By highlighting the critical role of knowledge, the potential of digital innovations, and the limitations of current technological capacities, it provides a roadmap for actionable change. With targeted investments and collaborative efforts, Nigerian universities can not only overcome these challenges but also position themselves as leaders in sustainability and innovation on the global stage.

To bridge the identified gaps, the study recommends targeted investments in infrastructure, capacity-building, and policy reforms. Universities should prioritise partnerships with industry and government to secure funding and technical expertise. In addition, international bodies promoting the circular plastic economy should extend their support to Nigerian universities, enabling them to access cutting-edge technologies and best practices.

Future research should explore the scalability of digital innovations like web applications in promoting sustainability actions. Given their proven impact in this study, these tools could serve as a stepping stone toward broader technological adoption. Research should also investigate the socio-cultural factors influencing the uptake of 3D printing technologies, providing insights into how universities can better engage students and staff in sustainability efforts.

Acknowledgements This work was supported by the British Council Innovation for African Universities Programme and the Sustainable Manufacturing and Environmental Pollution (SMEP) programme funded with UK aid from the UK Government Foreign, Commonwealth and Development Office (FCDO) (IATI reference number GB-GOV-1-30012).

References

Adefila A, Abuzeinab A, Whitehead T, Oyinlola M (2020) Bottle house: utilising appreciative inquiry to develop a user acceptance model. Built Environ Proj Asset Manag

Agyemang M, Kusi-Sarpong S, Khan SA, Mani V, Rehman ST, Kusi-Sarpong H (2019) Drivers and barriers to circular economy implementation: an explorative study in Pakistan's automobile industry. Manag Decis

Alamelu R, Sudha M, Purushothaman R, Alamelu R, Sudha M, Purushothaman R (2024) Adoption of circular economy strategies with artificial intelligence: technology to hasten the shift [WWW Document]. https://doi.org/10.4018/979-8-3693-6205-1.ch007

Alcayaga A, Hansen EG (2024) Smart circular economy as a service business model: an activity system framework and research agenda. RD Manag. https://doi.org/10.1111/radm.12707

Alzhrani RF, Alyahya MY, Algahtani MS, Fitaihi RA, Tawfik EA (2024) Trend of pharmaceuticals 3D printing in the Middle East and North Africa (MENA) region: an overview, regulatory perspective and future outlook. Saudi Pharm J 32:102098. https://doi.org/10.1016/j.jsps.2024.102098

Antikainen R, Lazarevic D, Seppälä J (2018) Circular economy: origins and future orientations. In Lehmann H (ed) Factor X: challenges, implementation strategies and examples for a sustainable use of natural resources. Springer International Publishing, Cham, pp 115–129. https://doi.org/10.1007/978-3-319-50079-9_7

Baike P (2016) 3D prosthetic printing breathes new life to those in need of limbs. The Observer

Balogun VA, Otanocha OB, Ibhadode AO (2018) The impact of 3D printing technology to the Nigerian manufacturing GDP. Mod Mech Eng 8:140–157. https://doi.org/10.4236/mme.2018.82010

Barrie J, Anantharaman M, Oyinlola M, Schroeder P (2022) The circularity divide: what is it? And how do we avoid it? Resour Conserv Recycl 180:106208

Barua R, Datta S, Roychowdhury A, Datta P (2021) Importance of 3D printing technology in medical fields. In: Research anthology on emerging technologies and ethical implications in human enhancement. IGI Global, pp 704–717

Bell J, Waters S (2018) Ebook: doing your research project: a guide for first-time researchers. McGraw-Hill Education, UK

Berg A, Antikainen R, Hartikainen E, Kauppi S, Kautto P, Lazarevic D, Piesik S, Saikku L (2018) Circular economy for sustainable development

Besliu R (2018) Want to build a 3D printer? Look no further than your electronic junkyard. Yale-Global Online [WWW Document]. https://archive-yaleglobal.yale.edu/content/want-build-3d-printer-look-no-further-your-electronic-junkyard (accessed 12.20.24)

Birtchnell T, Böhme T, Gorkin R (2017) 3D printing and the third mission: the university in the materialization of intellectual capital. Technol Forecast Soc Change 123:240–249

Bressanelli G, Adrodegari F, Perona M, Saccani N (2018) Exploring how usage-focused business models enable circular economy through digital technologies. Sustainability 10:639

Bressanelli G, Saccani N, Perona M (2024) Are digital servitization-based circular economy business models sustainable? A systemic what-if simulation model. J Clean Prod 458:142512. https://doi.org/10.1016/j.jclepro.2024.142512

Cagno E, Neri A, Negri M, Bassani CA, Lampertico T (2021) The role of digital technologies in operationalizing the circular economy transition: a systematic literature review. Appl Sci 11:3328

Chatzoglou PD, Michailidou VN (2019) A survey on the 3D printing technology readiness to use. Int J Prod Res 57:2585–2599

Corvellec H, Stowell AF, Johansson N (2022) Critiques of the circular economy. J Ind Ecol 26:421–432

Cruywagen M (2017) Additive manufacturing in South Africa. RAPDASA. https://site.rapdasa.org/additive-manufacturing-in-south-africa/ (accessed 12.19.24)

Davis College Akilah (2016) Why Africa should embrace 3D printing. https://blog.akilahinstitute.org/why-africa-should-embrace-3d-printing-1131d7c75138
Dawood A, Marti BM, Sauret-Jackson V, Darwood A (2015) 3D printing in dentistry. Br Dent J 219:521–529
de Beer D, Du Preez W, Greyling H, Prinsloo F, Sciammarella F, Trollip N, Vermeulen M, Wohlers T (2016) A South African additive manufacturing strategy. Comm Dep Sci Technol Repub South Afr, pp 4–5
Desiderio B (2018) 3D printing: shaping Africa's future. Atl Counc. https://www.atlanticcouncil.org/in-depth-research-reports/issue-brief/3d-printing-shaping-africas-future/ (accessed 12.19.24)
Fahfouhi K, Craveiro F, Bártolo H (2024) The role of construction 3D printing in advancing sustainability and digitalization in Africa. In: Galvão JR, da CS, Brito P, Neves, F dos S, Almeida H de A, Mourato S de JM, Nobre C (eds) Proceedings of the 3rd international conference on water energy food and sustainability (ICoWEFS 2023). Springer Nature Switzerland, Cham, pp 613–622. https://doi.org/10.1007/978-3-031-48532-9_57
Ford S, Minshall T (2019) Where and how 3D printing is used in teaching and education
Gall M, Wiener M, de Oliveira CC, Lang RW, Hansen EG (2020) Building a circular plastics economy with informal waste pickers: recyclate quality, business model, and societal impacts. Resour Conserv Recycl 156:104685
Galvão GDA, de Nadae J, Clemente DH, Chinen G, de Carvalho MM (2018) Circular economy: overview of barriers. Proc Cirp 73:79–85
Garmulewicz A, Holweg M, Veldhuis H, Yang A (2016) Redistributing material supply chains for 3D printing. Proj. ReportAvailable Online. Accessed 16 July 2019
Geissdoerfer M, Savaget P, Bocken NM, Hultink EJ (2017) The circular economy—a new sustainability paradigm? J Clean Prod 143:757–768
Geng Y, Sarkis J, Bleischwitz R (2019) How to globalize the circular economy. Nature 565:153–155
Grdic ZS, Nizic MK, Rudan E (2020) Circular economy concept in the context of economic development in EU countries. Sustainability 12:3060
Hair JF, Sarstedt M, Pieper TM, Ringle CM (2012) The use of partial least squares structural equation modeling in strategic management research: a review of past practices and recommendations for future applications. Long Range Plann 45:320–340
Hariyani D, Hariyani P, Mishra S, Kumar Sharma M (2024) Leveraging digital technologies for advancing circular economy practices and enhancing life cycle analysis: a systematic literature review. Waste Manag Bull 2:69–83. https://doi.org/10.1016/j.wmb.2024.06.007
Huleihil M (2017) 3D printing technology as innovative tool for math and geometry teaching applications. In IOP conference series: materials science and engineering. IOP Publishing, p 012023
Kirchherr J, Reike D, Hekkert M (2017) Conceptualizing the circular economy: an analysis of 114 definitions. Resour Conserv Recycl 127:221–232
Kolade O, Adegbile A, Sarpong D (2022) Can university-industry-government collaborations drive a 3-D printing revolution in Africa? A triple helix model of technological leapfrogging in additive manufacturing. Technol Soc 69:101960
Kolade O, Odumuyiwa V, Abolfathi S, Schröder P, Wakunuma K, Akanmu I, Whitehead T, Tijani B, Oyinlola M (2022) Technology acceptance and readiness of stakeholders for transitioning to a circular plastic economy in Africa. Technol Forecast Soc Change 183:121954
Korhonen J, Nuur C, Feldmann A, Birkie SE (2018) Circular economy as an essentially contested concept. J Clean Prod 175:544–552
Madhav CV, Kesav R, Narayan YS (2016) Importance and utilization of 3D printing in various applications. Int J Mod Eng Res, pp 24–29
Mahapatra RK, Kaliyath Y, Shet, VNS, Satapathi GS, Mahapatro SR, Naidu ML (2024) 3D-printing technology: a review. In: 2024 second international conference on intelligent cyber physical systems and internet of things (ICoICI). Presented at the 2024 second international conference

on intelligent cyber physical systems and internet of things (ICoICI), pp 528–532. https://doi.org/10.1109/ICoICI62503.2024.10696498
Manero A, Smith P, Koontz A, Dombrowski M, Sparkman J, Courbin D, Chi A (2020) Leveraging 3D printing capacity in times of crisis: recommendations for COVID-19 distributed manufacturing for medical equipment rapid response. Int J Environ Res Public Health 17:4634
Manickam P, Duraisamy G (2019) 3Rs and circular economy. In: Circular economy in textiles and apparel. Elsevier, pp 77–93
Matthews C (2016) This innovative west African lab is turning e-waste into 3D printers and robots [WWW Document]. https://www.vice.com/en/article/upcycling-e-waste-into-3d-printers-and-robots-at-togos-woelab/ (accessed 12.20.24)
Minetola P, Galati M (2018) A challenge for enhancing the dimensional accuracy of a low-cost 3D printer by means of self-replicated parts. Addit Manuf 22:256–264
Morseletto P (2020) Targets for a circular economy. Resour Conserv Recycl 153:104553
Murray A, Skene K, Haynes K (2017) The circular economy: an interdisciplinary exploration of the concept and application in a global context. J Bus Ethics 140:369–380
Nikolaou IE, Tsagarakis KP (2021) An introduction to circular economy and sustainability: Some existing lessons and future directions. Sustain Prod Consum 28:600–609. https://doi.org/10.1016/j.spc.2021.06.017
Noorani R (2017) 3D printing: technology, applications, and selection. CRC Press
Okoya SA, Oyinlola M, Ajala O, Kolade O, Adefila A, Akinlabi E (2024) Assessing the determinants of participation in the circular plastic economy by Nigerian students. Int J Sustain High Educ. ahead-of-print. https://doi.org/10.1108/IJSHE-04-2023-0132
Olatunji G, Osaghae OW, Aderinto N (2023) Exploring the transformative role of 3D printing in advancing medical education in Africa: a review. Ann Med Surg 85:4913. https://doi.org/10.1097/MS9.0000000000001195
Oyelaran-Oyeyinka B, Adebowale BA (2017) University-industry collaboration as a determinant of innovation in Nigeria. Inst Econ, pp 21–46
Oyinlola M, Kolade O, Okoya SA, Ajala O, Adefila A, Adediji A, Babaremu K, Tijani B, Adejuwon J, Wambui F, Akinlabi ET (2024) Entrepreneurship and innovation in Nigerian universities: trends, challenges and opportunities. Heliyon 10. https://doi.org/10.1016/j.heliyon.2024.e29940
Oyinlola M, Okoya SA, Whitehead T, Evans M, Lowe AS (2023) The potential of converting plastic waste to 3D printed products in Sub-Saharan Africa. Resour Conserv Recycl Adv 17:200129. https://doi.org/10.1016/j.rcradv.2023.200129
Oyinlola M, Schröder P, Whitehead T, Kolade O, Wakunuma K, Sharifi S, Rawn B, Odumuyiwa V, Lendelvo S, Brighty G (2022) Digital innovations for transitioning to circular plastic value chains in Africa. Afr J Manag, pp 1–26
Pagoropoulos A, Pigosso DCA, McAloone TC (2017) The emergent role of digital technologies in the circular economy: a review. Proc CIRP 64:19–24. https://doi.org/10.1016/j.procir.2017.02.047
Pavlo S, Fabio C, Hakim B, Mauricio C (2018) 3D-printing based distributed plastic recycling: a conceptual model for closed-loop supply chain design. In: 2018 IEEE international conference on engineering, technology and innovation (ICE/ITMC). IEEE, pp 1–8
Pilogallo A (2018) 3D printing: global impact: transforming manufacturing & industry [WWW Document]. https://infomineo.com/technology-telecommunication/additive-manufacturing-africa-middle-east/#_ftn6 (accessed 12.20.24)
Pîrjan A, Petroşanu D-M (2013) The impact of 3D printing technology on the society and economy. J Inf Syst Oper Manag 7:360–370
Potting J, Hekkert MP, Worrell E, Hanemaaijer A (2017) Circular economy: measuring innovation in the product chain. Planbur. Voor Leefomgeving.
Ramalingam B, Hernandez K, Martín PP, Faith B (2016) Ten Frontier Technologies for international development
Reike D (2024) Understanding the circular economy: from synthesized conceptual foundations to system-oriented progress measurement [WWW Document]. https://doi.org/10.33540/2543

Rogge MP, Menke MA, Hoyle W (2017) 3D printing for low-resource settings. The Bridge 47:37–45
Sæterbø M, Solvang WD (2023) A readiness model for facilitating the implementation of metal additive manufacturing at SMEs. In: 2023 IEEE conference on technologies for sustainability (SusTech). Presented at the 2023 IEEE conference on technologies for sustainability (SusTech), pp 91–98. https://doi.org/10.1109/SusTech57309.2023.10129602
Sanchez FAC, Boudaoud H, Camargo M, Pearce JM (2020) Plastic recycling in additive manufacturing: a systematic literature review and opportunities for the circular economy. J Clean Prod 264:121602
Sanchez FAC, Boudaoud H, Hoppe S, Camargo M (2017) Polymer recycling in an open-source additive manufacturing context: mechanical issues. Addit Manuf 17:87–105. https://doi.org/10.1016/J.ADDMA.2017.05.013
Schröder P, Oyinlola M, Barrie J, Bonmwa F, Abolfathi S (2023) Making policy work for Africa's circular plastics economy. Resour Conserv Recycl p. 190
Scott C (2017) Elephab aims to become Nigeria's primary supplier of 3D printed parts—3DPrint.com | The Voice of 3D Printing/Additive Manufacturing [WWW Document]. https://3dprint.com/190034/elephab-nigeria-3d-printing/ (accessed 12.19.24)
Severini C, Derossi A (2016) Could the 3D printing technology be a useful strategy to obtain customized nutrition? J Clin Gastroenterol 50:S175–S178
Simon (2020) 3D printed prosthetics get Ugandan schoolchildren back on their feet [WWW Document]. 3ders.org. http://www.3ders.org/articles/20150603-3d-printed-prosthetics-get-ugandan-amputees-back-on-their-feet.html (accessed 12.20.24)
Skýpalová J (2024) The concept and development of the circular economy. https://vilniustech.lt/bm. https://doi.org/10.3846/bm.2024.1276
Swiss BH (2018) Silicon Savannah: Africa's Tech Hub. Glob Oppor
Uçar E, Dain M-AL, Joly I (2020) Digital technologies in circular economy transition: evidence from case studies. Proc Cirp 90:133–136
Weston R, Gore PA Jr (2006) A brief guide to structural equation modeling. Couns Psychol 34:719–751
Yeh C-C, Chen Y-F (2018) Critical success factors for adoption of 3D printing. Technol Forecast Soc Change 132:209–216

Determinants of Consumer Green Product Consumption: Analyzing the Role of Green Marketing and Consumer Attitudes

Muhammad Tabish and Saima Munawar

Abstract The average consumption of clothes consumed worldwide is rising rapidly. Most individuals nowadays tend to update their wardrobes to reflect the changing seasons and fast-evolving fashions, which raises the average frequency of clothing consumption per person. The textile industry is addressing consumer demand; however, this is leading to the depletion of natural resources. By 2030, it is anticipated that the industry will need 118 billion of water. This study examines the factors influencing customers' intentions to purchase environmentally friendly products despite relatively few brands adopting sustainable production practices. Data was collected from a sample of 394 respondents, primarily from Karachi, Pakistan, through a questionnaire. The hypotheses were analyzed using Smart PLS, and the results demonstrate the impact of these factors on Pakistani customers' green product consumption. The findings indicate that all proposed hypotheses were supported.

Keywords Green price · Green product · Greenwashing concern · Consumer attitude · Subjective norms · Green product consumption · Theory of reasoned action

Chapter Objectives

- To Understand the role of green marketing in shaping consumer attitudes toward environmentally friendly products.
- To explore how consumer concerns about greenwashing affect their perception and attitude toward green products.
- To study the relationship between consumer attitudes towards green products and their actual consumption behavior.

M. Tabish (✉) · S. Munawar
Institute of Business Management (IoBM), College of Business Management (CBM), Karachi, Pakistan
e-mail: muhammad.tabish@iobm.edu.pk

S. Munawar
e-mail: saima.munawar@iobm.edu.pk

S. A. R. Khan et al. (eds.), *Circular Economy and Technological Innovation*, Industrial Ecology, https://doi.org/10.1007/978-981-96-5650-9_14

- To assess how societal and cultural norms influence consumer behavior regarding green product consumption.
- TRA will be used to explain the behavioral patterns behind green product consumption, focusing on attitudes and subjective norms.

Learning Outcomes
By the end of this chapter, readers should be able to:

- Understand the factors influencing green product consumption, particularly the roles of green marketing and greenwashing concerns.
- Evaluate the effectiveness of green marketing strategies in changing consumer behavior towards sustainable products.
- Critically assess how greenwashing impacts consumer trust and the potential adverse effects on green product consumption.
- Analyze the role of subjective norms in shaping consumer behavior using the theory of reasoned action as a framework.
- Apply empirical data analysis techniques like PLS-SEM to evaluate consumer attitudes and behaviors toward green products.

These objectives and outcomes focus on theoretical understanding and practical application based on the research discussed in the chapter.

1 Introduction

The significance of understanding green consumers in modern society has grown due to the repercussions for marketers who cannot understand and communicate green purchasing patterns. From the beginning of the 1980s, it started affecting daily activities; this concern has dominated, and now consumers are playing their role in minimizing this problem by opting for green or organic products (Reddy et al. 2023). For the protection of our environment, consumers have started demanding green products that are harmless and eco-friendly, as well as organic products. They consume less energy and can easily be recycled or reused. So, by considering the demand of consumers' organizations started green product development and green marketing (Wang et al. 2024). As the globe sees the depletion of resources, deforestation, water shortages, and global warming, the dire environmental situations are receiving the well-deserved attention they deserve.

Green marketing has been considered an essential environmental factor for many decades. Now, companies are evolving around eco-friendly products to get the green price from their green consumers (Pathak et al. 2024). The late 1980s and early 1990s saw the realization of the importance of green marketing by academics and marketing experts (Alhamad et al. 2023b). Climate change has affected humanity much faster, and people have now started accepting it as a reality. Green consumers are the targeted consumers nowadays for the business because consumers are more interested in eco-friendly products (Devi Juwaheer et al. 2012). Many companies are involved in green product development and advertising green. These green-promoting companies may include Perm Glaze, Mayville, Michelin, and Toyota Mauritius Ltd, continuously promoting products that will be harmless to the environment.

Consumers' awareness of environmental concerns and eco-friendly products has significantly risen (Shehawy and Khan 2024). Research indicates a positive correlation between favorable attitudes towards eco-friendly products and increased purchase intent, highlighting that consumers are more inclined to buy these products when they perceive their benefits (Malhotra and Srivastava 2024). Effective marketing strategies and consumer education play crucial roles in enhancing awareness (Al Zubaidi 2020). Promotional activities targeting eco-friendly products have been shown to significantly influence consumer decisions (Kumar and Sharma 2024). Consumers are encouraged to research products and seek certifications to make informed choices, boosting their awareness and willingness to adopt sustainable practices (Usha Rani and Senthil Kumar 2024). For example, Levi's has also implemented its worldwide sustainability methods to minimize consumption per person, using less water and producing jeans with a longer lifespan (Suhartanto et al. 2024).

Patterns of human behavior significantly alter environmental quality. The effects of historical actions that have seriously degraded the quality of the environment and are now being carried out in Pakistan are being felt by the existing population of the planet (Lavuri et al. 2024). The pressure on the industry to embrace green products and prices will increase as more individuals adopt pro-environmental activities (Shafiei and Maleksaeidi 2020). An environmental agency, "terra choice," studied greenwashing concerns, and the results show that over 79% of global brands are engaged with greenwashing concerns (Lim et al. 2013). Green marketing to the general public or consumers has doubled the mind regarding green marketing. Previous research on consumer environmental behavior has identified several antecedents, such as individual brand awareness and the green positioning of products. Additionally, studies on the purchase intention of green products have highlighted various factors influencing consumer environmental behavior, including consumer expectations, perceptions of a company, ecological concerns, self-image congruence with green product consumers, and customer experiences with green products (Alhamad et al. 2023a). Despite its significance, the collectivist cultural context has received little attention in the literature as an antecedent of green product purchase intention.

This study contributes to the literature by selecting consumers' attitudes toward green products. Consumer attitude plays a vital role when purchasing any product because if consumers are unsatisfied with a specific product, they will not buy it. However, we have connected green marketing and greenwashing concerns with consumer attitudes toward green products. Consumer attitudes vary in both cases. Most consumers positively value green products because they also understand their importance. Secondly, the constantly increasing rate of global warming and various disorders are affecting the population. So, most consumers show a positive attitude toward green products. However, concerns about greenwashing negatively influence consumers' attitudes toward these products.

2 Literature Review

2.1 Definitions of the Study Variables

2.1.1 Attitude Towards Green Products

Consumer's attitude towards green products refers to the consumer's intention towards eco-friendly or environmentally friendly products. Green products are organic products that can be reused or recycled (Boncinelli et al. 2023).

2.1.2 Green Marketing

Green marketing, also known as environmental marketing, promotes environmentally friendly products and services (Gill et al. 2023). It refers to the comprehensive range of eco-friendly product strategies. Green marketing includes only products that are safe for the environment. It relates to selling those products that benefit the environment. It focuses on sustainable, eco-friendly brands (Putra et al. 2024).

2.1.3 Greenwashing Concern

Greenwashing refers to activities that claim to be environmentally friendly (Jog and Singhal 2024). Greenwashing makes unsustainable claims about its products to let consumers believe that their products are environmentally friendly or that the products or services are eco-friendly (Apaolaza et al. 2023).

2.1.4 Subjective Norms

Subjective norms refer to an individual's beliefs and whether they align with or differ from a particular behavior (Nogueira et al. 2023). The coherence of a community or group that connects individuals, sharing, participating, and influencing each other's decisions is sometimes called subjectivity (Pham et al. 2023).

2.2 *Theoretical Underpinning*

The study deploys the Theory of Reasoned Action (TRA) to explain the factors influencing green product consumption. In 1975, the theory of reasoned action (TRA) was proposed by Fishbein and Ajzen (Hale et al. 2002). TRA focuses on observing two components, i.e., subjective norms and attitude. Subjective norms are the representation of an individual's perception relating to any product. Attitude is how a person feels – positively or negatively—while achieving a goal. In their perspective, behavior is influenced by purpose. In turn, an individual's attitude and subjective norms influence the intention (Coleman et al. 2011).

In this study, the intention to consume green products is the behavior being examined, and the variables (green marketing, greenwashing concerns, consumer attitude, and subjective norms) are aligned with the components of TRA. The variable "attitude towards green products" is evaluated as a critical predictor of green product consumption. "Green marketing" can be seen as a factor that strengthens positive attitudes towards green products. "Greenwashing concerns" tests the negative relationship between concerns and consumer attitudes toward green products. "Green product consumption" represents the behavioral outcome influenced by the consumer's attitude toward green products and the pressure from "subjective norms".

2.3 *Hypothesis Development*

2.3.1 Green Marketing and Attitude Towards Green Products

To communicate one's attitude, one must evaluate a specific item using positive or negative criteria (Sia and Jose 2019). Consumers' attitudes toward green products lead to their intention to buy organic food (Kashif and Rani 2021). Green products are environment-friendly products. They include the purchase or use of those products that impact the environment at the lowest level, mainly biodegradable products or products that can be reused or recycled (Iqbal et al. 2023). Businesses may achieve long-term operating and manufacturing expense reductions using green marketing strategies and product development (Yan and Yazdanifard 2014). Businesses can reduce the adverse environmental and health effects by standardizing product modification and raw materials management through "green product development" approaches (Nair and Aithal 2023). Consumers have seen positive attitudes toward green products when a brand uses green marketing to promote them. Brands increasingly actively participate in green marketing practices (Šagovnović and Stamenković 2023). Therefore, this study posits that green marketing positively influences consumers' attitudes towards the consumer.

H1: There is a direct relationship between green marketing and consumer attitude towards the green product.

2.3.2 Greenwashing Concern and Attitude Towards Green Products

As global warming increases day by day, everyone is becoming more concerned about it (Sia and Jose 2019). Therefore, it has been observed that consumers are increasingly choosing environmentally friendly products to mitigate the effects of global warming. Unfortunately, many consumers cannot distinguish between green and non-green products (Lim et al. 2013). Many brands are unethically promoting their products as green, as many make false claims about their brand, which creates a negative impact (Ioannou et al. 2023). From the above discussion, it can be seen that consumers negatively impact greenwashing and attitudes toward green products.

H2: There is a negative relationship between greenwashing concerns and consumers' attitudes toward green products.

2.3.3 Attitude Towards Green Products and Green Product Consumption

Green products, in general, can easily be recycled or reused (Alhamad et al. 2023a). It also includes those products that minimize the environmental impact (Suhartanto et al. 2024). Green products use renewable or non-renewable resources (Alhamad et al. 2023b). Consumers have consistently maintained a favorable perspective regarding environmentally friendly products. 85% of the global population favors green marketing, and consumers are inclined to purchase environmentally friendly products (Chaihanchanchai and Anantachart 2023; Krissanya et al. 2023). The consumption of ecological products is also high when consumers have a positive attitude toward them.

It is widely recognized that global warming is an undeniable reality, and there is a growing understanding of the potential for mitigating its effects through the widespread adoption of environmentally friendly products in our daily lives (Lavuri et al. 2024). As individuals become increasingly conscious of the environment, they are increasingly drawn to products that prioritize the health and safety of our planet (Srivastava and Gupta 2023). Using environmentally friendly products can help slow down the rate of global warming.

H3a: Consumers' attitude towards green products directly relates to green product consumption.

2.3.4 Attitude Towards Green Products and Subjective Norms

With a rise in environmental consciousness, people are more focused on themselves and tend to use products that can benefit the environment (Alalei and Jan 2023). Over the past few years, consumers' attitudes toward green products have increased sufficiently (Kumar et al. 2023). Due to this, brands are more concerned about being greener towards their product and showing the customers as the "green" brand (Li et al. 2023).

Based on influence, subjective norms impact the purchasing habits of regular customers. Consumer's attitude toward green products is positively influenced by subjective norms (Srivastava and Gupta 2023). Consumers agree with the other's behavior as they accept the concept of "green." Even brands align their products with the "green" concept to gain customers' attention and improve the environment (Van Tonder et al. 2023). Therefore, we propose the hypothesis below.

H3b: Consumer's attitude towards the green product positively relates to subjective norms.

2.3.5 Subjective Norms and Green Product Consumption

Subjective norms are a person's beliefs and how well they align with a given situation (Natarajan et al. 2024). The paper primarily discusses how individuals perceive societal expectations regarding accepting or rejecting a particular system or behavior (Sun et al. 2020). The primary explanation for subjective norms is the extent to which individuals feel compelled to adopt or reject a particular system or behavior (Li et al. 2023). Extensive research has been conducted on purchasing behavior, with well-established methods such as TRA that can accurately predict green product consumption (Prentice et al. 2019). It is crucial to predicting purchasing behavior (Ahmad and Zhang 2020). This statement highlights the importance of considering various factors influencing a consumer's decision to purchase a particular product or service (Chen et al. 2010).

From a consumer and marketing standpoint, sustainability is rising (Minton et al. 2018). Green products influence a consumer's behavior; environmentally friendly products are positively correlated with subjective norms (Shang et al. 2023). The following hypothesis is based on the fact that individuals are ingesting green products to combat global warming, which is experiencing a significant increase (Minton et al. 2018).

H4: Subjective norms influence the consumer's attitude towards green product consumption.

Based on all the above hypotheses, we propose the following conceptual framework (Fig. 1):

3 Methodology

We have selected an audience from Pakistan to carry out this study. A convenience sampling strategy was utilized to gather primary data, comprising individuals who voluntarily consented to participate. The participants completed an online survey regarding cultural collectivism, green products, and their inclination to purchase environmentally friendly items. Various communication channels were utilized to distribute the online survey.

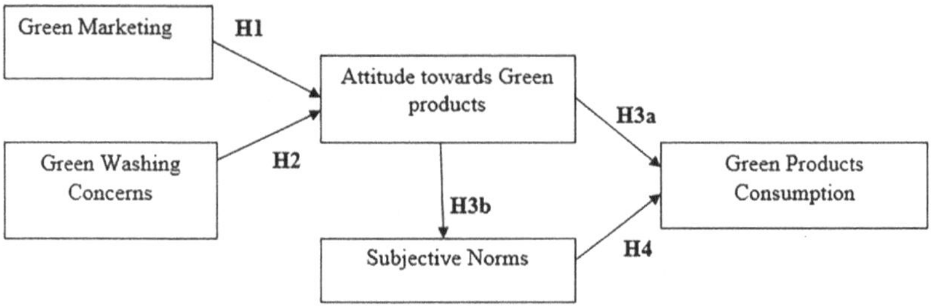

Fig. 1 Conceptual framework

A sample size of 1000–2500 is sufficient for countryside investigations. Regional researchers have an abundance of sample sizes ranging from 200 to 1000. A sample size of 100 to 200 would be enough for structural equation modeling (SEM). Nevertheless, the sample size was increased to 394 to adopt a more comprehensive perspective on the research.

All of the constructs employed in this investigation have been modified and adapted. All constructs are adapted from previous researches; green marketing (Dangelico and Vocalelli 2017), greenwashing concern (Torelli et al. 2020), consumer attitude towards green products (Mehta and Chahal 2021), subjective norms (Manning 2009), and green product consumption (Paul et al. 2016). The respondents rated the construct variables in an online survey through a five-point Likert scale ranging from 1 (strongly disagree) to 5 (strongly agree). The questionnaire was distributed to residents of Karachi, Pakistan. The Smart PLS instrument is employed to evaluate the responses of the respondents.

4 Results of Data Analysis

The sample data was analyzed using the partial least square structural equation modeling (PLS-SEM) technique to test the hypothesized relationships. SEM is a technique that can be applied to test hypotheses and analyze data from several sources (Henseler et al. 2015). PLS is an excellent tool for evaluating route models' performance.

4.1 Descriptive Statistics

Descriptive statistics were examined to ensure univariate normality existed (see Table 1). Skewness and Kurtosis are acceptable in the +2 to –2 range (Sharma and Ojha 2020).

Table 1 Descriptive statistics

Constructs	Mean	Std. Deviation	Skewness	Kurtosis
GM	3.24	1.01	–0.46	–0.23
GC	3.21	1.02	–0.50	–0.92
ATGP	3.20	1.02	–0.30	0.30
SN	3.45	0.95	–0.84	0.87
GPC	3.47	0.94	–0.90	0.94

Table 2 Cronbach alpha value for reliability analysis

Constructs	Cronbach Alpha (α)	Mean	SD
GM	0.793	3.24	1.01
GC	0.816	3.21	1.02
ATGP	0.760	3.20	1.02
SN	0.761	3.45	0.95
GPC	0.818	3.47	0.94

4.2 *Reliability of the Constructs*

The internal consistency of the constructs was tested through Cronbach's alpha. The Cronbach's Alpha should be 0.7 or more for each construct (Jayaweera 2015). Table 2 shows that all the constructs in the model had Cronbach alpha above 0.7, which shows their internal consistency.

4.3 *Exploratory Factor Analysis*

Exploratory factor analysis was used to determine the suitability of the data, and the following results were obtained (see Table 3):

Table 3 Exploratory factor analysis (EFA)

Constructs	KMO	BToS	CFL (%)
GM	0.699	294.335	71.01
GC	0.705	329.508	73.121
ATGP	0.678	237.777	67.648
SN	0.784	337.490	67.732
GPC	0.759	446.009	64.773

Table 4 Correlation analysis

Constructs	GM	GC	ATGP	SN	GPC
GM	–				
GC	0.593**	–			
ATGP	0.765**	0.667**	–		
SN	0.739**	0.634**	0.684**	–	
GPC	0.671**	0.488**	0.649**	0.724**	–

Note ** Correlation is significant at 0.01 level (2-tailed)

Table 5 Reliability of the constructs and variance explained

Constructs	Cornbrash's Alpha	AVE	Mean	SD
GM	0.793	0.709	3.28	0.94
GC	0.816	0.730	3.23	0.97
ATGP	0.760	0.676	3.25	0.95
SN	0.761	0.677	3.24	1.07
GPC	0.818	0.646	3.33	0.83

4.4 Correlation Analysis

Correlation is investigated to determine the extent to which the variables under investigation are connected. The correlation test shows that constructs are strongly associated with significant r values (Table 4).

All construct relationships are found to be different from one another and complimentary of multicollinearity because they all remain between 0.3 and 0.9.

4.5 Convergent Validity

Convergent validity indicates how well one measure correlates with another, assuming they both assess the same phenomenon (Cheah et al. 2018). Based on AVE and Cronbach's alpha, which both meet the requirements of surpassing 0.5 and 0.7, respectively, the constructs were developed to maintain convergent validity under this study (as shown in Table 5).

4.6 Discriminant Validity

Discriminant validity shows the uniqueness of the constructs in the model. The values of discriminant validity in Table 6 show that constructs are significantly different from

Table 6 Discriminant validity

Constructs	GM	GC	ATGC	SN	GPC
GM	**0.822**				
GC	0.668	**0.855**			
ATGP	0.768	0.607	**0.821**		
SN	0.665	0.505	0.686	**0.804**	
GPC	0.685	0.636	0.740	0.736	**0.836**

each other. An analysis of these relationships was initiated by comparing them with the square root of the AVE. The square roots of each construct are higher than its correlation with other constructs, confirming the discriminant validity (Rönkkö and Cho 2022).

4.7 *Structural Equation Modeling*

The model was analyzed using Partial Least Squares Structural Equation Modeling (PLS-SEM) with Smart PLS 4.0 software (Tables 7–9). The model fit is sufficient since the Standardization Root Mean Square Error (SRMR) is below 10% or 0.1 (Shi et al. 2020).

In the current study, subjective norms mediate the interaction between attitudes and green product consumption. Our study's findings are comparable to those of other research, showing a sizable mediating influence between attitudes and consumption of green products.

The 394 gathered answers were assessed using the bootstrapping approach to account for the model's complexity (Fig. 2). Because R-square and Adjusted R-square values surpassed 0.2, the combined effect of the independent factors on

Table 7 Model fit

	Saturated model	Estimated model
SRMR	0.082	0.096
Chi-Square	3482.524	3674.831
NFI	0.545	0.520

Table 8 R-square

	R Square	*R* Square (Adj)
ATGP	0.706	0.701
SN	0.469	0.468
GPC	0.590	0.588

Table 9 Hypotheses results

	Relationship	*T* statistics	*P* values	Hypothesis
H1	GM → ATGP	4.038	0.000	Supported
H2	GC → ATGP	3.142	0.002	Supported
H3a	ATGP → SN	3.057	0.002	Supported
H3b	ATGP → GPC	2.171	0.030	Supported
H4	SN → GPC	7.154	0.000	Supported

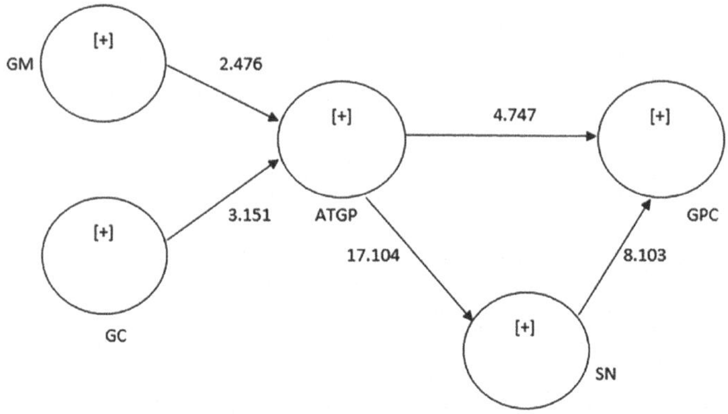

Fig. 2 *t*-values

attitude, subjective norms, and green product consumption was determined to be favorable (Bar-Gera 2017).

4.8 *Discussion*

This research first examined the relationship between green marketing and attitude towards green products. Previous studies have shown the significance of this hypothesis. Our analysis also agrees with the research earlier that green marketing has shown a positive and direct relationship with the consumer's attitude towards green products (Iftikhar et al. 2022). In the literature review, we discussed a positive relationship between these two variables, and our results also show the relationship between these two variables.

In hypothesis 2, we have discussed the direct relationship between greenwashing concerns and consumer attitudes toward green products. The results also show the positive and direct connection between these two variables. The greenwashing issue frequently contradicts earlier studies by demonstrating a favorable effect on mindset and, as a result, norms (Iqbal et al. 2023). This can be because of demographics or because respondents misunderstood the phrase in the construct's items. Other uncontrolled circumstances can have contributed to the unexpected outcomes.

Hypothesis 3a has shown a positive relationship between consumer attitude towards green products and consumption. Through a favorable impact on attitude, the danger of the environment and human coping mechanisms favorably influence green product consumption (Jaiswal et al. 2022). However, in this study's findings, greenwashing also tends to contradict earlier studies by favoring attitudes and, as a result, purchasing intentions. This may also be the consequence of a shift in demography or an incorrect understanding of the word in the construct's items; there might also be other uncontrolled circumstances that contributed to the unexpected results (Sahioun et al. 2023).

Hypothesis 3b shows the relationship between consumers' attitudes towards green products and subjective norms. Previous studies have also demonstrated the relationship between these two variables, and the results mentioned in this study also show a positive relationship between these two variables (Sewwandi and Dinesha 2022). Hypothesis 04 has shown the relationship between subjective norms and green product consumption. Subjective Norms have been used in various studies where they have served with green product consumption (Kim 2021). Similarly, this study has tested the relationship between these two variables and has a direct and positive relationship.

5 Conclusion

The study successfully analyzes the determinants of green product consumption, focusing on the impact of green marketing, greenwashing concerns, consumer attitudes, and subjective norms. The results support the proposed hypotheses, indicating that green marketing positively influences consumer attitudes, while greenwashing concerns negatively affect them. Furthermore, consumer attitudes and subjective norms are significant predictors of green product consumption, emphasizing the importance of personal beliefs and social influences. These findings suggest that companies adopt transparent and authentic green marketing strategies to foster positive consumer attitudes and increase green product consumption. The study also highlights the role of subjective norms in shaping environmentally responsible behavior, suggesting that societal and cultural factors are critical in promoting sustainable consumption.

5.1 Theoretical Implications

This study provides significant theoretical contributions by extending the **Theory of Reasoned Action (TRA)** to the context of green product consumption. The research confirms the relevance of TRA in explaining consumer behavior, particularly the influence of attitudes and subjective norms on purchasing decisions. Integrating variables such as green marketing and greenwashing concerns further enriches the theoretical understanding of consumer attitudes toward environmentally friendly products. By highlighting the positive role of green marketing and the negative impact of greenwashing on consumer attitudes, the study underscores the need for companies to adopt authentic and transparent green marketing strategies. The findings also demonstrate that subjective norms are crucial in shaping consumer behavior, indicating that social influence is a powerful driver in promoting sustainable consumption practices. This broadens the applicability of TRA to include culturally specific and environmentally focused consumer behavior.

5.2 Implications for Managers

Due to a lack of thorough research in this area's geographic region of Asia, this research was conducted (Yadav and Pathak 2016). Marketing professionals and organizational managers might pay attention to the implications presented in the study after considering the findings of this study (Al-dmour et al. 2023). We have shown that green pricing is relatively successful at encouraging green product consumption (Rausch and Kopplin 2021) and encouraging purchase behavior. Therefore, discounting these items will probably encourage Pakistani consumers to buy green products.

Similarly, perceptions of the seriousness of environmental issues and the effectiveness of appropriate responses have positively influenced green product consumption (Mehraj et al. 2023). Consequently, a green marketing strategy that raises awareness of the severity of global environmental conditions and promotes effective coping mechanisms could foster positive green product consumption among Pakistani consumers by shaping their attitudes and subjective norms (Nguyen-Viet 2023). It is recommended that this region be further investigated to exploit it to the textile business's advantage while preserving the environment. The greenwashing issue has revealed results contrary to earlier studies in the West.

5.3 Research Limitations and Future Research Directions

Most of the samples utilized in this investigation originated from Karachi, Pakistan. As a result, the results may not apply to the entire population of Pakistan and other Asian countries. Consequently, future research may acquire a more comprehensive sample, resulting in more generalizable conclusions for Pakistani consumers. The sample was obtained for the sake of expediency. Marketers may obtain superior outcomes and establish a strong foundation by employing more advanced sampling techniques. The primary age groups were the focus of the study's sample, which included both men and women. The findings were founded on shared effects.

Collecting more significant, more precise samples may be necessary to identify age- and gender-specific influences on and fostering green product consumption that stakeholders can successfully exploit. It is imperative to conduct additional research in this field, utilizing a variety of methodologies and perspectives, to determine the factors that motivate Pakistani consumers to purchase environmentally friendly products and those that discourage them from doing so. There is still significant potential for researchers and subject matter specialists to identify the factors that may promote an environmentally responsible perspective and generate revenue in this field of research. Additionally, it is imperative to assess a variety of triggers to enhance the field and ascertain which triggers most potently evoke a sense of the surrounding threat and the activation of coping mechanisms.

Appendix A

Questionnaire

Constructs and Items	Source
Green Marketing	(Rajadurai et al. 2021)
Utilizing environmentally friendly products can help the environment	
I'm likely to buy environmental products in the future	
Eco-labels and environmentally friendly product certifications are familiar to me	
I believe that businesses' environmental claims regarding their products are accurate and sincere	
Greenwashing Concern	(de Freitas Netto et al. 2020)
It concerned enterprises that misrepresent their products as environmentally friendly	
I doubt the reliability of businesses' environmental claims for their products	
Businesses should be more open about how their products affect the environment	
The possibility of greenwashing influences my decisions to purchase environmentally responsible products	
Laws and regulations should be more transparent and explicit to prevent businesses from making false environmental claims	
Attitude towards Green Products	(Sun and Wang 2020)
I believe that using eco-friendly products can benefit the environment	

(continued)

(continued)

Constructs and Items	Source
I believe that environmentally friendly products are the most effective and of the highest quality	
I am willing to pay more for eco-friendly products	
I am inclined toward selecting eco-friendly products over conventional ones	
Subjective Norms	(Hasan and Suciarto 2020)
The opinions of my peers and family influence my decision to utilize eco-friendly products	
I believe that society expects us to use ecological products	
I believe that others would support my decision to use eco-friendly products	
My motivation to use green products is derived from the actions of influential individuals or organizations	
Social pressure compels me to implement eco-friendly practices	
Green Products Consumption	(Testa et al. 2021)
In the future, I intend to purchase more eco-friendly products	
I frequently purchase green products	
I now only use eco-friendly alternatives to conventional products	
I would encourage others to use eco-friendly products	
I place a high priority on using eco-friendly products	

References

Ahmad W, Zhang Q (2020) Green green product consumption: effects of electronic service quality and customer green psychology. J Clean Prod 267:122053. https://doi.org/10.1016/j.jclepro.2020.122053

Alalei A, Jan MT (2023) Factors influencing the green purchase intention among consumers: an empirical study in Algeria. J Glob Bus Insights 8(1):49–65

Al-dmour H, Hadad H, Al-dmour R (2023) The impact of the adoption of green marketing on corporate performance of non-profitable organizations: empirical study. Soc Resp J 19(1):1–19

Alhamad A, Ahmed ER, Akyürek M, Baadhem AMS (2023) The impact of environmental awareness and attitude on green purchase intention: an empirical study of turkish consumers of green product. Malatya Turgut Özal Üniversitesi İşletme Ve Yönetim Bilimleri Dergisi 4(1):22–36

Alhamad AM, Jaafar ZM, Salem AM (2023) Influence of consumer environmental responsibility on green consumption intention iniraqi universities: the role of purchase convenience and availability of green products. Int J Eng Sci 13(7):41–49

Al Zubaidi N (2020) The relationship between collectivism and green product green product consumption: the role of attitude, subjective norms, and willingness to pay a premium. J Sust Market 1(1). https://doi.org/10.51300/josm-2020-23

Apaolaza V, Policarpo MC, Hartmann P, Paredes MR, D'Souza C (2023) Sustainable clothing: why conspicuous consumption and greenwashing matter. Bus Strateg Environ 32(6):3766–3782. https://doi.org/10.1002/bse.3335

Bar-Gera H (2017) The target parameter of adjusted R-squared in fixed-design experiments. Am Stat 71(2):112–119. https://doi.org/10.1080/00031305.2016.1200489

Boncinelli F, Gerini F, Piracci G, Bellia R, Casini L (2023) Effect of executional greenwashing on market share of food products: an empirical study on green-coloured packaging. J Clean Prod 391:136258

Chaihanchanchai P, Anantachart S (2023) Encouraging green product purchase: green value and environmental knowledge as moderators of attitude and behavior relationship. Bus Strateg Environ 32(1):289–303. https://doi.org/10.1002/bse.3130

Cheah JH, Sarstedt M, Ringle CM, Ramayah T, Ting H (2018) Convergent validity assessment of formatively measured constructs in PLS-SEM: on using single-item versus multi-item measures in redundancy analyses. Int J Contemp Hosp Manag 30(11):3192–3210. https://doi.org/10.1108/IJCHM-10-2017-0649

Chen YH, Hsu IC, Lin CC (2010) Website attributes that increase consumer green product consumption: a conjoint analysis. J Bus Res 63(9–10):1007–1014. https://doi.org/10.1016/j.jbusres.2009.01.023

Coleman LJ, Bahnan N, Kelkar M, Curry N (2011) Walking the walk: how the theory of reasoned action explains adult and student intentions to go green. J Appl Bus Res 27(3):107. https://doi.org/10.19030/jabr.v27i3.4217

Dangelico RM, Vocalelli D (2017) "Green Marketing": an analysis of definitions, strategy steps, and tools through a systematic review of the literature. J Clean Prod 165:1263–1279

Devi Juwaheer T, Pudaruth S, Noyaux ME, M. (2012) Analysing the impact of green marketing strategies on consumer purchasing patterns in Mauritius. World J Entrep Manag Sust Dev 8(1):36–59. https://doi.org/10.1108/20425961211221615

de Freitas Netto SV, Sobral MFF, Ribeiro ARB, Soares GRDL (2020) Concepts and forms of greenwashing: a systematic review. Environ Sci Europe 32:1–12

Gill MS, Kaur K, Vij TS, Mohideen AS, Lakshmi MR (2023) Green marketing: a study of consumer perception and preferences in India. J Survey Fish Sci 10(3S):6612–6619

Hale, J. L., Householder, B. J., & Greene, K. L. (2002). The theory of reasoned action. In: The persuasion handbook: Developments in theory and practice, vol 14, pp 259–286

Hasan HN, Suciarto S (2020) The influence of attitude, subjective norm and perceived behavioral control towards organic food purchase intention. J Manag Bus Environ 1(2):132

Henseler J, Ringle CM, Sarstedt M (2015) A new criterion for assessing discriminant validity in variance-based structural equation modeling. J Acad Mark Sci 43(1):115–135. https://doi.org/10.1007/s11747-014-0403-8

Iftikhar F, Asghar A, Khan M (2022) The impact of green marketing and environmental awareness on consumers green and conscious consumption of green products. Acad J Soc Sci 6(2):077–094

Ioannou I, Kassinis G, Papagiannakis G (2023) The impact of perceived greenwashing on customer satisfaction and the contingent role of capability reputation. J Bus Ethics 185(2):333–347

Iqbal A, Kazmi SQ, Anwar A, Ramish MS, Salam A (2023) Impact of green marketing on green purchase intention and green consumption behavior: the moderating role of green concern. J Posit School Psychol 975–993

Jayaweera T (2015) Impact of work environmental factors on job performance, mediating role of work motivation: a study of hotel sector in England. Int J Bus Manage 10(3):271–278. https://doi.org/10.5539/ijbm.v10n3p271

Jaiswal D, Singh B, Kant R, Biswas A (2022) Towards green product consumption: effect of green marketing stimuli and perceived environmental knowledge in Indian consumer market. Soc Bus Rev 17(1):45–65

Jog D, Singhal D (2024) Greenwashing understanding among indian consumers and its impact on their green consumption. Glob Bus Rev 25(2):491–511. https://doi.org/10.1177/0972150920962933

Kashif M, Rani T (2021) Customers' attitude towards green packaging. 3(1)

Kim H (2021) Use of mobile grocery shopping application: Motivation and decision-making process among South Korean consumers. J Theor Appl Electron Commer Res 16(7):2672–2693. https://doi.org/10.3390/jtaer16070147
Krissanya N, Sholikhah S, Berutu MB, Sari DAP (2023) Exploring the role of green brand positioning in determining green product purchase intention. Int J Appl Econ Financ Acc 15(2):88–95
Kumar S, Gupta K, Kumar A, Singh A, Singh RK (2023) Applying the theory of reasoned action to examine consumers' attitude and willingness to purchase organic foods. Int J Consum Stud 47(1):118–135. https://doi.org/10.1111/ijcs.12812
Kumar A, Sharma A (2024) Social media marketing activities for influencing voter citizenship behaviour: brand relationship quality as a mediator. J Mark Commun 1–33
Lavuri R, Parida R, Singh S (2024) Unveiling ways to examine the purchase intension of green products in emerging markets. Benchmark Int J 31(5):1385–1401
Li X, Dai J, Zhu X, Li J, He J, Huang Y, Liu X, Shen Q (2023) Mechanism of attitude, subjective norms, and perceived behavioral control influence the green development behavior of construction enterprises. Human Soc Sci Commun 10(1):1–13
Lim WM, Ting DH, Bonaventure VS, Sendiawan AP, Tanusina PP (2013) What happens when consumers realise about green washing? A qualitative investigation. Int J Glob Environ Issues 13(1):14. https://doi.org/10.1504/IJGENVI.2013.057323
Malhotra G, Srivastava H (2024) Green purchase intention in omnichannel retailing: role of environmental knowledge and price sensitivity. J Strateg Mark 32(4):467–490
Manning M (2009) The effects of subjective norms on behaviour in the theory of planned behaviour: a meta-analysis. Br J Soc Psychol 48(4):649–705
Mehraj D, Qureshi IH, Singh G, Nazir NA, Basheer S, Nissa VU (2023) Green marketing practices and green consumer behavior: demographic differences among young consumers. Bus Strateg Dev 6(4):571–585. https://doi.org/10.1002/bsd2.263
Mehta P, Chahal HS (2021) Consumer attitude towards green products: revisiting the profile of green consumers using segmentation approach. Manage Environ Qual Int J 32(5):902–928
Minton EA, Spielmann N, Kahle LR, Kim C-H (2018) The subjective norms of sustainable consumption: a cross-cultural exploration. J Bus Res 82:400–408. https://doi.org/10.1016/j.jbusres.2016.12.031
Nair SB, Aithal PS (2023) An assessment of green marketing tools and strategies for increasing the consumption pattern of Khadi textile products among millennials in Kerala. Int J Manag Technol Soc Sci 8(3):340–355
Natarajan T, Geetha Raveendran Nair J, Jayapal J (2024) Subjective norms as a moderator in the consumption behaviour of branded functional beverages post-COVID-19 pandemic: a pragmatic view. Asia-Pac J Bus Admin 16(2):307–330
Nguyen-Viet B (2023) The impact of green marketing mix elements on green customer based brand equity in an emerging market. Asia-Pac J Bus Admin 15(1):96–116
Nogueira M, Dias F, Santos V (2023) Sustainable mobility choices: exploring the impact of consumers' values, attitudes, perceived behavioural control and subjective norms on the likelihood to choose sustainable mobility options. J Consum Behav 22(2):511–528. https://doi.org/10.1002/cb.2144
Pathak K, Prakash G, Jain M, Agarwal R, Attri R (2024) Do eco labels matter for green business strategy and sustainable consumption? A mixed method investigation on green products. Bus Strateg Environ 33(5):4271–4291. https://doi.org/10.1002/bse.3687
Paul J, Modi A, Patel J (2016) Predicting green product consumption using theory of planned behavior and reasoned action. J Retail Consum Serv 29:123–134
Pham VH, Nguyen TKC, Nguyen TBL, Tran TTT, Nguyen TVN (2023) Subjective norms and entrepreneurial intention: A moderated-serial mediation model. J Entrep Manag Innov 19(1):113–140

Putra AHPK, Mariam S, Tafsir M, Rosanti N (2024) Deciphering the green marketing puzzle: understanding the interplay of green marketing strategic orientation, attitude towards green marketing, brand integrity, and purchase intention. Int Rev Manag Mark 14(4):210–229

Prentice C, Han XY, Hua LL, Hu L (2019) The influence of identity-driven customer engagement on green product consumption. J Retail Consum Services 47(November 2018):339–347. https://doi.org/10.1016/j.jretconser.2018.12.014

Rajadurai J, Zahari AR, Esa E, Bathmanathan V, Ishak NAM (2021) Investigating green marketing orientation practices among green small and medium enterprises. J Asian Finance Econ Bus 8(1):407–417

Rausch TM, Kopplin CS (2021) Bridge the gap: Consumers' green product consumption and behavior regarding sustainable clothing. J Clean Prod 278:123882. https://doi.org/10.1016/j.jclepro.2020.123882

Reddy KP, Chandu V, Srilakshmi S, Thagaram E, Ch, Sahyaja, Osei B (2023) Consumers perception on green marketing towards eco-friendly fast moving consumer goods. Int J Eng Bus Manage 15:18479790231170960. https://doi.org/10.1177/18479790231170962

Rönkkö M, Cho E (2022) An updated guideline for assessing discriminant validity. Organ Res Methods 25(1). https://doi.org/10.1177/1094428120968614

Šagovnović I, Stamenković I (2023) Investigating values of green marketing tools in predicting tourists' eco-friendly attitudes and behavior. J Ecotour 22(4):479–501. https://doi.org/10.1080/14724049.2022.2075003

Sahioun A, Bataineh AQ, Abu-AlSondos IA, Haddad H (2023) The impact of green marketing on consumers' attitudes: a moderating role of green product awareness. Innov Mark 19(3):237

Sewwandi JPN, Dinesha PKC (2022) The impact of green marketing tools on green product purchase behavior: the moderation effect of consumer demographics. Asian J Market Manag 1(01). http://journals.sjp.ac.lk/index.php/ajmm/article/view/5469

Shang D, Wu W, Schroeder D (2023) Exploring determinants of the green smart technology product adoption from a sustainability adapted value-belief-norm perspective. J Retail Consum Serv 70:103169

Shehawy YM, Khan SMFA (2024) Consumer readiness for green consumption: the role of green awareness as a moderator of the relationship between green attitudes and purchase intentions. J Retail Consum Serv 78:103739

Srivastava V, Gupta AK (2023) Price sensitivity, government green interventions, and green product availability triggers intention toward buying green products. Bus Strateg Environ 32(1):802–819. https://doi.org/10.1002/bse.3176

Suhartanto D, Dean D, Amalia FA, Triyuni NN (2024) Attitude formation towards green products evidence in Indonesia: Integrating environment, culture, and religion. Asia Pac Bus Rev 30(1):94–114. https://doi.org/10.1080/13602381.2022.2082715

Shafiei A, Maleksaeidi H (2020) Pro-environmental behavior of university students: application of protection motivation theory. Glob Ecol Conserv 22. https://doi.org/10.1016/j.gecco.2020.e00908

Sharma C, Ojha CSP (2020) Statistical parameters of hydrometeorological variables: standard deviation, SNR, Skewness and kurtosis. Lect Notes Civil Eng 39. https://doi.org/10.1007/978-981-13-8181-2_5

Shi D, Maydeu-Olivares A, Rosseel Y (2020) Assessing fit in ordinal factor analysis models: SRMR vs. RMSEA. Struct Equat Model 27(1):1–15. https://doi.org/10.1080/10705511.2019.1611434

Sia SK, Jose A (2019) Attitude and subjective norm as personal moral obligation mediated predictors of intention to build eco-friendly house. Manag Environ Quality Int J 30(4):678–694. https://doi.org/10.1108/MEQ-02-2019-0038

Sun S, Law R, Schuckert M (2020) Mediating effects of attitude, subjective norms and perceived behavioural control for mobile payment-based hotel reservations. Int J Hosp Manag 84(June 2019), 102331. https://doi.org/10.1016/j.ijhm.2019.102331

Sun Y, Wang S (2020) Understanding consumers' intentions to purchase green products in the social media marketing context. Asia Pac J Mark Logist 32(4):860–878

Testa F, Pretner G, Iovino R, Bianchi G, Tessitore S, Iraldo F (2021) Drivers to green consumption: a systematic review. Environ Dev Sustain 23:4826–4880

Torelli R, Balluchi F, Lazzini A (2020) Greenwashing and environmental communication: effects on stakeholders' perceptions. Bus Strateg Environ 29(2):407–421

Usha Rani J, Senthil Kumar JP (2024) Unveiling student intention towards entrepreneurship development—a bibliometric investigation. J Educ Bus 99(5):323–332

Van Tonder E, Fullerton S, De Beer LT, Saunders SG (2023) Social and personal factors influencing green customer citizenship behaviours: the role of subjective norm, internal values and attitudes. J Retail Consum Serv 71:103190

Wang L, Chen L, Li C (2024) Research on strategies for improving green product consumption sentiment from the perspective of big data. J Retail Consum Serv 79:103802

Yadav R, Pathak GS (2016) Young consumers' intention towards buying green products in a developing nation: extending the theory of planned behavior. J Clean Prod 135:732–739. https://doi.org/10.1016/j.jclepro.2016.06.120

Yan YK, Yazdanifard R (2014) The concept of green marketing and green product development on consumer buying approach. 7

Revolutionizing Sustainability: The Impact of Circular Economy Innovations on CO_2 Emissions

Moneeba Iftikhar, Amjad Ali Shah, Syed Hassan Raza, and Shahzad Ahmad Khan

Abstract This chapter seeks to grasp the transformational function of the Circular Economy in acquiring Sustainable Development Goals (SDGs) among global conservational crises and financial differences. By modifying from a conventional linear economy to a circular model, the circular economy emphasised—reducing, recycling, reusing, and renewing resources, in that way minimising waste and greenhouse gas adversities. Through an in-depth analysis of the Netherlands' ground-breaking circular economy initiatives, this study shed light on the circular economy's strategies to augment resource efficacy, lessen CO_2 emissions, and endorse sustainable resource administration in supply chain, customer goods, and business sectors. This chapter explains how sophisticated digital technologies, such as blockchain and artificial intelligence, can be incorporated to support foretelling analytics and lifespan supervision of resources. To this point, this study also addresses the circular economy's broader macroeconomic influence, demonstrating its ability to steer innovation, decline economic disparities, and promote robust business practices.

Keywords Sustainability · Circular economy innovations · Carbon emissions · SDG · Digital technologies

---

M. Iftikhar
Department of Mass Communication, Lahore College for Women University, Lahore, Pakistan
e-mail: moneeba.iftikhar@lcwu.edu.pk

A. A. Shah
Institute of Media and Communication Studies, Bahauddin Zakariya University, Multan, Pakistan

S. H. Raza (✉)
School of Media and Communication, Taylor's University, Subang Jaya, Malaysia
e-mail: Hassanraza.syed@taylors.edu.my

S. A. Khan
College of Business, University of Buraimi, Al Buraimi, Sultanate of Oman
e-mail: shahzad@uob.edu.om

S. A. R. Khan et al. (eds.), *Circular Economy and Technological Innovation*, Industrial Ecology, https://doi.org/10.1007/978-981-96-5650-9_15

1 Introduction

Amongst the intensifying environmental catastrophes and economic discrepancies, the notion of a "Circular Economy" (CE) has harvested recognition as a rational mechanism for attaining Sustainable Development Goals (SDGs) (Vann Yaroson et al. 2024). Circular Economy (CE) has become a top agenda of researchers, policy-makers, and stakeholders of businesses to recognize its impression on the Sustainable Development Goals (SDGs) (Garcia-Saravia Ortiz-de-Montellano et al. 2023). The trend to adopt the imperative of transitioning to a circular economy (CE) currently prevails rapidly within the global congregation. This epitomizes a significant shift from the conventional linear economic model typically in practice (Dosi 2023). In contrast to the linear model's ' end-of-end service' approach, CE is adaptive to the tenets of rejuvenation and the enduring reuse of materials strategically devised to minimize waste and curtail pollution (Jain 2021). CE underscores a cyclical system of decreasing, reusing, recycling, and retrieving the existing resources. The customary linear economy, driven by dense exposition and consumption, depletes resources and imposes substantial environmental damage (Joyia et al. 2024). Conversely, CE could dramatically lessen the global market for biomass, metals, fossil fuels, and minerals (Akbarian et al. 2022). Unlike the linear economy, which saps raw materials through extraction and disposal, CE secures the sustainable and continuous availability of resources (Puntillo et al. 2021). The Circular Economy is built upon a fundamental commitment to entrepreneurship, innovation, and collaboration.

The climate hazards executed due to climate change and the limited resources of nature spawn paradigm transferals at the neck and neck of economic, societal, and ecological strategies and policies. It Promotes the ideologies of circular economy and sustainable development as a priority worldwide (Apostu et al. 2023). The Circular Economy (CE) is an essential tool for countering carbon dioxide (CO_2) emissions associated with resource management, utilization, and disposal. Consequently, it is climactic regarding deteriorating greenhouse gas (GHG) emissions (Yang et al. 2023). The adaptation of CE offers practical choices for achieving the SDGs (Dantas et al. 2021). It is ascertained that shifting towards a circular economy can mitigate damaging outcomes, reduce monetary disparities, and preclude further environmental degradation (Yang et al. 2023). The circular economy also correlates significantly with persistent digital transformation, which consists of big data, cloud computing, blockchain, artificial intelligence (AI), and other digital technologies (Schöggl et al. 2023). Specialists claim that adopting the circular economy model is merged with digitalization to enable predictive analytics, surveillance, and monitoring throughout the product life cycle (Liu et al. 2022).

This current study analyses the potential link between the circular economy (CE) and CO_2 emissions in the Netherlands, concentrating on both from the perspective of time and frequency. The Netherlands sets a benchmark as a model for CE, evidenced by its pioneering waste-to-recycling endeavors and avant-garde energy-generation technologies. With a vision of progressive and sustainable environmental policies, the country is a leader within the Eurozone and ranks among the world's most innovative users of natural resources (Sileryte et al. 2022). Further, the Netherlands is reinforced by a refined mechanism of transportation, communications, information technology, logistics, and systems to innovate, reuse, and recycle (Wijewickrama et al. 2021). The country has ascertained vital precedent for adapting the Circular Economy (CE) model for waste management. The Dutch government has set enterprising points to accelerate CE adoption (Rataj et al. 2024):

1. Production processes are optimized to enhance resource efficiency, reducing the demand for raw materials.
2. There is a strategic emphasis on utilizing sustainably sourced, renewable raw materials, such as biomass derived from plants, trees, and organic waste, to minimize dependence on fossil fuels.
3. There is a focus on advancing circular manufacturing technologies and developing innovative products that support the CE framework.

Implementing various waste management policies in the Netherlands reflects a solid commitment to circular transition. In 2016, in the Netherlands, "the Circular Economy (CE) by 2050" program was intended to reduce mineral use (van de Gronden 2022). It targets five industries, consumer goods, construction, manufacturing, plastics, food, and biomass, to efficiently consume and reuse raw materials with minimal destructive emissions. The strategy emphasizes responsible material sources for public, environmental, and social benefits (Hsiao and Hu 2024). CE anticipates benefiting the environment by reducing reliance on inadequate imported resources (Bianchi and Cordella 2023). The system also concentrates on various regions and cities, fostering sustainability through waste reduction, renewable resources, and long-lasting outcomes. The buildings and new construction require reused, zero-emission materials (Selvaraj et al. 2024).

This project's innovations are marked by a shift towards leveraging groundbreaking technologies, proffering high-tech production, and adopting pioneering managerial and surveillance strategies (Egbelakin et al. 2024). This conversion impacts the dynamics of microeconomics and macroeconomics, demonstrating the benefits of new economic models and promoting resource-efficient and waste-free technologies (Adamowicz 2022). With the increase in industrial activities, which pose environmental risks, there is a crucial necessity to enhance living standards to safeguard the environment (Zhang et al. 2022). It poses the need to integrate circular economy precepts to counter the adverse effects of resource depletion and environmental pollution due to rapid socio-economic progress (Nunes et al. 2023). These challenges of justifying a circular economy's benefits are paramount for its adaption in industries, transportation sectors, and human activities. These challenges required developing a new economic model incorporating the informatization of components and business approaches (Tavares et al. 2023).

Addressing environmental protection and mitigating the negative impacts is required for effective waste management and disposal (Abubakar et al. 2022). In this context, the principles of the circular economy arise as a vital approach, enabling resource conservation and reducing production and processing costs. These processes are critical macroeconomic development indicators of economic growth and stability

(Kuzior et al. 2023). The primary objective of this study is to determine the main macroeconomic trends within the circular economy framework (Kuzior et al. 2023). It probes the circular economy principles and their application through information and innovative technologies to enrich the application, consequently optimizing these tools, methods, and forms (Hariyani et al. 2024). The study also aims to establish these processes' foundational tendencies and interactions by analyzing these macroeconomic trends (Kuzior et al. 2023). The increasing significance of the circular economy as a driver of macroeconomic advancement is underscored by integrating innovative technological informatization throughout all phases of economic development (Hondroyiannis et al. 2024).

2 Circular Economy

Circular Economy (CE) enforces the 3R principle- concentrating, reusing, and recycling to progress broader sustainable development goals (Zorpas 2024). These goals include preventing polluted land, cutting greenhouse gas emissions, optimizing resource procurement, and handling dangerous waste (Awewomom et al. 2024). Like other sustainability practices, CE faces limitations and challenges (Roos Lindgreen et al. 2022). The core concept of CE involves recognizing critical dimensions of the 5Rs, including reuse, recycle, remanufacture, restore, and retrieval, and leveraging them to shape future patterns. Most often, recycling is emphasized in the literature (Kirchherr et al. 2023). This concept entails various recovery processes where waste materials are recycled, and new goods and materials are produced to be utilized for their original purpose and applications (da Silva et al. 2021). Recycling and reusing involves the reproduced use of a product to expand its lifecycle (Pérez-Martínez et al. 2021). Reuse entails reapplying non-waste materials or components for their intended original purposes (Moalem et al. 2023). The concept of Circular Economy (CE) has recently attained traction as a strategy for replacing and reusing materials to enhance a firm's ability to serve the needs of future generations (Hofstetter et al. 2021). CE has been increasingly acknowledged for managing end-of-life products through reprocessing, re-managing, and re-utilization, along with proffering zero waste initiatives (Ezeudu et al. 2024). Zero Waste strives to avoid trash yard disposal by either upcycling (improving product quality by redesigning the same parts or components) or downcycling (creating new products from existing parts or elements (Mahanta et al. 2022). The primary objective of zero waste is to eliminate waste by continuously repurposing materials (Zaman 2022).

The Ellen MacArthur model underlines the significance of recycling and recovery programs in restraining waste (Voukkali et al. 2023). As detailed above, this model endorses the constant circulation of technological and biological nutrient-manufactured products within the economic system (Salinas-Velandia et al. 2022). Thus, component reuse and recycling strategies are pivotal to minimizing greenhouse gas emissions and environmental importance (Nguyen et al. 2021). Firms with the resources to execute and reuse components can attract internal and external stakeholders and gain incalculable ecological perspicuity. As a result, companies can refine their waste knowledge management techniques and move toward green innovation with reinvigorated management activities (Chen et al. 2023). Likewise (de Oliveira and Oliveira 2023). It was suggested that companies could further ascertain and espouse circularity gauges in the context of corporate objectives and business tactics (Bag 2023; Khan et al. 2024a). Moreover, the gaps are opportunities for further research and potential approaches for improving the relevance of circularity indicators for sustainability. Hence, leveraging organizational knowledge management becomes a cornerstone in promoting environmental sustainability across the product life cycle (Hariyani et al. 2024).

The knowledge management (KM) strategies employed to achieve environmental advantages are influenced by determining internal and external drivers of organizational green innovation (Shehzad et al. 2024). Managers employ knowledge yielded by external stakeholders, which creates the conditions necessary to minimize the distribution of knowledge. In this context, knowledge is acquired sequentially and informally (Biloslavo and Zornada 2022). Following insights from the literature, one critical observation is that few studies have focused on the circular knowledge economy (Ul-Durar et al. 2023). The circular economy (CE) concept provides a practical framework for apprehending circular knowledge management (Silvério et al. 2023). The CE two-tier organizational planning process promotes a more environmentally responsible production and consumption system (Mandal and Pal 2021). It develops the lifespan of materials (to reduce waste and enhance ecosystem efficiency) to meet sustainable goals (Ogunmakinde et al. 2022). The knowledge management (KM) literature has evolved to address the knowledge economy (EK) (Ul-Durar et al. 2023) as crucial for sustainability initiatives (Kohl et al. 2022). EK is a fundamental knowledge resource that enables organizations to align their systems with present and future environmental challenges (Bresciani et al. 2023). Therefore, analysing the circular knowledge economy (CKE) is indispensable. The knowledge economy strives to devise a harmonious production system that supports technological and scientific innovation (Skene 2022). CKE is based on the mechanisms that foster organisations to re-accumulate, re-internalize, re-utilize, and re-share knowledge-intensive activities, focusing on resource productivity and eco-efficiency to maximize product, component, and material utility for customers and society, thus contributing to renewal and material management innovation. However, a deeper understanding of CE practices still needs to be devised, and they are in their early stages in developing countries.

3 Literature Review

The notion of a circular economy has garnered attention due to increasing environmental challenges and measures to stimulate economic sustainability with the tiniest ecological blow (Akter et al. 2024). Numerous studies in the past have analysed the circular economy and its affinity with CO_2 in countering capacities (Hagelüken and Goldmann 2022). For instance, it assessed the degree to which the circular economy has been adopted. The findings indicated that the circular economy is still a novel concept, with its development in the preliminary stage (Santa-Maria et al. 2021). Furthermore, the current approaches and application processes need to be improved for the industry, as there is a need for standardised strategies at a macro level (Rincón-Moreno et al. 2021).

Likewise, studies too have scoured the circular economy's wreck on CO_2 markdowns, offering substantial evidence reinforcing its role in declining emissions (Hu 2024). In this regard, the circular economy's contribution to minimising CO_2 across various sectors, including manufacturing, energy, and transportation, was later investigated (Razmjooei et al. 2024). Their findings suggest that while the circular economy does not initially contribute to CO_2 reduction due to increased raw coal output and consumption (Tiwari et al. 2024), it shows a decline in emissions over time, steered by reducing dependency on carbon-intensive energy sources (Thomaßen et al. 2022). Besides, the energy, industry, and transportation sectors possess the most significant potential for cost-cutting through circular methods (Dey et al. 2022). This affinity is further discussed, and the relation between circular economic policies and CO_2 emissions is underscoring the effect of environmental concerns, waste management, and agricultural activities that have the potential to reduce dependence on traditional resources (Paes et al. 2022).

Several studies have examined the level of circular economy development and its effects on environmental emissions (Hailemariam and Erdiaw-Kwasie 2023). European countries have grown substantially due to their firm technological bases and economic rise. Some nations are leading the shift towards circular economies, creating success stories (Mhatre et al. 2021). For instance, it determined a long-term affinity between the circular economy and CO_2 reduction attributed to enhanced resource management (Velenturf and Purnell 2021). Their results also indicated that short-term emissions are compelled by the high demand for materials prompted by investment and consumption. In the long run, however, the circular economy enables ecological growth and enriches environmental quality (Kandpal et al. 2024).

Similarly, research proved that emissions are caused mainly by the construction and transportation sectors, with the circular economy as a critical factor in declining CO_2 (Ye et al. 2022). In the Netherlands, recent literature indicates that the country is at the fore of the circular economy shift, contributing to mitigating environmental challenges (Marino and Pariso 2021). According to (Raihan 2024), recycling and e-waste dumping have significantly decreased CO_2 emissions, alleviating climate change. Furthermore, the circular economy aids in value creation. It plays a pivotal role in digital transformation (Cudečka-Puriņa et al. 2022). It studied the growing importance of the circular economy as a path to attaining sustainable development goals (SDGs) while indicating that strategic innovation promotes enterprises to manage sustainability matters while retaining their competitive edge.

Technological innovation is essential for advancing the circular economy and helping environmental issues (Khan et al. 2022). In this context, the role of innovation in the circular economy within EU nations is examined. Their determinations revealed that technical invention is influential in propelling circular economy development (Dagilienė et al. 2024). Further, it stresses the significance of social and environmental characteristics in the evolution to a circular economy, stressing the relevancy of technology in this transformation (Chauhan et al. 2022). They validated the importance of technical progress while studying the impact of technological innovation on the transition from an unbent to a circular economy (Siwal et al. 2022). Their findings indicate that innovation enhances recovery, recycling, and reuse processes, which can reduce emissions (Khan and Khurshid 2024). Similarly, Germany probed technological innovation in developing renewable energy, indicating that invention is a significant factor in energy conversion, which helps minimize harmful environmental effects (Özkan et al. 2023). Lastly, it found a positive correlation between the circular economy and reduced emissions to understand their dynamics and practical applications better (Hailemariam and Erdiaw-Kwasie 2023).

The literature on the circular economy and CO_2 interaction is extensive. However, more in-depth studies are still needed to understand their dynamics and practical applications better (Xie et al. 2023). Therefore, the current research examines the time-frequency lead-lag relationship between the circular economy and CO_2 in the presence of technological innovation (TI) (Khan and Khurshid 2024). Previous research has largely overlooked the role of TI despite its critical importance in the circular economy transition (Carreira et al. 2023). The interplay between the circular economy and CO_2 becomes more compelling when considering technological advancements, as they play a vital role in the circular transition and contribute to mitigating environmental issues (Wang et al. 2023).

Moreover, present investigations must sufficiently estimate the joint impact of the circular economy and CO_2 because ecological pollution is one of the world's most imperative hazards (Wang et al. 2023). Transitioning to a circular economy can reduce carbon dioxide emissions, making this change the primary urge (Zhang et al. 2024).

Conventional methods used to examine the circular economy and CO_2 mainly focus on the whole sample, violating subsamples and overseeing spatial and temporal aspects that could help identify lead-lag connections (Xu and Yi 2022). Traditional practices must also be modified to avoid constraints such as false regression results, unwieldy model specifications, and excessive time waste. These methods must provide an integrated framework for scrutinizing changes in time and frequency.

Among the researchers who have researched the fundamental principles of the circular economy and improvements in waste management (Goyal et al. 2021) earmarked their introspections to the subjects of the "circular economy," global changes and their impact on national economies (Lila et al. 2022). These scholars recognized the core principles of macroeconomic development in the genre of environmental and economic challenges, offering solutions to incorporate best practices from other nations (Agbonifo 2021). The authors' stance is convincing, as the circular economy enhances ecological conditions and boosts competitiveness and operational efficiency at both the enterprise and national levels (Khan et al. 2023).

Waste management has been a critical focus of prominent researchers (Silvério et al. 2023), who analyzed European backgrounds and the direction of national policies on solid waste management. While recognizing the significance of preliminary scientific contributions to this case (Batista et al. 2021), further study should be conducted to justify and purify the oddities of macroeconomic trends and indicators linked with the circular economy (De Noni et al. 2021). Particularly, Ukraine mandates more adaptation of circular economy approaches, which would foster its development of innovative partnerships (Bashynska et al. 2024).

The circular economy is also defined by Truong et al. (2024) as an economy marked by a vital and self-contained nature. It minimizes the consumption of immediate raw materials and processed resources while reducing waste (Kara et al. 2022) claim that the circular economy presents options to standard economic models by recuperating resources and using them in a closed-loop form throughout the value chain. It is asserted that the circular economy is based on resource recovery, health protection, and safeguarding socio-eco-economic systems, providing efficiency across all levels, from households and small firms to the global economy (Mandpe et al. 2023). However, these principles have ultimately fully applied to Ukraine's international exertions, specifically in innovative technologies. It further highlights the relevance of this research (Honcharuk et al. 2024). According to Kara et al. (2022), the circular economy is underpinned by new business models to reduce resource consumption and enable reuse and closed-loop production. These scholars present the circular economy in the context of shaping the strategic prospect for businesses and provide a methodological foundation to ensure industrial security through a circular economy course (Blomsma et al. 2023).

Research in macroeconomic indicators has gained Special attention from scholars such as (Adrangi and Kerr 2022), who examined the dynamics of gross domestic product (GDP) and the reasons and factors influencing it. These researchers also explored the relationship between GDP and government revenues, employing various comparative analysis methods and macroeconomic regulation approaches (Hein and Martschin 2021). However, certain aspects of the domestic macroeconomic situation, particularly the impact of resource-saving and waste recycling on GDP growth, need to be adequately investigated. Such factors could contribute to a considerable increase in GDP share (Kuzior et al. 2022).

Meanwhile, domestic scholars have focused on managing innovation processes and logistical support (Mikhno et al. 2021). These scientists assert that logistical support contains the mobilization, expansion, and distribution of resources, innovation in business processes, information support, and execution of planning, control, and monitoring tasks (Nour 2022). These courses aim to optimize the use of economic resources and mitigate dangers. The informatization of the national economy and the shaping of economic foundations for originating the information society have increasingly evolved topics of scientific investigation for both domestic and international researchers (Ievdokymov et al. 2023). For example, it emphasized societal and governmental expansion is only possible with information exchange and robust information support. Moreover, adopting digital technologies enhances public administration's transparency, reduces corruption, and increases public trust by involving citizens in decision-making (Afiyah 2024).

4 Governance and Digitalization

The rise of industrial revolutions and the expansion of digital technologies resulted in the rapid integration of information technology (IT) across various economic sectors, from local to multinational levels. This transformation has mainly contributed to developing an information society (Van Veldhoven and Vanthienen 2022). Researchers assert that IT, alongside artificial intelligence (AI), has expedited the adoption of digital technologies across multiple factors of society (Dąbrowska et al. 2022). Simultaneously, the expanded use of IT is reshaping conventional communication courses between governments and entrepreneurs, transitioning to more digital-oriented relations. It will necessitate OK and open communication channels (Tigre et al. 2023). As a result, e-governance, defined as the provision of public services through the Internet and IT in the public sector, emerged as a critical development. Studies reveal that e-governance operates with many IT tools in external and internal governmental functions (Aziz and Sallow 2022). It facilitates communication strategies across different levels, resulting in resource consumption, including capital, labor, and natural resources. Successful e-governance implementation hinges on stakeholder involvement and ensuring adequate digital literacy (Nwachukwu and Unachukwu 2023).

Previous literature shows that IT nonlinearly impacts a nation's social, economic, political, and ecological advancement. The scope of this impact is affected by intermediate elements such as trade openness, industrial structure, productivity, corruption, financial development, and public trust in the government (Sharma et al. 2021). Moreover, some studies indicate that the strength of digitalization harms economic growth and government effectiveness in developing countries, which could exacerbate unemployment, worsen inequality, and widen income disparities (Wang and Shen 2024). In these cases, governments must implement proactive policies, such as lifelong education, digital literacy programs, and training subsidies for government employees (Ciesielska et al. 2022). Stresses limited internet access as the primary barrier to maximizing the potential of e-governance for a country's growth (Manoharan et al. 2023).

In developing nations, e-governance enhances public trust by transitioning from inefficient to effective governance systems. It significantly reduced corruption through increased transparency in public services (Alam et al. 2023). Researchers using FGLS (Feasible Generalized Least Squares) and PTR (Panel et al.) models have demonstrated a U-shaped relationship between e-governance and corruption (Zou et al. 2023). It also implies that while e-governance can initially reduce corruption, excessive levels may lead to revitalization (Abdulnabi 2024). Gulf Cooperation

Council (GCC) countries' studies prove the e-government index's positive impact on economic growth, although this result varies across nations (Mutambik et al. 2023). For example, Bahrain, Kuwait, and Saudi Arabia have shown positive development, while Oman and Qatar have experienced different outcomes.

Scholars further assert that digitizing governance services helps achieve sustainable development goals (SDGs) and improves environmental rendition (Ionescu et al. 2022) A literature review also points out that much research has been devoted to analyzing the efficacy of monitoring systems in achieving SDGs through IT (Trane et al. 2023). Digitalization can boost trade openness by enabling countries to sell goods to a broader range of markets using digital platforms (Sturgeon 2021). Evidence of a positive correlation between internet penetration and trade openness is further supported by empirical studies showing that digitalization contributes positively to economic growth and trade openness (Abendin and Duan 2021).

Digital technologies have also been instrumental in modernizing industrial sectors, reshaping their structure, and influencing energy consumption patterns through investments in research and development (R&D) (Wang et al. 2022). Furthermore, Industry 4.0 and AI technologies are crucial in enhancing energy security, mainly through renewable energy development. Scholars have confirmed that industrial structure mediates the relationship between digitalization and a nation's green growth (Hao et al. 2023). Using data from Chinese cities between 2011 and 2019, researchers applied mediating effect models, benchmark regression models, and spatial Durbin models to empirically verify that digitalization fosters green innovation, with trade openness and industrial structure serving as intermediaries (Luo et al. 2023). Additionally, investment in R&D has been found to mediate the connection between the digital economy and carbon emissions, facilitating the relationship between digitalization and ecological progress (Ma et al. 2022).

5 E-Governance and Clean Energy Access

A review of the theoretical discourse on the link between digitalization and energy development reveals a need for more consensus on the nature and direction of this relationship (Brenner and Hartl 2021). The concept of an open energy market, essential for achieving SDGs, relies on digitalizing governance to provide clean and affordable energy (Miskiewicz 2022). Underscore the importance of management in the era of Big Data, particularly in addressing gaps in household electricity access in India (Pelz et al. 2021). Research on Nigeria's progress toward SDG 2030 has also shown that local e-governance contributes to combating climate change by promoting the use of renewable energy (Omweri 2024). Similar conclusions are drawn from studies of Italy, where digitalization has been found to facilitate SDG achievements (Secundo et al. 2022).

Increased governance efficiency in the energy sector can be realized through expanding digital technologies in households and developing intelligent cities (Li 2022). Studies confirm that the relationship between governance efficiency and the spread of digital technologies is complex and context-dependent (Castelnovo and Sorrentino 2021). E-governance has been linked to enhanced energy efficiency by increasing the share of renewable energy, closing gaps in electricity access, and improving the affordability of clean energy (Ullah et al. 2021). Investments in R&D and industrial structural energy intensity reduction have also been associated with the spread of digital technologies (Zeng et al. 2023). However, some studies indicate that digitalization may increase energy consumption due to the rebound effect. In Nepal, e-governance projects have expanded rural access to electricity and promoted renewable energy use (Sarker et al. 2021). These findings underscore the need to investigate further the hypothesis that e-governance significantly impacts clean and affordable energy (Lyulyov et al. 2024).

6 Ecological Modernization

Ecological Modernization Theory (EMT) examines the intersection of modernization and environmental preservation (Asghar et al. 2024). The early stages of ecological modernization globally coincided with China's reform period and opening to international markets. This period saw twin challenges: industrial modernization and the environmental protection needed for ecological sustainability (He 2023). EMT advocates for coordinated progress in green industrialization, urbanization, and environmental modernization. Technological and ecological synergies are emphasized in this framework (Ma and Shi 2023). Information technologies are pivotal in China's environmental modernization efforts, supported by initiatives like the State Informatization Development Strategy (2006–2020), which aims to create a nationwide information infrastructure, promote independent innovation, and bolster information security (Shi and Wei 2024).

China has embraced a point-line-plane strategy to develop high-tech industrial parks to enhance its international competitiveness and optimize its industrial structure (Di Vaio et al. 2022). Prominent regions such as the Pearl River Delta, the Yangtze River Delta, and the Bohai Area are leading this effort, with technological, industrial, and trade revenue growing significantly (Hou et al. 2024). National Electronic Information Industrial Parks have been established in key coastal areas to accelerate information-oriented development further, focusing on supporting IT and systems development (Suraj 2022). These industrial parks are essential to the country's efforts to align high-tech advancements with environmental goals, ultimately contributing to economic and ecological progress (Song et al. 2023).

7 Eco-Symbiosis

Eco-symbiosis is a sustainable approach where systems collaborate within a larger framework. Eco-industrial parks exemplify this concept, demonstrating how synergistic and mutually beneficial systems can coexist (Buch et al. 2023). This circular economy (CE) aspect begins at the enterprise level. It can expand to industrial parks, cities, and even regions, fostering a gradual accumulation of experience that informs decision-making at each stage (Kirchherr et al. 2023). For instance, eco-industrial parks operating within a broader community, such as a city or province, may exhibit eco-symbiotic relationships across various levels, akin to the human body's circulatory and respiratory systems working together (Inglese et al. 2024). The interaction among these systems and their adaptation to their environment is essential for improving environmental and economic conditions (Sharifi 2021).

From an information technology (IT) and information system perspective, the implications for such organizations revolve around open-source and distributed communication systems at multiple levels. The Internet, e-commerce, and other inter-organizational collaborations are critical to sharing knowledge, expertise, and data (Runeson et al. 2021). This system represents one of the less-developed organizational innovations that transcends traditional boundaries. These interconnected organizations and adaptive and dynamic information systems are managed as geographic information systems (GIS) and mobile technologies—are necessary (Shou et al., 2024). Moreover, IT tools that facilitate waste exchanges across organizations, forming a virtual eco-industrial symbiosis, could prove invaluable. An example of such a tool is China's construction industry's 'Web fill,' an e-commerce platform encouraging the reuse and recycling of residual construction materials across various sites (Han 2023).

8 Green Supply Chain Management

Green or Environmental Supply Chain Management (GSCM) is an organizational innovation that incorporates environmental considerations into an organization's inter-organizational value chain activities. Supply chain management (SCM) encompasses the management of resources—whether informational, knowledge-based, economic, material, or labor-related—that flow between organizations (Dahinine et al. 2024). GSCM is still emerging in China, with more developed aspects such as internal green supply activities, while other areas, like reverse logistics, are still evolving (Feng et al. 2022).

IT can play a pivotal role in greening supply chains by substituting the movement of information for the physical movement of goods and materials, leading to more excellent transportation and storage efficiencies (Gawusu et al. 2022). It means that materials are not unnecessarily transported, produced, or stored. Linking life cycle analysis, design-for-environment strategies, and green purchasing systems across organizations are essential to achieve these efficiencies (Sharm 2024). Unfortunately, such technologies and systems are underutilized in Chinese organizations, partly due to insufficient information and systems supporting these activities across supply chains (Feigenbaum and Nelson 2022).

9 Environmental Innovation

The world's natural resources, the most complex ecosystems sustaining biodiversity, are at risk of depletion or extinction (Mondal and Palit 2022). In this context, eco-innovation moves toward genuine sustainable development (Tomashuk and Baldynyuk 2023). A central feature of environmental innovation is enhanced resource efficiency. Environmental Innovation, Ecological Innovation, and Green Innovation are those terms that are often used interchangeably. Broadly, environmental innovation refers to producing goods, services, processes, marketing methods, organizational structures, and institutional arrangements intentionally or not, reducing ecological impacts compared to alternative practices (Rodríguez-Rebés et al. 2021).

Circular economy (CE) is a highly debated notion, defined by Suárez-Eiroa et al. (2021) as a dual-loop regenerative system focused on the effective and efficient utilization of ecosystem resources, worthwhile for optimizing environmental and economic performance. European Union policies prod the adoption of CE principles. Management, marketing, and institutional frameworks at the manufacturing level can help achieve sustainability and resource efficiency goals (Kazancoglu et al. 2021). The most widely accepted CE definition states that it maximizes resource utilization, including recycling at the end of its lifecycle (Spreafico 2022). This process provides minimal waste during manufacturing and after the product's life, completing resource loops (Kara et al. 2022).

In exploring the development of resource-efficient products, a literature review of 40 studies on environmental innovation (Dimakopoulou et al. 2023; Ul-Durar et al. 2023) A paper was presented that provides an overview of EI knowledge and introduces a capability-based framework from 1970 to 2014. The authors suggest that environmental, learning, and marketing capabilities, as operating capabilities, are essential to driving eco-innovation (Khan et al. 2024b, 2024c). While their findings align with existing EI literature, they focused mainly on the capability stance, leaving room for added inquiry into the micro-level determinants of CE initiatives that influence ecological innovation. Further, other literature reviews underline the capability perspective.

10 Discussion and Conclusions

This chapter is fundamental to address the contemporary concept of the circular economy, which is the most pressing need globally, whether in developed or underdeveloped nations. The chapter begins by explaining the linear economic model to understand how it shifts into the circular economy. This shift focuses on reducing, reusing, rethinking, recycling, and retrieving resources to minimize waste and pollution, thus achieving sustainability. CE reduces raw material use and greenhouse gas emissions and supports resource management. The Netherlands model is a prime example that challenges new economic models and provides evidence of effective waste management. The three Rs—reduce, reuse, and recycle—extend to five Rs: refuse, manufacture, restore, retrieve, and the Ellen MacArthur model is one of the best applications of this system.

The world must survive and achieve climate goals and environmental sustainability to be protected from environmental hazards. Every nation requires this concept, and comprehensive knowledge about green innovation is crucial for effectively enhancing resources. The circular economy (CE) is the only solution, aiming to reduce CO_2 emissions by optimizing resource use. Evidence from the literature supports this benefit, as the linear economy increased emissions due to higher material demand and minimal reuse and recycling. This is why the world is now unanimously more concerned about climate change, which impacts all sustainability categories—from social to economic and beyond.

The literature and previous expert findings show that technology is significant and crucial to advancing the circular economy. This includes improving recycling and reducing ecological impacts. The world, including its people and nations, needs e-governance and digitalization to support CE goals. These technologies can reduce many hard materials and tangible products, saving resources. This can also be achieved by enhancing public service efficiency, renewing energy use, and incorporating eco-symbiosis to improve environmental and economic conditions. There is a need for green supply chain management (GSEM), which integrates ecological considerations with information and technology for effective optimization. There are many gaps in this area, and more research is needed to establish the relationship between the circular economy and CO_2 emissions, which contribute to global warming. Climate and environmental communication should focus on how technological innovations influence the circular economy. This will be very helpful in refining methodologies for better analytical results, allowing the global economy to achieve sustainability targets in all aspects. Additionally, there is a need to work on the e-waste management system to turn waste into valuable resources. Extracting metals and precious metals such as gold, silver, and copper from e-waste will benefit underdeveloped areas and other parts of the world. **It is recommended that policymakers enhance support for technological innovations and robust e-waste management systems to drive circular economy goals.**

References

Abdulnabi SM (2024) Issues and challenges of implementing e-governance in developing countries: a comprehensive analysis of civil service models. Cogent Bus Manag 11(1):2340579

Abendin S, Duan P (2021) International trade and economic growth in Africa: the role of the digital economy. Cogent Econ Fin 9(1):1911767

Abubakar IR, Maniruzzaman KM, Dano UL, AlShihri FS, AlShammari MS, Ahmed SM, Al-Gehlani WA, Alrawaf T (2022) Environmental sustainability impacts of solid waste management practices in the global South. Int J Environ Res Public Health 19(19):12717

Adamowicz M (2022) Green deal, green growth and green economy as a means of support for attaining the sustainable development goals. Sustainability 14(10):5901

Adrangi B, Kerr L (2022) Sustainable development indicators and their relationship to GDP: evidence from emerging economies. Sustainability 14(2):658

Afiyah S (2024) The impact of E-government services, citizen participation, and transparency on public trust in government. Glob Int J Innov Res 2(6):1246–1261

Agbonifo PE (2021) Renewable energy development: opportunities and barriers within the context of global energy politics. Int J Energy Econ Policy 11(2):141–148

Akbarian A, Andooz A, Kowsari E, Ramakrishna S, Asgari S, Cheshmeh ZA (2022) Challenges and opportunities of lignocellulosic biomass gasification in the path of circular bioeconomy. Biores Technol 362:127774

Akter MMK, Haq UN, Uddin MA (2024) Sustainable development and circular economy. In: Waste management in the circular economy, pp. 133–152. Springer International Publishing, Cham

Alam T, Aftab M, Abbas Z, Ugli KMM, Bokhari SAA (2023) Impact of e-government initiatives to combat corruption mediating by behavioral intention: a quantitative analysis from emerging economies. Sustainability 15(3):2694

Apostu SA, Gigauri I, Panait M, Martín-Cervantes PA (2023) Is Europe on the way to sustainable development? Compatibility of green environment, economic growth, and circular economy issues. Int J Environ Res Public Health 20(2):1078

Asghar M, Leghari S, Ullah S, Nobanee H (2024) Balancing environmental sustainability: socio-economic drivers and policy pathways in oil-importing nations. Energ Strat Rev 55:101497

Awewomom J, Dzeble F, Takyi YD, Ashie WB, Ettey EN, Afua PE, Sackey LN, Opoku F, Akoto O (2024) Addressing global environmental pollution using environmental control techniques: a focus on environmental policy and preventive environmental management. Discov Environ 2(1):8

Aziz ZA, Sallow AB (2022) Concepts of E-governance development: a review. Eurasian J Sci Eng 8(1):51–64

Bag S (2023) Restorative supply chain practices in a circular economy and supply chain sustainability performance: the moderating effect of the perceived professional status of supply chain managers. Benchmarking Int J

Bashynska I, Lewicka D, Filyppova S, Prokopenko O (2024) Green innovation in Central and Eastern Europe. Taylor & Francis

Batista M, Caiado RGG, Quelhas OLG, Lima GBA, Leal Filho W, Yparraguirre ITR (2021) A framework for sustainable and integrated municipal solid waste management: barriers and critical factors to developing countries. J Clean Prod 312:127516

Bianchi M, Cordella M (2023) Does circular economy mitigate the extraction of natural resources? Empirical evidence based on analysis of 28 European economies over the past decade. Ecol Econ 203:107607

Biloslavo R, Zornada M (2022) Development of a knowledge management framework within the systems context. In: Strategic human resource management at tertiary level, pp 137–164. River Publishers

Blomsma F, Tennant M, Ozaki R (2023) Making sense of circular economy: understanding the progression from idea to action. Bus Strateg Environ 32(3):1059–1084

Brenner B, Hartl B (2021) The perceived relationship between digitalization and ecological, economic, and social sustainability. J Clean Prod 315:128128
Bresciani S, Rehman SU, Giovando G, Alam GM (2023) The role of environmental management accounting and environmental knowledge management practices influence environmental performance: mediated-moderated model. J Knowl Manag 27(4):896–918
Buch R, O'neill D, Lubenow C, DeFilippis M, Dalrymple M (2023) A transdisciplinary approach to an ethical circular economy
Carreira RJ, Ferreira JV, Ramos AL (2023) The consumer's role in the transition to the circular economy: a state of the art based on an SLR with bibliometric analysis. Sustainability 15(20):15040
Castelnovo W, Sorrentino M (2021) The digital government imperative: a context-aware perspective. In: Digital government and public management. Routledge, pp 77–93
Chauhan C, Parida V, Dhir A (2022) Linking circular economy and digitalisation technologies: a systematic literature review of past achievements and future promises. Technol Forecast Soc Chang 177:121508
Chen P, Sauerwein M, Steuer B (2023) Exploring greenhouse gas emissions pathways and stakeholder perspectives: in search of circular economy policy innovation for waste paper management and carbon neutrality in Hong Kong. J Environ Manag 341:118072
Ciesielska M, Rizun N, Chabik J (2022) Assessment of E-government inclusion policies toward seniors: a framework and case study. Telecommun Policy 46(7):102316
Cudečka-Puriņa N, Atstāja D, Koval V, Purviņš M, Nesenenko P, Tkach O (2022) Achievement of sustainable development goals through implementing a circular economy and developing regional cooperation. Energies 15(11):4072
da Silva TR, de Azevedo AR, Cecchin D, Marvila MT, Amran M, Fediuk R, Vatin N, Karelina M, Klyuev S, Szelag M (2021) Application of plastic wastes in construction materials: a review using the concept of life-cycle assessment in the context of recent research for future perspectives. Materials 14(13):3549
Dąbrowska J, Almpanopoulou A, Brem A, Chesbrough H, Cucino V, Di Minin A, Giones F, Hakala H, Marullo C, Mention AL, Mortara L (2022) Digital transformation, for better or worse: a critical multi-level research agenda. R&D Manag 52(5):930–954
Dagilienė L, Varaniūtė V, Banionienė J (2024) Cultivating a sustainable and circular economy: the role of institutional logics in manufacturing companies. J Clean Prod 434:140363
Dahinine B, Laghouag A, Bensahel W, Alsolami M, Guendouz T (2024) Modelling the combined effect of green leadership and human resource management in moving to green supply chain performance enhancement in Saudi Arabia. Sustainability 16(10):3953
Dantas TET, de-Souza ED, Destro IR, Hammes G, Rodriguez CMT, Soares SR (2021) How can the combination of circular economy and industry 4.0 contribute towards achieving the sustainable development goals? Sustain Prod Consum 26:213–227
De Noni I, Ganzaroli A, Orsi L (2021) Green invention as leverage for economic growth in locally collaborative European regions. In: Rethinking clusters: place-based value creation in sustainability transitions. Springer International Publishing, Cham, pp 17–31
de Oliveira CT, Oliveira GGA (2023) What do Circular economy indicators measure? An overview of circular economy principles and sustainable development goals. Resour Conserv Recycl 190:106850. https://doi.org/10.1016/j.resconrec.2022.106850
Dey PK, Malesios C, De D, Budhwar P, Chowdhury S, Cheffi W (2022) Circular economy to enhance the sustainability of small and medium-sized enterprises. In: Supply chain sustainability in small and medium-sized enterprises. Routledge, pp. 10–45
Di Vaio A, Hassan R, Chhabra M, Arrigo E, Palladino R (2022) Sustainable entrepreneurship impact and entrepreneurial venture life cycle: a systematic literature review. J Clean Prod 378:134469
Dimakopoulou AG, Chatzistamoulou N, Kounetas K, Tsekouras K (2023) Environmental innovation and R&D collaborations: firm decisions in the innovation efficiency context. J Technol Transf 48(4):1176–1205

Dosi G (2023) The foundations of complex evolving economies: Part one: Innovation, organization, and industrial dynamics. Oxford University Press.
Egbelakin T, Ogunmakinde O, Sojobi A (2024) Innovations, disruptions and future trends in the global construction industry. In: Omotayo T (ed). Routledge
Ezeudu OB, Tenebe IT, Ujah CO (2024) Status of production, consumption, and end-of-life waste management of plastic and plastic products in Nigeria: prospects for circular plastics economy. Sustainability 16(18):7900
Feigenbaum EA, Nelson MR (2022) Taiwan's opportunities in emerging industry supply chains. Carnegie Endowment for International Peace
Feng Y, Lai KH, Zhu Q (2022) Green supply chain innovation: emergence, adoption, and challenges. Int J Prod Econ 248:108497
Garcia-Saravia Ortiz-de-Montellano C, Samani P, van der Meer Y (2023) How can the circular economy support the advancement of the Sustainable Development Goals (SDGs)? A comprehensive analysis. Sustain Prod Consum 40:352–362. https://doi.org/10.1016/j.spc.2023.07.003
Gawusu S, Zhang X, Jamatutu SA, Ahmed A, Amadu AA, Djam Miensah E (2022) The dynamics of green supply chain management within the framework of renewable energy. Int J Energy Res 46(2):684–711
Goyal S, Chauhan S, Mishra P (2021) Circular economy research: a bibliometric analysis (2000–2019) and future research insights. J Clean Prod 287:125011
Hagelüken C, Goldmann D (2022) Recycling and circular economy—towards a closed loop for metals in emerging clean technologies. Miner Econ 35(3):539–562
Hailemariam A, Erdiaw-Kwasie MO (2023) Towards a circular economy: implications for emission reduction and environmental sustainability. Bus Strateg Environ 32(4):1951–1965
Han Y (2023) Development of integrated e-waste management system based on resource-saving in China.
Hao X, Li Y, Ren S, Wu H, Hao Y (2023) The role of digitalization on green economic growth: does industrial structure optimization and green innovation matter? J Environ Manage 325:116504
Hariyani D, Hariyani P, Mishra S, Sharma MK (2024) Leveraging digital technologies for advancing circular economy practices and enhancing life cycle analysis: a systematic literature review. Waste Manag Bull
He J (2023) Integration degree of China's the new development pattern of dual circulation and industrial green development. PLoS ONE 18(7):e0288160
Hein E, Martschin J (2021) Demand and growth regimes in finance-dominated capitalism and the role of the macroeconomic policy regime: a post-Keynesian comparative study on France, Germany, Italy and Spain before and after the Great Financial Crisis and the Great Recession. Rev of Evol Polit Econ 2(3):493–527
Hofstetter JS, De Marchi V, Sarkis J, Govindan K, Klassen R, Ometto AR, Spraul KS, Bocken N, Ashton WS, Sharma S, Jaeger-Erben M (2021). From sustainable global value chains to circular economy—different silos, different perspectives, but many opportunities to build bridges. Circ Econ Sustain 1(1):21–47
Honcharuk V, Bugaenko T, Shevchuk I, Liubchenko N, Bezlatnia L (2024) Educational innovation and digital transformation: interconnection and prospects for Ukraine. Futur Educ 4(2):61–85
Hondroyiannis G, Sardianou E, Nikou V, Evangelinos K, Nikolaou I (2024) Circular economy and macroeconomic performance: evidence across 28 European countries. Ecol Econ 215:108002
Hou J, Shi J, Chen L, Zhang Z, Kuang E (2024) Exploring the spatial spillover effects of Yangtze River Delta ports on urban economic growth. PLoS ONE 19(8):e0307770
Hsiao CJ, Hu JL (2024) Biomass and circular economy: now and the future. Biomass 4(3):720–739
Hu P (2024) Physical versus behavioural emissions reductions: quantifying and comparing emissions reduced by behaviour and emissions reduced by technology of net-zero communities. Master's thesis, University of Waterloo
Ievdokymov V, Oliinyk O, Polupanova K, Khadzhynova O, Iefimova G, Legeza D, Tarasiuk H, Yashchyshyna I, Sarancha I, Mazur N, Bogoyavlenska Y (2023) Digitalization of economics: inter-disciplinary and inter-branch approach

Inglese G, Lucibello S, Rotondi C (2024) Resilience envelopes: the "fourth environment" as a source of inspiration, a place for speculation and a territory for experimenting with new models of life. In: For nature/with nature: new sustainable design scenarios. Springer Nature Switzerland, Cham, pp 1039–1060

Ionescu AM, Clipa AM, Turnea ES, Clipa CI, Bedrule-Grigoruță MV, Roth S (2022) The impact of innovation framework conditions on corporate digital technology integration: institutions as facilitators for sustainable digital transformation. J Bus Econ Manag 23(5):1037–1059

Jain Y (2021) Regenerative economies: a new approach towards sustainability. In: No poverty. Springer International Publishing, Cham, pp 761–771

Joyia MAK, Ahmad M, Chen YF, Mustaqeem M, Ali A, Abbas A, Gondal MA (2024) Trends and advances in sustainable bioethanol production technologies from first to fourth generation: a critical review. Energy Convers Manage 321:119037

Kandpal V, Jaiswal A, Santibanez Gonzalez ED, Agarwal N (2024) The economics of sustainable energy transition and the circular economy. In: Sustainable energy transition: circular economy and sustainable financing for Environmental, Social and Governance (ESG) practices. Springer Nature Switzerland, Cham, pp 53–87

Kara S, Hauschild M, Sutherland J, McAloone T (2022) Closed-loop systems to circular economy: a pathway to environmental sustainability? CIRP Ann 71(2):505–528

Kazancoglu I, Sagnak M, Kumar Mangla S, Kazancoglu Y (2021) Circular economy and the policy: a framework for improving the corporate environmental management in supply chains. Bus Strateg Environ 30(1):590–608

Khan K, Khurshid A (2024) Are technology innovation and circular economy remedies for emissions? Evidence from the Netherlands. Environ Dev Sustain 26(1):1435–1449

Khan SAR, Sheikh AA, Ahmad Z (2023) Developing the interconnection between green employee behavior, tax avoidance, green capability, and sustainable performance of SMEs through corporate social responsibility. J Clean Prod 419:138236

Khan SAR, Sheikh AA, Tahir MS (2024a) Corporate social responsibility—an antidote for sustainable business performance: interconnecting role of digital technologies, employee eco-behavior, and tax avoidance. Environ Sci Pollut Res 31(3):4365–4383

Khan SAR, Sheikh AA, Hassan NM, Yu Z (2024b) Modeling the intricate association between sustainable service quality and supply chain performance: moderating role of blockchain technology and environmental uncertainty. Sustainability 16(11):4808

Khan SAR, Tahir MS, Sheikh AA (2024c) Sustainable performance in SMEs using big data analytics for closed-loop supply chains and reverse omnichannel. Heliyon 10(16)

Khan SAR, Umar M, Asadov A, Tanveer M, Yu Z (2022) Technological revolution and circular economy practices: a mechanism of green economy. Sustainability 14(8):4524

Kirchherr J, Yang NHN, Schulze-Spüntrup F, Heerink MJ, Hartley K (2023) Conceptualizing the circular economy (revisited): an analysis of 221 definitions. Resour Conserv Recycl 194:107001

Kohl K, Hopkins C, Barth M, Michelsen G, Dlouhá J, Razak DA, Abidin Bin Sanusi Z, Toman I (2022) A whole-institution approach towards sustainability: a crucial aspect of higher education's individual and collective engagement with the SDGs and beyond. Int J Sustain High Educ 23(2):218–236

Kuzior A, Arefieva O, Poberezhna Z, Ihumentsev O (2022) The mechanism of forming the strategic potential of an enterprise in a circular economy. Sustainability 14(6):3258. https://doi.org/10.3390/su14063258

Kuzior A, Arefiev S, Poberezhna Z (2023) Informatization of innovative technologies for ensuring macroeconomic trends in the conditions of a circular economy. J Open Innov Technol, Market Complex 9(1):100001

Li B (2022) Effective energy utilization through economic development for sustainable management in smart cities. Energy Rep 8:4975–4987

Lila A (2022) The development of the circular economy in China as a national strategy

Liu Q, Trevisan AH, Yang M, Mascarenhas J (2022) Digital functions and mechanisms are a framework of digital technologies for the circular economy. Bus Strateg Environ 31(5):2171–2192

Luo S, Yimamu N, Li Y, Wu H, Irfan M, Hao Y (2023) Digitalization and sustainable development: how could digital economy development improve green innovation in China? Bus Strateg Environ 32(4):1847–1871

Lyulyov O, Pimonenko T, Saura JR, Barbosa B (2024) How do e-governance and e-business drive sustainable development goals? Technol Forecast Soc Chang 199:123082

Ma Q, Shi F (2023) New urbanization and high-quality urban and rural development: based on the interactive coupling analysis of industrial green transformation. Ecol Ind 156:111044

Ma Q, Tariq M, Mahmood H, Khan Z (2022) The nexus between digital economy and carbon dioxide emissions in China: the moderating role of investments in research and development. Technol Soc 68:101910

Mahanta NR, Samuel AK, Sachan D (2022). Emerging trends of zero waste in the built environment and a paradigm shift toward sustainability. Emerging Trends Approaching Zero Waste, 1–35

Mandal A, Pal B (2021) Effects of green innovation and advertisement in an imperfect production-based competitive supply chain under the two-tier credit facility. Math Methods Appl Sci 44(17):13227–13251

Mandpe A, Paliya S, Gedam VV, Patel S, Tyagi L, Kumar S (2023) Circular economy approach for sustainable solid waste management: a developing economy perspective. Waste Manage Res 41(3):499–511

Manoharan AP, Mossey S, Zhao H, Viswanath S (2023) Municipal E-governance in Asia. Global encyclopedia of public administration, public policy, and governance. Springer International Publishing, Cham, pp 8363–8373

Marino A, Pariso P (2021) The transition towards to the circular economy: European SMEs' trajectories. Entrep Sustain Issues 8(4):431

Mhatre P, Panchal R, Singh A, Bibyan S (2021) A systematic literature review on the circular economy initiatives in the European Union. Sustain Prod Consum 26:187–202

Mikhno I, Koval V, Shvets G, Garmatiuk O, Tamošiūnienė R (2021) Green economy in sustainable development and improvement of resource efficiency

Miskiewicz R (2022) Clean and affordable energy within sustainable development goals: the role of governance digitalization. Energies 15(24):9571

Moalem RM, Remmen A, Hirsbak S, Kerndrup S (2023) Struggles over waste: preparing for re-use in the Danish waste sector. Waste Manage Res 41(1):98–116

Mondal S, Palit D (2022) Challenges in natural resource management for ecological sustainability. In: Natural resources conservation and advances for sustainability. Elsevier, pp 29–59

Mutambik I, Lee J, Almuqrin A, Alkhanifer A, Baihan M (2023) Gulf cooperation council countries and urbanisation: are open government data portals helping? Sustainability 15(17):12823

Nguyen TK, Ngo HH, Guo W, Nguyen TL, Chang SW, Nguyen DD, Varjani S, Lei Z, Deng L (2021) Environmental impacts and greenhouse gas emissions assessment for energy recovery and material recycling of the wastewater treatment plant. Sci Total Environ 784:147135

Nour R (2022) Enhancing the Logistics 4.0 firms through information technology. Sustainability 14(23):15860

Nunes AMM, Coelho Junior LM, Abrahão R, Santos Júnior EP, Simioni FJ, Rotella Junior P, Rocha LCS (2023) Public policies for renewable energy: a review of the perspectives for a circular economy. Energies 16(1):485

Nwachukwu LC, Unachukwu CL (2023) Adoption and utilization of E-Government in human resource management in Nigerian public service: opportunities and challenges. Jalingo J Soc Manag Sci 5(2):1–23

Ogunmakinde OE, Egbelakin T, Sher W (2022) Contributions of the circular economy to the UN sustainable development goals through sustainable construction. Resour Conserv Recycl 178:106023

Omweri FS (2024) A systematic literature review of e-government implementation in developing countries: examining urban-rural disparities, institutional capacity, and socio-cultural factors in the context of local governance and progress towards SDG 16.6. Int J Res Innov Soc Sci 8(8):1173–1199

Özkan O, Alola AA, Adebayo TS (2023) Environmental benefits of nonrenewable energy efficiency and renewable energy intensity in the USA and EU: examining the role of clean technologies. Sustain Energy Technol Assess 58:103315

Paes LAB, Bezerra BS, Jugend D, Agudo FL (2022) Prospects for a circular bioeconomy in urban ecosystems: proposal for a theoretical framework. J Clean Prod 380:134939

Pelz S, Chindarkar N, Urpelainen J (2021) Energy access for marginalized communities: evidence from rural North India, 2015–2018. World Dev 137:105204

Pérez-Martínez MM, Carrillo C, Rodeiro-Iglesias J, Soto B (2021) Life cycle assessment of repurposed waste electric and electronic equipment compared to original equipment. Sustain Prod Consum 27:1637–1649

Puntillo P, Gulluscio C, Huisingh D, Veltri S (2021) Reevaluating waste as a resource under a circular economy approach from a system perspective: findings from a case study. Bus Strateg Environ 30(2):968–984

Raihan A (2024) A review of the potential opportunities and challenges of the digital economy for sustainability. Innov Green Dev 3(4):100174

Rataj O, Kemp R, Mordaszewska K (2024) They are mainstreaming innovative circular economy solutions—a comparative study between entrepreneurs in developed versus emerging markets and developing economies. Bus Strat Environ

Razmjooei D, Alimohammadlou M, Ranaei Kordshouli HA, Askarifar K (2024) A bibliometric analysis of the literature on circular economy and sustainability in maritime studies. Environ Dev Sustain 26(3):5509–5536

Rincón-Moreno J, Ormazábal M, Álvarez MJ, Jaca C (2021) Advancing circular economy performance indicators and their application in Spanish companies. J Clean Prod 279:123605

Rodríguez-Rebés L, Navio-Marco J, Ibar-Alonso R (2021) Influence of organisational innovation and innovation in general on eco-innovation in European companies. J Intellect Cap 22(5):840–867

Roos Lindgreen E, Opferkuch K, Walker AM, Salomone R, Reyes T, Raggi A, Simboli A, Vermeulen WJ, Caeiro S (2022) Exploring assessment practices of companies actively engaged with the circular economy. Bus Strat Environ 31(4):1414–1438

Runeson P, Olsson T, Linåker J (2021) Open data ecosystems—an empirical investigation into an emerging industry collaboration concept. J Syst Softw 182:111088

Salinas-Velandia DA, Romero-Perdomo F, Numa-Vergel S, Villagrán E, Donado-Godoy P, Galindo-Pacheco JR (2022) Insights into circular horticulture: knowledge diffusion, resource circulation, one health approach, and greenhouse technologies. Int J Environ Res Public Health 19(19):12053

Santa-Maria T, Vermeulen WJ, Baumgartner RJ (2021) Framing and assessing the emergent field of business model innovation for the circular economy: a combined literature review and multiple case study approach. Sustain Prod Consum 26:872–891

Sarker T, Tandukar S, Dey SR (2021) Promoting sustainable development through realizing the demographic dividend opportunity in the digital economy: A case study of Nepal (No. 1225). ADBI Working Paper Series

Schöggl JP, Rusch M, Stumpf L, Baumgartner RJ (2023) Implementing digital technologies for a circular economy and sustainability management in the manufacturing sector. Sustain Prod Consum 35:401–420

Secundo G, Schena R, Russo A, Schiavone F, Shams R (2022) The impact of digital technologies on the achievement of the Sustainable Development Goals: evidence from the agri-food sector. Total Qual Manag Bus Excel 1–17

Selvaraj VK, Subramanian J, Dutt SS (2024) Integrating circular economy principles in achieving net zero toward sustainable futures: India's perspective. Mater Circ Econ 6(1):1–23

Sharifi A (2021) Co-benefits and synergies between urban climate change mitigation and adaptation measures: a literature review. Sci Total Environ 750:141642
Sharma R, Shahbaz M, Kautish P, Vo XV (2021) Analyzing the impact of export diversification and technological innovation on renewable energy consumption: evidences from BRICS nations. Renewable Energy 178:1034–1045
Sharma S (2024) Fostering green product design and innovation for a sustainable future. In: Waste management and life cycle assessment for sustainable business practice. IGI Global, pp 86–110
Shehzad MU, Zhang J, Dost M, Ahmad MS, Alam S (2024) Knowledge management enablers and knowledge management processes: a direct and configurational approach to stimulate green innovation. Eur J Innov Manag 27(1):123–152
Shi Y, Wei F (2024) Comparative analysis of digital economy-driven innovation development in China: an international perspective. J Knowl Econ 1–43
Shou M, Jia F, Yu J, Wu Y (2024) Challenges in developing information and communication technology (ICT) use for rural e-governance: an ecology perspective. Inf Syst J
Sileryte R, Sabbe A, Bouzas V, Meister K, Wandl A, van Timmeren A (2022) European waste statistics data for a circular economy monitor: opportunities and limitations from the amsterdam metropolitan region. J Clean Prod 358:131767
Silvério AC, Ferreira J, Fernandes PO, Dabić M (2023) How does circular economy work in industry? Strategies, opportunities, and trends in scholarly literature. J Clean Prod 412:137312
Siwal SS, Sheoran K, Saini AK, Vo DVN, Wang Q, Thakur VK (2022) Advanced thermochemical conversion technologies used for energy generation: advancement and prospects. Fuel 321:124107
Skene KR (2022) The circular economy: a critique of the concept. Towards a circular economy: transdisciplinary approach for business. Springer International Publishing, Cham, pp 99–116
Song Y, Yang L, Sindakis S, Aggarwal S, Chen C (2023) Analyzing the role of high-tech industrial agglomeration in green transformation and upgrading of manufacturing industry: the case of China. J Knowl Econ 14(4):3847–3877
Spreafico C (2022) An analysis of design strategies for circular economy through life cycle assessment. Environ Monit Assess 194(3):180
Sturgeon TJ (2021) Upgrading strategies for the digital economy. Glob Strateg J 11(1):34–57
Suárez-Eiroa B, Fernández E, Méndez G (2021) Integration of the circular economy paradigm under the just and safe operating space narrative: twelve operational principles based on circularity, sustainability and resilience. J Clean Prod 322:129071
Suraj E (2022) Information systems management and sustainable urban development: a case study. Doctoral dissertation, Walden University
Tavares TM, Ganga GMD, Godinho Filho M, Rodrigues VP (2023) The benefits and barriers of additive manufacturing for circular economy: a framework proposal. Sustain Prod Consum 37:369–388
Thomaßen G, Redl C, Bruckner T (2022) Will the energy-only market collapse? On market dynamics in low-carbon electricity systems. Renew Sustain Energy Rev 164:112594
Tigre FB, Curado C, Henriques PL (2023) Digital leadership: a bibliometric analysis. J Leadership Organ Stud 30(1):40–70
Tiwari S, Mohammed KS, Mentel G, Majewski S, Shahzadi I (2024) Role of circular economy, energy transition, environmental policy stringency, and supply chain pressure on CO_2 emissions in emerging economies. Geosci Front 15(3):101682
Tomashuk I, Baldynyuk V (2023) Eco-innovation as a basis for sustainable development. Three Seas Econ J 4(1):71–87
Trane M, Marelli L, Siragusa A, Pollo R, Lombardi P (2023) Progress by research to achieve the sustainable development goals in the EU: a systematic literature review. Sustainability 15(9):7055
Truong D, Duc KN, Dinh NC (2024) Circular economy essentials. In: Navigating the circular age of a sustainable digital revolution. IGI Global, pp 1–26

Ul-Durar S, Awan U, Varma A, Memon S, Mention AL (2023) Integrating knowledge management and orientation dynamics for organization transition from eco-innovation to circular economy. J Knowl Manag 27(8):2217–2248
Ullah A, Pinglu C, Ullah S, Abbas HSM, Khan S (2021) The role of e-governance in combating COVID-19 and promoting sustainable development: a comparative study of China and Pakistan. Chin Polit Sci Rev 6(1):86–118
van de Gronden N (2022) The circular economy discourse among dutch policy actors: discussing the prospects for the circular economy in the Netherlands
Van Veldhoven Z, Vanthienen J (2022) Digital transformation as an interaction-driven perspective between business, society, and technology. Electron Mark 32(2):629–644
Vann Yaroson E, Chowdhury S, Mangla SK, Dey P, Chan FTS, Roux M (2024) A systematic literature review exploring and linking circular economy and sustainable development goals in the past three decades (1991–2022). Int J Prod Res 62(4):1399–1433. https://doi.org/10.1080/00207543.2023.2270586
Velenturf AP, Purnell P (2021) Principles for a sustainable circular economy. Sustain Prod Consum 27:1437–1457
Voukkali I, Papamichael I, Loizia P, Lekkas DF, Rodríguez-Espinosa T, Navarro-Pedreño J, Zorpas AA (2023) Waste metrics in the framework of the circular economy. Waste Manage Res 41(12):1741–1753
Wang F, Shen S (2024) Does the digital economy development improve or exacerbate income inequality? International evidence. Manag Decis Econ
Wang J, Wang B, Dong K, Dong X (2022) How does the digital economy improve high-quality energy development? The case of China. Technol Forecast Soc Chang 184:121960
Wang M, Hossain MR, Mohammed KS, Cifuentes-Faura J, Cai X (2023) Heterogenous effects of circular economy, green energy and globalization on CO_2 emissions: policy-based analysis for sustainable development. Renewable Energy 211:789–801
Wijewickrama MKCS, Chileshe N, Rameezdeen R, Ochoa JJ (2021) Information sharing in reverse logistics supply chain of demolition waste: A systematic literature review. J Clean Prod 280:124359
Xie J, Xia Z, Tian X, Liu Y (2023) Nexus and synergy between the low-carbon economy and circular economy: a systematic and critical review. Environ Impact Assess Rev 100:107077
Xu X, Yi B (2022) New insights into the impact of local corruption on China's regional carbon emissions performance based on the spatial spillover effects. Sustainability 14(22):15310
Yang M, Chen L, Wang J, Msigwa G, Osman AI, Fawzy S, Rooney DW, Yap PS (2023) Circular economy strategies for combating climate change and other environmental issues. Environ Chem Lett 21(1):55–80
Ye M, Deng F, Yang L, Liang X (2022) Evaluation of regional low-carbon circular economy development: a Sichuan province, China case study. Int J Clim Change Strat Manag 14(1):54–77
Zaman A (2022) Zero-waste: a new sustainability paradigm for addressing the global waste problem. The vision zero handbook: theory, technology and management for a zero casualty policy. Springer International Publishing, Cham, pp 1195–1218
Zeng G, Wu P, Yuan X (2023) Has the development of the digital economy reduced the regional energy intensity—from the perspective of factor market distortion, industrial structure upgrading and technological progress? Sustainability 15(7):5927
Zhang L, Xu M, Chen H, Li Y, Chen S (2022) Globalization, green economy, and environmental challenges: state of the art review for practical implications. Front Environ Sci 10:870271
Zhang Y, Hassan NM, Sheikh AA (2024) Unboxing the dilemma associated with online shopping and purchase behavior for remanufactured products: a smart strategy for waste management. J Environ Manage 351:119790
Zorpas AA (2024) The hidden concept and the beauty of multiple "R" in the framework of waste strategies development reflecting to circular economy principles. Sci Total Environ 952:175508

Zou Q, Mao Z, Yan R, Liu S, Duan Z (2023) Vision and reality of e-government for governance improvement: evidence from global cross-country panel data. Technol Forecast Soc Chang 194:122667

Greening the Workforce for Product Recycling and Energy Conservation

Hina Zafar, Yuwei Sun, Bader Unnisa Mehdi, and Amine Lekmiti

Abstract This chapter explores the impact of workforce greening in promoting sustainable business practices, emphasizing recycling of products and energy saving. The chapter highlights the incorporation of Green Human Resource Management (GHRM) practices as a fundamental element for embedding sustainability within organizations, focusing on key areas such as environmentally friendly recruitment, performance evaluation, training, and employee engagement. It is important to support the principles of a circular economy by equipping employees with the necessary knowledge and skills to enhance resource efficiency, minimize waste, and foster eco-innovation. The chapter explores the impact of green training on supply chain processes, explaining how collaboration among different stakeholders—including companies, governments, customers and suppliers—boosts the implementation of green practices in the organization. It pinpoints the significance of a sustainability-focused organizational culture through dedicated leadership and cross-departmental teamwork. Additionally, the chapter directs the stumbling blocks posed by skill gaps and resistance to change, while recognizing the opportunities brought by new technologies, leadership enhancement and strategic collaborations to address these challenges. The chapter positions workforce greening as an important strategy for achieving organizational objectives, boosting organizational resilience, and sustaining global competitiveness. It offers practical insights and case studies for policymakers, organizations and educators to harmonize operational strategies with wider green goals, paving the way for a more sustainable future.

H. Zafar (✉) · A. Lekmiti
University of Newcastle, Callaghan, NSW, Australia
e-mail: hina.zafar@newcastle.edu.au

A. Lekmiti
e-mail: c3412483@uon.edu.au

Y. Sun
University of Wollongong, Wollongong, NSW, Australia
e-mail: ysun@uow.edu.au

B. U. Mehdi
Western Sydney University, Penrith, NSW, Australia
e-mail: b.unnisa@westernsydney.edu.au

S. A. R. Khan et al. (eds.), *Circular Economy and Technological Innovation*, Industrial Ecology, https://doi.org/10.1007/978-981-96-5650-9_16

Keywords Green Human Resource Management · Circular economy · Sustainability · Green Workforce Development · Environmental training · Eco-Innovation

1 Introduction to Green Workforce Development

Organizations are increasingly focused on incorporating sustainability principles into their business practices. This is not possible without the development of green workforce (Zafar et al. 2024). Organizations design training programs to equip employees with the necessary skills to engage in eco-friendly practices (Saeed et al. 2019). Employees are the main players who can help the organizations through their green actions (Sabokro et al. 2021). Nowadays, organizations are strategizing to align their strategies with their sustainability goals. Green Human Resource Management (GHRM) plays a vital role in this regard (Zafar and Suseno 2024). Green practices such as green performance management, green training and recruitment help the organizations in developing a green workforce (Zafar et al. 2023; Zafar and Suseno 2024). By incorporating sustainability principles into their operations, organizations can groom their employees to implement innovative and sustainable approaches, ultimately fostering green creativity and competitiveness in the changing economic landscape. This approach affiliates with green goals while optimizing systematic efficiency and developing trust with the workforce who is committed to sustainable practices. GHRM not only affects the positive behavior of employees but also affects the positive image of the organization in the community.

Organizations should focus on corporate digital responsibility by promoting the ethical and sustainable use of technology. Concepts like corporate digital responsibility and sustainability are getting the attraction of organizations. Establishing green goals for employees is critical in transforming green goals into actionable steps. This approach ensures that every individual of the organization is aware of the organizational sustainability vision and plays a central role in promoting eco-friendly practices (Shah 2019). The effectiveness of these sustainable initiatives depends on employees' environmental knowledge and green values, which can be enhanced through focused training and development programs (Raza and Khan 2022). For instance, organizations that prioritize green training programs, are able to enhance employee engagement and sustainable performance. A sustainable commitment of the organization is viewed positively by the employees (Zafar et al. 2023). Employees feel pride in being part of a green organization because green organizations are focused on the well-being and safety of the people living on earth. Such organizations have positive reputation in the eyes of the general public and employees feel respected being part of such organizations.

1.1 *Objective and Motivation*

This chapter intends to examine the important role of development of sustainable workforce in promoting sustainable business practices, with an emphasis on energy conservation and product recycling. Through analysis of GHRM practices, skill development, and collective efforts within the supply chain, this chapter seeks practical insights for organizations that want to achieve sustainability. This chapter provides a detailed account of how organizations can adopt environmental practices, aligning their efforts with global sustainability goals, such as the circular economy and reducing carbon emissions.

The motive behind this chapter arises from the need to address the environmental challenges. As concerns over resource depletion, climate change and waste management continue to grow, businesses face substantial pressure to implement green practices. However, the success of these initiatives depends largely on the actions of employees—specifically, its skills, level of engagement and values. By viewing employees as catalysts for change, this chapter highlights the significance of GHRM practices to develop a green workforce that actively contributes to green organizational goals.

This chapter highlights the benefits of creating a green workforce. Organizations can enjoy a sustainable competitive advantage by adopting and implementing GHRM practices. The chapter highlights that organizations should focus on developing sustainable workforce. For example, organizations can associate rewards with green behavior and actions of employees. By synthesizing current research and best practices, this chapter aims to inspire organizations, policymakers, and educators to focus on development of a green workforce to address the environmental challenges.

Section 2 covers the explanation of green workforce. This section spotlights the integration of environmental management into human resource practices through GHRM. It emphasizes the significance of embedding sustainability into HR functions such as recruitment, training, and performance evaluation to cultivate a green workforce. Section 3 explains that sustainability-focused skill development of employees is required to achieve sustainability objectives. Sections 4 and 5 highlight the significance of green training, opportunities, and challenges in the development of green workforce, respectively.

2 Integration of Environmental Management and HR Practices

Alignment of human resource practices into organizational practices is important in different sectors like manufacturing and hospitality. In these sectors, minimizing environmental impact is not only desirable but significant for enhancing operational efficiency and compliance with regulations (Soomro et al. 2021). Thus, organizations can not only benefit in terms of achieving sustainability goals but also achieve cost savings through waste reduction and optimum resource utilization.

Leaders play a significant role in promoting GHRM practices. Different leadership styles such as green servant leadership (Zafar et al. 2022), green transformational leadership (Al-Ghazali et al. 2022; Hoang et al. 2024) play a significant role in promoting sustainability in the workplace. The behavior and attitudes of leaders affect the adoption, implementation, and success of GHRM initiatives (Sheikh et al. 2024). Thus, organizations can foster a green organizational culture to promote the green behavior of employees. When leaders try to lead by example by carrying out green behaviors, employees follow them and try to show their dedication by engaging in green activities. Effective leaders have the ability to position the organization as leaders in sustainability (Inam et al. 2021).

External factors such as societal expectations, regulatory requirements and stakeholder pressures significantly affect the adoption of GHRM practices by an organization. These factors can serve as motivators for the organization to incorporate sustainability into human resource practices. Organizations have to actively respond to these factors to meet their sustainability objectives. Sustainable organizations have a positive reputation in society and can enjoy a sustainable competitive advantage because customers favor organizations that focus on sustainability (Napathorn 2022; Naseer et al. 2023).

Organizations should focus on the integration of sustainability into their practices to ensure enhanced operational efficiency in terms of sustainability (Sharma et al. 2022). These practices may involve reduction of carbon footprints, waste reduction, and adoption of sustainable supply chain. Nowadays, businesses are focusing on green certifications, effective waste management systems and energy-efficient technologies for alignment of their operations with environmental objectives. Previous research indicates that management practices can play an imperative role in fostering green behavior among organizational employees (Zafar et al. 2022) and contribute to a sustainable performance of the organization (Rubel et al. 2020). Organizations should incorporate green practices into their practices, policies and procedures to promote environmentally friendly behavior among employees (Khan et al. 2023b). This move can lead to environmental outcomes for the organization. For instance, hiring the individuals who share green values can help the organization in achieving its organizational objectives (Saifulina et al. 2020) (Fig. 1).

Organizations have started utilizing digital tools such as online portal for leave applications, tracking of attendance, virtual platforms for interviews and management of employees' salaries. Organizations can adopt green practices such as sustainable production, recycling of products and green manufacturing (Khan et al. 2023a). Additionally, paperless strategies, use of public support, teleworking and carpooling should be promoted to promote sustainability. Furthermore, organizations should focus on utilizing green payroll systems, maintenance of electronic records to reduce paperwork, and running energy conservation awareness campaigns for reinforcement of sustainable behaviors.

Implementing GHRM practices not only improves green behavior of employee through targeted recruitment and sustainability-focused incentives; but also boosts

Fig. 1 Recent trends. *Image Source* Sharma et al. (2022)

their commitment to ecological objectives. Such green initiatives can contribute to the greening of both the organization and its employees. Masri and Jaaron (2017) highlight the significance of green recruitment in enhancing the environmental performance of the organization. Organizations and communities should work together to achieve broader sustainability objectives (Soomro et al. 2021). Organizations should incorporate GHRM into their human resource systems to effectively incorporate environmental sustainability into their policies and practices. For instance, integration of environmental considerations into job responsibilities and roles at all levels ensures that sustainability is rooted within the organizations' structure (Khan et al., 2024b).

Recruitment advertisements of the organizations should demonstrate the commitment of the organizations to sustainability and purpose to attract candidates who share green values. By involving in such green practices, employees become more clear of their role within an environmentally conscious sustainable organization (Dumont et al. 2017). Sustainable organizations foster a sense of pride among employees for being part of a green organization. This pride makes their connection stronger with the organization and motivates them to engage in voluntary green behaviors, such as promoting ecological practices beyond their job responsibilities. Employees feel a deeper connection, loyalty and attachment with the organizations that demonstrate a stronger commitment to environmental sustainability. Such organizations value the green contributions of their employees and their green values are aligned with the green values of the organization (Rayner and Morgan 2018).

Implementation of GHRM practices affects the entire organization, not just an individual employee. For example, when sustainability principles are integrated into performance management and training; employees are not only encouraged to adopt green behaviors but are also provided with the skills and knowledge required to efficiently implement sustainable practices. Employees who view their organizations as sustainable are more inspired to advocate for the company, which in turn positively affects its reputation among stakeholders, including suppliers, customers, retailers and investors (Hassan et al. 2023; Khan et al. 2024a; Zhang et al. 2024). This advocacy not only strengthens the organization's competitive advantage but also supports broader societal efforts to tackle environmental issues (Rehman Khan et al. 2022). Thus, GHRM fosters a unique approach focused on achieving both environmental and business objectives.

Ethical considerations are increasingly valued by the organizations to promote sustainability efforts. Organizations focus on the development and implementation of green policies, practices that enhance workplace well-being, such as minimizing exposure to harmful substances, efforts to improve indoor air quality and offering wellness programs to employees. Fair trade and ethical practices are also gaining attraction to ensure that green initiatives benefit not only the environment but also the whole community that is part of the supply chain. This holistic approach highlights the connection between environmental sustainability and social responsibility (Fig. 2).

Eco-innovation refers to development of new technologies and processes to minimize harmful environmental impact. Organizations are increasingly investing in research and development for creation of products and services that are both eco-friendly and economically profitable. This may include innovation in renewable energy, energy-efficient production processes and biodegradable materials. Adoption of eco-innovation, organizations comply with environmental regulations and position themselves as sustainable leaders in transitioning to the circular economy.

Fig. 2 Green HRM *Image Source* https://www.youtube.com/watch?v=gHm8pMk9sF4

3 Skill Development for Circular Economy Objectives

For achieving circular economy objectives, development of relevant skills has become critical in fostering sustainable business practices. These practices focuse on resource efficiency, promotion of sustainable production, waste reduction and consumption models. Organizations should invest in green training and implement innovative green human resource strategies to meet green objectives. GHRM practices ensure that employees are not only aware of environmental challenges but also have the skills to address these challenges (Vasilev et al. 2024). Waste management can be reduced by arranging training programs. Green innovation and creativity can play an important role in this regard. GHRM promotes sustainability initiatives of the organizations (Tanveer et al. 2024).

When employees feel that their organization is focused on greening, they try to engage in green activities to support the green objectives of the organization (Zafar et al. 2023). This is the responsibility of the organization to encourage employees to focus on adopting green behaviors such as printing double-sided, turning off the lights when leaving their offices and using recycling cups, etc. Organizations can also associate green rewards with the green behaviors and actions of employees. When employees notice that organization is rewarding employees for their green performance. They will be highly motivated to perform green tasks and their voluntary green participation will increase. Thus, a green climate perception will be developed within the minds of employees that organizations encourages and values green actions of employees. Organization can provide professional development opportunities to employees to develop their green skills. Organizations should also collaborate with universities to promote awareness of advanced technologies in enhancing sustainability. A comprehensive approach is required for skill development related to circular economy objectives. This includes integration of GHRM practices, fostering a supportive organizational culture, and engaging with external partners. Through investment in employee training and aligning human resource strategies with sustainability goals, organizations can effectively move to a circular economy, enhance their environmental performance and sustainable competitive advantage.

4 The Role of Green Training in Product Recycling and Energy Conservation

In this section, we will explore what is green training and how does green training impact product recycling and energy conservation through the supply chain.

4.1 What is Green Training?

It is important to encourage individuals' pro-environmental behaviour and increase the sustainability of corporate supply chain through the multilateral cooperation of key stakeholders, such as government, corporates, customers and suppliers (Teixeira et al. 2016).

a. Government

As one of the most important stakeholders, government support organisations' green training through educating individuals and organisations about the environment-protection regulations and requirements, making policy and propose relevant initiatives. For example, the United States Environmental Protection Agency (EPA), a federal agency established in 1970, is responsible for protecting residents' health and the local environment. EPA enforces regulations that limit pollution, manage the conservation of natural resources, and oversees environmental policies (US EPA 2024b). EPA hosts regular training webinars to help stakeholders explore development of renewable energy. For example, EPA hosts webinars to help stakeholders explore the application of renewable energy on current or previously contaminated land, such as landfill and mine sites. New Jersey, Massachusetts, and Illinois have implemented extensive programs that have successfully led to the creation of numerous megawatts of new renewable energy projects at re-powering sites (the number of re-powering projects across the US can be seen in Fig. 3). These initiatives have brought a wide range of benefits, including financial incentives, procurement preferences, streamlined permitting processes, liability relief, and direct assistance for developing new renewable energy projects (US EPA 2024a).

The re-powering initiatives also make use of existing infrastructure, shorten project cycle times through streamlined permitting and zoning, enhance project financials by lowering land costs and bring tax incentives, foster community support through land renewable initiatives, and help conserve open space (US EPA 2024a). The diagram below shows the advantages of re-powering initiatives in the US (Fig. 4).

In Canada, an initiative aimed at providing green training to approximately 20,000 apprentices and skilled workers was proposed under the new Sustainable Jobs Stream of the Canadian Apprenticeship Strategy's Union Training and Innovation Program (UTIP) (Olivero 2024). This initiative involved an investment of over $95 million over a five-year span, which enables Canadian tradespeople to stay current with in-demand skills as industries transition to low-carbon solutions and global partners seek to invest in Canadian clean technologies (Olivero 2024).

b. Corporates

Organizational green training refers to ongoing education and on-the-job training designed to help companies meet their environmental management goals and objectives (Daily and Huang 2001). This type of training is typically implemented through GHRM initiatives. GHRM highlights that human resource policies should be designed to promote sustainable use of resources and should support green

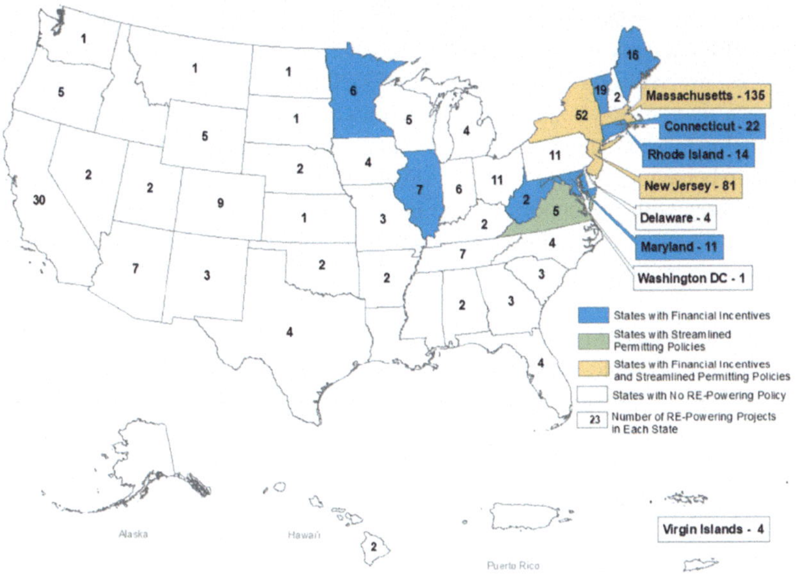

Fig. 3 The number of re-powering projects by state and territory as of November 2023 (US EPA 2023)

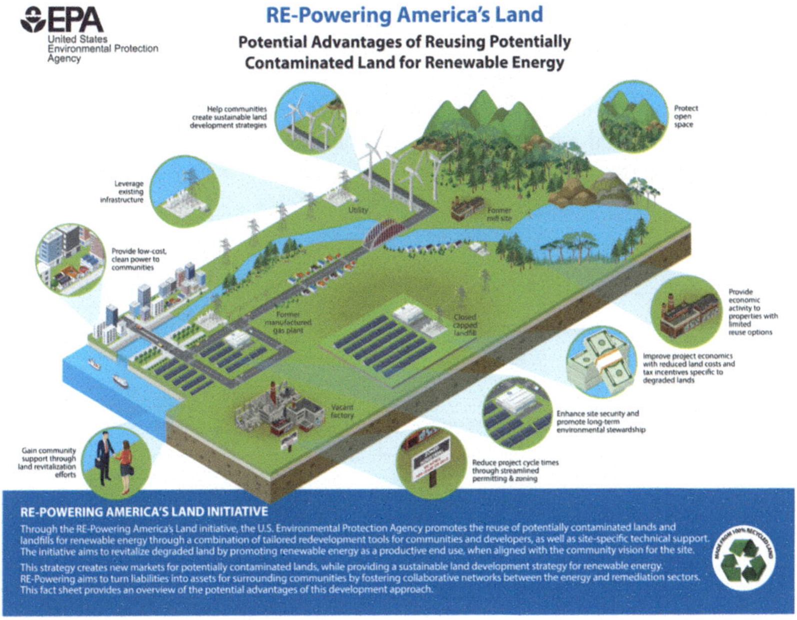

Fig. 4 The potential advantages of re-powering initiative (US EPA 2024a)

initiatives of the organization (Ahmad 2015; Mampra 2013). Such practices may involve different activities like providing green training, recognizing and rewarding employees' green efforts (Renwick et al. 2012). GHRM promotes sensitivity among employees towards environmental protection (Jabbour 2011; Usman et al. 2023). Additionally, these practices can play an important role in promoting organizational citizenship behavior among employees (Daily et al. 2009). GHRM practices provide the employees with the opportunity to help each other in performing green tasks. Thus, organizations can reduce their carbon footprint and enhance their commitment to environmental responsibility (Jabbour 2011; Pham et al. 2020; Pinzone et al. 2019).

Integration of GHRM philosophy into human resource policy is becoming popular day by day. For example, green training and developing activities will help employees know more about the environment management and embrace different methods of energy conservation within workplace, such as reducing the consumption of paper and turning off the light when leaving (Ahmad 2015). Additionally, Usman et al. (2023) also posited that green training also influences employees' beyond-work pro-environmental behaviors, such as the consumption of eco-friendly products, reuse of items and materials, and reduced consumption of resources, such as water, electricity, and water (see Fig. 5).

c. Customers and suppliers

Green training has been extended from internal employees to the whole supply chain– including customers and suppliers (Teixeira et al. 2016). Involving customers and suppliers in the decision-making processes related to green issues across the supply chain is beneficial to overcome the challenges of stakeholder inclusion in initiating environmental actions (De Abreu et al. 2015). The conceptual model of green supply chain can be seen in Fig. 6.

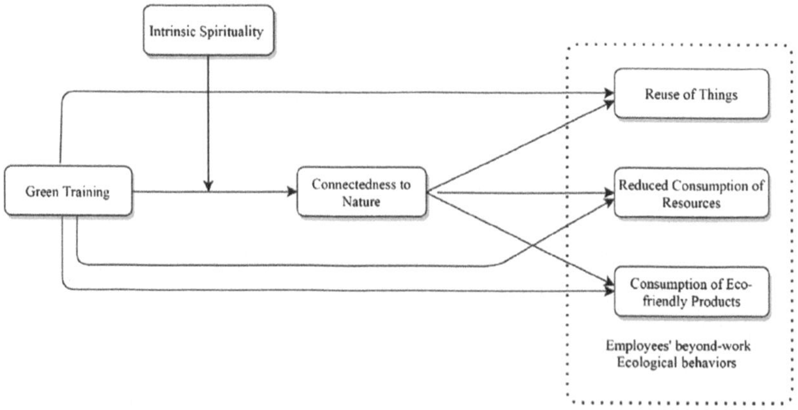

Fig. 5 The theoretical framework of how green training will impact employees' beyond-work ecological behaviours (Usman et al. 2023, p. 356)

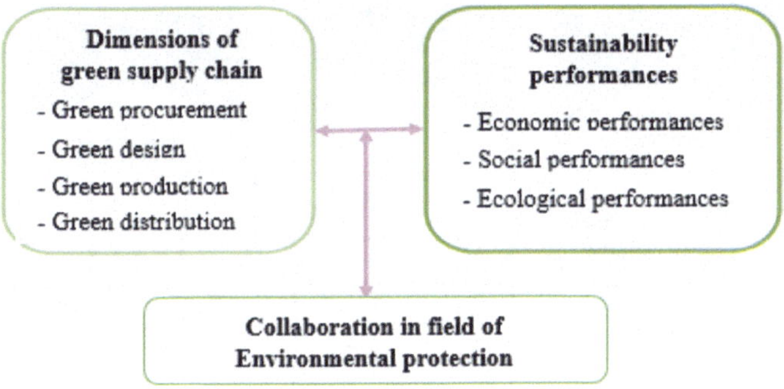

Fig. 6 Conceptual model of the green supply chain (Veljković et al. 2022, p. 36)

A survey conducted by De Abreu et al. (2015) on Brazilian firms with ISO 14001 certification revealed a strong positive relationship between green training and the adoption of environmentally conscious supply chain practices. The findings show that green training not only improves collaboration with the customers, but also supports environmentally friendly purchasing practices among the suppliers. These findings emphasize the significant role of green training in development of a green supply chain management.

4.2 *Significance of Green Training*

In this section, we will use product recycling and energy conservation as examples to show how green training benefit the society as a whole.

a. Product recycling

Product recycling is the process of collecting and processing used up materials (waste) that would otherwise be thrown away as rubbish and turning them into new products. Product recycling plays significant roles in fulfilling the cycle of sustainable supply chain. It does not only require end-users to put rubbish in the right place, but also need producers to print on-package recycling information on the products.

For example, in Australia, the Australian Recycling Label (ARL) provides consumers with clear, on-package recycling information that reduce consumer confusion about which bin to throw (recycle or general waste) and lower the amount of waste sent to landfill. There are three variations of ARL labels: recyclable, conditionally recyclable, and not recyclable (see Fig. 7). The ARL reduces the likelihood that end-users place non-recyclable items in the recycling bin, which can contaminate the recycling system and make it more expensive to process.

Except for the industry-wide standard, an increasing number of organisations are implementing recycling programs as part of the corporate social responsibilities (Ahmad 2015). Some leading multinational companies in the US, such as Intel, Estee

Fig. 7 Three variations of ARL (Department of Climate Change 2023)

lauder, and Texas Instruments, stand out for their commitment to environmental stewardship, especially in product recycling and waste management—They have received external certification, such as ISO 14001 standard, across their facilities. Besides, of the total waste produced by those companies, more than 85% is recycled.

The recycling of coffee cups has long been a challenge for some major coffee-consuming countries, especially Australia. An estimated 1.84 billion single-use cups are used by Australians every year. The challenge of recycling those single-use coffee cups lies in separating paper and plastic lining (which keeps beverage warm), causing most coffee cups to end up in landfills without being recycled. To combat the challenge of recycling disposable coffee cups, Simply Cups, an Australia-based paper cup recycling company, created disposable coffee cups made from a combination of paper and plastic (Waste360 Staff 2016). With this new disposable coffee cups, the paper fibers and the polyethylene lining can be easily separated, or they can be fully reprocessed into a polymer to produce new products, such as trays and coasters (Waste360 Staff 2016).

b. Energy conservation

Conservation of energy within the workplace can have a significant environmental impact. Corporate around the world have introduced several energy-saving initiatives to reduce the environmental footprint. Common practices include cutting down the use of traditional power sources, introducing substitute energy, encouraging carpooling and public transport. For example, the HR department in UK of Sky has initiated a campaign where employees are asked to turn off devices and lights when leaving, and use 100% renewable energy, including solar lighting (Ahmad 2015).

Another common practice of energy conservation involves reducing the consumption of paper. Going paperless in the office is easier said than done. Common office tasks, such as sketching designs, signing contracts, and taking notes all require paper and pen. However, Ideal Rebel, a Vancouver-based digital agency, introduced the zero-waste policy and has achieved 100% paperless. Jamie Garratt, the owner of Ideal Rebel, introduced a number of eco-friendly policies and invested in digital equipment to facilitate the transition from traditional office to a paperless office. For example, pay slips are sent by emails; paper pay slips are no longer provided. Contract signatures are collected using the SignEasy software, and Mac Preview is used to insert them into the documents (Borzykowski 2013). And every employee has two computers and an iPad at the desk, enabling them to read multiple documents at once without needing to print (Borzykowski 2013).

5 Challenges and Opportunities in Greening the Workforce

The transition towards a greener workforce represents a complex yet rewarding journey for organizations across various industries. As sustainability becomes a central focus in business operations, companies face the dual challenge of integrating environmental considerations into their practices while also equipping their workforce with the necessary skills and competencies to support these initiatives. A very significant challenge is to provide employees with comprehensive green training opportunities. Most of the employees do not have the required skills and green knowledge to actively contribute to green organizational practices. Majority of the employees have unmet training needs which hampers their ability to actively and efficiently contribute to sustainability objectives of the organization (Robin et al. 2019).

This highlights the pressing need for green training that can equip the employees with knowledge, skills, learning and can help them adapt to evolving environmental practices. Organizations should invest in green training because it is central to foster sustainable change in the organization and to promote green empowerment among employees. Green empowerment inspires employees to alter their tasks in terms of sustainability and can help organizations in achieving high level of green performance (Hameed et al. 2020; Zhang et al. 2019).

One challenge that organizations have to face is resistance to change by employees. Employees may consider green practices as extra load and may not understand the significance of sustainability initiatives (Atan et al. 2021). Organizations should focus on implementing efficient change management strategies for the smooth engagement of employees in sustainability. Clear and transparent communication about the benefits and rewards of sustainable practices can play a significant role in reducing resistance to change. Participation of employees in decision making and encouraging their suggestions for dealing with environmental issues can promote their engagement in green activities and their commitment to sustainability (Eimontaite et al. 2022).

Despite several challenges, sustainable organizations have the opportunity to attract talented employees who have strong environmental and ethical values (Foley et al. 2021). Organizations should offer green jobs, should invest in skill development of employees to establish themselves as leaders in sustainability (Hall et al.

2020). The development of a green workforce can enhance the organizational environmental performance, bolster its image and improve its market position. Technological innovations can enhance the development of green workforce. For instance, the use of robotics can lessen the physical demands on workers and promote organizational sustainable practices, ultimately increasing the green performance of the organization (Kuhlmann et al. 2018).

Organizations that adopt the latest technologies can not only enhance their efficiency, but also contribute to broader sustainability goals. Additionally, the educational curriculum should be well-aligned with industry needs to ensure that recent graduates are aware of the required skills for sustainable jobs (Jessup et al. 2024). Internship programs should be arranged to provide graduates with practical experience in sustainable practices and prepare them for a green economy (Madsen et al. 2024). Such partnerships between industry and educational institutions can create a talented workforce that can help the organizations in achieving its green objectives.

6 Conclusion

This chapter stresses the role of sustainable workforce in achieve environmental objectives of the organizations. The chapter highlights that GHRM practices play important role in fostering green behavior among employees. GHRM practices such as green training, green rewards, green recruitment, green empowerment and green performance management can help the organizations in development of a green workforce. Integrating GHRM into human resource practices opens a way for employees to align the green behavior of employees with green organizational objectives. Implementation of green initiatives can foster a green workplace climate, ultimately fostering green performance of the organizations.

This chapter also emphasizes that organizations may have to face challenges in the development of a green workforce. These challenges may involve resistance to change and lack of awareness of the significance of sustainability initiatives among employees. At the same time, sustainable organizations may enjoy a sustainable competitive advantage in the long run. Such organizations can get the attraction of employees who possess green values and can develop strategic partnerships. The journey towards sustainability involves the collaborative efforts of all the stakeholders. Organizations should understand the significance of the development of a sustainable workforce to achieve global sustainable goals. Sustainable organizations should focus on green innovation and creativity to position themselves as leaders in sustainability and eco-innovation. The insights of the chapter provide a roadmap for organizations to balance profitability with environmental stewardship.

References

Ahmad S (2015) Green human resource management: policies and practices. Cogent Bus Manag 2(1). https://doi.org/10.1080/23311975.2015.1030817

Al-Ghazali BM, Gelaidan HM, Shah SHA, Amjad R (2022) Green transformational leadership and green creativity? The mediating role of green thinking and green organizational identity in SMEs. Front Psychol 13. https://doi.org/10.3389/fpsyg.2022.977998

Atan A, Ozgit H, Silman F (2021) Happiness at work and motivation for a sustainable workforce: evidence from female hotel employees. Sustainability 13(14):7778. https://doi.org/10.3390/su13147778

Borzykowski B (2013) How one company went completely paperless. The Global and Mail. https://www.theglobeandmail.com/technology/tech-news/how-one-company-went-completely-paperless/article12522284/

Daily BF, Huang S-C (2001) Sustainability through human resource factors achieving sustainability through attention to human resource factors in environmental management. Int J Oper Prod Manag 21(12):144–3577. http://www.emerald-library.com/ft

Daily BF, Bishop JW, Govindarajulu N (2009) A conceptual model for organizational citizenship behaviour directed toward the environment. Bus Soc 48(2):243–256. https://doi.org/10.1177/0007650308315439

De Abreu MCS, Cunha LT Da, Barlow CY (2015) Institutional dynamics and organizations affecting the adoption of sustainable development in the United Kingdom and Brazil. Bus Ethics 24(1):73–90. https://doi.org/10.1111/beer.12074

Department of Climate Change, Energy the Environment and Water (2023) Recycling packaging. Australian Government. https://www.dcceew.gov.au/environment/protection/waste/packaging/australasian-recycling-label

Dumont J, Shen J, Deng X (2017) Effects of green HRM practices on employee workplace green behavior: the role of psychological green climate and employee green values. Hum Resour Manage 56(4):613–627. https://doi.org/10.1002/hrm.21792

Eimontaite I, Cameron D, Rolph J, Mokaram S, Aitken JM, Gwilt I, Law J (2022) Dynamic graphical instructions result in improved attitudes and decreased task completion time in human-robot co-working: an experimental manufacturing study. Sustainability 14(6):3289. https://doi.org/10.3390/su14063289

Foley K, Attrill S, Brebner C (2021) Co-designing a methodology for workforce development during the personalisation of allied health service funding for people with disability in Australia. BMC Health Serv Res 21(1):680. https://doi.org/10.1186/s12913-021-06711-x

Hall GS, DeSouza L, Starr E, Wheeler K, Schleyer K (2020) Sustaining passion: findings from an exploratory study of the OST program workforce. J Youth Dev 15(1):9–23. https://doi.org/10.5195/jyd.2020.821

Hameed Z, Khan IU, Islam T, Sheikh Z, Naeem RM (2020) Do green HRM practices influence employees' environmental performance? Int J Manpow 41(7):1061–1079. https://doi.org/10.1108/IJM-08-2019-0407

Hassan NM, Khan SAR, Ashraf MU, Sheikh AA (2023) Interconnection between the role of blockchain technologies, supply chain integration, and circular economy: a case of small and medium-sized enterprises in Pakistan. Sci Prog 106(3):1–22. https://doi.org/10.1177/00368504231186527

Hoang HT, Ho NTT, Pham NT (2024) Green transformational leadership, green human resource management, big five personality traits, and hotel employees' green behavior in Vietnam. In: Green human resource management, pp 197–211. Springer Nature Singapore. https://doi.org/10.1007/978-981-99-7104-6_11

Inam A, Ho JA, Sheikh AA, Shafqat M, Najam U (2021) How self leadership enhances normative commitment and work performance by engaging people at work? Curr Psychol. https://doi.org/10.1007/s12144-021-01697-5

Jabbour CJC (2011) How green are HRM practices, organizational culture, learning and teamwork? A Brazilian study. Ind Commer Train 43(2):98–105. https://doi.org/10.1108/00197851111108926

Jessup B, Proudfoot F, Cross M, Barnett T (2024) Are recent health, welfare and care graduates part of a rural and remote workforce solution? Evidence from Tasmania, Australia. BMC Health Serv Res 24(1):652. https://doi.org/10.1186/s12913-024-11087-9

Khan SAR, Ahmad Z, Sheikh AA, Yu Z (2023a) Green technology adoption paving the way toward sustainable performance in circular economy: a case of Pakistani small and medium enterprises. Int J Innov Sci. https://doi.org/10.1108/IJIS-10-2022-0199

Khan SAR, Sheikh AA, Ahmad Z (2023b) Developing the interconnection between green employee behavior, tax avoidance, green capability, and sustainable performance of SMEs through corporate social responsibility. J Clean Prod 419. https://doi.org/10.1016/j.jclepro.2023.138236

Khan SAR, Sheikh AA, Hassan NM, Yu Z (2024a) Modeling the intricate association between sustainable service quality and supply chain performance: moderating role of blockchain technology and environmental uncertainty. Sustain (Switzerland) 16(11). https://doi.org/10.3390/su16114808

Khan SAR, Sheikh AA, Tahir MS (2024b) Corporate social responsibility-an antidote for sustainable business performance: interconnecting role of digital technologies, employee eco-behavior, and tax avoidance. Environ Sci Pollut Res Int 31(3):4365–4383. https://doi.org/10.1007/S11356-023-31377-9

Kuhlmann E, Batenburg R, Wismar M, Dussault G, Maier CB, Glinos IA, Azzopardi-Muscat N, Bond C, Burau V, Correia T, Groenewegen PP, Hansen J, Hunter DJ, Khan U, Kluge HH, Kroezen M, Leone C, Santric-Milicevic M, Sermeus W, Ungureanu M (2018) A call for action to establish a research agenda for building a future health workforce in Europe. Health Res Policy Syst 16(1):52. https://doi.org/10.1186/s12961-018-0333-x

Madsen ER, Schaffer K, Hare Bork R, Yeager VA (2024) On-the-job learning: bright spots of governmental public health employee reflections on the COVID-19 response. J Public Health Manag Pract 30(3):372–376. https://doi.org/10.1097/PHH.0000000000001880

Masri HA, Jaaron AAM (2017) Assessing green human resources management practices in Palestinian manufacturing context: an empirical study. J Clean Prod 143:474–489. https://doi.org/10.1016/j.jclepro.2016.12.087

Napathorn C (2022) The development of green skills across firms in the institutional context of Thailand. Asia-Pacific J Bus Adm 14(4):539–572. https://doi.org/10.1108/APJBA-10-2020-0370

Naseer SA, Mukhtar S, Gul M (2023) Green HRM; job performance: unveiling pathway through job satisfaction. J Soc Res Dev 4(2):410–419. https://doi.org/10.53664/JSRD/04-02-2023-15-410-419

Olivero T (2024) Canadian government invests in green training for skilled trades. Our Great Minds. https://theogm.com/2024/06/24/canadian-government-invests-in-green-training-for-skilled-trades/

Pham NT, Vo Thanh T, Tučková Z, Thuy VTN (2020) The role of green human resource management in driving hotel's environmental performance: interaction and mediation analysis. Int J Hosp Manag 88. https://doi.org/10.1016/j.ijhm.2019.102392

Pinzone M, Guerci M, Lettieri E, Huisingh D (2019) Effects of 'green' training on pro-environmental behaviors and job satisfaction: evidence from the Italian healthcare sector. J Clean Prod 226:221–232. https://doi.org/10.1016/j.jclepro.2019.04.048

Rayner J, Morgan D (2018) An empirical study of 'green' workplace behaviours: ability, motivation and opportunity. Asia Pacific J Hum Resour 56(1):56–78. https://doi.org/10.1111/1744-7941.12151

Raza SA, Khan KA (2022) Impact of green human resource practices on hotel environmental performance: the moderating effect of environmental knowledge and individual green values. Int J Contemp Hosp Manag 34(6):2154–2175. https://doi.org/10.1108/IJCHM-05-2021-0553

Rehman Khan SA, Ahmad Z, Sheikh AA, Yu Z (2022) Digital transformation, smart technologies, and eco-innovation are paving the way toward sustainable supply chain performance. Sci Prog 105(4):1–26. https://doi.org/10.1177/00368504221145648

Renwick DWS, Jabbour CJC, Muller-Camen M, Redman T, Wilkinson A (2012) Special issue: green (environmental) HRM in theory and practice. Int J Hum Resour Manag 23(16):3498–3499. https://doi.org/10.1080/09585192.2012.705092

Robin N, Castrucci BC, McGinty MD, Edmiston A, Bogaert K (2019) The first nationally representative benchmark of the local governmental public health workforce: findings from the 2017 public health workforce interests and needs survey. J Public Health Manag Pract 25(2):S26–S37. https://doi.org/10.1097/PHH.0000000000000939

Rubel MRB, Kee DMH, Rimi NN (2020) The influence of green HRM practices on green service behaviors: the mediating effect of green knowledge sharing. Empl Relat 43(5):996–1015. https://doi.org/10.1108/ER-04-2020-0163

Sabokro M, Masud MM, Kayedian A (2021) The effect of green human resources management on corporate social responsibility, green psychological climate and employees' green behavior. J Clean Prod 313:127963. https://doi.org/10.1016/j.jclepro.2021.127963

Saeed BB, Afsar B, Hafeez S, Khan I, Tahir M, Afridi MA (2019) Promoting employee's proenvironmental behavior through green human resource management practices. Corp Soc Responsib Environ Manag 26(2):424–438. https://doi.org/10.1002/csr.1694

Saifulina N, Carballo-Penela A, Ruzo-Sanmartín E (2020) Sustainable HRM and green HRM: the role of green HRM in influencing employee pro-environmental behavior at work. J Sustain Res 2(3). https://doi.org/10.20900/jsr20200026

Shah M (2019) Green human resource management: development of a valid measurement scale. Bus Strateg Environ 28(5):771–785. https://doi.org/10.1002/bse.2279

Sharma C, Sakhuja S, Nijjer S (2022) Recent trends of green human resource management: text mining and network analysis. Environ Sci Pollut Res 29(56):84916–84935. https://doi.org/10.1007/s11356-022-21471-9

Sheikh AA, Shan A, Hassan NM, Khan SN, AbdAlatti A (2024) Impact of green human resource management practices on hotels environmental performance: a mediation and moderation analysis. Sustainable Futures 8:100409. https://doi.org/10.1016/j.sftr.2024.100409

Soomro MM, Wang Y, Tunio RA, Aripkhanova K, Ansari MI (2021) Management of human resources in the green economy: does green labour productivity matter in low-carbon development in China. Environ Sci Pollut Res 28(42):59805–59812. https://doi.org/10.1007/s11356-021-14872-9

Tanveer MI, Yusliza MY, Fawehinmi O (2024) Green HRM and hospitality industry: challenges and barriers in adopting environmentally friendly practices. J Hosp Tour Insights 7(1):121–141. https://doi.org/10.1108/JHTI-08-2022-0389

Teixeira AA, Jabbour CJC, De Sousa Jabbour ABL, Latan H, De Oliveira JHC (2016) Green training and green supply chain management: evidence from Brazilian firms. J Clean Prod 116:170–176. https://doi.org/10.1016/j.jclepro.2015.12.061

US EPA (2023) Re-powering America's land initiative: project tracking matrix, pp 1–44. https://www.epa.gov/system/files/documents/2023-11/re-on-cl-tracking-matrix-112823.pdf

US EPA (2024a) What is re-powering. https://www.epa.gov/re-powering/what-re-powering

US EPA (2024b) The origins of EPA. United States Environmental Protection Agency. https://www.epa.gov/history/origins-epa

Usman M, Rofcanin Y, Ali M, Ogbonnaya C, Babalola MT (2023) Toward a more sustainable environment: understanding why and when green training promotes employees' eco-friendly behaviors outside of work. Hum Resour Manag 62(3):355–371. https://doi.org/10.1002/hrm.22148

Vasilev V, Stefanova D, Icheva M (2024) Green human resource management as a component of sustainable organizational development in environmental and natural economics. In: Environment. Technologies. Resources. Proceedings of the international scientific and practical conference vol 1, pp 402–407. https://doi.org/10.17770/etr2024vol1.7966

Veljković J, Milovanović G, Talić M (2022) Green supply chains and global competitiveness of companies. Ekonomika 67(3):29–43. https://doi.org/10.5937/ekonomika2203029v

Waste360 Staff (2016) Simply cups launches pilot disposable coffee cup recycling program in Australia. Waste360.

Zafar H, Ho JA, Cheah J-H, Mohamed R (2022) Catalyzing voluntary pro-environmental behavior in the textile industry: environmentally specific servant leadership, psychological empowerment and organizational identity. J Clean Prod 378:134366. https://doi.org/10.1016/j.jclepro.2022.134366

Zafar H, Ho JA, Cheah J, Mohamed R (2023) Promoting pro-environmental behavior through organizational identity and green organizational climate. Asia Pacific J Hum Resour 61(2):483–506. https://doi.org/10.1111/1744-7941.12347

Zafar H, Suseno Y (2024) Examining the effects of green human resource management practices, green psychological climate, and organizational pride on employees' voluntary pro-environmental behavior. Organ Environ 37(4):581–609. https://doi.org/10.1177/10860266241241532

Zafar H, Suseno Y, Ho JA (2023) Pro-environmental behavior and GHRM: effects of organizational and coworker support for environment. Acad Manag Proc 2023(1). https://doi.org/10.5465/AMPROC.2023.15434abstract

Zafar H, Tian F, Ho JA, Roh T, Latif B (2024) Understanding voluntary pro-environmental behavior among colleagues: roles of green crafting, psychological empowerment, and green organizational climate. Bus Strateg Environ. https://doi.org/10.1002/bse.4001

Zhang Y, Hassan NM, Sheikh AA (2024) Unboxing the dilemma associated with online shopping and purchase behavior for remanufactured products: a smart strategy for waste management. J Environ Manag 351. https://doi.org/10.1016/j.jenvman.2023.119790

Zhang Y, Luo Y, Zhang X, Zhao J (2019) How green human resource management can promote green employee behavior in China: a technology acceptance model perspective. Sustain (Switzerland) 11(19). https://doi.org/10.3390/su11195408

The manufacturer's authorised representative in the EU is Springer Nature Customer Service Centre GmbH, Europaplatz 3, 69115 Heidelberg, Germany. If you have any concerns regarding our products, please contact ProductSafety@springernature.com

Printed and bound by CPI Group (UK) Ltd, Croydon, CR0 4YY
01/10/2026
02225921-0011